ART IS A TYRANT

ART IS A TYRANT

THE UNCONVENTIONAL LIFE OF ROSA BONHEUR

CATHERINE HEWITT

ICON

First published in the UK in 2020
by Icon Books Ltd, Omnibus Business Centre,
39–41 North Road, London N7 9DP
email: info@iconbooks.com
www.iconbooks.com

Sold in the UK, Europe and Asia
by Faber & Faber Ltd, Bloomsbury House,
74–77 Great Russell Street,
London WC1B 3DA or their agents

Distributed in the UK, Europe and Asia
by Grantham Book Services,
Trent Road, Grantham NG31 7XQ

Distributed in Australia and New Zealand
by Allen & Unwin Pty Ltd,
PO Box 8500, 83 Alexander Street,
Crows Nest, NSW 2065

Distributed in South Africa
by Jonathan Ball, Office B4, The District,
41 Sir Lowry Road, Woodstock 7925

Distributed in India
by Penguin Books India,
7th Floor, Infinity Tower – C, DLF Cyber City,
Gurgaon 122002, Haryana

ISBN: 978-178578-621-1

Typeset in Bembo MT by Marie Doherty

Printed and bound in Great Britain
by Clays Ltd, Elcograf S.p.A.

Contents

'Art is an absorbent — a tyrant. It demands heart, brain, soul, body, the entireness of its votary. Nothing less will win its highest favour. I wed art. It is my husband — my world — my life-dream — the air I breathe. I know nothing else — feel nothing else — think nothing else.'

—Rosa Bonheur

Prologue

The temperature had dropped on 25 October 1899 as Parisians, their outer garments pulled tight, made their way up and down the tree-lined Boulevard de la Madeleine. Beyond the bustling flower market, in the shadow of the majestic Église, horse-drawn carriages rumbled past attendant omnibuses and the occasional cyclist. The roar of a motorcar was not an uncommon feature of boulevard life these days, and heads would turn as a member of the elite paraded their affluence. But pedestrians still outnumbered vehicles. Men accessorised with top hats and canes went about their business, while long skirts swished to and fro as women circulated between the boulevard's grand apartment buildings and shops. The younger, more fashion-conscious fin-de-siècle ladies chose dresses to accentuate the waist. So far did contemporary fashion go, critics objected, that women had become veritable 'packets', no longer voluptuous beacons of fertility but prisoners in their own bodices. But whatever her stance on the trends of the day, every woman could be glad that, today at least, the autumnal drop in temperature had not also obliged her to carry an unwieldy umbrella as well as her usual bags or parcels.

Leaving the boulevard's cacophony of voices, hooves and carriage wheels, the narrower, tangential Rue de Sèze offered a reprieve for a person more accustomed to a quieter way of life.

Presently, a woman could be seen making her way along the macadam of this side street. Her curious appearance invited a second look. Though hardly more than 40, in her left hand she gripped a cane and the sharp-eyed observer would notice that she walked with a limp.

Notwithstanding, she carried herself well and her undulating mane of wiry, chestnut brown hair had been drawn back into a loose bun. The chignon rested behind an oval face with a high forehead, full lips and pale blue eyes which would become animated if she smiled. And despite a nose which was a little too prominent for her face, no one who passed her could doubt her femininity.

The outward signs of frailty were deceptive; she was a resilient American and she possessed titanic inner strength. She needed that quality now.

The American stopped before the door of the building at number 8. The meeting she was about to attend filled her with trepidation. There was certain to be conflict, dispute and heartrending emotion. But she had a delicate task to perform; she had made a promise. A force more powerful than she had brought her here.

The woman instigating this meeting was, quite simply, unique – the very antithesis of 19th-century society's feminine ideal. She was educated, she shunned traditionally 'feminine' pursuits, she rejected marriage and she wore trousers. Though her origins were modest, her aspirations were grand. Problematically for a 19th-century female, she was determined to paint. Dismissing society's prejudice, bearing the cruellest forms of ridicule, she had persevered in her craft and gone on to win medals, commendations and become the first woman ever to be made Officier de la Légion d'Honneur. Her company was sought by kings and courtiers, celebrities and statesmen. She dined and debated with John Ruskin, she talked thoroughbreds with Buffalo Bill, her work was summoned by Queen Victoria and she was decorated by the Empress Eugénie of France, Emperor Maximilian of Mexico and King Alphonso XII of Spain. She kept lions and monkeys in her home, she rode her horse resolutely astride and was often mistaken for a man. But exceptionally, the society whose gendered rules she spurned accepted her – because by the mid-19th century, this woman was perhaps the greatest painter of animals France had ever seen.

And around her persona lingered tantalising questions: was she really descended from royalty? How many taboos would she violate for love? Most of all, why would a woman so devoted to family give her entire fortune to an outsider?

Of one thing at least the American was certain: such greatness must be protected. The promise had to be kept. Her story must be told.

The door of number 8, Rue de Sèze swung open. Bracing herself, the American stepped inside.

I

Two Houses

When she arrived at the Mairie of Bordeaux on 21 May 1821, Sophie Marquis had cause for apprehension. She was about to do something radical.

Fine-boned with dark hair and eyes, a delicate nose and even features, at 24, Sophie was a pretty girl. She was bright and accomplished, and had received an education fitting for a lady of her station. She was well read, spoke competent Spanish, and could sing and dance beautifully. Her piano playing held audiences enraptured. Any lingering recollection of her first two years in her native Germany had now been subsumed by a library of memories of life in France with her adoptive father, M. Dublan de Lahet, and his family.[1]

Jean-Baptiste Dublan de Lahet was well qualified to supervise a refined young lady's maturation. Dignified and decorous with a slim face and aquiline nose, M. Dublan was said to have served as page to Queen Marie Antoinette in his youth, before exercising the profession of merchant, and his father had been treasurer for King Louis XV. Like many aristocrats, M. Dublan had been forced to flee France during the Revolution. He returned chastened, but with sufficient fortune intact to enjoy a comfortable existence. His assets included a home in Bordeaux at number 15, Cours de l'Intendance, while his family had property in the nearby commune of Quinsac, to the south-east of the city.[2]

How M. Dublan had come to bring Sophie and her German nurse back with him to France remained a mystery, one Sophie herself had never satisfactorily resolved. The household servants were studiously cagey. But with M. Dublan's exemplary treatment, persistent questioning might have seemed churlish or disrespectful. Sophie wanted for nothing and had been raised as one of her adoptive father's own children. And when M. Dublan's wife, Jeanne Clothilde Julie Ketty Guilhem, died while Sophie was still in her teens, the presence of his adoptive daughter rewarded the widower's benevolence.[3] He now had even more time to invest in his ward, on whom he doted.

Sophie had the utmost respect and affection for her adoptive father. And that made what she was about to do even harder. She knew that M. Dublan vehemently disapproved.

Experience had sensitised M. Dublan to the significance of class – with all its inconveniences and its obligations. He knew drawing to be a prized female accomplishment in elegant society, and accordingly, once Sophie was of age to profit from it, M. Dublan had procured his ward a teacher. He was determined that Sophie should learn from the best to be found – and he soon met an instructor more than equal to the task.

In his early twenties with blue eyes, a round face and a crown of bouncing, golden blonde curls, Raimond Bonheur resembled a cherub from a Rococo painting. He had studied at the drawing school in Bordeaux, where one of his teachers was the esteemed painter and engraver Pierre Lacour.[4] The bespectacled polymath Lacour was a well-regarded figurehead of Bordeaux's arts scene. On his father's death in 1814, Lacour had taken over as curator of the Musée des Beaux-Arts de Bordeaux and teacher at the city's free drawing school in the Rue Saint-Dominique. A man of royalist sympathies who deferred to institutions, Lacour was a reverent disciple of the neoclassical tradition. His syllabus centred on the close study of nature, antiquity and the great masters, with keen emphasis being placed on drawing. Raimond Bonheur had been shaped by a formidable mentor.

At the time Raimond entered Lacour's classroom in the early part of the 19th century, the doctrines of the Romantic movement were being trumpeted across Paris. The importance of emotion and feeling were being advocated over what were felt to be the repressive constraints and artifice of neoclassicism. An impressionable youth, Raimond Bonheur was easily seduced by this impassioned movement centred in the capital. Lacour's reproof was immediate: these were dangerous doctrines indeed, the older man cautioned, expounded as they were by men dissatisfied by the monarchy and extolling the abandonment of order.[5] The pupil was quickly swayed by his mentor. Raimond drank in his teacher's views, and made them his own.

Under Lacour's tuition, Raimond developed a style which was reassuringly conservative, a more reliable approach to painting in uncertain times.[6] Even so, making a living by one's brush was always a precarious business, so, his studies complete, Raimond began giving lessons in his turn. The young artist–teacher was an immediate success, as much due to the enthusiasm he inspired in his pupils as the results they achieved under his instruction. That Raimond Bonheur was also remarkably handsome merely heightened his appeal.

So striking was Raimond's divine appearance that people in Bordeaux had baptised him Angel Gabriel.[7] Then with his enthusiasm

Raimond Bonheur, *Self Portrait*, c. 1822,
oil on canvas, 73 x 58 cm, Musée des
Beaux-Arts-Mairie de Bordeaux.
Photo: F. Deval. No. d'inventaire: Bx E 1164

for art and his dynamic presence, Raimond Bonheur exuded magnetism. M. Dublan was certainly impressed by his credentials and Sophie's lessons commenced.

Sophie was naturally creative and proved a receptive pupil to Raimond's tuition. In fact, Raimond was only a year older than the young woman and the more the pair worked together, the closer they became. Sophie's work progressed and all parties seemed content with the arrangement. But then one day, the nature of the student–teacher relationship shifted – and both Sophie and Raimond realised they had fallen deeply, hopelessly in love.

When he learned of the nascent attraction, M. Dublan was vexed. That Raimond Bonheur had abused his role as teacher was a secondary concern; the young man's background (what little was known of it) signalled a yawning class disparity. Word had it that Raimond came from a long line of chefs.[8] His father François was said to have been head cook for the Cambacérès household in Toulouse. The Cambacérès dynasty included not only the Archbishop of Rouen, Étienne-Hubert de Cambacérès, but his brother, Jean-Jacques Régis de Cambacérès, the renowned nobleman, statesman and lawyer who had served as Second Consul to Napoleon Bonaparte and was famed for drawing up the Civil Code. Cambacérès' gastronomic excesses and his indifference to women were a talking point in high society.[9] But for all that his 'appetites' provoked titillation, Cambacérès' table was the finest to be found, his dinners unsurpassed.

As a young man, François Bonheur had met the daughter of an invalided soldier, a girl named Eléanore Marie Perard, with whom he settled before he turned 40. The couple subsequently had a daughter, whom they named Elisabeth, and a few years later, Raimond was born. But unlike his father, Raimond was more attracted by pencils than by pastry. Those who knew the family recounted that he had first shown his flair by sketching his father's lavish butter sculptures.[10] Raimond's mother was a culturally astute woman and when she noticed her son's gift, she encouraged him. The parents agreed to let their son follow his calling.

Cooking was an admirable trade. Historically, some chefs had even been raised to nobility and the association with the Cambacérès' superior table gave no cause for shame.[11] Notwithstanding, cooking remained an artisanal occupation – like painting. The art teacher-son of a chef was no serious marital prospect for an aristocrat – and that was how M. Dublan saw Sophie.

Defying her father's wishes did not sit comfortably with Sophie. But Raimond's presence was irresistible. Besides, Sophie was no longer a minor and she had no birth certificate to testify to her parentage. An approved affidavit was all she required to legitimate a marriage.

Therefore, earlier that month, the banns had been published. And with no formal opposition lodged, Sophie now found herself about to become Mme Raimond Bonheur. If M. Dublan's absence sufficed to convey his feelings, Raimond's parents could have little grounds on

Raimond Bonheur, *Portrait of Sophie Bonheur*, undated.
Collection Atelier Rosa Bonheur

which to object. But the couple's marriage certificate immediately justified M. Dublan's misgivings over their class difference; François Bonheur declared that he had no profession. Nor was he able to sign the document; he had never learned how.

Concerns of class had little place in the happy couple's minds as they left the Mairie that spring afternoon. Buoyed by the euphoric glow of their nuptials, the teacher and his pupil set up home on the corner of the narrow Rue Saint-Jean-Saint-Seurin, a short walk from the imposing 11th-century Saint-Seurin church.[12] And then, a new life began.

&

With a population of more than 89,000 and an important maritime industry, 1820s Bordeaux was a hub of animation and activity. After its golden era in the 18th century, the largely monarchist Bordelais had felt jaded by the Bonapartist regime.[13] The Restoration received a warm welcome, a response ignited by nostalgia and fuelled by hope. The renewed sense of confidence found expression in a number of dramatic topological developments. The fate of the Fort of Hâ, the Fort Saint-Louis and the Château Trompette had already been called into question at the end of the 18th century and in 1816, the Château Trompette was demolished. Bordeaux was opened up to the world and symbolically, the vast Place des Quinconces was built, providing an open space which begat social exchange. As citizens circulated through Bordeaux's streets and squares, sailboats bobbed up and down on the Garonne, while along the quayside, men hammered and repaired wooden vessels as horses heaved up heavy cargo.

But for all the progressive architectural change, Bordeaux's economy was stagnant. Recent history had taught prudence. Jobs in industry were scarce, so many clung to the familiar but erratic commercial activity they knew: the sea. Activity in the port had slumped in the early 19th century when Napoleon Bonaparte blocked maritime relations with England. The introduction of steamboats from 1818 offered some assistance by creating more jobs. But the maritime industry was notoriously unpredictable and dangerous. And in any case, Raimond Bonheur was no seafarer. He was a servant to passion – and his passion was art.

Raimond and Sophie's marital life began auspiciously. Raimond's reputation as a teacher brought him a steady stream of clients. And while his income was not sufficient to sustain a luxurious lifestyle, Sophie found that she could supplement their funds by offering piano lessons. If not wealthy, the couple were at least comfortable.

Once he had made peace with the notion of Sophie working, M. Dublan had to concede that the couple's love showed no signs of waning. Their commitment was admirable. Sophie's guardian softened and he began to accept that his ward had made her choice.

Through necessity, the newlyweds lived with François and Eléanore Bonheur. At nearly 70, François was increasingly infirm and reliant on his son. Still, Eléanore was able to repay Raimond and Sophie in kind by helping with the housework, so enabling Sophie to dedicate herself to her husband and her teaching. She could focus more closely on her health too, and that was important; just a few months after their marriage, Sophie discovered she was pregnant.

In families blessed with financial security, the announcement of a pregnancy was cause for celebration. The 1789 Revolution had underlined the importance of family values, with social discourse regularly equating a well-balanced home life with a stable state.[14] Families without children were widely considered incomplete. As the bearer of the family name, increasingly in the 19th century, offspring were treated as an extension of the self, as little people to be nurtured and cherished. 'Forming mothers' remained the primary goal of girls' education throughout the 19th century, while concern over France's declining birth rate only increased the social pressure on newlyweds to procreate.[15]

Even so, Sophie and Raimond could hardly ignore the financial implications of their imminent arrival. Added to which, for a woman of delicate constitution like Sophie, pregnancy and childbirth were loaded with anxiety.

With the majority of women giving birth at home, labour was a distinctly feminised realm. Nineteenth-century propriety erred away from male involvement.[16] A doctor was costly; in many families, he was only called as a last resort and as a result, his appearance in the birthing chamber was taken as a grim harbinger.[17] With no mother of her own to consult, pregnancy naturally encouraged a more intimate acquaintance between Sophie and her mother-in-law. Female friends like the Spaniard Victoria Silvela were of even greater importance too.

Victoria was the daughter of the Spanish writer, lawyer and magistrate Manuel Silvela.[18] The Silvelas had been living in Bordeaux since 1813 following the fall of the French government in Madrid, a body installed when Spain was considered a client state of the First French Empire.[19] Manuel had fraternised with the *afrancesados*, those who supported the political and social progress following the French Revolution, and in Madrid he had served on the government of Joseph Bonaparte during the Peninsular War. Now, the former statesman was living in exile in France, reduced to teaching Spanish to make ends meet. Notwithstanding, he positively radiated culture, and his circle of acquaintances included the brightest members of Europe's literati, notably the poet and playwright Leandro Fernández de Moratín. The Silvelas were an erudite family and although Sophie was several years older, with both their childhoods coloured by exile and their households each receptive to literary pursuits, Sophie and Victoria had much in common.

Victoria Silvela now offered a vital support to Sophie. And as a proficient letter writer, the expectant mother had a ready means of communication at her disposal.

As the New Year 1822 began, Sophie was nearing her travail. Finally in the middle of March, she went into labour, leaving the remaining Bonheurs to wait anxiously as they prepared to welcome their latest member.

When at last a healthy baby was delivered at 8 o'clock in the evening on 16 March, the relief was universal. Sophie emerged from the ordeal depleted, but the family consoled itself that her strength would surely return.[20]

The infant was a robust and plump little creature, with Raimond's round face and impressively strong limbs. By contemporary standards (or stereotypes), the child's hearty physique was deceptive; the baby was a girl.

On 18 March, Raimond and his parents went to the Mairie to announce the arrival. The new father was elated. Social discourse pitched a child as the means of overcoming one's own mortality. His sense of pride stirred, Raimond informed the authorities that the baby would share his initials. They would call her Marie-Rosalie, or Rosalie for short.

Sophie Bonheur's entrance into motherhood was timely. By the mid-19th century, maternity had become a fashionable commodity. In the second half of the previous century, Jean-Jacques Rousseau's *Émile* (1762) had called for a reassessment of motherhood, and accordingly, maternal sentiment was de rigueur. While during the 18th century, new, particularly upper-class mothers had been accustomed to sending their infants out to be cared for by a wet nurse, women were now being encouraged to breastfeed their babies themselves and to play a more active part in their child's upbringing.[21]

It was a role perfectly suited to Sophie's temperament. But as the days passed and Rosalie grew, it soon became clear that the path to maternal bliss would not afford a smooth passage. Rosalie was a hungry and purposeful child, and her determined grip caused the frail Sophie much discomfort. The new mother persevered. Treatises like Abbé Besnard's *Perils Faced by Children Whose Mothers Refuse to Breastfeed Them* (1825) left women like Sophie in little doubt of society's expectations in the 1820s.[22] Meanwhile, the 18th century's artistic legacy of happy mothers was still being actively promoted by genre painters keen to satisfy bourgeois sensibilities. Every year, the Salon walls filled with sickly — but saleable — scenes of maternal and familial bliss.[23] It was hard for women not to read these images as prescriptive. Increasingly, the use of wet nurses was becoming a lower-middle and working-class phenomenon, a means resorted to only when a woman's income was indispensable to the household budget.[24] Sophie reasoned that the feeding routine would surely get easier. It did not.

Eventually, Sophie realised that she must resign herself to handing her precious little girl over to be cared for by a nurse. Ever since the Bureau Général des Nourrices et Recommanderesses pour la ville de Paris had first begun uniting parents and wet nurses in 1769, private bureaus had been springing up across France.[25] In 1813, the local *Calendrier de la Gironde* encouraged wet nurses equipped with the requisite certificate and potential employers to visit a Mme Lacroix in the Rue Pont-Long.[26] But even if such a concern was inaccessible or unaffordable, around a large city like Bordeaux, there was no shortage of peasant women eager to earn some extra francs. However, sourcing a reliable, lactating individual so quickly was a more complicated matter.

Finally, an obliging peasant was found. But between Rosalie's rapid development and the nurse's inability to produce sufficient breastmilk, for much of the time, the little girl was fed cow's milk from a spoon. With animal milk as yet untreated, it was a bold move; feeding a child this way too early could have devastating consequences.[27] But Rosalie was a vigorous baby and she thrived under the nurse's care. And the nurse was clearly in raptures over Rosalie. She cuddled and caressed her as though she were her own, and went out herself to milk the best cow so that her charge might go to sleep with a full little belly. Her attention, though irreproachable, filled Sophie with envy. She was painfully aware of what she could only read as her own shortcomings as a mother. Only later did she confide in Victoria Silvela that she could hardly bear to see the nurse approaching the house.[28]

Still, for all Sophie's misgivings and insecurities, and the financial strain of having another mouth to feed, the family's daily life was punctuated by many happy interludes.

Young Rosalie was brought up under a tender shield of familial protection. The Bonheur household now included three generations, and the child's grandfather and grandmother – her *pépé* and *mémé* in the local parlance – became an accepted presence at home as she learned to sit up, crawl, then toddle. The family was by no means affluent, but their Sunday walks in the countryside around Bordeaux offered a reminder of their spiritual riches. Raimond's sister Elisabeth was based in the city too. A cultured woman, well read and artistically adroit, her lively character could animate a family gathering, even if those same qualities could sometimes try the family's patience.[29]

Beyond the family home, M. Dublan's doors were always open to Sophie and her brood. Shortly after Rosalie was born in April 1822, M. Dublan had purchased two of the domains previously owned by his family in Quinsac, a verdant little commune in vine-growing country on the Garonne river. This included a rolling estate to which he could receive his family.[30] He proved a warm and affectionate grandfather in spite of himself, and the Bonheurs often found themselves spending lengthy stays at his property.

However, the year after Rosalie was born, there was an alteration to the family's surroundings and routine. Aunt Elisabeth – or Tatan as she was called in front of Rosalie – announced that she was moving to Paris.

The capital had always held an important place in the eyes of France's provincials. Whether glorified or mistrusted, Paris's significance was undeniable. Although the large proportion of France's population who lived and worked in the country was growing steadily, migration to the cities had long been a feature of rural life.[31] In the first half of the 19th century, the populations of Paris and Toulouse particularly started to creep up, setting the trend for other large cities.[32] Gradually, increased employment opportunities were tempting more and more Frenchmen to establish themselves in the city.

Now its magnetic draw had lured Elisabeth, convincing her that her skills as a teacher might flourish there. The change heralded new possibilities. Elisabeth quitted Bordeaux, leaving her brother to meditate on her decision.

But the Bonheurs could not mourn Elisabeth's departure for long. François was growing weaker. By contrast, Rosalie was becoming more stolid and boisterous by the day. Then in the spring of 1824, Sophie fell pregnant again.

Though in many respects a joy, another pregnancy could only have a detrimental effect on Sophie's health – and on the family budget.

Poverty regularly forced women like Sophie to give their babies up. The abandoned child was an all-too-familiar figure in Bordeaux. A fearful establishment had been set up on the Garonne river (known forebodingly as 'the factory') to deal with the countless children that society had rejected.[33] An 'accident' which threatened to compromise upper-class reputations lay behind many cases of abandon. But parents' poverty explained the majority. Upon arrival at 'the factory', unwanted infants had any trace of their original identity effaced and replaced by a number. Without family, they were subsequently sent out into the world alone. For a tender, nurturing soul like Sophie, the consequences of poverty were apt to send a shiver down the spine.

While Raimond tried to keep money flowing into the house, Sophie busied herself preparing for the birth. The baby was due at the end of the autumn. A move to the Rue Fondaudège between the births of their two children had added another challenge to their mountain of tasks, and when September arrived, the couple were not yet prepared to receive the baby.[34]

'I've still got lots of things to get ready,' Sophie exclaimed to Victoria Silvela.[35]

Their experience with Rosalie as a newborn had decided the couple to hire a nurse for her little brother or sister. But only six weeks before the birth, a suitable woman had still not been found.

'One from La Souille came by today,' Sophie told her friend. 'She seems decent and looks fresh and healthy [...] She suits me perfectly, but we can't pay what she's asking.'

The family's finances were already stretched. When Sophie gave birth to a baby boy on 4 November 1824, the money situation could only deteriorate further.

While the mother convalesced, the new baby, Auguste, made his presence known, and Raimond Bonheur struggled to keep the household afloat, Rosalie spent as much time as possible outdoors.[36] She was now two and a half, and she conducted herself with gusto. Fearless and sturdy, she showed great interest in the world around her. Whenever she was taken to Grandfather Dublan's, there was long grass to march through, oxen to pet and cow barns to visit. The occupants of these shelters fascinated the child, and she was the perfect height to enjoy the warm, moist sensation of a cow licking her head as it was being milked.[37]

When she was a little older and had become more familiar with the estate, Rosalie enjoyed following M. Dublan's sons when they went hunting so that she could watch the wild rabbits bounding through the fields. On one occasion, an attempt to imitate them resulted in her falling in a ditch and losing a shoe; there were charged emotions as a rescue attempt was hastily launched.[38]

But Rosalie's mother was anxious that her daughter's time should not be given entirely to play. Sophie appreciated her own education, and so as soon as she deemed her daughter old enough, she began giving Rosalie informal lessons. But reading and writing failed to engage the youngster. Reciting the alphabet caused her particular anxiety. Years later, she remembered beads of sweat actually collecting on her brow as she attempted to keep up with her mother's lessons. Words lacked the immediacy of lived experience; Rosalie preferred gallivanting outdoors. Pictures, however, were a different matter. She delighted in creating images, and she found soil and sand acted as a perfect canvas on which to sketch out the full array of creatures she could see pecking around M. Dublan's poultry yard. Often, local peasant children were treated to an impromptu exhibition of this kind.

'Rosalie is a dear little thing,' Raimond enthused that year in a letter to his sister. 'I must tell you that already she has begun to show a taste for the arts. She often seizes my crayon and scrawls on the door and then calls to me: "Papa, papa, Lalie (Rosalie) makes picture." And she draws rounds and strokes innumerable.'[39]

Observing her daughter's natural inclinations more critically, Sophie could see that her current teaching strategy was fundamentally flawed. But then she had an idea: if she could incorporate pictures into their lessons, perhaps Rosalie would make more progress. At the next class, Sophie asked Rosalie to draw an animal next to each new letter of the alphabet – an ass for A, a bull next to B and so on. It was an inspired idea. Sophie had her pupil's attention; Rosalie began to learn.

Her drawing was developing, too. Rosalie was captivated by her father's work, and to her mother's horror, she helped herself to his paint pots and smeared colour wherever she could. Once when she showed an interest, Raimond explained that sometimes people would sit for him so that he could draw or paint them. To the little girl, this practice seemed marvellous. She immediately took her favourite Punch doll and posed him so that she too could produce a portrait like papa.

A curious child, as she watched her little brother growing, Rosalie began to wonder how he had come to join them. Grandfather Dublan struck her as a wise authority figure, and so she put her question to him: where had she come from? M. Dublan's response was instantaneous: why, a steamboat had delivered her to Bordeaux.

This news was revelatory. The following day, Rosalie tore down to the water's edge to see if the tidal Garonne river might bring another baby brother, or even a sister. It did not.

Subsequent trips were no more fruitful and Rosalie's faith began to waver. But she continued to visit the riverside, just in case the day she abandoned her quest was the same day nature finally granted it. On one occasion, Rosalie lay down on the shore to wait and drifted off to sleep. She was abruptly woken by her nurse who had come out looking for her, and she found herself being scooped up and rushed back home, dripping but alive.

The Garonne was an omnipresent backdrop to Rosalie's childhood. Once, on a moonlit walk, she was awestruck as she gazed down at the glittering reflection of the stars and the moon dancing on the water.

'Mama,' she exclaimed squeezing Sophie's dainty hand as hard as she dared, 'let's go to the end of the world, we'll see them so much better there.'[40] At that moment, anything seemed possible.

As she grew, the steamboat bearing siblings was just one aspect of the world Rosalie struggled to comprehend. Another incongruity was the ritual her mother observed whenever she went shopping. Rosalie watched in amazement as Sophie handed over a large amount of money and received in exchange, not just the desired item, but more money. Mme Bonheur tried to explain that she was being given change, but to no avail. To the daughter, this business of purchasing money was wondrous.

Sensitive to social customs, every weekend Sophie dressed Rosalie in her Sunday best. This comprised a white dress, pantaloons and a pair of red shoes. The ceremonial ritual of wearing this attire made it superb in Rosalie's eyes. Her innocent delight in her appearance touched her father, and he immediately set about painting a portrait of his beloved daughter, who would not appear for such an important picture without her favourite Punch doll.

Raimond Bonheur, *Portrait of Rosa Bonheur as a Child*, c. 1826, oil on canvas, 40 x 32 cm.
Collection Atelier Rosa Bonheur

Sundays were often spent with M. Dublan. For the Bonheur family, his company and routine invariably gave a taste of life for a social class decidedly above their own. In elegant society, music recitals were an integral part of such gatherings, and M. Dublan enjoyed accompanying Sophie on his flute as she sang and played the harpsichord. Often, Rosalie sat by their feet busily cutting out silhouettes of animals and their keepers while the music wafted over her. On one occasion, Rosalie remembered M. Dublan pulling her mother up and urging her to play more softly. Sophie tried the piece again, and when Rosalie approached her to study her playing more closely, the mother stopped what she was doing and scooped her daughter, her 'Rosa', up into her arms, covering her with kisses.[41]

Whatever the Bonheurs' monetary concerns, for Rosalie, life was full of happiness. Years later, she remembered that the family even owned a pet parrot, which could imitate Sophie's voice with uncanny precision.[42]

Rosalie had just turned five when providence finally granted her wish and another little brother was delivered. His name, her parents told her, was Isidore. It was incredible; Rosalie had not even noticed the steamboat arrive.

The big sister felt even more tenderly towards this second sibling. Notwithstanding, it was with Auguste that Raimond Bonheur painted her that year in a bucolic scene, with the little boy's hand hovering poignantly above the head of a puppy, close to his sister's belly, a subtle nod towards the expansive nature of family.

The Bonheurs' social life was not confined to their immediate circle. The Silvelas and several other Spanish families from Bordeaux's little colony of emigrants were close friends. The year after Auguste was born, Victoria Silvela had married Nicolas Figuera and now, soirées and dinners with the Silvelas and the Figueras were a regular fixture in the Bonheurs' diary.

Raimond now found himself mingling in a cultural milieu he could only ever have dreamed of frequenting before his marriage to Sophie. At one such gathering, the family made the acquaintance of Manuel

Raimond Bonheur, *Portrait of Rosa and Auguste Bonheur as Children*, 1826, oil on canvas, 94.8 x 80.6 cm, Musée des Beaux-Arts-Mairie de Bordeaux.

Photo: F. Deval. No. d'inventaire: Bx E 1168

Silvela's good friend, the poet and playwright Leandro Fernández de Moratín, who was now in his late fifties. With eyes like glinting pieces of coal, a large nose and full, rosebud lips, Moratín was an audacious and charismatic figure of the Spanish Enlightenment, whose acquaintances included the great printmaker and painter now living in Bordeaux, Francisco José de Goya. Moratín had translated Molière and Shakespeare into Spanish and he also wrote plays and poetry, using his writing as a vehicle for social and literary critique.[43] Like his friend Manuel, Moratín had supported Joseph Bonaparte and he had also served as royal librarian. He too had been forced to flee Spain and was now living in France in exile. Though considerably older than Raimond, their shared reverence for the neoclassical tradition gave them an important point of contact. Moratín thought young Bonheur's girl charming, and he good-naturedly played with the child, whom he nicknamed 'pretty little cabbage' and called his 'round ball'.[44] Sometimes, Rosalie drew him pictures and those who knew the Spaniard insisted that he treasured every one.

17

At these literary and artistic gatherings, glasses chinked while ideas and thoughts circulated like cigarette smoke, and Raimond found his creativity excited. It was consequently with heavy heart that he learned shortly after Isidore's birth that Manuel Silvela was planning to move his family to Paris, just as his sister had done. Silvela said that in the capital, his teaching skills would gain him more financial security. The family left Bordeaux.

Raimond's despondency at having lost his sister and now his friend was compounded by the exacerbation of difficulties at home. The financial strain of struggling to support the growing clan on an art teacher's income was becoming unworkable. There were now three children and two pensioners dependent on Raimond and Sophie. Art classes were a luxurious commodity; families could do without them when times got hard. Then François Bonheur's reliance on his son only increased each year, while Raimond's ageing mother was becoming less able to help with the housework. The family was on a downward trajectory. There seemed little chance of their situation improving in Bordeaux.

Raimond's sister and his friend Silvela had given him reason to hope. He could command higher prices in the capital. Perhaps he would even find an environment in which his art might flourish.

So it was that in the month of Rosalie's sixth birthday, the little girl received some devastating news: her papa was going to leave them.

2

Where Angels Fear

Eighteen twenties Paris was 'a statue composed of the vilest sediment and the most beautiful gems', proclaimed a contemporary tourist guide, citing Voltaire.[1] 'Its qualities are inseparable from its faults,' the author explained.

But for an aspirational provincial like Raimond Bonheur, the capital's virtues outweighed its flaws. In his mind, Paris was a utopian centre where dreams were realised and fears would melt away.

Nor was this belief without foundation; by comparison with the turbulent reign of Napoleon Bonaparte, the re-empowered Bourbon dynasty offered some semblance of stability.[2] On the surface, Restoration France under Louis XVIII and then Charles X provided an uneventful backdrop against which citizens could launch quests for personal glory. The value of foreign trade had increased in the first year of the sexagenarian King Charles X's reign, while with Joseph de Villèle as head of government, finances stabilised.[3] Many post-Revolutionary administrative ventures remained unchanged, too. The division of the country into *départements*, the tax system and the Banque de France, established by Napoleon Bonaparte in 1800, were now familiar features of bureaucratic life.[4]

Then Paris had long been a crucible of the arts. Institutions like the world-renowned Académie des Beaux-Arts, founded in the 17th century, assured the continuation of the capital's historic prestige and superior position as an arbiter of taste.[5] Paris was also the home of the Salon, the most important event in an artist's year. Painters slaved over canvases for months, sometimes years, in the hope of having their work displayed. If the notoriously conservative and exacting Salon jury agreed that a submission would be accepted, a painter could rejoice: it offered the surest indication that the following twelve months would be financially and professionally gratifying. The Paris Salon was where trends were set, careers launched and reputations made.

At the same time, for the novice tourist, Paris was undeniably the centre of progress.

Since the early 1800s, oil lamps had been illuminating the streets when dusk fell. With the introduction of gas lights from 1817, the capital rejected natural order, elongating Parisians' days and altering routines.[6]

Topographical changes reflected the future-focused mentality, too. Under the Restoration, the Rue de Rivoli, that grand street begun by Napoleon Bonaparte, continued to expand.[7] The rejuvenated Bourse was inaugurated in 1826 in the recently completed Palais Brongniart, while the proliferation of ornate, covered shopping arcades like the Passage des Panoramas tempted a newly enfranchised bourgeoisie to rid themselves of their capital. Even if the close controls to which the arts were subjected were not fully relaxed with Emperor Napoleon's departure, artistic life was still more vibrant in Paris than in other French cities. Meanwhile, social expansion beckoned, as citizens now made their way around the capital in horse-drawn omnibuses, sitting with their knees pressed up against strangers they might never have encountered otherwise.[8]

But to perceive only these advances was to assume a rose-tinted view of the urban metropolis. In reality, the centre of power was far from stable. Like Louis XVIII before him, King Charles X was attempting to steer things in the aristocracy's favour. Yet the scars incurred by the Revolution of 1789 could not be effaced so easily, nor the nation established in its aftermath swiftly dismantled. Charles X's pompous coronation at Reims confirmed how out of touch the King was with his people, on whom grand religious gestures no longer made an impression.[9] The rise of the Ultras, that group who supported the

Bourbons so fervently that they were considered more royalist than the King, gave the populace further cause for concern. Riled by the assassination of the Duc de Berry in 1820, the Ultras had since been accruing power with ominous hunger. Those at the top seemed intent on reinstating the divine right of kings. Their mission might not have struck such a controversial note were it not for the fact that for society's lower echelons, life in Paris was decidedly bleak.

Contrary to the glowing accounts of Paris retold in the provinces, unemployment was a very real part of city life. Under the Restoration, more than half of the city's 224,000 households were estimated to be living in poverty.[10] Many residential areas had fallen into decrepitude. Indeed, in Paris, penury and prosperity were frequently neighbours; around the majestic edifice of the Louvre, the dreary labyrinth of narrow side streets were filthy, contaminated and unsafe. Houses awaited demolition. Rubbish was deposited daily on the streets, preventing water from flowing away. With an inadequate sewage system, the pungent odour of untreated waste made the stomach turn, while dubious sludge collected on the paving slabs as foul-smelling liquid trickled towards the Seine. Overcrowding made it difficult to spot Paris's 30,000-odd thieves and pickpockets at work in this dim warren of alleyways and side streets.[11] Even in daylight, these areas were a hotbed of vice and crime. When night fell, they became positively terrifying.

It was April when Raimond Bonheur arrived in the city. For the traveller of modest means with luggage to convey, the most commonly used form of transport was the *diligence*. These huge, towering covered carriages were dangerously top-heavy.[12] They lurched forward as they set off, then creaked and swayed precariously as the five horses pulling them negotiated often unmade routes. 'Travellers are not only obliged to suppress their every need,' criticised a contemporary publication for young adults, 'but they are forced to suffer the society of people whose opposing tastes and education destroy any charm the trip might have held from the outset.'[13] The wealthier passenger could at least treat him- or herself to a little more comfort by booking a sheltered seat at the front, the *coupé*. But if a traveller's budget could not stretch to such luxuries, they could take a seat inside or, for the particularly thrifty voyager, *à l'Impérial*, on the roof at the very front – and at the mercy of the elements. Still, wherever a person sat, the journey in a *diligence* invariably left passengers bruised and bewildered, and accidents were common.

Night travel was a recent development at the time Raimond made his pilgrimage to Paris. Averaging 12 km an hour, a *diligence* leaving Bordeaux took a minimum of two days and three nights to reach Paris in the late 1820s.[14] Even when a passenger opted for one of the cheaper fares, travel by *diligence* was expensive. In a top price seat, a person could pay as much as 116 francs to travel between Bordeaux and Paris – more than a month's board and lodgings for the economic migrant once they arrived in the capital.[15] For Raimond, returning to Bordeaux was not an option. He had to make this work.

No sooner had he dropped off his bags than Raimond seized a pen and began a letter home. It abounded with determined optimism:

'I have just arrived after an excellent journey,' he informed Sophie. 'I went first to my sister's lodging, where I deposited my trunk, and am now with the Silvelas, who are most kind to me.' Then as though to reassure: 'But neither their kindness nor the noise of Paris can fill the void I feel away from you and all my loved ones.'[16]

In a vast and bustling new city, the pang of loneliness made itself felt even more keenly. Bursting with discoveries he wanted to share, Raimond wrote to Sophie again the very next day.

'I have had a glimpse of the Tuileries. It is quite fairy-like,' he gushed. Then remembering to assure his addressees that they had not been forgotten: 'But how much more fairy-like it would seem to be transported to your side, dear one, and to be with poor mother and father and my darlings, Rosalie and Auguste. Kiss them for me.'[17]

Back in Bordeaux, Rosalie gladly accepted the kiss that her mother recited for her. But she would sooner have received it in person.

Despite Raimond's assurances, it had been hard not to fret as her papa had explained that he would travel to Paris, that faraway city, just as Tatan and M. Silvela had done. Grandfather Dublan was watching over them as Raimond had said he would. But despite her father's insistence that they would all be together again, he had been unable to say when. And in his absence, the promise that he would send for them as soon as he had established a comfortable home now seemed empty.

Sophie could not bear to see her daughter pining. She tried to accommodate as many of Rosalie's interests as possible.

'Rosalie has gone mad since the May bugs arrived,' Sophie exclaimed in a letter to her husband shortly after he had left. 'She has dozens of them, I no longer have enough containers to keep them in.'[18]

'Rosalie asks every day when you are coming back,' read another letter written in June, when Raimond had already been gone two months. 'She longs to see you again. She is painting you some little men to send.'[19]

The summer arrived, and still Raimond had no home to offer them. Added to which, he was missing his children's important life events.

'Our Rosalie is doing well,' Sophie told him, 'she speaks of you constantly. She was quite unwell with whooping cough, which set back her reading, something she struggles with. I cannot understand how this child, who is quite bright, has so much difficulty learning; I think it is carelessness, but she has a good heart.'[20]

Sometimes, Sophie's letters arrived with a gift: 'Rosalie is sending you in the box her first tooth which has come out, and a picture, with the promise of nicer ones in the future.'[21]

At the end of one letter, Sophie implored her husband: 'Do thank her for her gift and write to her, because it brings her so much pleasure.'[22]

The truth was, living in Paris was proving far harder than Raimond had anticipated. The Silvelas were running a boarding school in the capital and they had invited their friend to stay with them while he made more permanent arrangements. Raimond was deeply appreciative when they steered some much-needed clients his way. But the pay was poor and the trickle of income he received was still not enough to fund his family's move to Paris. Raimond was expected to pay 69 francs a month for board and 9 francs 16 sous for lodging, sending whatever he had left back to Sophie.[23]

To compound his misery, with only a few contacts in the city, the sociable Raimond was bitterly lonely.

'The lack of friendship, which is such an imperious need of my nature, would make me altogether melancholy and deprive me of all energy, if I had not you, dear Sophie, to know and love me,' he told his wife. 'Perhaps my outward defects, my impulsiveness, my bluntness, may prejudice people against me and conceal my real nature,' he conceded.[24]

Alone with time for self-reflection and longing for like-minded companions with whom to share the new thoughts that his experience of the city inspired, Raimond was perhaps more susceptible than most to the assorted currents of social doctrines being aired in the capital. Initially, he gravitated towards the group of followers who surrounded Pierre-Jean de Béranger, a dedicated nationalist and critic of the restored Bourbon monarchy whose popular songs and poems aroused controversy. But then, in between his lessons and visits to his sister or the Silvelas, he began to remark the recurring name of Comte Henri de Saint-Simon. The late theorist had been convinced that society should be reorganised with industrialists and scientists forming the backbone of any government (on account of their beneficial effect on moral and physical welfare).[25] Saint-Simon had defended the industrial or working class, which in his conception encompassed anyone plying a trade which served the wider good. During his lifetime, his sermons had fallen on deaf ears. But now, a handful of energetic young disciples – including Olinde Rodrigues, Saint-Amand Bazard and the incorrigible charmer, Barthélemy-Prosper Enfantin – were promulgating and developing his theories. They had even founded a journal, Le Producteur, designed to spread Saint-Simon's teachings. With its altruistic and fraternal bent, and its advocation of merit-based reward and the enfranchisement of women, the burgeoning cult of Saint-Simonianism caught Raimond's interest. It provided intellectual fuel as he struggled to make a home to receive his family.

The New Year 1829 arrived but the long-desired family reunion seemed no closer to being realised. In the breaks between her piano teaching, Sophie continued to update Raimond on their children's trials and triumphs.

Rosalie was now nearing seven years old, yet she exhibited none of the usual behavioural traits of a girl her age. She was stout, courageous and bold, and far more interested in the physically energetic games her brothers played than the ladylike pastimes which had formed such an intrinsic part of her mother's development. François Bonheur was struck by his granddaughter's masculinity.

'You imagine you have a daughter,' the old man proffered. 'It is a mistake. Rosalie is a boy in petticoats!'[26]

Sophie had to concede that her little girl was a conundrum. She was determined and expressed her opinions assuredly. She looked and behaved like a boy but when she drew, she did so with feminine sensitivity.

'I don't know what Rosalie will be,' Sophie confessed in one of her letters to her husband, 'but I have a conviction that she will be no ordinary woman.'[27]

At last, not a few months as he had said, but nearly a year after Raimond Bonheur's departure, his family received the letter they had so eagerly been anticipating: he had found a home. It was time for them to join him in Paris.

M. Dublan was anxious. He knew his son-in-law's predisposition to enthusiasms, and he worried Sophie would be taking the children to their new home too early. Desperate for her adoptive father's blessing, Sophie begged and pleaded, and finally, M. Dublan gave in. He even agreed to pay their travel.[28]

Just before they left, Sophie, Rosalie and the rest of the family received a final letter from Raimond with instructions for their trip. 'Be sure, dear mother, to take every precaution during your three days' journey,' the art teacher urged his elderly parent. 'Here, we will try to forget our troubles. And you too Sophie – I think of your present fatigue. Try not to be too sad in leaving the old place. Think of my

25

having been alone so long, and of our meeting again. And you, my little ones, try to be good. Look round and fix in your memory the spot you are leaving, for many years may go by before you see it again.' His closing line was designed to rouse excitement: 'at last you are about to become Parisians!'[29]

⌘

However much the family longed to see Raimond, their departure would not be with made without regrets. The emotional tear was all the greater since they would also be waving farewell to François Bonheur. With his deteriorating health, it had been agreed that the old man should stay in Bordeaux rather than undertaking the strenuous journey to Paris. A carer had been found, but that scarcely consoled the rest of the group.

On the day of their departure, Sophie readied Rosalie, Auguste and Isidore. Then, she prepared to leave her childhood home forever.

As the passengers boarded the *diligence*, M. Dublan was joined by his housekeeper, the kindly Mme Aymée, whose eyes brimmed with tears while parting embraces were exchanged and tender wishes offered.

Brushing her skirts aside and hoisting herself into the *diligence*, Rosalie could not fully have comprehended the significance of the journey she was about to make, by far the longest she had ever taken. For an intrepid seven-year-old, a ride in a bumpy stagecoach was a marvellous adventure. All at once, the usual routine was abandoned. Food and mealtimes altered, sleep patterns were disrupted. For the next few days, the family's focus would be the more primitive objective of survival and striving to satisfy the most basic physical needs. Still, the spirit was not entirely neglected; there were new sights to take in too, if only from a distance. But after two interminable days and three uncomfortable nights, the novelty was inclined to wear thin on even the most venturesome of youngsters. When limbs were aching and sleep had been lacking, the first glimpse of Paris's rooftops through the carriage window was cause for jubilation.

For a father wanting his children to experience Paris's finer face, the area Raimond had settled on was ideally situated. The family's new home was an apartment in the Rue Saint-Antoine, a broad if rather tired-looking thoroughfare, the continuation of the Rue de Rivoli. The street was lined with houses, apartments and shops – a hub of commerce and trade. As a main artery across Paris, all day long, there was noise; local people were constantly moving to and fro, with many more passing through. The world-famous Louvre was just a few minutes' walk away, while the elegant 17th-century church of Saint-Paul-Saint-Louis was a feast for the eyes a little closer to home. And wherever a person stood, there was a sense that great edifices of historic glory were close at hand, sitting guarded behind some more banal building or other.[30]

Paris was quite different from Bordeaux. But with her child's curiosity, Rosalie was far more captivated by the life-sized wooden sculpture of a boar which stood outside the pork butcher's shop opposite the family home.[31] In the absence of the real livestock she had enjoyed watching in Bordeaux, this creature mesmerised the little girl. She imagined him to be awaiting slaughter.

'More than once when I went out I stopped to caress the poor animal!' she remembered years later.[32] It was a highlight in her new routine – one of the few.

Paris was big and noisy and eventful – just as Rosalie had been told. But after the glittering accounts she had been given in Bordeaux, the youngster found herself decidedly disenchanted with the reality.

'I didn't like the great capital,' she recalled candidly. 'Even the bread seemed insipid when compared to our southern loaves, which were salty and so to my taste. Moreover, I yearned for the sun of my native town, especially as the early spring days of that year were cloudy and chilly.'[33]

Even at home, it was impossible to escape people. The Bonheurs' apartment was located above a private bath establishment, in a building in which a small school had also been established. The institution was run by a M. Antin, a man of Jansenist persuasion (an alternative,

Catholic-based religious movement). Raimond Bonheur had immediately warmed to the spiritual deviant, and when his children arrived in the capital, he was proud to introduce them. M. Antin was delighted with the three young Bonheurs and it was quickly agreed that Auguste should join his classes, and even little Isidore could acquire some basic skills. But then when the schoolmaster beheld Rosalie, a novel idea occurred to him: why didn't she join the boys' class too? The suggestion thrilled Raimond, who thought it inspired that a girl should be educated. Henceforward, Rosalie went to class like a boy and was taught the same syllabus.[34]

A small establishment in a busy street where space was at a premium, the school sent its pupils out to spend their break times in the nearby Place Royale, with its enormous quadrilateral lawn flanked by resplendent, 17th-century buildings.[35] It was an unconventional playground, quite unlike any a child would encounter in Bordeaux. And after what seemed an eternity confined to a classroom, M. Antin's boys liked nothing better than letting off steam with hearty rough-and-tumble. Rosalie was often the self-appointed leader of the group, and she did not hesitate to use her fists whenever she felt the need to defend herself. She fought, played and chased, and even giggled with them at a pale and sickly-looking girl they often saw in the Place Royale, invariably wearing a strange-shaped hat and a green shade over her eyes.[36]

With her father's intense interest in common welfare and spiritual matters, Rosalie was perhaps more aware than most children her age of the political climate in her city of residence. Politics featured prominently in the Bonheur family's private life, acting as a lens through which all their experiences were filtered. Still, a child who had only recently turned eight could scarcely be conscious of the extent and implications of the mounting dissension towards the King.

As early as 1825, the declaration that financial indemnities would be awarded to *émigrés* dispossessed of their property during the 1789 Revolution had given the bourgeoisie cause for alarm. In addition, handing education and the keeping of civil registers over to the clergy had signalled a new regime ready to pander to the Catholic Church.

Now, Parisians were afraid that a return to the pre-Revolutionary system of monarchical dictatorship might be close at hand. The fear seemed all the more credible since the King had reshuffled the Cabinet in the spring of 1829, elevating a number of unpopular but like-minded ministers to positions of power.[37]

But if all this escaped a small child, Rosalie could hardly ignore her father's increased involvement with the group who revered the late Saint-Simon and his spiritual philosophy. One facet of the silent expansion of Saint-Simonianism since the thinker's death was a series of lectures at which devotees could pay homage and detractors be converted. Raimond had an inherent need to discuss and debate any new ideas he encountered; the family could not fail to notice his growing attraction for the cult-like faith.

But neither Raimond's nascent Saint-Simonianism nor Rosalie's own school life made the sudden impact of a very harrowing piece of news they received one day: before the year was out, François Bonheur passed away.

Then, as if nature sought to impress its cyclical character, in November, Sophie discovered she was pregnant again.

Neither Rosalie nor her brothers were given any suspicion of their parents' anxiety at having another mouth to feed. And in truth, Raimond's attention was focused on humanity as a whole when, on 19 July 1830, Sophie gave birth to a little girl whom the couple named Juliette.

But before the family had time to adjust to its new configuration, life in Paris was turned on its head. Dissatisfaction with the regime had been mounting since Charles X's declaration that opposition would be overcome by force was greeted in the Chamber by an address of no confidence. The King had dissolved the Chamber and kept his ministers as the opposition gathered support. Now, just a week after Juliette's birth, the King invoked article XIV, which empowered him to make 'the necessary regulations and ordinances for the execution of the laws and for the safety of the state'. For the people of Paris, the ordinances published on 26 July 1830 were akin to a coup d'état: the liberty of the press was suppressed, the Chamber was dissolved, the law was altered so that the electorate was reduced to a body composed almost entirely of landed proprietors and the date for the new elections shifted.[38]

The people would no longer suffer in silence. In the offices of *Le National*, the paper's co-founder Adolphe Thiers and fellow journalists drew up a protest which contested what they felt to be the government's undemocratic character. On 27 July, *Le National* ran an article with a thinly veiled call to arms: it was for the country to decide 'how far she ought to carry resistance against tyranny.'[39]

Paris was quick to respond. That day, word trickled back to the Bonheur household that citizens were massing outside the Palais-Royal, just a few minutes' walk from the Rue Monsigny where the Saint-Simonians held their meetings, and worryingly close to the Bonheur family's home. In the streets, the tension was palpable. Something was going to happen.

By the evening of 27 July, riots had escalated into fighting, the Royal Guard having been unable to repress the disturbances. Before the end of the day, the first civilian blood had been shed. For a mother like Sophie with three young children and a baby to protect, the sounds of unrest outside induced panic. But to many men of Saint-Simonian persuasion, this development represented change – and that meant new freedom, advancement and possibility.[40]

Rosalie was to be profoundly affected by what happened next and its far-reaching consequences.

The following day, as Sophie lay convalescing and Rosalie grew better acquainted with her new baby sister, the on-duty Major General of the Royal Guard, Maréchal Auguste de Marmont, the veteran famed for betraying Napoleon Bonaparte, neatly summarised what Sophie and Raimond now suspected. He wrote a memo and instructed one of his aides to take it to the King: 'Sire, it is no longer a riot,' read the note, 'it is a revolution'.[41]

3

Hear the People

'Never did so great a change take place in the aspect of the city in so few hours,' exclaimed the Countess of Blessington, a pretty and vivacious Irish literary hostess, on 28 July 1830.[1] Paris had been transformed.

The first barricade had been constructed the day before, a hastily erected obstacle fashioned from an upturned omnibus and designed as a means of defence. Meanwhile, street lights – which were suspended from ropes stretching from one side of the street to the other – had been smashed, plunging the city into darkness and wreaking havoc at nightfall. Word spread that the Royal Guard had opened fire on civilians and that evening, the corpse of one of the victims had been paraded through the streets to rouse citizens' fighting spirit.[2]

On the morning of 28 July, Parisians awoke to find that all the shops were shut. No omnibuses or carriages circulated, and the absence of usual noise made the sounds which had replaced it more terrifying. From daybreak, shouting and distant gunshots could be heard against a backdrop of galloping horses and insistent church bells. Then every now and then, all would fall silent again 'so that for a time one could believe that everything in the city was normal'.[3] Overnight, more barricades made of stones, furniture and carts had gone up, and suppliers of arms had been pillaged. The people were readying themselves to confront the enemy.

Daily life had spiralled into a vortex of fear and uncertainty – and the Bonheur family found themselves at the very heart of the drama.

On the sweltering hot afternoon of 28 July, some 2,000 members of the Royal Guard took up position at the Place de la Bastille, a short walk from the Bonheurs' home. Panic rippled out through the side streets as residents warned each other: 'close your windows!'[4] A cannon had been stationed just outside the Bonheurs' front door. Fascinated as people raced past their house to confront the enemy, Auguste scrambled up onto a *porte cochère* to get a better look. The first shot from the cannon was fired towards the Place de la Bastille, shaking the surroundings so violently that Auguste came tumbling down from his lookout perch and fell by Rosalie's feet.[5]

'Firing in file and in platoon succeeded each other without intermission, and the report of cannon was heard every three or four minutes,' recorded Leonard Gallois, an invalid who watched the events unfold from his apartment on the nearby Boulevard Saint-Antoine.[6]

Workmen, artisans and labourers with arms ranging from pistols to pitchforks marched forward determined, spurred on by calls of '*Vive la liberté!*'[7]

Auguste Bonheur picked himself up from his fall unscathed. Meanwhile, Rosalie watched in disbelief as the Royal Guard charged towards the people. Onlookers felt a surge of triumph as civilians moved forward to meet them, shouting, driving them back.[8]

From upstairs windows, resourceful Parisians hurled stones, paving slabs, furniture – whatever they could lay their hands on – as King Charles's soldiers passed. All around, people fell, many of them wounded, some fatally.

Eventually, as the numbers diminished and fatigue set in among those remaining, the Royal Guard retreated back to the Bastille. Before long, they were called away to the centre of the city. But the aftermath of the conflict around the Place de la Bastille was horrifying. The Bonheurs' neighbourhood had been brutally scarred; windows in houses nearest the centre of the action had not a pane of glass remaining and that evening, countless families dressed wounds, while others mourned. The Bonheurs had reason to be thankful that none of their number had been injured – or worse. And still the King would not withdraw the ordinances.[9]

The following day was warm, 'lovely', Leonard Gallois reported, 'with a slight mist'.[10] There was now a barricade in nearly every street, and the Bonheurs' *quartier* witnessed flurries of activity throughout the day. At one point, the appearance of the National Guard on the Boulevard Saint-Antoine provoked cheers and whoops of delight. Uniformed soldiers from the policing and military reserve force (composed largely of middle-class citizens and operating independently from the army) marched past to the beat of a drum and expressions of popular support. But the centre of the action had now moved. The Bonheurs' neighbourhood was again 'tranquil, whilst blood was flowing in the centre of Paris'.[11]

Among this united front of citizens, word spread rapidly with updates of the progress being made by comrades elsewhere in the city. The Louvre had been captured; the Hôtel de Ville had been invaded; the Tuileries Palace had been seized and people learned that revolutionaries were running riot, looting, tipping furniture into the Seine and quaffing fine wine out of crystal glasses. The Royal Guard and the Swiss Guard were retreating. Then finally, the news reached the Rue Saint-Antoine that a provisional government had been formed.

'It is all over,' exclaimed an eyewitness in the Bonheurs' *quartier*. 'We have a provisional government. General Lafayette is at the head of the National Guard: he has under his orders the brave General Gérard [...] This will be one of the grandest festival days Paris ever saw. Liberty is saved, and for ever will dwell with the French.'[12]

That evening, *Le Globe* could print a triumphant declaration on its front page: 'Paris has delivered France: our enemies are in full retreat.'[13]

Having witnessed the action on their doorstep, the Bonheurs could well appreciate the ecstatic celebrations which followed. Citizens returning from the centre of Paris were jubilant. Rounds of musket shot were accompanied by shouts of joy: 'Down with the Bourbons! Lafayette for ever!' Victorious cries were answered in kind by people leaning out of windows, while the *Marseillaise* could be heard on every corner.[14]

On 2 August, the King formally abdicated and his son renounced his right to the throne as well. Charles X's cousin, the 57-year-old Duc d'Orléans, Louis-Philippe, was offered the crown, but it came with a proviso; Louis-Philippe would not rule by divine right – he was king of the French and the monarchy would only ever be conditional.

'The citizens are masters of the city,' declared *Le Figaro* as Paris adjusted to a new government and fresh leadership.[15]

The wake of the 1830 revolution was an extraordinary time for eight-year-old Rosalie to be growing up in Paris. The National Guard were the heroes of the hour. The principal armed force in the city, they could be seen everywhere. 'For the present there is only one living thing in Paris,' remarked Honoré de Balzac.[16] 'It is the National Guard! Everywhere, blue, red uniforms, *pompoms*, *aigrettes*, shakos, spurs, sabres.'

Louis-Philippe proved himself every bit the citizen king France had demanded. He took the Palais-Royal as his home, not Versailles, that legacy of bygone royal splendour so loaded with implication; he enjoyed daily walks through the streets attired in the familiar bourgeois uniform of top hat and coat, with an umbrella under his arm, and he carolled the *Marseillaise* heartily whenever the opportunity arose. Several evenings a week that summer, the Palais-Royal was open to visitors and the King and his wife Marie-Amélie appeared on the balconies to thunderous applause. This was a king to whom people raised their hats, and he talked to and made time for everyone.[17]

Louis-Philippe's administration took on decidedly bourgeois character, too. Censorship was abolished, military service decreased, the National Guard was restructured and the King's allowance reduced. The time of royal dictatorship had passed; Paris belonged to the bourgeoisie.

But the Bonheur family were not bourgeois. Nor were countless others in the city. And in the following months, the growing pains of a new administration and the conviction that the end of revolution heralded freedom saw an explosion of political clubs and organisations bent on social reform. All at once, people had been brought into politics – and the Saint-Simonians were one of several groups who felt that finally, their moment had come.

In public, the Saint-Simonians declared themselves apolitical; in practice, the revolution had sparked an atmosphere of hope, anticipation and a longing to effect concrete social change.[18] To many, the Saint-Simonians' proclamations all too often assumed a political shape. There seemed a new impetus behind the movement and the weekly meetings at the group's headquarters in the Rue Monsigny became increasingly animated, as thoughts on the way society should be restructured were aired and debated. The group called for the common ownership of goods, an end to the right of inheritance, and the enfranchisement of women, and that autumn, they acquired the paper *Le Globe* as the official organ of their movement, a publication which they distributed free of charge. The round-faced Bazard and the younger, charismatic Enfantin with his assured, penetrating gaze, were now the recognised authority figures or Supreme Fathers, and a series of lectures or sermons attracted a growing number of disciples. Many of the adherents had trained at the prestigious École Polytechnique and they included some of France's brightest young minds, such as the politically disposed Hippolyte Carnot, financiers and engineering enthusiasts Émile and Isaac Pereire, and the Talabot brothers, the engineer Paulin and the legally trained Edmond. In many people's eyes, the Saint-Simonians' membership conferred upon the group a near-Masonic prestige. The number of conversions grew. On Tuesdays, Thursdays and Saturdays there were evening discussions, and Sundays were given to meetings of 'the Family'. At these gatherings, the sparsely furnished rooms at the Rue Monsigny would come alive with music, singing and dancing, and the spirited soirées soon became the fashionable evening haunt of Paris's more curious intellectual.[19] Rosalie's father was among the group's most enthusiastic followers.

But Saint-Simonianism failed to shore up the Bonheur family's livelihood. For all the hopes the revolution had inspired among their fellow citizens, finances in their own household were stretched. After recent events, few Parisian families considered drawing lessons a priority. Raimond struggled to find enough clients to keep the family, and in any case, his mind was consumed with his Saint-Simonian *éducation sentimentale*. Ever practical, Sophie began taking in sewing work making cheap garters. It was intellectually undemanding and it helped feed the family. But for a woman of aristocratic breeding, the work was utterly demeaning.

Still, there was little choice. With the growing family, the strain on their budget seemed unlikely to ease, and in October, Raimond announced that they would be moving to more suitable accommodation in the Rue des Tournelles, just minutes away from their current home. The street was narrower and less peopled than the Rue Saint-Antoine – closer in character to the Rue Saint-Jean-Saint-Seurin in Bordeaux where Rosalie was born. However, to Rosalie's mind the upheaval brought little compensation.[20]

The family's new home was an imposing old house dating back to the time of Louis XIII. Once inside, their apartment was accessed via an enormous stone staircase which filled Rosalie with dread.

'It was so gloomy that I was frightened to go up it alone, especially as underneath us lived an undertaker's man,' she recalled.[21]

When she was still acclimatising to her Parisian surroundings, the sudden move to the strange, dull and dank old building was dispiriting. But the change of address brought one curious and unexpected consequence.

The wife of the undertaker who lived below made shuttlecocks and other children's toys, and she purchased the skin she required from a woman named Mme Micas. A stout and solemn individual, Mme Micas never smiled, rarely spoke and even when she did, issued only careful, measured phrases. From time to time, Rosalie would see Mme Micas delivering her stock to the building and gradually, the Bonheur family came to learn a little more about her.

The Micases were of Iberian origin. M. Micas's family had suffered cruelly during the Revolution of 1789, after which he had worked in the printing trade and subsequently directed a company which made assorted covers and casings. Mme Micas ran their workshop of some twenty female staff, an employment strategy which harmonised with Raimond Bonheur's Saint-Simonian principles. They had a daughter – an ashen-faced, lanky little girl two years younger than Rosalie. It was said that the parents fussed and cosseted the child as though she were made of glass. They even insisted on her wearing a visor to protect her eyes when she was taken out for her daily walks in the Place Royale. It quickly became clear that their daughter was none other than the little girl at whom Rosalie had so often laughed with her peers during her break times.[22]

As that turbulent year drew to a close, Sophie channelled her energies into caring for her brood, while Raimond kept his gaze fixed on the betterment of humanity. However, one day in December, an urgent message arrived at the Bonheur house: M. Dublan was ill – gravely so. Sophie must come at once.

Disregarding how any borrowed money might be repaid, Sophie set off for Bordeaux. Rosalie never forgot what she was told had happened next.

Once she arrived, Sophie raced to the old man's bedside. She was just in time; M. Dublan was hovering precariously between life and death. When he saw the young woman enter, he struggled to pull himself up.

'Sophie,' he faltered, 'you are my daughter, my very own daughter.' All at once, everything became clear.[23]

Sophie was both distraught and elated. By some cynical twist of fate, she was finding a father and losing him at the same time. A final question burned inside her: if he were her real father, who was her mother?

M. Dublan could barely speak now. 'My child, I promised never to reveal it, but in my writing desk, you will find papers which will tell you.'[24]

The old man seemed to be trying to say something more, but his voice trailed off. He was slipping away. Abandoning their conversation,

Sophie busied herself around the invalid, doing her best to nurse and comfort him. M. Dublan passed away on 18 December 1830.

Sophie's heart was heavy with grief when, preparing to return to Paris, she remembered her father's final instruction. She went to his writing desk as he had advised, hoping that the papers might bring her some comfort by giving her what she had never known: a mother.

But when she approached the desk, Sophie had a shock: it was already open. The lock had been forced, the contents rifled through, and no trace of any documents relating to her birth remained. Sophie could not guess at the identity of the perpetrator; her distress by her father's bedside had been all-consuming and she had noticed no one else in the room who might have overheard the dying man's words.

Those papers could have radically altered the Bonheur family's fortune. With their disappearance went hope. Now, Sophie's family must live by their merits and industry alone.

Even at her young age, Rosalie noticed a change in her mother from that point. As the Saint-Simonians claimed more and more of Raimond, Sophie's strength had to be found deep within – and her reserves were now depleted.

The New Year 1831 unfolded, and the Saint-Simonians turned their attentions to the working classes in a hope to rally disciples, while Raimond set about making his own conversions. He firmly believed that the path to enlightenment had been revealed to him. One of the first acquaintances he chose to honour with his findings was his former tutor, Pierre Lacour.

'I little ever imagined that I, moved by a religious sentiment, would address myself to you,' Raimond Bonheur began his letter on 1 March 1831. 'You will pardon my confidence, my hope, that I may be able to give you something in exchange for your lessons,' Raimond continued, adding appreciatively that 'it was due to you that I turned my back on the dangerous doctrines of Boulanger and company.'[25]

A lengthy essay on the tenets of Saint-Simonianism followed, and Raimond concluded his letter with the request that its contents be communicated to the Philanthropic Society.[26]

Former classmates from Raimond's time under Lacour's tuition received similarly compelling letters.[27] Raimond had become one of the Saint-Simonians' most loyal disciples.

Whatever her true feelings, Sophie was ill placed to challenge her husband's principles. She had always encouraged him to follow his heart. She agreed to join him in whatever Saint-Simonian projects he might undertake.

With Raimond's enthusiasm and Sophie's submissive cleavance, it was impossible for Rosalie and her siblings not to absorb something of the Saint-Simonian ethos. A spiritual reference point was now more necessary to the family than ever; 1831 brought still more challenges.

The death of Raimond's mother Eléanore that year compounded the family's distress, adding new impetus to Raimond's quest for peace. He moved the family again to a property near the Place de la Bastille. But they could not settle there either. Finally, Raimond found a home which he believed suited even better, in the Rue Taitbout – conveniently, the same street where the Saint-Simonians had opened a meeting house and gave Sunday lectures.

A young and impressionable little girl consumed by filial devotion, Rosalie watched as Raimond's faith consumed more and more of their lives while her mother grew increasingly distant.

The Saint-Simonians proposed to establish a missionary station in each of the city's twelve districts. Every one would have its own physician, director and directress, and Raimond and Sophie were designated director and directress of the eighth district. The aim was to coax the poor into a system of communal living. In the event, budgetary limitations obliged the Saint-Simonians to scale down their original plan and Raimond alone was named an adjunct of one of the stations.[28]

The Saint-Simonians remained optimistic. However, as 1831 progressed, a rift was becoming evident within the movement. In many people's eyes, Enfantin's proposals, particularly those regarding women, were becoming more radical. He argued for the reform of marriage and the renewal of society through love. If God was indeed androgynous, it followed that Enfantin, who now presented himself as a Pope-like figure, should be accompanied by a 'popesse'. Enfantin insisted that a female Messiah, 'the mother', was coming; once she arrived, the next step would become clear. Tension was growing increasingly apparent between the mystical Enfantin and Bazard, who took issue with his colleague's views on marriage and female emancipation. In November, the final schism occurred. The now ailing Bazard, who had suffered a stroke that summer, consciously distanced himself from Enfantin's teachings, while the latter assumed leadership of the movement and the activity in the Rue Monsigny. To complicate matters, the authorities were growing uneasy about the order. The 1830 revolution had taught prudence where the populace was concerned. Suspicious of conspiracy and anxious to safeguard itself, Louis-Philippe's ministry clung to article 291 of the 1810 penal code, which specifically stipulated that 'no association numbering more than 20 persons, which meets daily or on certain fixed dates, and whose aim is of a religious, literary, political, or other nature, can be formed without the consent of the government'.[29] In January 1832, the house at the Rue Monsigny was ransacked by two attachments of Municipal Guards, a squad of National Guards, a company of troops and a squadron of hussars. Then, the hall in the Rue Taitbout was closed by the authorities.[30]

Things finally came to a head that April, just as poor sanitation and poverty were escalating into one of the worst cholera epidemics the capital had ever known. All at once, citizens were falling. Within hours of contracting the disease, victims became crippled with diarrhoea, vomiting, cramps and life-threatening dehydration. Horrified onlookers watched corpses with sunken eyes and bluish skin being carried from houses. A death toll of ten became twenty, then 100. Each day it mounted, as if a silent and deadly killer was roaming the streets of Paris. Without proper treatment or adequate sanitation, death was virtually inevitable once cholera took hold. Dancers taken ill at balls deteriorated so rapidly that they had to be buried in their costumes. Undiscriminating and unpredictable, the disease could strike anywhere. The bracing odour of chlorine identified those houses needing disinfecting and as the Bonheur family went about the streets, snatches of overheard conversation centred entirely on the fearful illness. People hissed that the government were to blame, the King even, that the wells had been poisoned.[31]

Rosalie had only just turned ten, but she never forgot the chilling scenes.

'It was dreadful,' she recalled. 'Carts filled with corpses were continually in the streets.'[32]

Everyone knew someone who had been affected. One of the first victims was Enfantin's mother. Her death – on the same day that *Le Globe* abruptly ceased publication having proved itself financially inviable – marked the turning point in the Saint-Simonian project.

A flamboyant procession of Saint-Simonians attended Mme Enfantin's funeral. Afterwards, the mourners returned with their leader back to the deceased's home in the Rue Ménilmontant, where Enfantin delivered a stirring speech and selected 40 disciples to remain with him – permanently. The brothers would make Ménilmontant their home. Each man must make a vow of celibacy, wear a beard and undertake household chores, for there would be no domestic staff. The chosen ones could not leave the retreat – and Raimond Bonheur was among that group.

Raimond did not refuse. He was one of several married men to take up the post. The male-only retreat would, Enfantin believed, counteract accusations that the movement encouraged lust and sinful behaviour.

And so, for the second time in her life, Rosalie was obliged to bid farewell to her father.

❦

High above the rooftops of Paris in Ménilmontant, life in the retreat was strictly regimented. Raimond was responsible for sounding the trumpet at 5.00 am. The brothers then took breakfast at 7.00, their midday meal at 1.00, their evening supper at 7.00 and they were in bed each night by 10.00. Food was bland and living conditions spartan.

During the day, each man had specific responsibilities and duties, be it cooking, cleaning or tending the garden. This last task, Rosalie remembered, was also entrusted to her father.[33]

The houseful of men, most in their 30s, swearing celibacy and performing domestic chores – considered 'women's work' – quickly became a titillation point among Parisians. Every Sunday, citizens could visit the convent and watch the spectacle of the Saint-Simonians on parade. Up to 10,000 people flocked to Ménilmontant to gawp at the men of this strange cult with their curious customs and peculiar songs. So enormous was the crowd that it had to be cordoned off with ropes. The authorities' unease mounted.[34]

On Wednesdays, the house also accepted private visits. Henceforward, that became the most eagerly awaited day in Rosalie's week.

On the day of these visits, Sophie ensured that her children were made smart and dressed appropriately. Then, the family set off, with Sophie leading her brood along the meandering route across Paris to the north-east of the city, so that they could snatch a few precious moments with their father.

To accomplish this ritual, Rosalie had to wear her Saint-Simonian bonnet with a tassel. She knew her father loved to see her dress this way, but the moment she put on that hat, Rosalie became the subject of ridicule. Street children jeered and taunted and some even threw stones. But Rosalie held her head high and accepted the persecution as validation of the nobility of her father's cause.[35]

Besides, there were new friendships to be made through Saint-Simonianism. On one of the Bonheur family's visits to the retreat, Rosalie joined with some other Saint-Simonian children throwing fallen apples over a wall. Passing youngsters on the other side started catching the fruit and their squeals of delight as they fought over the booty merely increased the Saint-Simonian group's zeal. Among the gaggle of youngsters to whom Rosalie was throwing fruit was a strange-looking child – a tall girl with pale skin and a protective visor over her eyes. But absorbed in the game, Rosalie had little time to recognise the child as someone she had met before.[36]

The reception Raimond gave his family every Wednesday seemed to make all their pains of the week worthwhile. 'What a warm welcome he would give his wife,' Rosalie remembered sadly. 'It was always accompanied by some fine words.'[37]

Words, Rosalie now knew, came easily to her papa.

'Whenever things got difficult, my father would become truly eloquent; he always rekindled my mother's faith by giving her a glimpse of the New Christianity's imminent triumph.'[38]

But there were some obstacles against which even Raimond's rhetoric was powerless. By May, cholera had claimed 18,402 victims.[39] That same month, the family were grieved by a personal loss; their old friend from Bordeaux, Manuel Silvela, finally expired after a long, drawn-out illness. And it was then that Sophie learned of the Saint-Simonians' dire financial situation.

The group had repeatedly accepted loans from investors who believed in the movement. That May, Rosalie overheard someone confiding in Sophie that the treasurer, Père Bouffard, needed some 200,000 francs to cover debts. There were only 75 francs in the kitty.[40]

Irrespective of his family's needs and concerns, Raimond's faith showed no signs of waning. 'Father, I believe in you as I believe in the sun,' he declared in one of his professions to Enfantin. 'You are in my eyes the son of humanity: you warm it with your love, which is the living image of the Infinite love of God.'[41]

On 6 June, the brothers performed the ceremony for the formal adoption of the habit. Raimond was actually credited with having designed the uniform.[42] This consisted of simple trousers (white, symbolising love), a white waistcoat trimmed with red (the colour associated with work) and a blue-violet frock coat, whose colour was intended to signify faith. The waistcoat fastened at the back so that the wearer was purposely obliged to turn to one of his brothers for assistance whenever he dressed. The costume thus served as a daily reminder of the members' co-dependency.

It was an overcast and thundery day when Sophie took Rosalie and her siblings along to Ménilmontant to watch the event, the first public ceremony of this kind. The occasion coincided with a small Republican insurrection in the Rue Saint-Martin, where a barricade had even been constructed. The unrest, though ultimately inconsequential, served as a poignant reminder of the social unease Saint-Simonianism proposed to tackle.[43]

Uncharacteristically, Raimond demonstrated some reluctance when he was called forward in his turn and Rosalie later learned that he had become uneasy about 'the Family's' precarious situation. Still, the participation of some of his more esteemed colleagues reassured him and he allowed himself to be ordained.[44]

For the Saint-Simonians, the ceremony marked a new chapter. News that the government had made a case for the indictment of Enfantin, Michel Chevalier and Charles Duveyrier gave cause for dismay but not despair. Raimond remained committed to Enfantin, determined to continue his life at Ménilmontant.[45]

But that summer brought more difficulties for the group, and the Bonheur family were directly affected.

As though to herald the closure of a certain era of Saint-Simonianism, on 29 July, Bazard passed away. And less than a month later, the Saint-Simonians went to court.

Rosalie vividly remembered the first day of the hearing. On 27 August 1832, the Saint-Simonians marched down from Ménilmontant behind Enfantin, dressed in their full raiment and accompanied by music. Crowds rushed to watch them pass as they made their way to the Palais de Justice. With their flamboyant costumes and the scandalous accusations of immorality and public disorder, the court case became the fashionable event of the moment. All Paris wanted to attend.[46]

Raimond stood as one of Enfantin's defence witnesses and he refused to testify, as he had been instructed. Indeed, Enfantin had planned his defence carefully. The court rose to his bait, making itself look antiquated when it rejected the two women he had nominated as part of his legal counsel.

Despite the group's best efforts, Enfantin, Chevalier and Duveyrier were ultimately sentenced to one year's imprisonment, to start in

December. And even before that, there was to be a second trial. In October, the group were tried for having obtained money by fraudulent means and being unable to repay their staggering loans. This time they were acquitted and a celebratory banquet thrown. However, as the date of Enfantin's sentence approached and money became scarcer, cracks were appearing in the Saint-Simonian veneer.

It was decided that the Saint-Simonians should disperse. Some left the group voluntarily, their disenchantment with the movement finally supplanting their credence. The faithful were urged to go out and spread the word and a Saint-Simonian expedition to Egypt was even discussed.

But this put Raimond in a difficult situation. Ménilmontant and merely weekly interviews with his family were acceptable to Raimond; as a married man with children, leaving the country was not. Late in 1832, he returned home.[47] His resentment did little to buoy Sophie's spirit.

Often, Raimond grew so impassioned when discussing the Saint-Simonian cause that he openly advocated celibacy. These throwaway lines invariably reduced Sophie to tears and Rosalie remembered her mother holding her tightly as she sobbed. The scene, replayed so many times, fixed marriage with a distinctly negative connotation in the little girl's mind.

Rosalie was struck by her mother's despondency during those dark days. On one occasion, when Rosalie had begged her mother to sing as she used to in Bordeaux, Sophie's voice sounded so plaintive and sad that Rosalie begged her to stop.

'What a baby you are,' the little girl remembered her mother exclaiming. 'So grab a stick and dance.'[48] Rosalie did so, momentarily appeased and delighted. But her happiness was short-lived.

Raimond's art classes were no longer drawing clients. Sophie accepted more sewing work and took in as many pupils for music lessons as could be found, snatching any spare slots between caring for Juliette. Going out to see students at least afforded a change of scene. It was Sophie's only contact with the outside world, save her early morning trip to the market to obtain the cheapest vegetables, now the family's mealtime staple.

Sophie was merely a shadow of the person she had once been when Rosalie contracted scarlet fever. Rosalie recalled the look of concern in Sophie's usually bright eyes when she bent over to give her daughter her medicine. She placed her hand on her child's forehead to ascertain her temperature and Rosalie responded by wrapping her arms around her mother's neck and kissing her eyes. Sophie could barely hold back her tears.[49]

Rosalie recovered. Sophie never did.

Not long after Rosalie recuperated, Sophie herself was taken ill with an indefinable malady. Sophie had survived the 1830 revolution, the cholera epidemic and the strain of her husband's spiritual mission. Now, she was simply worn out.

That May, Rosalie's life changed forever. Early in the month, Sophie Bonheur passed away. Raised as a princess, she died a pauper and was buried in a common grave.

At eleven years old, Rosalie Bonheur could no longer be a child; it was time to be the extraordinary woman her mother had foreseen.

4

Trying for Size

In a society which prized the family, widowers were a subject of pity. Nineteenth-century social discourse pitched the mother as the centre of this all-important institution, and art and literature followed suit. Novels equated the mother's absence with disorder and a loss of sensitivity, while painting frequently cast the widower as a figure of misfortune. The arts' tendency towards melodrama had its roots in the creative output of the previous century. Enthusiasm for English literature had fixed melancholy as a fashionable topos in the second half of the 18th century and still in the 1830s, sentimental genre painting offered viewers anecdotal scenes which played to bourgeois sensitivities. Exaggerated gestures and expressions were commonplace in pictures which tugged at the heartstrings. The Salon walls abounded in works which continued the thematic enterprises of popular 18th-century artists like Louis-Léopold Boilly and Pierre-Alexandre Wille.[1] Moreover, if strict etiquette regarding the duration of mourning was observed – six months typically being advised for the death of a wife – it was hard for a grieving spouse to conceal his predicament.[2] Children merely accentuated the tragedy. The figure of the single father fell firmly outside the model society projected as normative.

Raimond could paint and draw and teach. But he was a novice when it came to running a home. However close the Bonheurs were as a family, it was Sophie who had cared for and brought up the children. Grieving, plagued by debt, Raimond's load had become too much.

It was Mme Aymée, M. Dublan's former housekeeper, who came to his aid. The old lady had adored Sophie; anything she could do to help the deceased's poor, motherless children would be a delight. She sent word to Raimond, insisting that it would be her pleasure to take Rosalie to live with her while he found his footing.

Although struggling, Raimond was reluctant. At eleven, Rosalie was able to look after herself. She was also of immense practical assistance when the family were all at home and she proved a great strength to her brothers in their mourning, too. Isidore particularly looked up to her.

Yet supporting a family of five on an art teacher's income would be difficult, perhaps even impossible. And Mme Aymée's offer was generous. Raimond considered his other children.

The boys, he reasoned, would suffer if forced to leave Paris, where more schools increased their chances of receiving superior education. That naturally meant greater job prospects. And the father could no doubt pay their lessons in kind in exchange for art classes.

Raimond resolved that he could more easily spare three-year-old Juliette, for whom some time in the countryside could do no harm. No sooner had he decided than Juliette and her belongings were expedited to Bordeaux.

Fortunately, Raimond had now found a job at a boarding school and even in his grief, he was able to negotiate a place each for Isidore and Auguste (aged six and nine respectively). That just left Rosalie. With no means of paying school fees, Raimond appealed to his sister Elisabeth, Rosalie's Tatan.

However much she may have wished to help, Elisabeth herself could offer little in the way of childcare. Using her own money, the aunt sent Rosalie to board with a friend of hers.

Mme Pélèrin lived in the Allée des Veuves near the Champs-Élysées, where she looked after and gave basic instruction to several children.[3]

Where girls were educated in 19th-century France, the feminine arts of sewing and embroidery, and above all, the cultivation of lady-like attributes such as modesty and good manners, were often given as much emphasis as reading, writing and arithmetic.

A budding teen, Rosalie was a curious child. But while she took keen interest in the world around her, she showed no special aptitude for academia. Nor did she fit the refined model of femininity educators of women typically extolled. She wore a girls' dress, but her square jaw and firm features were hardly delicate and her mannerisms recalled nothing of Sophie Bonheur's grace. Her mother's absence soon told in her appearance, too, for her dress scarcely varied and through necessity, she wore her hair short; with no one to arrange a plait or set it in ringlets, cascading locks were an encumbrance. What Rosalie did do, and extremely well, was draw. Wherever she went, she studied her surroundings intently, with almost scientific assiduity. Nature captivated her. And the sketches she produced – nearly always of animals – showed an inherent flair.

The time outside Mme Pélèrin's establishment afforded her the opportunity to express herself in pictures. People later reported seeing a sturdily built girl sketching in the dust by the roadside, thoroughly absorbed. One story ran that a stranger's compliment on her work elicited a self-effacing response: any talent came directly from her father.[4]

Whenever father and daughter were reunited, Raimond had occasion to examine the studies Rosalie was producing. Her gift was undeniable. Nothing in Rosalie's scholastic career to date had given proof of excellence or suggested another talent which might be nurtured. Rosalie was creative and practical; she was decidedly not academic. However, Raimond was anxious that she should not follow in his professional footsteps. Drawing and painting was a difficult career for a man. For a woman, it would be inviting a lifetime of struggle. Even the celebrated portrait artist Élisabeth Vigée-Lebrun acknowledged it to be a 'misfortune to be a woman'.[5] Vigée-Lebrun's success was exceptional and as a female, she was rarely entrusted with the profits. 'M. Le Brun took charge of all my earnings,' the artist explained, 'telling me that he would use them to advantage in his business […] It was more usual, in fact, for M. Le Brun himself to receive the money, and very often he failed to tell me I had been paid.'[6] Raimond believed

Rosalie would do better to train and acquire a creative but manual – and importantly, lucrative – skill.

As soon as his work found him able to be based at home again, he seized the opportunity to take Rosalie back to live with him. Then, he set about finding her a position as an apprentice.

The widower took a home on the Quai de l'École, close to the Pont Neuf, an area pulsing with activity. The street's name harked back to the 13th century, when it was used as the main through way of scholars heading towards the cloister of Saint-Germain l'Auxerrois.[7] A muddle of fishermen's huts had since been destroyed, opening up the space, and by the time Raimond Bonheur moved to the area, there was talk of further development. From the ground floor of tall, multi-storey buildings, shops and cafés conducted vibrant industry while barges, steamboats and rafts charged with wood chugged and drifted up and down the Seine. Along the quayside, vessels loaded or deposited people and cargo – just as Rosalie remembered them doing in Bordeaux. Meanwhile, a whole cross-section of Parisian society could be seen traversing the Pont Neuf, itself a hub of social inter-action. Buffeted by noise and people and movement, an observer got the sense that nothing was ever standing still.

But the animation merely heightened Raimond's sense of isolation. Though work satisfied the family's material needs, Raimond had never tolerated the neglect of his spirit. With Sophie gone and the brother-hood at Ménilmontant disbanded, Raimond's soul craved something deeper. The move to the Quai de l'École provided it – and Raimond found that spiritual salvation in the most unlikely of places.

In the 18th century, the Café du Parnasse near the Pont Neuf had made its name as a favoured drinking haunt of the Revolutionary pol-itician and orator Georges Jacques Danton. There, Danton met – and later married – Antoinette Gabrielle Charpentier, daughter of the landlord, Jérôme François Charpentier. With its prime location and history of celebrity patrons, the venue remained a lively meeting place of some of the foremost thinkers and theorists of the day. During one of his breaks from teaching, Raimond found himself passing the door of the establishment. Spiritually lost and longing for companionship, the art teacher was drawn towards the welcoming glow and hum of voices emanating from the café. In the amalgam of chinking glasses, chatter and cigarette smoke, he struck up a conversation with a mesmerising stranger.

Tall with receding hair, a well-defined bone structure and dark, twinkling eyes, Dr Bernard-Raymond Fabré-Palaprat was arresting for a man in his 60s. He was also fiercely intelligent. Ordained as a priest, qualified in medicine, Fabré-Palaprat had been made director general of the Société Médico-philanthropique in 1803. His publications ranged from treatises on medical innovations to historical and religious essays, while his bravery and valour during the 1814 Battle of Paris had earned him the title of Chevalier de la Légion d'Honneur.[8] But his most noteworthy achievement had been in 1804, when he founded the Order of the Temple.

Fabré-Palaprat's organisation represented an effort to resurrect the 11th-century order the Knights Templar. Originally set up to defend Christian pilgrims on their journey to the Holy Land, the Catholic military order united knightly and monastic concerns. Recognised by the Pope in the 12th century when Hugues de Payens was made the very first Master of the Temple, the group became an autonomous corporate body answerable only to the Pope. One of the most skilled fighting units of the Crusades, the order also created a banking system which proved so efficient that monarchs and church leaders were soon entrusting their money and assets to the Templars. The group accumulated power and magnificent wealth. But by the 14th century, those riches were provoking unease – and jealousy. Added to which, the loss of the Holy Land saw the Templars' supporters dwindle. Then there were secrets; people whispered about a mysterious initiation ceremony and suspicion mounted. Finally, King Philip IV of France ordered the arrest of the Templars and, not long after, the execution of the current Master of the Temple, Jacques de Molay. The order was disbanded and its property dispersed. However, many suspected that the Templars had survived as an underground movement.[9]

In the early 19th century, Fabré-Palaprat had made it his mission to revive the order. Napoleon Bonaparte had demonstrated his approval and ever since, the Order of the Temple had been expanding. Fabré-Palaprat even claimed to hold important relics in his home, notably the helmet and breastplate of Jacques de Molay.[10] To further support his cause, Fabré-Palaprat pointed to the recently discovered Larmenius Charter (or the Charter of Transmission), which named the successive Grand Masters of the Templars and was ostensibly written in the 14th century. Mistrustful, critics denounced Fabré-Palaprat's assumption of leadership. The doctor had formed the Johannite Church in 1812, a Gnostic Christian denomination which set out to perpetuate the Christian teachings of John the Baptist and John the Apostle. Now, Fabré-Palaprat appeared to be introducing a faith-based element into the Templars. Notwithstanding, the resurrected Templars continued to attract supporters. And with the movement's emphasis on morality and chivalrous behaviour, as well as the vestimentary pageantry of their white robes emblazoned with scarlet crosses, the Order of the Temple had all the components to appeal to Raimond Bonheur.

The Templars were not unknown to Raimond. Fellow Saint-Simonian Hippolyte Carnot had been involved with the group before joining Enfantin's movement. In fact, the similarity between the Templars and the Saint-Simonians did not pass unnoticed with the Parisian public. 'Go and die of despair in your dungeon, Père Enfantin,' exclaimed a reporter for the *Messager des Dames* in 1833. 'There is a new cult in Paris and you are not invited!'[11] Carnot was ultimately disappointed with what he considered to be the order's resistance to progress. But Raimond did not concur. Smart, eloquent and persuasive, Fabré-Palaprat was a silver-tongued orator. It took little for his enthusiastic apologia to mollify the pliant listener. In no time at all, Raimond Bonheur had found his latest calling.

Nevertheless, as a single parent, he could no longer rely on his spouse to carry the burden of child-rearing whenever a novel interest beckoned. The Bonheurs' new home established, it was time to settle Rosalie in a profession.

Working-class families had long been sending their children out to earn as soon they became employable. Although social theorists had begun to object to child labour by the 1830s, the concerns they raised were yet to make any measurable impact.[12] A young adult was viewed as another potential wage earner. In single-parent families, these youngsters became especially important. In time, a skilled artisan could expect a reasonable degree of job security and respectable wages, and so Raimond could feel pleased when he found his daughter a position training alongside a seamstress named Mme Ganiford.[13]

The garment trade was a prudent area to launch a career. Even when times were hard, everyone needed clothes and as foreigners had often observed, Paris was where 'fashions were determined and judged', for 'every minute a new one was born'.[14] Besides, the rich were always prepared to spend on maintaining their image. 'There are many balls,' observed a social commentator in an 1830s women's journal. 'It is truly exhausting running from party to party; but if one has a charming outfit, it is admired every time and by as many people as possible, and the swell in pride will make one forget even the most pronounced fatigue.'[15] Paris's fashion industry depended on a steady supply of laundresses, seamstresses and milliners to satisfy these demands.

A seamstress's work was repetitive and the hours long. A girl was expected to arrive punctually for an early start. She had to familiarise herself with the basics, perfect all manner of stitches and then apply them to an array of different fabrics. Most importantly, the work had to be carried out with speed and precision at all times. A simple midday meal taken in the workshop usually served to break the monotony. But it was a fleeting interlude; soon, the afternoon's tasks were upon the apprentice and work continued into the evening, with deteriorating visibility and days lasting up to twelve hours.

Rosalie found the work tedious. Fashion in the 1830s spawned excess. If occasion wear was flamboyant, everyday dress was often sombre. The resurgence of the corset had restricted female waists, but mutton-leg sleeves and longer skirts obliged seamstresses to manhandle swathes of often heavy fabric.[16] The simplest repairs were invariably the most exasperating.

But to brighten Rosalie's working day, her employer's husband had a workshop next door where he practised the intricate art of producing percussion caps, small cylinders made of metal containing shock-sensitive explosive material which were used in guns. Before long, Rosalie had stolen her way into the adjacent workshop and become engrossed in the work.

In the 19th century, percussion caps were made using a special press. This four-legged wooden contraption was not unlike a printing press and it had a large wheel on one side which had to be turned by hand to make the brass cups. These were then filled with percussion compound.

M. Ganiford was more biddable than his wife, and whenever Rosalie wandered into his room, he allowed her to turn the wheel.

This soothing, repetitive motion felt more instinctive to the young apprentice and, Rosalie remembered, 'suited me much better than stitching and hemming.'[17]

It suited Mme Ganiford less. Rosalie was dismissed.

Raimond did not have time to navigate his daughter's career path as well as his own. He was grateful when two friends of his, M. and Mme Bisson, offered Rosalie some work.

The Bissons produced heraldic painting and added colour to all kinds of plates and fashion engravings, a practice which immediately fascinated Rosalie.

Mme Bisson was an eccentric individual who was thrilled to find a girl eager to spend time with them. It had been her ardent wish to have a daughter; nature had granted her three sons. So keenly did she feel the urge for femininity that she had rebaptised all her boys with girls' names. Rosalie became great friends with the youngest, who answered to Éléonore.[18]

The husband and wife paid Rosalie what they could to produce simple drawings and colour kaleidoscope views. The money was pitiful, the work unchallenging. But that hardly mattered: for the first time in her life, Rosalie was taking home money for something she had drawn or painted. Years later, the very thought of those few coins still made her heart skip with joy.[19]

While Rosalie was contentedly working alongside the Bissons, Raimond's commitment to the Templars was growing more pronounced. Given his track record with the Saint-Simonians, those who knew him had cause to be concerned – and few people knew him better than his old friends the Silvelas.

The family's late head, Manuel Silvela, had boasted countless influential acquaintances. Before his death in 1832, Silvela had introduced Raimond to a very prominent professional contact. Now, that connection was to prove a lifeline.

Round-faced and balding with an upright stature and serious mien, Étienne Geoffroy Saint-Hilaire was one of the foremost scientists of the day. He had studied law and medicine in Paris and was barely twenty when he was made superior intendant of the Cabinet of Zoology at the Jardin des Plantes in charge of the menagerie. That same year, he became chair of Zoology at the newly created Musée National d'Histoire Naturelle. Saint-Hilaire's theoretical work included numerous publications and five collaborative texts with fellow naturalist Georges Cuvier. In the early 19th century, he first aired his ideas on 'the unity of composition', whereby he proposed that all living creatures were essentially variations on one basic blueprint. In 1798, Saint-Hilaire had joined the party of scientists and artists accompanying Napoleon Bonaparte's invasion of Egypt, where he collected important artefacts for museums and successfully defended them when they came under threat. Returning to Paris, he was made a member of the Académie des Sciences, and in 1809, Professor of Zoology at the Université de Paris. But his most high-profile exploit occurred in 1827, when he was asked to supervise the transportation of the first giraffe seen in Europe for centuries from its disembarkation at the port of Marseille up to Paris. The extraordinary procession travelled on foot, and by the time Saint-Hilaire and the giraffe arrived in Paris after a month's journey, both the naturalist and the animal had become celebrities. In the theoretical domain, a much-hyped debate between Saint-Hilaire and Cuvier (whose conjectures now diverged from the older naturalist's) at the Académie des Sciences in 1830 had cemented their respective positions in the spotlight. Cuvier died in 1832, leaving Saint-Hilaire one of the most eminent scientific personalities in the capital.[20]

Raimond Bonheur was acutely sensitive to scientific progress. In the early 19th century, Paris was widely seen as the scientific capital of Europe. The concept of time and space fascinated people. Chemist and physicist Joseph-Louis Gay-Lussac had attracted great attention in 1804 when he ascended 4,000 m in a hydrogen balloon to investigate the Earth's magnetic field and study the atmosphere.[21] By the mid-1820s, Jean-Baptiste de Lamarck had revolutionised understanding of the species he termed invertebrates.[22] Physicist François Arago held audiences enraptured with his public lectures on astronomy, while André-Marie Ampère had forged a place for the new science he called electrodynamics.[23]

Saint-Simonianism had provided countless opportunities for Raimond to encounter science. Broadly speaking, the movement supported scientific progress.[24] A man of progressive ideas, Raimond had long been teaching his students to regard nature as the ultimate model; from this perspective, scientific understanding could only be beneficial to artistic production.

His stance on science aside, Raimond's finances were faltering. It was a stroke of good fortune when, in the mid-1830s, the great Saint-Hilaire offered him freelance employment producing illustrations for the work he was undertaking at the Jardin des Plantes.

But though a propitious opportunity, it afforded Raimond even less time to supervise his children's development. The three youngest Bonheurs were attended to, but Rosalie was a continued source of anxiety. Her work with the Bissons was not blossoming into a fruitful career, and so Raimond decided to make one last attempt at educating her. A few more complimentary art classes were a small price to pay if it offset his daughter's tuition fees. Raimond enrolled Rosalie in a girls' boarding school run by a Mme Gibert in the Rue de Reuilly, a straight and busy street a little to the east of the Place de la Bastille.

From the moment she walked through the school gates, Rosalie was at odds with the administration.

'I became an element of discord,' she admitted.[25]

Mlle Bonheur was an avowed tomboy and soon her brazen manner saw her gathering disciples from the theoretically polite and refined student body. Rosalie's free spirit could not be tamed.

The girls were instructed to learn their lessons; Rosalie busied herself sketching a menagerie of animals and creating merciless caricatures of her teachers. Pupils were ordered to work on their arithmetic; Rosalie rolled up her caricatures, tied them with string and attached a chewed up wad of paper or bread to one end so that the whole construction would stick when she launched it at a flat surface. Classmates were at pains to smother their giggles when they saw effigies of their teachers dangling by their necks from the ceiling.[26]

The drawings were confiscated and punishment issued in exchange.

Playing the fool came to be Rosalie's reflex. As her mother's death became ever more distant, her nostalgia grew – and her academic progress stagnated. Only in art did she excel, putting Raimond in an uncomfortable position when prize-giving came round; invited to select the best drawing student, he had little choice but to present the award to his own daughter.

But Raimond did not allow Rosalie's disappointing academic record to shake his paternal aspirations. The Templars were still a dominant force in his life and it occurred to him that it would be marvellous for his daughter to be baptised as a Templar. So it was that one evening, Rosalie found herself being collected from boarding school in order to undertake a very special kind of ceremony.

Raimond led his daughter through the streets to the Templars' lodge in the notoriously squalid district of the Cour des Miracles. Upon arriving, Rosalie noticed countless souvenirs of the Templars' glorious past, not least in the form of the ancient altar, pulpit and baptismal font that had been preserved there. As she studied her surroundings, Rosalie was instructed to don a white robe.

'The ceremony was performed in their sort of chapel,' the teenager remembered, 'under a canopy of steel formed by the drawn swords of the knights in costume [...] full of solemnity, it appealed eloquently to my imagination.'[27]

By the time Raimond returned her to school, Rosalie was utterly convinced that she was truly a knight. And the young Templar was eager that her classmates should join her in the gallant missions her new status demanded.

'One day I proposed as a game a sham fight in the garden. We procured some wooden sabres and I ordered a cavalry charge.'[28]

Mme Gibert's prized flowerbed was the unhappy victim of the siege. It was entirely destroyed – and so was the teacher's patience. Raimond Bonheur was summoned and the young rebel expelled.

Rosalie's academic fate sealed, Raimond was instructed to take his daughter home.

The family's occupation of the property on the Quai de l'École had not lasted long. 'In my early youth we used to migrate with the birds', Rosalie later acknowledged, referring to her father's nomadic tendency.[29] She remembered the home she and her father returned to that day as being an apartment in the Rue des Tournelles, the same street the family had occupied when Sophie Bonheur was alive. They now lived at number six.

Since her mother's death, Rosalie had transferred all her filial affection onto her father. He had become an object of veneration whom she idolised. His pleasure meant everything; his disapproval was torturous. Waiting to be apprised of her fate was agonising.

Eventually, the father issued his verdict.

Setting a plaster cast down in front of her, Raimond began. It was clear, he explained, that all she excelled in was drawing. That left him only one choice: henceforward, the pencil and the brush would be her tools. She must learn to use them well, for with them she would earn her keep – she was to become an artist.[30]

Rosalie could scarcely contain her excitement. It was all she had ever dreamed of.

From that point, a glorious new routine established itself. Every morning, having set Rosalie a list of exercises for the day, Raimond left the apartment-cum-studio and set off for work. Then, Rosalie's training began.

Students in the leading art schools were traditionally set copying tasks as a way of perfecting their skills, and accordingly Raimond would leave Rosalie engravings to reproduce, and sometimes plaster casts to copy. But the art teacher considered studies from nature to be even more informative, and so he also set his daughter still lifes to work from.

Anxious to win her father's approval, Rosalie worked assiduously throughout the day, ignoring all interruptions, drawing, sketching and shading her way to her father's heart.

Each night on his return home, Raimond inspected and provided a critique of her day's production. Their relationship afforded her no special dispensation, and Rosalie often found the assessment harsh. But she absorbed every word. And through perseverance, her work began to improve.

Historically, academic teaching drilled students to acquire proficiency in line before they advanced to using colour. It was therefore a bold move when, one day, her father having left for work as usual, Rosalie decided to help herself to his paints. A bunch of cherries purchased as cheaply as possible and a small prepared canvas found in the studio provided all the additional material she required. Rosalie set to work.

Concentrating closely, her eye darting between her subject and her canvas, Rosalie toiled intently. Time seemed to telescope. She did not even hear her father return. Suddenly he was standing over her.

Surprise quickly gave way to anxiety. Raimond Bonheur's response was paramount.

'Why, that's quite pretty,' he observed at length.[31]

It was the endorsement Rosalie had so longed for. That day, every-thing changed. Her father's conclusion signposted the path that she should henceforward follow:

'You must now go to work in earnest,' he instructed.[32]

Rosalie asked nothing more. She would do just that.

5

Beasts and Benefactors

In 1835, one artist's name was on everyone's lips. Mme Élisabeth Vigée-Lebrun had just published her memoirs.

The preface to the work announced that hers was 'a life that resembles no other, one accompanied by the glory that appends superior talent and embellished by the love of work, countless successes and the most brilliant connections.'[1] Mme Vigée-Lebrun's appeal was greatly enhanced by her evident beauty and 'the warmth of her spirit'.[2] But her femininity was at once a latchkey and a prison; what might have remained mere criticism of the artist's technique or political leanings had she been a man escalated into scandalous gossip when her painting of Louis XVI's finance minister, the Comte de Calonne, sparked rumours of an illicit liaison.[3] Notwithstanding, Mme Vigée-Lebrun had proved that a woman could excel in the field of art, that it was possible for female talent to receive the acclaim it deserved.

Raimond Bonheur held Vigée-Lebrun aloft as a model to emulate, and Rosalie gladly accepted the challenge, striving as best she might to reach her father's gauge of perfection.

Barely fourteen years old, Rosalie remembered those first few months after her expulsion from school as some of the happiest of her life. Every day, she toiled at the work she loved. And each evening, she received a tutorial on her efforts.

If Raimond pushed his daughter, it was because he had detected in her the glinting nugget of potential – and not just Rosalie's own.

In the person of his daughter, the art teacher perceived the chance to realise his own unfulfilled ambitions, to choreograph the glittering career he himself might have led.

Rosalie's weekdays were thus spent perfecting her craft in the studio. But when the weekend arrived, Raimond encouraged a more recreational, though no less informative activity.

'At least once a week, everyone in Paris feels the need to get away from the bother of business,' proclaimed a contemporary social commentator, 'from that daily drudgery that must be resumed on Monday.'[4] It is, the writer went on, 'natural to yearn for the fields when one is confined to the great city.'[5] Raimond Bonheur was no stranger to this Parisian predilection.

By the 1830s, the environs of Paris had become a magnet to city dwellers at the weekend, especially in fine weather. 'At the first sign of spring, Parisians happily escape the city's confines,' observed a contemporary guide.[6] And there was no shortage of beautiful spots at which to gain a respite from city life.

The leafy Bois de Boulogne with its shaded alleys and pathways was where fashionable society was showcased and judged, where reputations were made – or sullied. To the east was Vincennes, with its 12th-century château and its forest, which, as one popular 1830s guide affirmed, 'abounds in game and animals suited to the chase'.[7] Then there were a myriad of other verdant spots accessible from the city centre, where a person could see horses and cattle and, for a time at least, believe they were really in the country.

Sunday walks to Paris's rural outskirts became a keenly anticipated feature of Rosalie's week, recalling as they did the strolls the family used to take around Bordeaux. The father and daughter were often joined by Raimond's friend, Justin Mathieu. Mathieu was the same age as Raimond and already a sculptor of some renown. The complement of this third viewpoint on the sights and sensations enriched the experience.

On one of the walks that Rosalie and her father took alone, Raimond proposed a hike out to Mont Valérien, a former pilgrimage site some 2 km to the west of Paris. The location's history could be traced back to the 3rd century, and it was said that Sainte Geneviève had pastured her sheep there in the 5th century. Under the Revolution, the sacred buildings which had been constructed over the centuries were all but destroyed and the religious function of the location gradually lost. Notwithstanding, in the early 1820s, a very unique kind of cemetery had been created, with the aim of offering a more elegant grave than was commonly available in Paris – for a price. It soon became the coveted resting place of the capital's richest, most well-to-do social elite. But from a purely artistic perspective, the views down over Paris from the top of its steep hill were spectacular.[8]

Having reached their destination, the father and daughter ambled in silence among the graves. Rosalie was struck by her father's pensive, preoccupied mien, which she attributed to the thoughts of her mother that the cemetery no doubt inspired. Its smart graves were quite unlike the one he had offered Sophie. Rosalie later described how, silently, respectful of her father's need to meditate, she remained a few paces behind him, conscious of the metaphorical as well as the literal sense in which she now walked in his footsteps. It dawned on her that one day, she would lose him as she had her mother.[9]

Such weekend visits invariably provided material for contemplation. And when the week began, Rosalie resumed her practice, revitalised. At a time when most girls her age were beginning to take notice of their toilette and contemplate husbands, Rosalie was engrossed in the dialogue between brush and experience, a journey happily oriented by the only man she could ever conceive of loving.

Her efforts were beginning to bear fruit, so much so that one day, Raimond announced that the moment had come to perform a very important rite: it was time to visit the Louvre.

❧

Described by a contemporary journalist as a 'magnificent palace which holds so many artistic treasures,' the Louvre was revered by scholars and eulogised by tourists.[10] For the latter, the pilgrimage often had no artistic motive at all. Many came 'from the provinces', with the sole purpose of being able to say on their return: 'I saw the Louvre.'[11]

Artists typically came with loftier aims. In a world where the official art bodies still deferred to academic tradition, the Louvre was considered an essential part of every artist's training.

A woman artist was not an unusual sight in the gallery. Still, for a female to draw in such an environment demanded courage and the acceptance that she would likely expose herself to ridicule. Any girl who took work modelling in an atelier could vouch for the cruel teasing inflicted on a female who betrayed her weakness. Added to which, Rosalie was especially young. She had every reason to feel nervous when, finally, the day of her first visit to the Louvre arrived.

Stepping inside the grand halls, where every sound reverberated, every error seemed magnified, Rosalie was instantly overwhelmed. With centuries of artistic brilliance peering down at her from the walls and a warning from her father about presumptuous male art students ringing in her ears, Rosalie was paralysed.

She returned home that night crestfallen. When Raimond examined her day's labour, he found nothing but blank pages; Rosalie confessed that she had been so terrified, she had been unable to draw a single thing.[12]

Determined to restore her father's faith, Rosalie resolved that the experience would not be repeated. The next time she entered the building, she strove to appear bold and self-possessed. Male heads still turned as she passed, but now, Rosa's coevals retained only the impression of her assured demeanour and the smart clack of her heels on the tiled floor as she marched with an emboldened step, so that her walk might project a confidence she did not possess. The students sniggered between themselves and called her 'the little hussar', but they all kept their distance. In any case, Rosalie soon realised she could avenge herself with her brush and pencil, and created devastating caricatures of anyone who dared cross her or question her right to be there.[13]

Henceforward, the stolid girl in her teens with her chequered cape and dress, and her brown hair which glinted copper in the sun, became an integral part of the gallery's human fabric. She arrived in the morning, worked diligently and did not leave until the end of the day, pausing only to take a few breaths of fresh air in the courtyard and a simple lunch of bread and fried potatoes, washed down with water from the hydrant. In time, Rosalie could boast one or two good acquaintances among the regular copyists.[14]

Gradually, Rosalie's portfolio of copies was building. Seventeenth-century art provided an especially rich source of training. She studied the dark, brooding landscapes of the rebellious Italian, Salvator Rosa; she marvelled at Dutchman Karel Dujardin's Italianate scenes of peasants and their livestock; she pored over the animal pictures of his fellow Dutchmen Paulus Potter, with his majestic steeds and strapping cattle, and Philips Wouwermans, who filled his landscapes with horsemen to create hunting and battle scenes and works like the *Parade with Fatted Ox* (*c.* 1650–1635), which had been in the Louvre since 1783.[15] Rosalie took in the radiant landscapes and pastoral scenes of the Dutch painter Nicolaes Pietersz Berchem. She tried to imitate the biblical scenes of the father of French classical painting, Nicolas Poussin, studying the carefully sculpted musculature of his figures. His *Arcadian Shepherds* (1637–1638) was duly copied as part of her training. Rosalie examined the meticulously worked religious painting of Eustache Le Sueur. Then there were more contemporary artists, like the recently suicided figure of Louis Léopold Robert, whose *Fishermen* (1835) was felt to 'rival the purity and poetry of the purest, most poetic works of Raphael' when it was shown at the Salon of 1836.[16] Rosalie reverently copied his celebrated *Arrival of the Harvesters* (1830).[17]

With her love of wildlife, Rosalie was naturally drawn towards contemporary painters of animals like the fellow Bordelais nearly eighteen years her senior, Jacques Brascassat, whose 1836 Salon entry one critic believed attained 'a level of verisimilitude' that left him 'without rival'.[18]

Occasionally, an English-speaking tourist peered around her easel to gape unashamedly at the work in progress, offering heavily accented praise: '*Très bien, très très bien.*' But commendations delivered in foreign languages escaped Rosalie, her English being even weaker than her French.[19]

Tangible recognition of her skill was less easy to ignore. The Bonheurs boasted numerous artistic contacts, and Rosalie was thrilled when her copy of *Henry IV* by the 16th–17th-century Flemish painter Frans Pourbus the younger found a buyer, and she received 100 francs.[20]

When she returned home at dusk, she did so weary, but happily satiated. Dining together on bread and broth from a nearby restaurant, the father and daughter shared their experiences of the day.

For all that he now embraced her artistic proclivity, Raimond viewed Rosalie's development as a holistic enterprise. Her mother had always fretted over the young girl's uncertain grasp of French, and Raimond was anxious that she should not abandon her literary studies. He himself dabbled in poetry and enjoyed composing verses. From time to time, he gave recitals of these writings, inviting friends and neighbours to join the family on Sundays at an informal salon. Guests remembered Rosalie's contribution being more musically oriented, and she would often perform popular songs and old ballads.[21] But Raimond would not allow her literary education to be neglected.

Thus when she returned from the Louvre, Rosalie's evenings were usually spent with a book. Sometimes, Raimond proposed reading aloud.

Rosalie's appreciation of literature remained subservient to her passion for art. Nevertheless, some of the writers her father recommended succeeded in engaging her.

The early 19th century saw foreign literature regaining some of the influence it had enjoyed before the Revolution of 1789, a phenomenon facilitated by the enriched literary and geographical nous of returning *émigrés* and the emerging notion of the professional critic.[22] Rosalie could soon count Walter Scott and James Macpherson among the reading list of her teenage years. Scott's *Redgauntlet* (1824) had been translated into French shortly after it appeared in English, and the powerful narrative of his poems and historical novels, with the skilful depictions of the Scottish landscape, made him a cherished addition to the Bonheur family library. 'Sir Walter's ardent love for animals drew me more closely to him,' Rosalie explained.[23] The epic poems of James Macpherson's Ossian had also appeared in their second French translation in 1810, and their wild, romantic quality particularly appealed to Rosalie.[24]

As French literature, Raimond encouraged Hugues-Félicité-Robert de Lamennais, the radical priest, writer and Christian Democrat. Well read but informally educated, Lamennais was thrust into the spotlight in 1817 with his *Essay on Indifference Towards Religion*, in which he urged the active practice of religion. Subsequent volumes of the treatise aroused controversy with the proposal that clerical authority was the principal solution to society's ills. Lamennais had then asserted that people should unite, with the church retaining spiritual authority. The founding of a religious congregation and a newspaper, *L'Avenir*, followed.

Rosalie first encountered Lamennais through his *Words of a Believer* (1834), a publication that had riled the church. With its thesis that the Gospels lay at the heart of democracy and its call for people to draw together to form a utopian republic, Lamennais' text spoke deeply to Raimond Bonheur.[25]

Under Louis-Philippe's *juste-milieu* regime, many artists were supported by the government. It was in their interest to remain discreet and dilute radical tendencies, and the period thus engendered something of a reconciliation between the Classicists and the Romantics. Raimond Bonheur had always vocalised his antipathy towards Romanticism. While not reneging on his views, in the 1830s, he found himself increasingly drawn to writers and thinkers revered by the Romantics, and Rosalie felt the effects.

'My father made me read Lamennais,' Rosalie explained, 'and Lamennais defined everything that I searched for.'[26]

The priest's contention that art should convey an object's or creature's spirit as well as its form resonated with both father and daughter. Rosalie also became familiar with the writings of Pierre

Leroux, the philosopher, economist and advocate of socialism linked to Saint-Simonianism who had founded *Le Globe* but broken with the movement when he felt Enfantin's sermons were growing too controversial.[27]

To complete Rosalie's education, Raimond urged her to study history from a reference book he had sourced cheaply. Touching history through paintings was one thing, but the dry tedium of the written word left her cold. 'History I thought little of,' Rosalie later admitted.[28] However, this schooling in the humanities was complemented by Raimond's expansions on the critical episodes of the country's past, a practice which ensured the events stayed rooted in her mind.

When she was not broadening her knowledge of history or literature, Rosalie could be found sitting by the flickering lamplight, sketching and shading the plaster casts of animals which sat around the studio. Many had been made by her father's younger friend, the sculptor Pierre-Jules Mêne. The chiaroscuro effect of the shadows in the gloaming made it an instructive exercise. The three-dimensional forms captivated the student, who began trying to sculpt her own models of assorted beasts. Through the absorbing, messy, physical practice, she gained a more profound understanding of animal anatomy, knowledge which could only benefit her painting.[29]

Raimond was delighted with his daughter's progress. That she had begun to sell a piece here and there was an additional boon. But while Rosalie was attaining creative fulfilment, her spirit was unsettled. Her mother's demise replayed in her mind. Years later, she was still haunted by the dreams of her early adolescence.

She distinctly remembered one night-time vision, where a pale-faced, sickly-looking girl appeared to glide down an old staircase towards her. In vain, Rosalie struggled to place the face. The dream stayed with her, though why she could not tell.[30]

One day not long after, a man called at the Bonheurs' door, visibly discountenanced. It transpired that the unexpected visitor was none other than M. Micas, the husband of the stout, grim-faced woman who used to supply the Bonheurs' neighbour in the Rue Saint-Antoine with skins to make her children's toys.[31] M. Micas quickly revealed the purpose of his visit.

His most precious possession was about to be taken from him. His daughter was ailing and almost certainly not long for this world. He and his wife would dearly love to capture a likeness of her cherished soul in paint so that part of her would remain with them always: would Raimond do them the honour of immortalising their little girl?

Rosalie later told friends that it was not her father's first encounter with M. Micas's daughter; Mlle Micas had been a pupil at one of the schools where Raimond had taught. With the pained father before him and his natural susceptibility to human suffering, Raimond agreed at once.

Conscious that time was of the essence, M. Micas brought his daughter to the Bonheurs' studio at the first available opportunity. The doting father presented his child: her name was Jeanne, but those who knew her called her Nathalie.

Unusually tall for a girl of twelve, and skinny, Mlle Micas looked a pitiful creature. The sallow complexion of her face was framed by dull brown hair, while below her aquiline nose sat a pair of thin, delicate lips. The father's concern was immediately comprehensible. Unmistakable too was his daughter's resemblance to Sophie Bonheur.

But Rosalie's shock had an altogether different cause: standing before her was the very girl she had dreamed about a few nights before.

The Bonheurs' warm welcome was soon reciprocated and Rosalie found herself being invited back to the Micases' apartment. Stepping inside their home, she was startled; their staircase was identical to the one she had seen in her premonitory dream where Nathalie had appeared.[32] For all her dour appearance, the matronly Mme Micas inspired sufficient confidence for Rosalie to discuss these strange occurrences.

The intimacy of the repeated sittings and shared confidences afforded a better acquaintance between the two families. And as Rosalie and Nathalie talked, a number of commonalities emerged. Nathalie, of course, was the child in the green visor whom Rosalie and her classmates had teased in the Place Royale She was also among the children to whom Rosalie had thrown apples on one of her Sunday visits to Ménilmontant.

As the sittings accumulated, the portrait of Nathalie progressed and pre-judgements were forgotten. A friendship began to blossom between Rosalie and the awkward model two years her junior. With her stories of the tomfoolery that routinely took place in the Bonheur household, Rosalie could make her younger listener laugh until she cried, while Nathalie's evident delight was profoundly reaffirming. The girls made a curious pair; one, pale and wiry yet bright, imaginative and supremely resourceful; the other, stocky and unfeminine, but astoundingly creative.

Raimond was also developing a soft spot for Nathalie, whom he affectionately called Nanette. This made M. Micas swell with pride. He was delighted by the attachment he could see forming between his marginalised little girl and the painter's daughter. Rosalie remembered how M. Micas referred to her as his 'little forest flower'.[33]

Often, the robust frame of Mme Micas would accompany Nathalie to her sittings. Rosalie remembered how the woman's heart was touched when mentions of Sophie Bonheur slipped into conversation. As her affection for her new friend's mother grew, Rosalie felt impelled to share another dream. She had seen her mother appear and she had tried to embrace her, only to find her limbs paralysed. When Rosalie called out to express her surprise that Sophie was not dead after all, the apparition smiled, shook her head and vanished. As Mme Micas listened, Rosalie expressed her conviction that her mother was watching over her.[34]

Inherently house proud, Mme Micas was quietly horrified when she saw the state in which the Bonheurs were living. Soon, Nathalie was being dropped off early for her sittings in order to perform some household chore or other.

This sense of purpose exhilarated the sickly young girl and she was visibly thrilled whenever some task she had undertaken earned her praise. And that was not her only reward; Rosalie was hardly domestic, and she expressed her gratitude to Nathalie through complimentary drawing lessons.

Nathalie relished the idea of being an artist, and Rosalie indulged her fantasy, offering hearty congratulations on her achievements. Though the student's drawing was manifestly inferior to the teacher's own, Rosalie was generous with her commendations to both the pupil and her public.

When Raimond's finished portrait of Nathalie was presented to the girl's father, M. Micas declared himself so satisfied that he would gladly commission Raimond to create one of himself and his wife. The friendship between the Bonheurs and the Micases deepened.

Raimond was in particular need of such social stability. In 1838, when Rosalie had turned sixteen, her father's good friend Justin Mathieu left Paris. And Raimond moved house again.

'When you left, I felt a great blank,' Raimond admitted to his friend, before expressing his concern that, away from Paris, his companion would be even lonelier than he. 'It is very sad to have to keep everything to oneself and to be understood by no one,' Raimond mused.[35]

He continued:

> I am no longer living in the Rue des Tournelles [...] I occupy a first floor in a nice house – 5 Rue de la Bienfaisance – where there is a wide view and a fine garden. The rent is 450 francs, which is apparently dear. But in the same house are two young ladies who, by the lessons they take, are worth 200 francs to me, and the relations I have formed in the house are good. I have a charwoman who keeps the rooms clean, and I am getting my eatables and cooking from outside until I shall have procured some kitchen utensils.[36]

Mathieu was sufficiently close to the family for Raimond to use Rosalie's more familiar name:

Rosa is well. She is doing nothing but work at her painting. My children are boarding near me, and if work does not come in as I should like, I can always earn enough to have bread and cheese, either through dealers or through lessons. I try, however, to avoid this poverty, for my past experience of it has much injured me. At present, I have orders to last.[37]

But Raimond was no closer to exorcising his itinerant tendencies. At the end of 1838, he relocated the family again, establishing their base at 29, Rue Faubourg-du-Roule.[38] This move had three fortuitous corollaries.

Firstly, it brought the Bonheurs closer to where Isidore and Auguste attended school, meaning family gatherings could become more frequent.

Another happy advantage was the accessibility of the Bois de Boulogne. The ancient, now fashionable forest enraptured Rosalie.

'There were grand old oaks of more than 300 years,' she enthused, 'and the smart lady and gentlemen riders drew my admiration.'[39]

Nature's ever-shifting kaleidoscope was inspiring, and Rosalie marvelled when the right time of day and conditions combined to bring dappled sunlight flooding in through the trees.[40]

The final, unexpected boon of the family's change of address came in the form of a very useful neighbour. He went by the name of Saint-Germain-Leduc.[41]

Just a few years younger than Raimond, Pierre-Etienne-Denis Leduc was a journalist and author who took a keen interest in agricultural economy and travel. Among his recent publications was the volume *Italy* (1834), and people said that his star-studded network of friends even included the great Honoré de Balzac.[42] Saint-Germain-Leduc became both a friend and a facilitator, for he enabled Raimond to form other valuable connections.

Diplomat, journalist, writer and collector Baron Félix-Sébastien Feuillet de Conches was one such contact. With wavy hair and dark eyes which sparkled with interest and intelligence, Feuillet de Conches was both learned and inquisitive. He had entered the ministry of foreign affairs shortly after Rosalie was born and in 1832, he was placed in charge of protocol. While he flourished in the role, his real passion was for collecting. Whether stamps, books or quirky memorabilia, to his mind, objects offered a key to the past. Bright and dynamic, Feuillet de Conches's lust for *curiosités* allied to his linguistic eloquence made him an engaging dinner guest.[43]

Another acquaintance who now became a significant part of the Bonheurs' lives was the elegant Polish Princess Anna Zofia Czartoryska (née Sapieha), who owned a property in the family's street and whose sons attended the same school as Isidore and Auguste.[44] Wife of the Prince Adam Czartoryski, the descendant of an ancient and noble family of Poles, the Princess had joined her husband when he left politically unstable Poland. Arriving in Paris, Princess Czartoryska had quickly established herself as a central participant on the capital's social scene. With her heart-shaped face and penetrating brown eyes, in her 40s, the Princess exuded gravitas and commanded respect. She could be spotted at the more erudite salons and dinners, invariably exhibiting, as one journalist put it, 'that zeal which distinguishes her'.[45] The Princess made herself a pinion for her fellow Polish expatriates and she frequented the Salon Brady, one of the more traditional salons of the day and a magnet for Polish emigrants. Princess Czartoryska devoted herself to charity work which would assist fellow Poles, and the annual sale for the benefit of sick, indigent Poles could count on her generosity during the 1830s.[46] Meanwhile, the charity ball for Polish indigents could boast her as one of the patronesses who capably ensured that the decor was eye-catching and the guests plentiful.[47]

Rosalie found the Princess to be kindness itself. Her Highness took to paying afternoon calls on the Bonheurs and, eager to help the cultured but financially disadvantaged family, even encouraged some of her wealthier acquaintances to solicit Raimond's services for tuition.

Word of the talented family of artists and their studio was spreading and soon, the great and glorious all wanted to pay the Bonheurs a visit. Though Raimond himself had not attained the artistic celebrity he hungered for, his sociability caused numerous illustrious names to cross the threshold of the Bonheur family home. Hence it was entirely plausible when people claimed that a portrait of a little boy by the revered artist Camille Corot was actually a picture of Rosalie.

'I remember in particular one little English lady,' Rosalie mused. She was 'rather eccentric, the wife of the admiral who was in command of the fleet that conveyed Napoleon to Saint Helena.'[48]

Jean-Baptiste-Camille Corot, *Portrait of a Child, c.* 1835, oil on wood, 32.1 x 23.5 cm, The Metropolitan Museum of Art, New York.
Photo by Francis G. Mayer/Corbis Historical via Getty Images

The wife (and third cousin) of the esteemed Admiral George Cockburn, Mrs Mary Cockburn, thought Rosalie charming. A little older than Raimond Bonheur, Mrs Cockburn was said to be of delicate constitution and was known to have lost a child.[49] Rosalie found her to be a social linchpin, for the Englishwoman declared she wished to take the youngster with her to Versailles.

Rosalie had never been anywhere so grand. Nothing in her wardrobe would suffice for such an occasion, and so it was to Mrs Cockburn, Rosalie remembered, that 'I owed my first white dress.'[50]

Through such influential admirers, Raimond gleaned a number of good-paying clients; the Bonheurs' situation improved. And in between these grand visitations, Rosalie continued to practise her drawing and painting. Her talent was developing. Wary of the taunting to which a girl with the surname Bonheur ('happiness' in French) might expose herself, her father suggested she sign her canvases 'Raimond'. Rosalie's refusal was respectful but firm.

Raimond was all too familiar with his daughter's wilful disposition. For all that he approved of feminine independence, he knew that to progress, such headstrong ways must be checked. But he could not deny his daughter's artistic skill. So in 1841, the father suggested an important and potentially life-changing development: it was time for Rosalie to enter work to the Salon.

Consideration by the Salon jury would be the biggest test to which Rosalie had ever subjected her artwork. But her father's confidence inspired her own. She worked assiduously to perfect two animal pictures. And her efforts were rewarded when both pieces were accepted.

With the Salon's alphabetical system of hanging, Rosalie's work appeared next to the landscape her father had submitted. He had now changed the spelling of his name to Raymond.

In a Salon where names like Eugène Delacroix and Camille Corot stole the show, and placed between interpretations of elevated themes such as Félix Boisselier's *Tobias and the Angel* and Paul Bonhomme's *Christ and St John the Evangelist*, to the critics, agreeable wall-fillers like Rosalie's *Two Rabbits* and *Goats and Sheep* scarcely seemed worth a mention. But that hardly mattered; Rosalie had been accepted to the most prestigious exhibition forum in France. Her career as an artist had begun.[51]

Meanwhile, Raymond's identity underwent further changes that year.

Rosalie gradually noticed that he had grown preoccupied. Something was clearly troubling him, but he seemed uncertain how to broach the subject.

The daughter told friends how, some evenings, she would accompany her father on a walk. He made his way through the streets of Paris, always stopping before one particular house. There he would wait and eventually, a young woman appeared. Rosalie remained a few paces behind Raymond and the mysterious lady as they walked. She could hear none of their conversation. With nothing else to do, her attention drifted to the flickering flame of the street lamps and the moths and bugs which hovered stupidly towards the light until, with an abrupt crackle, their lifeless bodies dropped to the ground. Rosalie filled her pockets with the sad little corpses and took them home to give them a more dignified burial.[52]

This evening ritual had not long been established when Raymond presented Rosalie with two pieces of news. The first was inconvenient, but characteristic: Raymond planned to move again.

The second item was more pivotal: Raymond Bonheur had fallen in love.

6

···

True Nature

The Rue Rumford was a short, unremarkable street to the north-west of Paris near the Plaine Monceau.[1] Few thoroughfares better encapsulated the complex, often contradictory nature of 1840s Paris and its social framework.

A modest 15 m in length, when the road opened in 1838, it did so without due authority. Not until 1840 was politician Pierre-Léon Bérard de Chazelles granted formal permission to inaugurate the two roads he had planned on land he owned around the old *hôtel particulier* of the Comte de Rumford. One of these became the Rue Lavoisier, in honour of the chemist Antoine-Laurent Lavoisier; the other took its name from the American-born British physicist Benjamin Thompson, the late Comte de Rumford, who founded the Royal Institution of Great Britain in London in 1799 before marrying Lavoisier's widow in 1804 following the chemist's death. With Mme Lavoisier's first and second husbands' namesakes now convivially adjoined, these new streets were at once expressions of urban progress and channels to Paris's shrinking rural outskirts. The Rue Rumford benefited from a water supply and gas lighting; but just a little way beyond it were fields and farms and dairies – a reminder of what the swelling capital was rapidly sweeping aside.[2]

As so often before in Paris's chequered history, progress wrestled with politics in the 1840s. Louis-Philippe's *juste-milieu* regime had taken important steps to establish economic prosperity and foster external peace, while rebuilding its colonial empire. The bourgeoisie, the majority of whom rejected the idea of a republic, were largely content, while for now, the gentle grumbles emanating from the working classes failed to erupt into cacophonous revolts.[3] Certainly, from time to time, there were demonstrations against the new regime or social conditions – or both. In 1831, an uprising of silk workers in Lyon had to be repressed, while in 1835, Louis-Philippe himself narrowly escaped assassination when Corsican Giuseppe Fieschi developed an 'infernal machine', a weapon designed to kill the King as he passed on the Boulevard du Temple.[4] Even the regime's more moderate detractors did not have to look far for evidence to justify their opposition. The purportedly democratic government used its 'September Laws' to tighten its grip on the penal system and the press, reconfiguring the decision-making process employed in the former and censoring the latter. More generally, too, birth rates in France were falling, while the capital's population was growing exponentially, placing even greater strain on amenities and living conditions.

Nonetheless, optimists could counter criticism with happier statistics. If France lagged behind Britain and remained a primarily agricultural country, industrialisation was firmly underway. The construction of canals continued (albeit sluggishly), particularly in the north, and in 1836, a scheme of local roadbuilding had been instigated, strengthening the country's transport skeleton.[5] Slowly, the railway was making its appearance, with the first proper line between Paris and Saint-Germain opening in 1837. Finances were respectable, while the Guizot Law of 1833 had revolutionised education by stipulating that every town should have a primary school for boys. Concomitantly, literacy was increasing. The provincial press was developing, while the affordability of the printed word meant that France could boast a larger reading public than ever before. Nor was its ruler indifferent to his people's passions; one of Louis-Philippe's boldest gestures to appease the populace was to have Napoleon Bonaparte's ashes returned to France in 1840 to be interred at the Invalides. Then with innovations like the daguerreotype in 1838 and literary landmarks such as Stendhal's

The Red and the Black (1831), Victor Hugo's *Notre-Dame de Paris* (1831) and Honoré de Balzac's *Le Père Goriot* (1835), culturally at least, France could hold its head high.[6]

But beneath the veneer of social and political stability, fracture lines were branching. And with the interweaving treatises of social theorists like Hugues-Félicité-Robert de Lamennais and an influx of foreign emigrants charged with their own political baggage and resentment, 1840s Paris was as much a simmering cauldron of revolutionary thought as it was the helm of economic change.

∞

The Bonheurs' new living quarters at 13, Rue Rumford were no more extraordinary than anywhere else they had lived; the property owed its uniqueness to the upstairs room of 4.5 x 5.5 metres, which was illuminated by a large vertical window. It was there that Rosalie and Raymond practised their art.[7]

With a light, airy space given entirely to painting alongside her beloved father, nineteen-year-old Rosalie was in her element. Whether working from studies or from nature reconstructed in the studio, she drew and painted tirelessly, scrutinising every corner of her composition so that the finished piece would come as close as possible to her measure of perfection. She worked for hours at a time, her gratification at work well done providing all the energy she needed. But so long as the family were disunited, her happiness could never be complete.

The brother closest to her in age, Auguste, was now a young man of seventeen. Tall and pallid with high cheekbones and blonde hair, he had a serious, pensive mien which made his true personality difficult to discern. Many people found him taciturn and indeed, he shared few characteristics with Rosalie, save maybe one: the family gift for painting.[8]

Once Auguste had completed his studies, it was agreed that he should go to work in education. He was clearly an excellent artist, but Raymond Bonheur was mindful of how difficult it was to succeed in the creative industry. Talent was not enough; a person's gift must be exceptional – like Rosalie's. Auguste was sent to work at a boarding school in the small town of Pithiviers, between Orléans and Paris. There, one further similarity with Rosalie became apparent: when cloistered away from the exhilarating milieu of practising artists, Auguste was deeply, unalterably miserable.

'My dear Pipon,' Raymond wrote using the family's affectionate soubriquet, 'you are as self-denying as a little sage, and patient resignation dwells beneath your cap.' The father went on:

> you, my dear boy, are surrounded by brawling children, who worry you from morning till night and who rob you of your best hours [...] It is my youth over again; for, like you, I have wept in secret far from my unhappy home [...] But there I learnt to ponder on many ideas [...] and later I came to realise that the greatest thoughts have their origin in the most painful experiences of our existence.[9]

The greatest thought that Auguste's experience inspired was soon acted upon. He had barely been at the school a few months when he announced his decision to resign; he meant to become an artist and would dedicate himself to his craft just as he had seen his sister do.

Auguste joined Rosalie and Raymond in the Rue Rumford, his objective clear and his drive to succeed unrelenting. He began painting portraits, and the wisdom of his career choice was quickly confirmed when commissions – and remuneration – began to flow in.

If Auguste's return was pleasing to Rosalie, the news that fourteen-year-old Isidore would also be coming home was elating. Rosalie had always been especially close to her youngest brother. Shorter than Auguste, Isidore possessed a light complexion with hints of auburn, while his natural curls and rounded face recalled those of his father.[10] Like his brother, he could appear solemn and reserved, even timid. But a little prompting coaxed him out of his shell, allowing a person to fully appreciate the warmth of his character. And once he made a friend, Isidore was unshakeably loyal.

Given his creative heritage, it was perhaps only natural that Isidore should also gravitate towards the arts. Initially, he too reached for the paintbrush. But for some time now, Rosalie had been experimenting with sculpture, primarily as a means of informing her painting rather than for show. It was not long before Isidore felt inspired to try modelling himself. Rosalie was proud to give him his first lessons and Isidore's little effigies of bulls and oxen soon began accumulating next to his paintings.

The studio in the Rue Rumford became a hive of industry. When Raymond left for work in the morning, the children ascended to their respective workspaces. Rosalie moved to her easel in the corner of the room and Auguste to his in the opposite corner, while Isidore worked around them, changing position depending on whether he was painting or modelling that day. Hour upon hour spent working alongside each other in an environment of intense creativity reinforced the bond between the siblings. And whenever Raymond returned, he took up his own place next to Auguste, from where he could survey his children's progress.[11]

All three students worked assiduously. But neither of the boys could match their sister's industry.

Raymond Bonheur had worked in the art world long enough to have repeatedly encountered the general prejudice which set women's artistic skill as being inferior to men's. Rosalie turned that stereotype on its head. She possessed both creativity and intellect, and was able to concentrate herself on a detail while never losing sight of the picture as a whole. The ingredients for success were inherent to her.

Raymond's belief that an artist should study from nature had become ingrained in Rosalie's practice, and the proximity of the studio to the Parc Monceau and the bucolic countryside of Paris's western suburbs made it possible to capitalise on nature's bounty.

Described by an 1830s tourist guide as a 'spot worthy of the traveller's visit', the Parc Monceau provided a verdant idyll in the heart of the city. The landscaped garden was informally planted 'in the English style' for the Duc d'Orléans at the end of the 18th century and was 'ornamented with Gothic grottos, Greek ruins' and 'superb peristyles'.[12] Only a few minutes' walk from the Rue Rumford, the Parc Monceau offered an easy access to nature in the winter when the weather was less clement. 'Tickets of admission may be obtained upon applying by letter,' advised a contemporary guide.[13] However, Raymond had acquired an entry card through a friend, meaning that Rosalie had ready access to this abundant resource.[14]

Loaded with drawing materials, Rosalie also made regular forays out to the nearby village of Villiers to capture the animals that were gradually becoming the central theme of her oeuvre. She considered studying the creatures' relationship to their natural habitat to be imperative. 'I discovered a delicious little corner of countryside at Villiers near the Parc de Neuilly,' Rosalie later enthused.[15]

Sometimes, her brothers joined her on these research trips. But whenever a more contracted period of study was required, Rosalie solicited the services of a hospitable peasant lady who had agreed to let her lodge in her humble home.

'I spent several months with her, on and off, at different times,' Rosalie remembered. 'I had here a good opportunity to study animals in their natural surroundings, which was of great advantage to my budding art development.'[16]

Cows, sheep and goats all became unwitting models. 'I loved capturing the rapid movement of the animals, the sheen of their coats, the subtlety of their characters, for each animal has its own individual physiognomy,' Rosalie remarked. 'Before beginning a study of a dog, a horse or a ewe, I familiarised myself with the anatomy, osteology and mythology of each,' she explained.[17] And she focused closely on the eyes – especially the eyes, for in them, Rosalie felt certain she could see an animal's soul.

Fortunately, Raymond's sensitivity to his children's creative needs meant that the studio was soon adapted in such a way that Rosalie was no longer obliged to go to Villiers to find her models.

Raymond allowed Rosalie to create a menagerie of her own at the Rue Rumford. A small terrasse adjoining the apartment was transformed into a miniature nature reserve, and before long, the space positively bloomed with interweaving plants and climbers.[18] The terrasse functioned as an urban pasture for the birds and beasts Rosalie was now collecting. She brought home rabbits, fowl and ducks which soon made their presence known.

The apartment also housed a squirrel, rats and butterflies. The Bonheurs were even joined by a sheep, whom they named Jocrisse. That tested the accommodation to its limits. The terrasse could hardly imitate the creature's natural environment, so every evening, either Auguste or Isidore was given the task of leading (or carrying) the animal down several flights of stairs so that it could graze and take the air around the Plaine Monceau.[19] Concerned they might be stymieing the ewe's natural sociability, the family introduced a goat into the apartment to keep it company.[20] The billy became a real playfellow to the Bonheur children, and would even join in their games of hide and seek, gleefully scampering down the stairs with them whenever it was time to be walked. When the goat died, a pair of lambs took his place.[21]

Henceforward, when guests arrived at the door of the Bonheur's apartment, they were greeted by the unmistakable odour of livestock and the sounds of bleating, chirruping and scuttling as all sorts of species scampered this way and that.

The animals were part of the family, so much so that Raymond knew Rosalie would be anxious to hear how they were faring when, in 1842, she went for a short working break to the commune of Annet, some 40 km to the east of Paris, where she lodged in the home of the Hèbres.[22]

'We are very glad you can study as you like with the worthy Mesdames Hèbres,' Raymond began. Knowing Rosalie's commitment to her art, he felt compelled to issue a warning: 'But be careful that you do not take cold in the damp weather. You know that it is dangerous to sit on the ground after a rainstorm.'[23]

Then followed the update he knew his daughter would be anticipating:

we are all well and all the live stock, too. The little goat is very tiring with its bleating, and smells strong. The squirrel has shut itself up like a hermit in Diana's head, but comes down regularly morning and evening to beg and play its tricks. The canaries are singing the 'Gloria Tibi, Domine', and the finch is getting steadier on its legs. The rats are off wandering somewhere or other, and the butterflies, transfixed by a pin in your box with the other insects, have not budged since their martyrdom. So you see that all those you care about are thriving.[24]

The questionable odours and pandemonium were not the only hazards human occupants had to contend with. The family indulged their pets' natural instincts, and on one occasion, an almighty crash from upstairs signalled catastrophe. There on the studio floor lay the enormous picture that usually hung above Raymond's easel, itself now crushed with the half-finished canvas it had supported ruined beside it. Kiki, the squirrel Rosalie had brought back from one of her Sunday walks and who usually slept inside a plaster cast or the mould of a mythological head, had lately taken to gnawing at the cord which held the heavy framed picture. It had finally given way.[25]

Rosalie sheepishly agreed to keep the creature encaged. But bearing witness to its captivity was intolerable and she regretfully let it go.

Daily life at number 13 was abuzz with artistic enterprise and bestial antics. Then when the evening came, the family members gathered together in the lamplight and each became absorbed in drawing, while one of them read aloud. In the summer when the days were longer, the party would sometimes take an evening walk across the expansive Plaine Monceau.[26]

Rosalie's great friend Nathalie Micas was a frequent visitor to the apartment. Quite unorthodox herself, she took the Bonheur menagerie in her stride. Rosalie remembered that one of the first portraits Auguste attempted in this chaos was a depiction of M. and Mme Micas.

After her debut at the Salon in 1841, Rosalie was ready to move forwards in her artistic career. In 1842, three of her paintings were accepted to the annual exhibition: *Animals Grazing, Evening Effect, Cow Lying in a Meadow* and *Horse for Sale*. This year, she also displayed a sculpture, a *Shorn Ewe* modelled in clay.

The review published in the *Revue étrangère de la littérature des sciences et des arts* typified the disproportionate amount of press space allotted to religious and history painting by comparison with genre and landscape, considered inferior categories.[27] In such a climate, it was extremely difficult for painters working in these fields to impress; for a woman, this became harder still. But as the stream of visitors flowed through the exhibition halls, contemporaries remembered *Animals Grazing* attracting interest and reported that Rosalie's *Shorn Ewe* even prompted an affinity to be drawn with the work of the celebrated Romantic sculptor of Raymond Bonheur's generation, Antoine-Louis Barye.[28] Such a comparison was sufficient gratification. Rosalie was gathering momentum.

That year, she had to exhibit without the support of her family beside her, too; neither Auguste nor Isidore was yet prepared for their work to be shown. None of Raymond's paintings appeared either. In fact, his attention had been diverted in an altogether different direction.

❧

At 29 years old, Marguerite Picard was some seventeen years younger than Raymond and less than ten years older than Rosalie – more a peer than a parent. She came from the Auvergne region in central France and was a widow, her husband François Hippolyte Peyrol having died the year before, leaving her with a nine-year-old son, also named Hippolyte.

As widowed single parents, Marguerite and Raymond had a shared understanding. In addition, Marguerite had quickly gauged how to strike that delicate balance of supporting yet reining in Raymond's flights of fancy as appropriate. Then she was experienced at dealing with youngsters and excelled at keeping a home. Marguerite seemed the missing piece to Raymond Bonheur's near-perfect life puzzle.

One day, Raymond announced to his children that their family would no longer be incomplete: he and Marguerite Picard were to marry. Their house would regain the sense of order only a matriarch could impart.

The wedding took place that summer and before the year was out, the new Mme Bonheur's son, Hippolyte Peyrol, had been sent for and had arrived at the Rue Rumford.[29]

Only time would tell whether the family's new configuration would prove workable for the Bonheur children – or if the eclectic but blissful chapter at the Rue Rumford had finally come to an end.

CR

If home life proved more challenging than she would have liked, Rosalie had ample demands from outside to excuse her absence. And not long after her father's remarriage, a very unique opportunity presented itself.

In 1843, Prince Czartoryski, husband of the family's great friend Princess Anna Zofia Czartoryska, made an extravagant purchase. Originally built for the financier Jean-Baptiste Lambert, the decadent, 17th-century Hôtel Lambert on the Ile Saint-Louis was an edifice to bygone splendour. Decorated by the esteemed painters Charles Le Brun, François Perrier and Eustache Le Sueur, the art-steeped mansion was a fitting headquarters for the Prince to welcome Polish exiles and undertake political activities.

Princess Czartoryska held the arts in high regard. Personally, she inclined towards embroidery, but drawing being an important female attribute in her social circle, she was keen that any princess in her care should take art lessons and, above all, that she should learn from a professional.[30] Now in need of such a tutor for one of the princesses, Anna Zofia had a very particular candidate in mind – for what could be better for an aspiring young lady painter than to train with one of her own sex, someone who could offer guidance on the woman art-ist's condition and how to navigate the tempestuous currents of the Paris art world? Rosalie Bonheur fitted the job description perfectly.

So it was that one day, Rosalie found herself arriving at the majestic Hôtel Lambert to commence lessons with a Polish princess.

The Hôtel Lambert was built around a central courtyard and its grand entranceway immediately gave visitors a hint of the luxurious interior they would find within. Room after room decorated in rich reds and gold preceded each other in a visual feast of high-ceilinged ostentatiousness, as Rosalie was led through the building to the sump-tuous Galerie Hercules, with its frescoes set in gold panelled walls.[31]

Attempting to master her sense of childlike wonder, Rosalie com-menced her class. Finding her student companionable, the teacher quickly lapsed into a state of juvenile playfulness. 'We did little else than slide up and down the highly-polished floor of the big gallery of the Hôtel Lambert,' she confessed afterwards.[32]

Rosalie could focus intently when working on a painting, channel-ling all her energy into the composition at hand – and such industry was rewarded when she had three pieces accepted to the Salon of 1843, with *Horses Returning from the Drinking Place* and *Horses in a Meadow* appearing in the painting section, and a plaster *Bull* on show with the sculptures. Sales of her work was the happy consequence of the exhibition.[33]

But with her working days so demanding, Rosalie's recreation often saw her regressing to enjoy the kind of boisterous, infantile pursuits she had indulged in at the Hôtel Lambert. Her stepbrother, Hippolyte, was struck by the child who lingered within the woman, now in her twenties.

'Sometimes she played horse with Isidore,' Hippolyte remembered. 'She would put into his mouth, as bit, a big drawing pencil, with a cord attached to either end, and thus harnessed, horse and driver would go rushing wildly about over the Monceau Plain and finally return home covered with dust and in a dripping perspiration.'[34]

The predisposition to fun and frolics were an intrinsic part of Rosalie's character. Yet her work ethic was unimpeachable. She had become her most exacting critic. Her morning was spent studying from nature, while the afternoon was given to arranging and refining her compositions.[35] Nothing was presented outside the home until she felt completely satisfied. Still, despite her best efforts, Rosalie was yet to receive substantial attention from the critics. In 1844, the young artist realised that she needed to demonstrate her commitment to her medium. Rosalie submitted only to the painting section of that year's Salon, sending *Cows Grazing on the Banks of the Marne*, *Sheep in a Meadow*, *The Meeting – Landscape with Animals*, and *A Donkey*. Her entries declared both her specialism and her sincerity. And to that end, she made one further, career-based change that year, too.

Sophie Bonheur had always addressed her affectionately as her 'Rosa'. That was how she would now identify herself. In so doing, something of her mother, whose faith in her had never wavered, would travel with her as she forged her career.

As though to confirm the sagacity of her approach, that year, Rosa received a press mention. Writing for *Le Moniteur Universel*, Fabien Pillet commended *Sheep in a Meadow*, in which he judged the models to be among 'the softest, cleanest, most abundant in fleecy wool' of their species.[36] It was a small tribute, but it was no less a landmark. People were beginning to stop in front of Rosa Bonheur's canvases.

Meanwhile, Raymond Bonheur was rediscovering the joys of married life. His new spouse brought colour and interest to his existence. That year, Marguerite introduced her husband to her native Auvergne and the powerful impression the area made on him was reflected in a landscape which appeared at the Salon of 1844.

The idea of one big, happy family cohabiting in the Rue Rumford appealed to Raymond. That same year, he set out for Bordeaux to tell Mme Aymé that Juliette could now come home. But the old woman's dismay at the thought of losing the child resigned Raymond to leave his youngest daughter where she was for the time being.[37]

Though her sister's return would have been a joy and she accepted rather than celebrated the woman she and her brothers now called 'Mamiche', Rosa found comfort and companionship in Nathalie

Micas. Nathalie was endlessly impressed by her friend's Salon appearances, which set her akin to a celebrity in the younger girl's eyes.

But Rosa would not allow herself to be distracted by flattery. She
knew that to progress, she must constantly be learning, improving,
perfecting. Painting animals, she had found her niche; to excel, she
must know her subject inside out – and there were few better places
to acquire such knowledge than in an abattoir.

⁂

The Abattoir du Roule was a large, quadrilateral arrangement of buildings grouped around a courtyard and just a few minutes' walk from the
Rue Rumford.[38] Completed in 1818, it was one of five slaughterhouses
whose construction was ordered by Napoleon Bonaparte in the early
19th century in an effort to improve conditions in central Paris. Up
until this point, butchers had driven cattle through the streets to reach
the private slaughterhouses in the city centre. As one 1840s guidebook
author remarked, 'these animals contributed to a great degree to render
the capital more dirty'.[39]

Though united with Paris's other slaughterhouses in its gruesome
function, the Abattoir du Roule was somewhat unique. An attractive
approach, an expansive esplanade in front of the main entranceway
and some generous planting around the perimeter gave it an aesthetic
advantage over the other abattoirs – 'a more agreeable aspect than one
would usually expect of such a building,' proclaimed the *Administrative
and Historic Dictionary of the Streets of Paris*.[40]

Napoleon's slaughterhouses remained objects of morbid fascination in the 1840s, so much so that in one contemporary guidebook,
tours were actually encouraged. 'Strangers should visit one of these
establishments,' came the advice. 'They must apply for a guide at the
porter's lodge, to whom a small fee is given.'[41]

The abattoir did not receive many visiting requests from single
women in their early twenties, but the administration nevertheless
obliged and Rosa was granted permission to see inside.

Any visitor to the abattoir had to suppress their sense of repulsion. The whole building emitted the sickening stench of blood and dirt.[42] Though Rosa was not an inherently dreamy or oversensitive girl, the environment was a test even for someone as pragmatic and stoical as herself. But the conditions were not the most unsteadying element. When the doors of the abattoir closed behind her, the young butchers' boys saw not a serious researcher but a defective quarry. The urge to goad was irresistible, their taunting merciless. The lads' most popular pastime became muttering lewd comments whenever Rosa passed to test how she reacted.

Their expectations were disappointed. Rosa was not upset but irritated by the persistent jibes. Eventually, her tolerance reached breaking point – and it was then that a powerful protector came to her aid.

The towering and corpulent frame of the slaughterhouse scalder Émile Gravel was apt to unsettle a new acquaintance. A swarthy man of some 40 years, he commanded infinite respect in the workplace. However, the brawny physique masked a kindly disposition and the most profound sensitivity. Noticing the fraught expression of the young woman he had seen visiting the abattoir, he asked the reason for her distress. Rosa explained her purpose and predicament. And as she did, M. Gravel became increasingly vexed.

As it happened, art was something for which he had a good deal of time.[43] Though his formal education was wanting, Gravel was a smart-witted man who abounded in common sense. He saw the worthy nature of Rosa's enterprise and decided to use his authoritative reputation to help her.

Without further ado, he turned to his co-workers: 'The first one of you who troubles this young woman will hear from me. You all know who I am and you also know that I always mean what I say. So remember, I am this girl's protector, and don't you forget it!'[44]

From that day, everything changed.

Observing that the lunch Rosa brought with her was often frugal, occasionally, Père Émile invited her back to his home so that she could take a good meal with him and his wife.[45]

But it was in the abattoir that Rosa really felt the benefits of Père Émile's protection. She could now make as many sketches of the unassuming beasts as she liked, studying them in their stalls, before scrutinising their most intimate engineering. Armed with an understanding of her subjects' bodies and a knowledge of their soul, she could bring the creatures to life on canvas.

In 1845, the Salon audience was treated to the fruit of Rosa's labour. One, more experimental piece was entitled *The Three Musketeers*, a genre painting Rosa later dismissed as being 'without importance', and a product of her admiration for Alexandre Dumas.[46] But the remaining five titles all announced her specialism as a painter of livestock. And the ultimate source of pride that year was that Rosa would not be the only Bonheur to appear; her efforts would hang next to two landscapes by her father and a work by Auguste, who was making his Salon debut.

As the day of opening approached, the whole family waited expectantly to discover how their work would be received.

Fortunately for Rosa, this tense period was broken by a pleasant distraction. Raymond still nursed the hope of Juliette returning to Paris, and there was always a chance that Rosa might be able to win round Mme Aymé. Before the results of the Salon could be gauged, Rosa boarded a stagecoach for Bordeaux.[47]

From Rosa's perspective, the diversion and the pleasure of time with Juliette were not the only attractions of the trip. Ever since Marguerite Picard had arrived at the Rue Rumford, Rosa's role in the house had been uncertain. Though she never publicly criticised her stepmother in those early years, the family's new configuration threw doubt onto her place as her father's confidante. Through necessity, she was becoming increasingly self-reliant. Time away from the family home brought space to think more clearly. It also provided a valuable opportunity to sketch the expansive pastures and woodland around her native Bordeaux. And she had become preoccupied by another matter, too.

The more settled her father became in his new marriage, the greater Rosa's urge to solve the riddle of her mother's origins. The trip to Bordeaux would afford the opportunity to subject to inquisition Mme Aymé, the only person who might be able to help.

Once she had clambered out of the coach and deposited her belongings, an audience with Mme Aymé was easily arranged. But Rosa soon realised that her efforts to uncover her ancestry would be fruitless. The old woman was empathetic but on the matter of Sophie Bonheur's identity, she was unmovable. Rosa was told politely but firmly to desist in her search. It would serve no purpose, Mme Aymé warned, particularly when Raymond Bonheur's own roots were so lowly. Reluctantly, Rosa promised to do as the housekeeper asked. But she later told friends that Mme Aymé would concede that Sophie Bonheur's mother had been a wellborn lady. She also made clear her animosity towards M. Dublan's manservant, whom Rosa suspected to be privy to the secret – and who was later said to have died in mysterious circumstances.[48]

Still, Rosa could not dwell on her frustration for long. On 14 June 1845, a letter arrived from her father.

'Let me tell you first of all a piece of news that will please you very much,' he began eagerly. 'Yesterday evening we received a big envelope from the director of museums, M. de Cailleux. The envelope was a large one with a big royal seal on it, and was brought by a tall attendant from the Louvre.'[49]

Then followed a playful diversion as, withholding the 'news', Raymond tantalised Rosa with an array of inconsequential trivia: what Tatan had been eating when the envelope arrived, where he had been, the work he was undertaking at the moment.

'I can fancy you scanning the lines hurriedly in order to get the explanation,' he teased.[50]

At last, at the bottom of the correspondence, Rosa's eyes alighted on a single sentence written in big, bold letters.

The news was incredible – her professional profile would never be the same again.

7

Life and Death

'Rosa Bonheur has received a [...] medal!'[1]
The composition *Ploughing* (1845) had earned Rosa a third-class prize. For a woman of only 23 years old, one who had received no formal tuition besides that from her father, it was an extraordinary achievement.

'Women painters prefer sentimental little scenes, flowers and portraits to landscape,' the art critic Théophile Thoré remarked disparagingly reviewing the female entrants to that year's competition.[2] Few were felt worthy of consideration as serious artists. But Rosa's painting was gutsy, powerful – masculine. Thoré was impressed.

'Mention must be made of Mlle Rosa Bonheur, whose grazing bulls are superior to those of M. Brascassat,' the critic opined.[3]

With his works reminiscent of the Dutch landscape artists, Jacques-Raymond Brascassat was a confirmed success at the Salon and one of the foremost painters of animals of the day. For such a comparison to be drawn by a well-regarded critic like Thoré, it was a momentous victory.

Rosa returned to Paris that summer haloed in glory. Now, she had to collect her prize from the organisers' offices in the city centre.

Raymond had instructed her to go unaccompanied; it would serve as a lesson in self-reliance, he explained. So on the appointed day, Rosa arrived alone, as well turned-out as she could manage.

The heavy metallic disc was solemnly presented by the Directeur des Beaux-Arts and words of commendation uttered as the medal was bestowed 'in the name of the King'.[4]

Rosa had never been in such a deferential position. With no notion of how she was expected to behave, she could draw only on her existing catalogue of social etiquette.

'Please thank the King from me,' she blurted, 'and be so kind as to add that I will try to do better next time.'[5]

☙

For the 19th-century Salon artist, a medal was far more than a symbol of recognition; an ascent in sales would surely follow. Rosa vowed to return all monetary rewards directly to her father.

Her whole entourage were elated, but no one more so than Nathalie Micas. The girls had become inseparable. Nathalie's admiration was unwavering and profound. She harboured no ambition to compete with her friend; her personal validation was found in serving Rosa. She was thrilled when the older girl allowed her to help with her work. In addition to performing household chores, Nathalie now became an unofficial technician. Rosa often entrusted her with tracing and transferring her drawings onto canvas. And the more the two girls worked together, the healthier Nathalie seemed to grow. Her insipid complexion flushed with colour, while her eyes danced with happiness. At the same time, the intimate companionship had brought Rosa stability and the luxury of being able to focus exclusively on her canvases.

Meanwhile, Raymond Bonheur had not yet resigned himself to his family's disjuncture. In 1846, Auguste travelled to Bordeaux to make some landscape studies. Raymond still longed for his youngest daughter to join them, and he hoped that Auguste might be able to effectuate his wish. Age was rendering his pining more acute.[6]

The father confided his melancholy to his itinerant son, penning a letter in April 1846. 'To tell the truth,' Raymond admitted, 'I have grown old, my heart is affected. I cannot walk as quickly as formerly, or run upstairs. I am forbidden to allow myself to get into a state of excitement, and so am very careful to let nothing put me out.'[7]

Fortunately, there was little in Auguste's trip to vex him: when Raymond's eldest son returned from Bordeaux, he brought with him a gift. As the door at the Rue Rumford was opened, there by Auguste's side stood Juliette, now a lovely young woman of nearly sixteen years old.[8]

With similar, fair colourings to Auguste, Juliette possessed the feminine grace that Rosa lacked. She shared the Bonheur family's square jaw and angelic face, but her features were more delicate than those of her sister. Below her soft gaze was a pair of sweet rosebud lips, while she wore her light hair arranged in a neat chignon. Juliette carried herself well and she possessed an elegance and a nurturing instinct which recalled those of her mother.[9]

Seeing her older siblings happily absorbed in the studio, Juliette wanted nothing more than to join them. She was found an easel and set to work, with Rosa guiding and supervising. The family gift soon became apparent.

Juliette reverently drank in everything Rosa taught her, gravitating towards sheep as her models of choice in those earliest canvases.

When engaged in her own work, Rosa's task was all-consuming. But, still in her mid-twenties, once her brushes had been set aside, she released her inner child. Her stepbrother Hippolyte remembered one excursion they took in 1846 to the Meudon Forest.

Meudon was a pretty village south-west of Paris which, as a contemporary guide for visitors explained, was 'principally remarkable for the château and park' once owned by Louis XIV.[10] The park had been laid out by Le Nôtre, while tourists were advised: 'the wood of Meudon is extensive, and is much frequented in the summer by the Parisians and inhabitants of the neighbourhood, particularly on Sundays, Mondays, and Thursdays, when a ball is given below the village.'

The Bonheurs were a family of avid walkers, and on this particular summer outing, their ramble lasted so long that a merciless thunderstorm broke while they were still far from home. As the sky blackened and rain dripped then pelted down, Rosa dived for shelter in a hut by the side of the road. But her move came too late: her patterned dress was soaked through so that 'she looked like a zebra,' her stepbrother Hippolyte recollected.[11] Still, Rosa was not given to vanity. 'She shared our fun at her expense, and finally we all got home, late in the afternoon, as wet as rats.'[12]

Rosa could justify such moments of frivolity; her hard work was now generating a stream of laudatory reviews and commissions.

'Mlle Rosa Bonheur's flock of sheep makes one want to be a shepherd, with a crook, a silk waistcoat and ribbons,' exclaimed her now loyal admirer Théophile Thoré when he beheld her submissions to the Salon of 1846 (of which there were six).[13]

Rosa's success was the sweet fruit of months of labour. She had now established a clear working method, and she often listed her tasks for the day before she began.

Whether she reached for a pencil or a brush, nature was always her starting point. Her equipment arranged before her model, Rosa watched the horse or lamb or cow intently, working quickly, her eye constantly flitting back and forth between her sitter and her page as she attempted to fix the creature on the blank surface. If the beast moved – as so often it did – she patiently started again. So doing, she soon amassed folder upon folder of studies. These scraps of paper were precious research tools; with them, she had the means to create a masterpiece.[14]

Sometimes, if a painting required a particular sky or a section of landscape, Rosa would study that independently. But for much of the time, she was alone with the animals. That was how she preferred it.

Entering into such an intimate relationship with a creature, Rosa came to understand its behaviour and inclinations better than most. Her insistence on anatomical accuracy even led her to attempt her own modest dissections on expired carcasses. For a woman to engage in such a practice would have been declared an outrage in elegant society. But acceptance in that kind of narrow-minded company had never been

Rosa's goal. She studied the animals' bodies, muscles and sinews with the scruples of a scientist – and she learned to know their characters with the unconditional love of a mother.

Her studies complete, the next step was to collate and refine them into a single composition which could be transferred to a primed canvas.

Collapsible tubes of paint had been available since the 1840s. Designed primarily to extend the life of premixed paint in the wake of the rapid expansion of mechanical colour grinding, they also offered the advantage that paint could be easily transported.[15] Above all, they saved time, an important consideration when an artist was attempting to capture the changing shades of nature. However, many painters complained that by not mixing the dry ground colour and the binder (frequently poppy oil) themselves, they lost the subtle distinctions in paint texture. Others disdained the business of mixing their own colours on the grounds that it reduced them to the status of artisans. Each painter had to weigh up the relative merits and inconveniences of each method. For now, Rosa adopted the traditional practice using ground colour, just as her father had taught her.[16]

Whenever she was working in oils, she began her canvas by broadly sketching out the forms in burnt red ochre. She was particular about her material, and she never used a linseed oil base, since she disliked the finish it gave.[17] Rosa accentuated the contours and coated the background with a neutral grey. The canvas then had to be left to dry. Once it was ready, Rosa began mixing and applying her oils, always choosing a rounded rather than a flat brush for ease of blending. She touched and reworked her canvas incessantly until she was satisfied that her animal looked true to life. And when she had finished for the day, Rosa cleaned up and washed her brushes meticulously, obsessively, refusing to entrust to anyone else a task she considered critical.

Romantic liaisons played little part in Rosa's timetable. Work took precedence. Not that she was unattractive; though hardly pretty by conventional standards, she possessed a number of striking features. Rosa was of medium height or a little under and was well built, while her square-shaped, cherubic face was finished with a high forehead. A crop of silky chestnut hair sat above this and her features were even. Her aquiline nose was slim and delicate, her mouth rather large and her lips often pursed in concentration. But perhaps her most striking attribute was her deep brown eyes. Like buttons of tempered chocolate, they gleamed with warmth, interest and purpose. Curiously given her stout physique, Rosa's hands were exquisitely elegant and fine with long, slender fingers. Indeed, the body betrayed the character within: Rosa possessed the stamina of a man and the delicacy of touch of a woman.[18]

Nor was she without admirers. Her visits to an apothecary's shop to obtain cocoa fostered the owner's affection and for a while, Rosa enjoyed his company. But 'we soon got tired of one another,' she explained. 'The courtship lasted a week! An apothecary's cannula did not inspire me with high respect!'[19] Besides, a true lover must also accept her lifestyle – and that meant her work and her animals. It was a lot to ask.

∾

By the time the Salon of 1846 closed its doors, Rosa was exhausted. Marguerite Picard's family had begged their relative to visit them in the Auvergne and the invitation had been extended to Rosa. While a protracted period with her stepmother and enforced separation from Nathalie had not featured in Rosa's scheme of ambitions, she was over-worked and in need of repose. Besides, the break might provide fresh material to inspire her next year's Salon entry. Rosa and her stepmother boarded a stagecoach and set off for the Auvergne.

In the mid-19th century, the Auvergne in central France remained one of the smallest and most sparsely populated regions in the country. Some 500 km south of Paris, communications and settlement were complicated by the area's hostile terrain. Constructed using the material available, the roads in the granite region were made of sharp, unforgiving stones, with those in the north connecting the Auvergne to Paris being among the worst.[20] Still, for the intrepid traveller, the destination offered sufficient reward for their pains. The region boasted breathtaking volcanic landscape and superb mountain vistas, punctuated by isolated farms and picturesque country lanes. It was visually dramatic yet eminently peaceful.

The long, mountainous route Rosa and Marguerite's carriage negotiated towards the town of Mauriac brought some spectacular scenery, and with the horses slowing to a mere walk whenever a hill approached, ample opportunity to enjoy it. Once she had arrived, letters to Nathalie and Mme Micas provided both an outlet for her impressions and a reassuring contact.

'The water is like crystal. It is wild and beautiful, beautiful a thousand times over,' the traveller enthused.[21]

In the Auvergne, there were breeds of cattle Rosa had never seen before, both traditional varieties and new crossbreeds. The docile, muscular Salers with their thick and scruffy red coat and their curved horns were virtually exclusive to the region. Well-adapted to the rugged terrain, they made excellent draft cattle, as well as being good milkers and offering succulent meat. The picturesque quality might not have been a farmer's most important consideration, but in Rosa's eyes, that was their defining characteristic. Her pencil fixed their sturdy musculature to her page, while her brush stroked the insulated curvature of their backs.[22] She took copious sketches and mental notes so that she could work her findings up on canvas or into clay as soon as she returned to Paris. But the trip inevitably required her to socialise with human company, too.

'People have been so eager to entertain me that I have not had a moment to myself,' Rose exclaimed. 'If I were not to run out of relatives and friends soon, I might die of indigestion. But it would be rude not to respond to their warm welcome.'[23]

Still, without her companion, Rosa's happiness was dilute.

'If you were here with me, I would be mad with joy,' she told Nathalie. 'I can only half enjoy a pleasure without you. The thing is, you see, you understand me, my dear Nathalie. It feels like a month since I saw you. And then life here is so different from that in Paris that I feel even farther away. I feel quite odd in the morning. When I wake, I am simply astonished not to be where I was. I long for news of you.'[24]

The pain of separation made Rosa's return to Paris even sweeter. Nor did she come back empty-handed; she brought with her some quail. Barring the windows and sectioning off a corner of her own room in the Rue Rumford apartment, she fashioned a mock hinterland out of heather and other hardy shrubs. The success of the encounter she engineered with some finches and canaries was difficult to gauge, since the mess the quail created was quickly agreed disproportionate to their value as models and they were evicted.[25] But in all other respects, the trip to the Auvergne had been productive.

As his daughter's friendship with Mlle Bonheur blossomed, M. Micas was developing a paternal fondness for the young artist. And he had become concerned; he could see Rosa's potential, but her work was not making enough to immunise her against financial anxiety.

'The year has not been fruitful and artists are not rich,' Rosa wrote to the statesman and art collector Adolphe Moreau *fils* on 19 June 1847.[26] Like his father before him, Moreau was an admirer of Eugène Delacroix, thus a shrewd choice of potential patron when Rosa found herself in financial need.

M. Micas considered such pleas unnecessary. Raymond Bonheur had come to rely too heavily on Rosa to nurture his other children's talents. Auguste, Isidore and Juliette were each progressing handsomely in their chosen field – but at what cost? M. Micas felt certain that Rosa's role as unpaid tutor to her siblings was holding her back.

Still, her submissions to the Salon of 1847 told a different story. Rosa, it seemed, could excel in both roles. Flanked by Auguste and her father, Rosa showed *Ploughing – Landscape with Animals (Cantal)*, *Sheep Grazing (Cantal)*, *Study of Thoroughbred Stallions*, and a piece simply entitled *Still Life*. The resulting accolades were her most glowing to date.

'Mademoiselle Rosa Bonheur is one of the leading painters of animals of the day,' lauded Théophile Gautier.[27]

'No one surpasses her,' seconded Paul Mantz.[28]

But by far the most powerful commendation came from Théophile Thoré:

'Mlle Rosa paints almost like a man.'[29]

In a single sentence, Thoré had pinpointed the presumption which lay at the heart of the Salon. It was an institution founded on prejudice, underpinned by convention. As a woman, Rosa had flouted them both. And in so doing, she was carving herself a niche of which she was fast becoming the reigning sovereign.

The success of Rosa's Auvergne-inspired pieces and her vivid accounts commended the region to Nathalie. She longed to share the experience, so once the Salon was over, the two friends persuaded each other that a summer holiday was in order.

'I can hardly tell you that I am bored,' Nathalie wrote to her mother once they had arrived. 'The image I had formed of this place is quite different from the reality. It is charming. The land is rich, and one can always find a spot of shade.'[30]

Then by way of reassurance: 'You tell me, good mother, not to do anything extravagant. I thank you, but if you were here, you would not even recognise me. I am and we are calm as can be. [...] It is only at sunset that we take our little walks together.'[31]

She continued: 'You, beloved mother, are the subject of our loveliest conversations. You also tell me, dear mother, not to get in my dear Rosa's way too much. I may deserve some blame, but as it is a long time since she has been able to create such beautiful studies, she gets carried away in spite of herself.'[32]

'I almost forgot to tell you,' Nathalie interjected, 'that I am feeling well as can be [...] You see, Mother, I am making progress.'[33]

At the end of the correspondence, Rosa herself added a line to the woman she now affectionately addressed as 'Mother Micas': 'If you only knew how happy I am,' she gushed. 'Everything has conspired to make it so, such kind hosts, such a rich landscape [...] And then,' she added, 'I am with my Nathalie.'[34]

The girls returned to Paris, drunk on the pleasure of their

adventure and companionship, with Rosa pepped and ready to resume work.

But as the year drew to a close, activity in Paris was assuming an ominous shape. If the capital's face shimmered seductively, beneath the surface the country's economy had been faltering for some years. The government was growing increasingly conservative. Those further up the class hierarchy objected that Louis-Philippe favoured the financial elite, while remaining indifferent to the needs of the industrial bourgeoisie and the middle classes. The voting system was considered grossly undemocratic, the electoral franchise being held by only a small minority. To these cries of discontent were added the resentful hollers of the common people. Harvests had been poor in 1846, with food prices and unemployment rising in consequence. Now, an economic depression had set in. The populace was turning against the Orléanist regime. When so many had hoped for so much, the disenchantment was crushing. But there was little chance to vent frustration; political gatherings and demonstrations had been banned. Dissension mounted. The idea of a republic began to take hold.[35]

Undeterred by the efforts to quash rebellion, the regime's most passionate opponents began holding so-called 'fundraising banquets' where discontent could legitimately be voiced. And in February 1848, one such banquet escalated into a full-scale political demonstration. All at once, daily life in Paris came to a shuddering halt.

Protesters took to the streets and formed barricades. The ghastly echo of 1830 pushed Louis-Philippe I to abdicate. A provisional government was hastily installed and a republic declared.

Rosa was well acquainted with the concept of revolution – and its implications. Her sister Juliette's birth remained inextricably linked to the 1830 uprisings in her mind. With her stepmother Marguerite Picard having fallen pregnant and approaching her final trimester, it was as though history was repeating itself. Raymond Bonheur's sociopolitical engagement and constant need to vocalise his feelings had made Rosa more cognisant than most when it came to the principles and practicalities of revolution. Rosa had witnessed only too clearly the tangible ways in which revolt could infringe on daily life – the sense of fear and uncertainty as a person walked the street, the price of bread rising so that the coins in one's pocket would no longer buy the familiar loaf.

She also knew to question utopian resolutions. The changes proposed by the Second Republic seemed liberal – suspiciously so. But for the time being, Rosa was distracted by another announcement. It heralded a change by which she stood to be even more personally affected.

Just days after the proclamation of the Second Republic, the newly formed provisional government's Minister of the Interior, Alexandre Auguste Ledru-Rollin, declared that for that year's Salon, there would be no jury, merely an organising committee to determine the distribution of prizes. Its members would be elected by the artists themselves.

Excitement rippled through the art world. Painters who might never have hoped to be accepted now busied themselves preparing work which would be seen – and judged – by all of Paris.[36]

The Bonheur household was in high spirits. It seemed the perfect moment for twenty-year-old Isidore to test the unpredictable waters of public opinion with his work. The studio in the Rue Rumford hummed with enthusiasm and feverish industry as canvases were planned, primed and perfected.

Now in his mid-twenties, Auguste Bonheur had left the family home and moved into a property in the Rue Blanche. He had been accepted to the prestigious École des Beaux-Arts where his work was benefiting from the tuition of the renowned history painter Paul Delaroche, who had been teaching there since 1832.[37] Even so, there was ample opportunity for the siblings to share their hopes and fears as the exhibition approached; Auguste had in mind a portrait of Rosa. For the duration of the sittings, Rosa would have to share the role of creator with her brother and also assume another, less comfortable position. Now, she would also become the object of enquiry.

Auguste decided to show his sister standing upright, her clasped hands resting on a table on which stood two of her sculptures, a bull and her *Shorn Ewe*; it was thus in her capacity as sculptor that he identified her, master – or mistress – of two strapping, working beasts. Wearing a plain, dark green dress and with her face angled towards the viewer so that one side was almost entirely in shadow, Rosa appeared intense, brooding and profound. Her dark brown eyes flashed with confidence as she fixed her viewer with a penetrating, sideways stare which seemed designed expressly to unsettle. Against the sombre background and clothing, the light which fell on Rosa's face made it virtually impossible to ignore the invitation to engage with her. Rosa was presented as a subject, but through her assured pose and stature, her brother empowered her, silently challenging prevailing gender stereotypes while using art to elevate and define her.

With the portrait of Rosa acting as figurehead to their family warship, the Bonheurs were ready to take on the Salon.

But before the siblings could gauge how their work would be received, something unexpected happened. Early in March, M. Micas, though only in his forties, was taken critically ill. From his bed, he called for Raymond. Rosa and Nathalie were privy to the men's conversation.[38]

As he lay languishing, the expiring father breathed out his heartfelt wish that, given how strongly the girls clearly cared for each other, they should henceforward be free to be together. Rosa felt as though she had been given a blessing. Less than a week later, M. Micas was dead.

Rosa now became an essential solace for Nathalie and Mme Micas. She had witnessed the terrible ache of a bereaved spouse; she had suffered the sharp, agonising pain of losing a parent. As the summer arrived, the rest of the Bonheur family prepared for Marguerite Picard's childbirth, while Rosa's attention was absorbed tending to Nathalie and her mother.

Emotions were already running high in the Bonheur household when, in May, the doors of this most unconventional of Salons opened to the public.

With Raymond, Rosa, Auguste and Isidore all exhibiting, the Bonheurs filled nearly an entire page of the Salon catalogue. But the family's wall space was dominated by Rosa, who exhibited no fewer than six canvases, and, having asserted her specialism as a painter, she also ventured two bronze sculptures of a ewe and a bull.

This year, viewers did not need to wonder at the kind of woman who could produce such strong, powerful paintings of animals; they could see the creator for themselves. Auguste's painting countered misconceptions, by showing his sister as bold, self-assured and more than equal to the task. Rosa's own submissions and Auguste's portrait worked together to present her as a brand.

Even so, Rosa was learning that a thick skin was vital as an artist grappled to make a success.

'This work is missing just one quality,' sneered a critic of her *Cows and Bulls, Cantal Breed*. 'That is the precise definition of osteology and mycology [...] It is skin we see, quite clearly skin, but skin that looks as though it has been stuffed.'[39]

Still, in a show which had received more than twice the number of entrants than the previous year and which had attracted, as Théophile Thoré put it, a 'mishmash of strange works', a 'bric-a-brac of paintings', for many, Rosa's carefully executed bucolic scenes of rural harmony provided a welcome visual respite.[40]

'What truth and what perfect observation,' proclaimed Théophile Gautier, in appreciation of her Cantal bulls. 'Nothing is forgotten, not even the white slaver that drips in a silvery foam from the corner of their mouths.'[41]

There were further comparisons with Brascassat, while Gautier placed Rosa in the same bracket as Paulus Potter, 'the Raphael of sheep'. Writing for *L'Illustration*, 'A J D' was both astounded and impressed that Rosa had 'not stayed around the sheep pen as a woman might naturally be inclined to do' but had actually 'gone out to study her *cattle* and her *bulls of Cantal* in the mountain air.'[42] The reviewer neatly summarised her position in Paris's eyes: 'Today, Rosa Bonheur is one of the art world's celebrities.'[43]

But there was scarcely time for Rosa to revel in her plaudits. As her stepmother neared her due date, unrest was building in the city.

The provisional government (composed largely of Republicans, many of bourgeois origin) might have achieved its goals of universal – significantly, male – suffrage and unemployment relief in Paris in the shape of National Workshops. But the April elections were framed by disturbances across the capital, as various social groups demonstrated their distrust of the Republic. Furthermore, the result of the vote had been a National Constitutional Assembly composed primarily of notables and middle-class men rather than workers, while the workshops proved unable to deal with the volume of demand.[44] In May, workmen had invaded the Assembly and been repelled. A battle of the classes was brewing.

On 19 June 1848, Marguerite Picard gave birth to an exceptionally tiny baby boy.[45] Soon afterwards, it was announced that the National Workshops were to be closed – and just days later, workers rose up in protest against what they felt to be the government and the Assembly's flagrant betrayal. Citizens once more took to the streets and barricades went up, while the all-too-familiar sound of gunshots echoed through the capital. When military forces led by the General Louis-Eugène Cavaignac were called in to suppress the revolt, the ensuing bloodbath lasted just a few days – the 'June Days'. But during that short time, of the tens of thousands of Parisians who participated, at least 12,000 were arrested and some 1,500 were killed.[46]

General Cavaignac was heartily applauded by his comrades. But the emerging Republican ship was clearly being steered by experienced Orléanists and Legitimists.[47] Politically speaking, it leaned to the right. And now in the aftermath of the revolution, it urgently needed to strengthen its position.

People and politics were at the forefront of Parisians' minds that summer when Rosa received two unexpected pieces of news.

The first arrived while she was absent from Paris. Her father's friend, Justin Mathieu, had invited her to his property in the *département* of the Nièvre, south-east of Paris. Mathieu now had two daughters and in recognition of his long-standing friendship with Raymond Bonheur, he had asked Rosa to become godmother to his youngest, who, according to custom, had been given Rosa's name.

While Rosa was enjoying time away from the hubbub of the capital, she learned that the Salon committee had shortlisted her to receive a prize.[48] When the results were announced, she discovered that her *Red Oxen of Cantal* had won a first-class prize.

'My daughter has had great success this year,' Raymond Bonheur boasted to his former tutor, Pierre Lacour. 'The Salon of 1848 has been one of the highlights of her life which will never be forgotten.'[49]

Nor did Raymond exaggerate the extent of Rosa's achievements. Even the acclaimed painter of battle scenes, Horace Vernet, who had immortalised Louis-Philippe in 1837, had approached Rosa to offer his congratulations.

It was an unequivocal triumph. But the second revelation that summer was even more momentous.

One day, Rosa received a curious memo. It came from the Ministry of the Interior, under whose jurisdiction the budget and purchase of artworks had now been placed – and its contents were scarcely believable: the government wished to commission her to produce a painting.

At first blush, pouring money into art when the capital was surfacing from one of the bloodiest episodes in recent history seemed preposterous. But in the resulting confusion, the Second Republic needed to shore up its foundations, and quickly. The Republican vision encompassed a wider public gaining access to higher cultural forms. Art was a powerful political tool and art patronage one of the fastest, most visible ways of demonstrating sensitivity to popular desires.[50]

History painting, which had long held such a privileged place in France and was inextricably linked to monarchic rule, had now fallen from favour. In the aftermath of national turmoil, the public no longer sought out dramatic moments in a distant historical past, but timelessness, peace and stability in a familiar context. The Republic needed a new iconography.[51]

In this non-monarchic era, the dictates of the Academy were increasingly rejected and many more prizes had gone to genre and landscape scenes than to history paintings in the 1848 Salon.[52] Republicans now turned towards the Barbizon school of painters, whose works

departed from the academic norms and depicted recognisable locations of national significance. Landscape painting – and most of all
the unspoiled French countryside – offered war-weary viewers the
peaceful refuge they craved. As Paris expanded, there was a new role
for landscape artists as pseudo-tourist guides.[53]

As the unlikely, but rising star of the art world, Rosa Bonheur was
agreed just the painter for the job. Her work found favour with both
left and right. And the added attraction was that nobody could accuse
the government of archaism – for what could be more progressive than
employing a woman to translate its ethos into paint?

A few days after the initial proposition, further details were released.
The Ministry of the Interior would pay a staggering 3,000 francs for
'a painting representing grazing animals'.[54] In that post-revolutionary
summer, it was a fortune. Most artists would have been thrilled to
receive a few hundred francs for a State commission.[55] At the end of
the correspondence, the gravity of the request was impressed: 'The
Ministry would like to think, Mademoiselle, that you will bring to the
execution of this task all the care that will justify the confidence that
has been placed in us.'[56]

Rosa could hardly refuse. Yet it was a dangerous mission. Recent
history had illustrated only too clearly the dim view the government
took of those hesitant to embrace its ethos. A commissioned picture
would be the focus of all eyes at next year's Salon. If the work were
deemed successful, the project could galvanise Rosa's reputation. But
if she faltered, the repercussions would be devastating.

There was plenty of encouragement from her immediate circle.
Raymond Bonheur was still overcome with pride at his daughter's
Salon success. He joyously reported to Pierre Lacour how, following
the show, Rosa's fellow artists had nominated her to be on the hanging committee (an invitation she ultimately refused on account of her
commission).[57]

At that time, Raymond had good reason to be in high spirits. He
had lately been asked to become director of the girls' drawing school
in the Rue de Touraine-Saint-Germain which had been founded by

Mme de Montizon in 1803.[58] Maintained at the expense of the government, the school was designed to teach 'young women destined for the arts or industrious professions', with an annual prize-giving ceremony and an exhibition of pupils' work.[59] Family members later intimated that it was Raymond's connections with former Saint-Simonians which had won him the position. Either way, it was a job offer Raymond was eager to accept, and Rosa's triumph seemed almost to endorse his nomination. It was as though Raymond's own unfulfilled ambitions were being realised through Rosa.

Despite the professional bolster, the value of money was making itself felt more keenly than ever in the Bonheur household. By the end of the summer, Isidore had received summons to complete his compulsory national conscription in the army. He had been unlucky in the lottery system used to staff the forces and had been posted to the Italian border.[60] There were no choices; the Bonheurs' finances were too erratic to make them one of those families fortunate enough to be able to afford a substitute. Rosa had to bid farewell to her adored younger brother as she turned her attention to her commission.

Another invitation to visit Justin Mathieu's family in the Nièvre arrived at a fortuitous moment. Rosa was settling on her subject for the commissioned canvas. If the government insisted on a landscape with animals, Paris was hardly a propitious place to start. She would surely find more material if she accepted Mathieu's offer.

Depicting a specific rural locale had earned her praise at that year's Salon. Parts of the former province of Nivernais were beautiful, rustic and untouched, visually charming with great stretches of lush green fields and pastures and dotted with little towns and farms. Its cattle were admired across France. But it was not an unproblematic choice of location. Peasants' lives were frequently impoverished and labour-intensive. A mix of radical and conservative forces could be detected and there had been a notable insurrection the previous March, when anger at the loss of grazing space had spurred some 800 peasants to retaliate with a revolt. With the *département*'s proximity and commercial links to the capital, Parisians – particularly the elite who had made investments – were naturally acquainted with activity in the area. And concern that the growing political consciousness of the rural population could be dangerous was spreading.[61]

For Rosa, it made the stakes even higher. If she could show this particular area in a favourable light, the canvas had the potential to catapult her career. But if she failed, she could be ruined.

With a leaden weight on her shoulders, but Nathalie by her side, Rosa prepared to leave Paris for the Nièvre. She was determined – she would and must succeed.

8

❖•❖

Cometh the Hour

Fifteen hundred francs was a lot of money to hold in one's hand. It would take Raymond Bonheur six months to earn that kind of amount in his new post as director of the girls' drawing school.[1] Rosa had never seen so much money, nor would she forget the feel of the three smooth, crisp banknotes she collected from the Ministry of Finance in the Rue de Rivoli that September. As she made her way home in the autumn sunlight through Paris's busy streets, it hardly felt as though she walked; it seemed rather that she was floating on air.

When Rosa pushed open the door at the family's new home in the Rue de Touraine-Saint-Germain, the appearance of such riches caused a furore. Raymond Bonheur had always entertained an ambivalent relationship with money. Though wealth impressed him, he abhorred the greed synonymous with the moneyed classes and proclaimed bitterly against what he called 'filthy lucre'.[2] Rosa never failed to be struck by her father's casual attitude towards remuneration; whenever he received money, he had the peculiar habit of scattering coins haphazardly around the studio, his thinking being that there would always be some cash to be found when times were hard. To Raymond, who had continually struggled to provide food for his children through art, the sight of Rosa clutching those banknotes symbolised the ultimate achievement.[3]

But Rosa did not allow the payment to distract her for long. Now, she had to earn it. Besides, it quickly became clear that money could not lift all the Bonheur family's worries.

Not long after Rosa had collected the first instalment of her commission fee, Raymond Bonheur fell ill. To the family's relief, the
malady was not protracted. But it left the man of the house and new
father depleted.

'My dear master,' Raymond wrote to his former tutor Pierre Lacour
in October 1848, 'you are one of those men to whom I would like to
write long letters, but I am just getting over an illness.'[4] He persevered:
'It seems there is so much I would like to say to you, I so wish I could
see you!'[5]

Raymond's children did their best to assist their father as he convalesced. Rosa at least was sufficiently qualified to share some of his
teaching responsibilities. But she could not afford her focus to be
diverted from the commitment she had made to the government. As
winter approached and a new year – and a new Salon – beckoned,
Rosa knew her canvas must be completed.

❧

There was no railway linking the *département* of the Nièvre to the
capital in 1848, so the most commonly used form of transport was
the stagecoach, a discomfort with which Rosa was familiar. But with
Nathalie once more sitting beside her, the trip became an adventure
rather than a chore. However, while the Auvergne had offered the
unpolished simplicity of a familial welcome, this time, the locus of the
girls' reception was closer to the setting of a novel.[6]

With parts dating back to the Middle Ages, the Château de la Cave
in the commune of Beaumont-Sardolles had been augmented over the
centuries to create a home which was grand, stately and imposing. It
had come into the Mathieu family after the Revolution of 1789, and
now, this elegant mansion sat on a sprawling estate, flanked by neatly
tended gardens planted with trees and ornamental bushes, and traversed
by regimented pathways. With little more than half the communes boasting a school in the 1840s, the Nièvre was a relatively undeveloped area.
However, at the Château de la Cave, there was little sense of deprivation.[7]

Now in his fifties, Justin Mathieu shuttled backwards and forwards between Paris and the Nièvre with his wife and daughters, travelling to the capital for business, retreating to the Château de la Cave whenever the need for quiet impressed itself. Always receptive to creative projects and anxious to help his old friend Raymond Bonheur, Mathieu was delighted to welcome Rosa so that she might complete her great commission.

As soon as the guests were comfortably installed in the château, Rosa began her work.

At first, locals were bemused to watch the peculiar young woman from Paris heaving her cumbersome drawing equipment up to the fields and back. In the provinces, popular stereotype cast the Parisienne as fashionable yet supercilious and aloof. But a few exchanges sufficed to spread the word that this particular city dweller was bright, friendly and genuinely interested in the country people and their ways. The area retained an affectionate memory of the painter from Paris, whom collective remembrance would fix as 'Mam'zelle Rosa'.

Surrounded by fields and farmland and all the activity associated with the year's end, Rosa's composition soon became clear in her mind. She would depict cattle ploughing.

Inspired yet conscious of the strain on time, Rosa worked quickly to capture the farm work, with the land, the soil, the oxen from different angles, as well as their human drivers. Once satisfied with her research, the real labour could begin.

Rosa was back in Paris to be able to write to Isidore on 2 November 1848, directing her letter to where he was now posted near Grenoble. She began by apologising for the tardiness of her correspondence, before updating him on life at home:

> First, M. and Mme Vernet are interesting themselves in your behalf. They intend to try and get you an unlimited furlough or have you put on the staff of hospital assistants at Versailles. You could then have more leisure to work.[8]

Rosa was frustrated that her earnings, though improved, were not yet sufficient to buy Isidore out of the army. But she tried to remain upbeat, filling him in on various daily trivia: her burgeoning friend-ship with the sculptor Mêne; how Horace Vernet had congratulated her at the prize-giving ceremony, invited her to his home and offered to lend her some Arab costumes. But in the middle of writing, such information suddenly seemed unimportant:

> My poor brother, I should have written all these little things to you sooner, for I know they please you. But sometimes I am so disgusted with everything that it seems they must have no importance for other people. Why talk to you about the good things that happen to me while you, poor lad, are carrying the knapsack?[9]

Then there was the matter of their father's health to address.

'We have had an anxious time with Papa, who was very ill for a while,' she shared. 'Happily, he is better now, and on Sunday next his pupils that have succeeded at the competitive examination are to receive their prizes. So he will be on his throne and I on mine.'[10]

Working together brought Rosa and Raymond mutual satisfaction. Raymond recognised his daughter's talent – and the headstrong tendencies which might jeopardise it. And though she had witnessed the havoc wreaked by his transient socialist passions, though she had heard his eloquent words, insistently voiced, always with sincerity but so often without action, publicly, Rosa turned a blind eye to her father's foibles. Instead, she celebrated his virtues: his essential goodness, his concern for humanity and his deep, unwavering love for his children.

Still, on the subject of her career and the conditions needed for it to flourish, Rosa was becoming more determined. M. Micas had always urged Raymond Bonheur to let Rosa take a studio of her own. With her father now having secured a good teaching position and her own work becoming more remunerative, not to mention space in the Bonheurs' apartment being at a premium, Rosa set out to honour M. Micas's wish. She turned to the capable Mme Micas for assistance, and in little time, found herself preparing to move into a well-appointed studio not far from where the Micas mother and daughter lived, at number 56, Rue de l'Ouest, near the Luxembourg Gardens.[11]

The building housed several studios and had become a thriving community of artists. Among Rosa's neighbours was the history and genre painter Émile Signol, while the artist Adolphe Yvon (who specialised in portraits and military scenes) was based in the nearby Rue Notre-Dame-des-Champs.[12]

The studio was reached by crossing an enclosed courtyard – and when the door swung open, the scene revealed looked something between a stable and a picture gallery. The ceilings were high, the floor finished in wood, while at one end of the room, an enormous, multi-paned window flooded the workspace with light. This was where Rosa's equipment and easel were set up, and a number of complete and half-finished canvases rested against the walls around it. This room was adjoined to the rest of the studio by a tall archway, through which the visitor passed to discover a kind of indoor smallholding. On the right, a set of small pens housed a sheep and goats which nibbled hay from a manger mounted on the wall in their enclosure. Opposite them was a larger feeding area for any more sizeable livestock Rosa might need. On the walls, amid mounted antlers, stuffed animal heads peered down at unsuspecting guests, and all around, buckets, baskets and straw gave visitors the sense that they had stepped into a farmyard, while every now and then a rabbit or other small creature darted out of nowhere before scampering off to hide.[13]

Rosa was delighted with her new workspace. Nathalie took up a virtually permanent place in the studio, arriving every morning to trace Rosa's drawings and act as a technician while the artist painted. Then, when the clock struck midday, the girls sat before the little wood-burning stove and roasted cuts of meat Nathalie had brought with her, which they devoured with a portion of fried potatoes. Immersed in paint and productivity, the pair were blissfully happy.[14] Still, for Rosa,

Rosa Bonheur's studio, illustration by Renard and Valentin, engraving by Best, Hotelin and Regnier, from *L'Illustration, Journal Universel*, No. 479, Volume XIX, 1 May 1852.

Photo DE AGOSTINI PICTURE LIBRARY/De Agostini via Getty Images

the pleasure was not without the occasional pang of nostalgia; it was the first studio she had occupied without her father.

In 1849, Rosa's brother Auguste painted Raymond Bonheur in a commanding portrait. Resting back in a chair, the father leant on a table, a book at his elbow bespeaking his intellect. His blonde curls had now turned grey and woolly, and had receded to the sides of his head, while he wore a bushy beard. On his balding pate, a cap had been positioned at an angle, so that he presented as the quintessential artist. The suggestion of a smile beneath his beard was confirmed by his twinkling blue eyes, around which multiple creases recorded a lifetime of tears and laughter, while radiating warmth and wisdom. The man in Auguste's portrait exuded strength and stability. The impression was deceptive: less than a week after Rosa's 27th birthday, Raymond Bonheur was dead.[15]

Nélie Jacquemart (after Auguste Bonheur), *Portrait of Raymond Bonheur*, after 1849, oil on canvas, 100.5 x 82.5 cm, Musée des Beaux-Arts-Mairie de Bordeaux.

Photo: F. Deval. No. d'inventaire: Bx E 1163

After a life spent at the service of his heart, that vital organ had eventually failed him. Rosa felt as though hers too had broken.

'M. Raymond Bonheur, landscape artist, has just died after a life-long battle against poverty,' reported the *Journal des Beaux-Arts* on 8 April 1849.[16] 'Only months ago, this artist took over as director of one of the state-funded drawing schools for girls run by the city.'

Raymond Bonheur had always benefited from contacts in high places. Just a few months earlier, he had casually mentioned his acquaintance with the Directeur des Musées, Philippe-Auguste Jeanron, in one of his letters to Pierre Lacour.[17] At his funeral, the full extent of his connections became clear. The deceased's fellow Saint-Simonian, Gustave d'Eichthal, spoke warmly of his colleague's 'touching devotion to his family', of 'his self-denial, his talent, his courage' and 'his deeply imbibed ideas of emancipation and of pacific progress for the human race'.[18] Afterwards, the infamous Père Enfantin wrote to Lamartine of 'that poor Raymond Bonheur [...] who has left in his daughter one of the greatest artists of the epoque'.[19]

It was Rosa who covered the funeral expenses – and she did so using the payment for the commission about which Raymond had been so excited, for the work which he would never see complete.

With neither her father nor Isidore at the Bonheur family apartment, home life lost its meaning for Rosa. The sense of isolation was profound. She had never shared an especially close bond with Auguste, and in any case, with him now absorbed in his career, his time was limited. Meanwhile, in her youthful innocence, Juliette seemed more accepting of their stepmother's presence than was her older sister. And to Marguerite Picard's delight, the nineteen-year-old got on remarkably well with her own son, Hippolyte Peyrol. Like Isidore, Hippolyte had begun sculpting animals and thanks to Raymond's intervention, had secured an apprenticeship with the great sculptor to whom Rosa had been compared, Antoine-Louis Barye, under whose supervision he was becoming accomplished in the art of bronze work.[20] As Hippolyte and Juliette progressed in their creative pursuits, their mutual affection was growing. Then with the intermittent cries of baby Germain, Rosa could tell that her own chapter at the family home had come to an end.

Nathalie and Mme Micas now had the chance to repay the debt of support that only a year ago Rosa had offered them.

Comfortably installed in an apartment in the Rue d'Assas, technically, Mme Micas was retired, though in practice her activity showed no signs of waning. Shrewd and pragmatic, the bespectacled and matronly Mme Micas was careful with her savings, yet generous when she felt someone deserved her confidence. Rosa told friends that it was good 'Mother Micas' who provided the funds to cover her father's remaining debts.

Working on her commission went some way to occupying errant thoughts and assuaging melancholy. But when the light faded and the working population of Paris began to make its way home, Rosa felt her spirits drop. Eventually, she asked Mme Micas if she might be able to move in with her and Nathalie, and the old woman gladly agreed.

It was consequently with the Micases that Rosa waited anxiously for that year's Salon to open. At last, she would discover if her attempt to remain blinkered to her grief and produce a successful work had paid off.

∝

The Salon of 1849 was noteworthy, both for Paris in general and for Rosa in particular. It was, to all intents and purposes, the first exhibition of the Republic. But the event was shrouded in confusion and uncertainty. The question of the form and role the Salon jury might take remained unclear until February, the location (when at last it was decided) was to move to the Tuileries Palace and even then, the show opened three months later than planned. Furthermore, with only 2,380 works submitted, the number of entrants had fallen, with many of the absentees being familiar, crowd-drawing names. The slump alarmed critic Théophile Gautier, who accused artists of neglecting their patriotic duty.[21]

The wider political situation only exacerbated matters. The Second Republic's first president had been elected at the end of 1848, and in an astonishing historical twist, Louis-Napoleon Bonaparte, nephew of the great man, won by an overwhelming majority. Short, with a pale complexion and a dark, bushy moustache, Louis-Napoleon seemed an unlikely leader. Pronouncing French with a German accent, his attitude was distant, his manners awkward and his face expressionless.[22] But the people had spoken. Indeed, the new president owed his victory largely to a now significant peasant faction among the electorate, many of whom felt disadvantaged under the Republic and nostalgically equated the Bonaparte name with the order they felt was lacking. But already by February that year, Louis-Napoleon was hosting grand balls from his residence in the Élysée Palace, where formal titles were used and the etiquette stringent. This swift and soundless assumption of near sovereignty boded ill. Then the elections for the Legislative Assembly in May saw the triumph of the Party of Order (formed by the monarchists and conservatives), painting a bleak picture for the future of the Republic. Just two days before the Salon opened, the army were called in to repress a left-wing uprising in the city, which was echoed in an insurrection in Lyon. As the Salon of 1849 welcomed its first visitors, the capital was in a state of high alert.[23]

But it was a disquieting show for Rosa on a personal level, too. This year, there was only one other family member listed on the same page as her in the person of Auguste. Isidore had now committed himself to sculpture and Rosa had quietly withdrawn from that component of the show, friends claimed, as a result. But perhaps more unusually – and certainly more perilously – Rosa had sent just one picture by which to be judged. The medal she won in the previous year had exempted her from jury scrutiny, but the Parisian public could be just as merciless. Her whole reputation hung on a single canvas. The question was: would the gamble pay off?

The show opened on 15 June and before long, the high-ceilinged halls of the Tuileries Palace began filling up with a varied cross-section of Parisian society. Skirts brushed frock coats, people mingled, necks were craned and judgements muttered as the public moved about inspecting what the new administration and its artists had to offer.

Visitors were guided by their peers and critics soon spotted a swarm of people lingering a little longer before one painting in particular. As the first wave of viewers moved aside, the scene was revealed to those behind them.

While horses and carriages clattered through the streets outside, while business pressed and people hurried, here was a slice of calm. In a sunlit field, six oxen walked in pairs, harnessed to a yoke, heaving an almighty plough, doing what they had done for centuries. As they strained diagonally across the field, linking background, middle-ground and foreground, the plough cut into the rich soil, digging it up, turning it over, revealing the source of nature's bounty. It was the very essence of constructive labour, a celebration of life's basic necessities.

Hoffbauer, *Salon of 1849 at the Tuileries*,
1875–1882, lithograph, 12.2 x 9.6 cm, published
in Theodor Josef Hubert Hoffbauer, *Paris à travers
les âges* (Paris: Firmin-Didot et cie, 1885).
Image courtesy of Brown University Library, Providence

And painted in such crisp, vivid colours, the group looked startlingly real. Such verisimilitude could hardly be a myth – for why would a person doubt their senses?

The response was immediate.

'Any work imbued with a true sense of rural harmony and which almost brings the smell of the fields to us is sure to be welcomed,' the critic F. de Lagenevais reasoned in the *Revue des Deux Mondes*. 'That is what we get in Mlle Rosa Bonheur's idyll.'[24]

'We will not delay any longer the commendation that we owe to

Mlle Rosa Bonheur,' added the reviewer for the *Journal des Beaux-Arts*. 'The truth and movement of her cattle are admirable, the drawing in her painting is firm and vigorous.'[25]

Fiercely loyal, Théophile Gautier was in raptures: 'Mlle Rosa Bonheur – and we say it with no gallant intention – is now at the very top of the field of animal painting. Her scene of Nivernais yoking is a masterpiece [...] We prefer Rosa Bonheur's cattle to Paul Potter's cows [...] Let us respect old reputations, but let us not indulge in degrading idolatry. Why should we suppose that nature cannot repeat itself, and with even more success the second time?'[26]

Gautier could not resist a reference to the early part of the 1846 novel *The Devil's Pool* by George Sand, which, for him, the scene called to mind. Nor was he the only reviewer to make the connection.[27] Before long, George Sand's virility, skill and independent spirit had been mapped onto Rosa and the press were tipping her to be the art world's answer to the successful female novelist.

'It is the women who steal the show this year,' declared Louis Desnoyers writing for *Le Siècle*. 'Have we in fact reached that era of emancipation [...] where women will be entirely enfranchised of the inferiority which weighs on their social condition? Where, while men take their turn at the housework, sewing and preparing stew for the nippers, these ladies will undertake the professions of representatives, state advisers, lawyers, bailiffs, prefects, judges and rural policewomen?'[28]

There were still criticisms amid the praise; the figures were not successful; cattle were an unworthy subject of great art; it was perhaps a little too good, the oxen improbably clean, the clods of mud simply not dirty enough. The full title *Ploughing in the Nivernais – Sombrage* was declared ill-fitting. *Sombrage* was not even a French word, the critic Desnoyers objected, and if it was being used to suggest that the scene was taking place at twilight (*sombre* translating as 'dark'), it was misleading; the colours were bright and radiant.[29] Rosa later defended herself on this count, insisting that the title was the result of an error in the catalogue. But on the whole, the verdict was resounding. Few quibbled the fact that the title adopted an outmoded name for the *département* (which had been known as the Nièvre since 1790), or that the cattle shown were clearly Morvan, a traditional breed which was fast disappearing as the Charolais cow became more common.[30] Passéism was comforting. This was the reassuring image people wanted. For Desnoyers, the work was 'without a doubt, the one which is proving the greatest success with the crowds and even with many art buffs'.[31] That Rosa had painted the 'truth' was not in question; the only contention lay in how well she had done it.

As critics saw it, Rosa's success was due primarily to her skill, but also to the delicious double significance of her surname (*bonheur* meaning 'happiness' in French) – and, of course, to the novelty of such a powerful work being painted by a woman.

'I do not know what [the Ministry of the Interior] paid for these six pairs of cattle,' mused 'A J D' in *L'Illustration*, 'but it certainly got a good deal.'[32]

So did Rosa. For once the Salon closed its doors, she was inundated with enquiries.

The business of dealing in modern pictures was still a relatively new phenomenon in 19th-century Paris. To begin with, it tended to be practised as a sideline, often by those who sold artists' equipment.[33] Rosa had already made the acquaintance of the shirt maker M. Bourges, who had a penchant for painting. Now, he increased his custom, regularly paying Rosa for pieces, either in cash or in kind, an arrangement which benefited several members of her family when they needed garments.

'I don't understand much about art,' Bourges's daughter Léonide remembered her father confessing, 'but I know a good sheep when I see one.'[34]

The well-regarded picture dealer M. Tedesco also became a recurrent buyer in the late 1840s. Since its inception in 1833, this family-run business had gone from strength to strength. Based in the Rue Saint-Martin, by 1846 the company was fully operational, and its first boss, Giacomo Tedesco, was conducting flourishing trade.[35]

Rosa's work schedule intensified. And as she was called on to play a more active role as the public face of her art, her character quirks were given wider airing.

'Rosa Bonheur's welcome was always frank and hearty,' remembered the minor painter Paul Chardin, who became a close acquaintance.

> Her chosen friends she treated as real companions without ever assuming an air of superiority. The dominating qualities in her nature were honesty, candour and uprightness. Her opinion she always expressed in plain, even blunt language [...] She consequently had a peculiar horror of flatterers and hypocrites.[36]

Chardin observed that 'she did not accept new friends easily' for 'she liked solitude, meditation, and felt free only in the company of those whom she had known for a long time.' Then, 'she gave free rein to her thoughts and bursts of gaiety which sometimes ended in real tom-foolery.'[37]

Still, Rosa was learning that playfulness must be kept in check. Now a celebrity, she needed to beware of sycophants and grovellers. She particularly distrusted dandies who tried to charm and reporters who sought to pry.

Repelling journalists and satisfying picture requests were not the only tasks Rosa now faced. Raymond Bonheur's death had left the drawing school without a director and Rosa was quickly agreed the logical replacement. She had acquired a good deal of teaching experience, not least working for the Princess Czartoryska and acting as her siblings' tutor. Rosa accepted the proposition and in little time, Paris's aspiring female art students were benefiting from her expertise.

One of the young women who profited from Rosa's weekly critiques remembered how she usually arrived wearing a short black jacket, a green or brown dress and a straw hat trimmed with green velvet. 'This hat she would toss onto one of the empty chairs and then begin her inspection,' the student recalled.[38] Her plain appearance often provoked amusement and furtive ridiculing. Furthermore, at 27, Rosa was only a little older than many of her pupils. Notwithstanding, the bulk of the student body revered her wisdom. Rosa later asserted proudly that when she spoke, 'you could have heard a fly on the wing'.[39]

Adhering to the approach traditionally adopted in art schools, Rosa insisted that her girls master the all-important skill of drawing before they progressed to using paint. She was compassionate but firm and she always reprimanded shoddy work. Those who had witnessed her weekly progress reviews reported that during one of her scoldings, she ordered a disappointing student to 'go back to your mother and darn stockings or do needlework'.[40] To Rosa's mind, domestic chores represented the most humiliating punishment an ambitious female artist could be issued. Indeed, she was capable of bringing a student to tears. But then so often, one of her unexpected witticisms would be uttered and the whole class – including the erstwhile victim – found themselves crippled with laughter.

For all her air of severity and her brusque manner, when the time came to award annual prizes and a speech was required, Rosa balked. The very thought of presenting a polished discourse to an expectant audience terrified her. Having wrestled with her anxiety for a while, she ultimately had to excuse herself.

By the time the autumn of 1849 arrived, the year had proved especially demanding. Another visit to the Mathieu family near Nevers seemed at once a fitting close and a welcome reprieve. However, news that Isidore was to receive another military posting impeded Rosa's peace of mind.

'How grieved I was to read your letter,' she exclaimed. 'What can I do? […] I will go back to Paris, if you think I can be useful. I was so relying on Mme Vernet. […] Oh! My dear old boy, I am so upset.'[41]

She wrote again once she had returned to the capital, assuring her brother that she was certain he would soon be discharged. But the New Year arrived and the military's needs prevailed.

In her next letter, Rosa told her brother that she had decided to send his captain a sketch. 'This will no doubt induce him to take more interest in you,' she reasoned hopefully.[42]

As she fretted for Isidore and attempted to sketch and pool money to buy him out of the army, Rosa also had her Salon submissions to prepare, her students to supervise and picture dealers to satisfy. And then there was Nathalie.

Nathalie Micas had become an indispensable cog in the Rosa Bonheur machine. Her attention kept their home in order, her technician work enabled the artist to concentrate on the business of creation, while her love, companionship and amusing eccentricities brought Rosa the very deepest kind of spiritual fulfilment.

But if the girls' gruelling work schedule was taking its toll on Rosa, Nathalie's more delicate constitution was showing even greater evidence of strain. Physically and mentally, she was at a low ebb when she contracted a fever from which she seemed unable to recover.

Rosa was alarmed. She had lost her mother, her father and now she had been separated from Isidore. She could not bear for Nathalie to suffer – or worse. When a doctor advised that a visit to the baths in the Pyrenees might be of benefit to them both, Rosa did not waste a moment.

Unusually, the Salon would not take place until December that year. In view of the unstable political climate, the government were nervous about large crowds massing at the Tuileries Palace. At the end of May, a law imposing eligibility criteria effectively ended universal suffrage, leaving many disenfranchised, left-wing workers embittered. Meanwhile, Louis-Napoleon's quiet quest for power continued as he prepared a fierce propaganda mission. Conditions were felt too inflammatory to risk a summer Salon. If Rosa were strategic and worked hard up until the moment of departure, she could still go away and be back in time for the opening.[43]

Expense and practicality decided the women that Mme Micas should stay at home. Nathalie and Rosa promised to keep in touch by letter, an only partially satisfactory solution, Mme Micas's written French being even less certain than her spoken grammar.

Nonetheless, as June approached, the girls could not suppress their excitement about their imminent departure. But when they turned their attention to packing, one final matter gave cause for concern.

To benefit fully from the trip, to be able to explore the countryside as they wished, to ride horses across the rough terrain, to paint and walk and hike through the mountains, their normal wardrobe would not suffice. With the heavy dresses and skirts of the day, feminine attire was deeply impractical. And without husbands to accompany them, they would have to tackle many of the practical tasks – and obstacles – themselves.

Rosa decided that there was only one way to proceed. It was daring, it was shocking, and without permission, it was illegal: to be truly liberated, they would have to dress and travel as men.

9

Changing Views

'**A**ny woman found wearing men's clothing [...] will be arrested and escorted to the *Préfecture de police*.'[1]

The ordinance issued on 7 November 1800 was abundantly clear: if a woman wanted to wear trousers, she had to apply to the *Préfecture de police* for a permit.

The decree was the fruit of a fearful post-Revolutionary climate, where establishing order and documenting status were perceived as key to controlling the populace. Freshly empowered, Napoleon Bonaparte was anxious about opposition to his regime. It was an era marked by repression, a period where the concern to protect the state from the misuse of titles and identities was at the forefront of the administration's collective mind.[2] The gender disparity was buttressed by the 1804 Civil Code, which reinforced male authority and reminded women – who had been active and even armed during the Revolution – just where their place was.[3]

The law professed to be protecting women with genuine cause from unwanted harassment. In practice, it meant that the authorities could accuse any woman wearing trousers without permission of usurping the masculine identity with malicious intent. In a society founded on male privilege, donning trousers gained the wearer unmerited freedoms. The potential ramifications were terrifying.

The police kept a file of requests lodged and the criteria for their being granted was stringent. A woman had to show a certified medical letter declaring a health condition or physical abnormality (such as a beard) that made it impossible to wear a skirt and go about her daily business. In short, permits were granted to those who did not conform. Should permission be given, the holder could not attend balls, shows or public meetings thus attired.[4] Even then, the permits were usually valid for just three to six months and only during carnival season would cross-dressing without one be tolerated.[5]

But there were tales of female triumph to inspire hope, cases passed where the medical 'need' seemed more oblique. Arriving in Paris in 1830, a certain Mlle Foucaud set about educating herself before getting a job in a printing press earning 2 francs 50 a day. But she quickly discovered that her male co-workers were carrying out the same tasks and earning 1 franc 50 more. Riled by the injustice, Mlle Foucaud asked to be admitted to the men's workshop. Impossible, her boss retorted – the sexes were not to be mixed. Mlle Foucaud promptly handed in her notice. Obtaining a permit, she cut off her hair, donned a pair of trousers and reapplied for a job in the men's workshop. She was accepted. There she worked for many years, saving diligently until she was able to buy some land and build a housing estate, which she managed as a superlatively efficient landlady.[6]

With a medical professional having prescribed both her and Nathalie a visit to a spa town where skirts could hamper their activity, Rosa felt confident that their cases would be heard favourably. And just as she had hoped, she and Nathalie were each presented with a smart certificate. Trading their taffeta for trousers, they were ready to depart.

ॐ

'Without doubt some of the finest scenery in France is to be found among the Pyrenees,' proclaimed an 1850s guide for travellers.[7]

It was the English who had first set the trend for Pyrenean sojourns in the mid-18th century, when the seemingly incongruous notion of travelling purely for leisure and health was still relatively novel. Stendhal's *Memoirs of a Tourist* had since appeared in 1838 and by the mid-19th century, the term *touriste* had become fixed in the French vocabulary. With an improving rail network and the vogue for summer holidays having taken hold among those with means, tourism was a rising commodity in mid-19th-century France.[8]

Rosa and Nathalie planned to base themselves in two or three well-appointed locations from whence they could make trips out to other places of interest. But on one matter they were immediately disappointed: 'the sunny atmosphere' which guidebooks assured travellers 'gives a warm glow to the landscape' was nowhere to be found; instead, the weather was unseasonably wet.[9]

They began their waterlogged adventure in Eaux-Bonnes, 'a fashionable resort, consisting of a row of 18 or 20 fine tall houses, chiefly modern, and Parisian in their style, and rather expensive, in a wild mountain nook.'[10]

The tricky inhabitants, with their smooth repartee and eloquent sales patter, left Rosa and Nathalie disenchanted.

'We have been [on] some beautiful walks,' Rosa informed Mme Micas, 'but done no real work, which is beginning to bore us.'[11]

Still, the companions had not travelled solely for work. The number of invalids visiting the Pyrenees was increasing by the year and a person's choice of spa was guided by the properties peculiar to each. Eaux-Bonnes, for example, boasted sulphurous water, and was particularly recommended to anyone suffering from complaints of the lungs.

Unfortunately, neither Rosa nor Nathalie found the purported remedial attributes of the baths to be apparent. But there were other causes of interest.

One day, word spread that a member of the Pyrenees' declining bear population had been killed near where the women were staying. Rosa's reflex was to write an excited letter informing Mme Micas. But she quickly checked her haste:

'Don't worry; the roads are quite safe and we don't go where there is the least danger,' she assured the old woman.[12]

Rosa was determined to take full advantage of the wildlife on show. It was not yet the end of June when she wrote to Isidore: 'I must confess to you that I have not been able to resist the desire to buy a mountain dog.'[13]

Such extravagances now seemed justified; Rosa had managed to gather enough money to buy a substitute to take her younger brother's place in the army.

On 16 June, she had written to Isidore in delight: 'I am just going to post you your money for the substitute. So now, my dear old boy, at last, everything is finished, and I shall see you soon, I trust.'[14]

Rosa now defended her canine purchase to her brother: after all, the hound had cost her only eighteen francs.

However, Rosa knew that, as her landlady, Mme Micas would need more convincing if she were to accommodate a mountain dog in her apartment.

'What a dog he is,' she urged. 'But how, after all, can one help doing things of this sort, when one is so apt as I am to fall into the besetting sin? [...] This creature will be a protection,' Rosa continued persuasively.[15]

Still, in their trousers and boots, Rosa and Nathalie scarcely gave the impression of travellers who needed protecting. When one of their excursions led them to Pau, a group of gendarmes took them for men and were greatly amused when they realised their mistake.[16]

'Ladies may be *carried* up to most points of interest in a chaise à porteur,' a popular guidebook reassured female travellers.[17] Rosa and Nathalie would hear of no such concession. Many of their excursions – including one to Gabas through the Ossau valley – were carried out astride a horse, which, travellers were assured, was 'the only way to see the Pyrenees to advantage'.[18]

'We are gaining quite a reputation as horsewomen,' Rosa proudly informed Mme Micas. And to Rosa's mind, such physical exertion demanded suitable fuel.

'Izard venison, game, ortolans, truffles, mountain-trout, green figs and strawberries are among the delicacies which await the traveller in the Pyrenees,' tempted one guidebook writer.[19] Rosa and Nathalie did not hold back.

'We tuck in a good deal,' Rosa updated Mme Micas.[20]

But such pleasures soon began to mount up. Their trip to Saint Sauveur was consequently conducted in the company of an abbot and his sister in order to split the travel costs.

The scenery en route was breathtaking. Nathalie was overwhelmed by Lourdes and its castle. They stopped for lunch in Bétharram, with its oppressive aura of melancholy, but were cheered by the expansive plains, with their orchards and their vines; they gained a glimpse of Argèles, lost their paints changing carriages and finally arrived in Saint Sauveur that evening, exhausted and glad of a hiatus. But the extolled 'charming walks' and 'fine scenery' were quickly overshadowed when the weary travellers were shown their room.[21]

'Inns are far inferior to those in the German watering places,' travellers to the Pyrenees were warned. 'They have all the fault of filth.'[22]

Rosa and Nathalie's room was no exception. Dingy and only eight feet by six, the ambience was scarcely cheered by a rickety table and a chequered green shawl in place of a rug. Then if they wanted to see their way around the claustrophobic space after dark, they had to provide their own candles. In addition, with attendants and waiters to tip at every point of interest, the expenses soon accumulated. Still, for Rosa, the value of the investment was beginning to show.

'I feel much better since I have taken two of these Saint Sauveur baths,' Rosa announced to a newly liberated Isidore, before adding a word of concern for the family: 'At present, our Pipon [Auguste] is in the country. It will do him good. Your task must be to encourage him, since, if he likes, he can show talent, the same as I and you.'[23]

'What I want,' Rosa pursued, 'is for us to be known as the three Bonheurs. As for Juliette, she has too much of the mothering instinct in her for my taste, and I am afraid she will get less happiness out of having children than from an artistic career.'[24]

A successful outcome at the Saint Sauveur baths was more needed than ever; Nathalie had contracted an eye infection and her fragile health suffered a notable relapse. Though dressed as a man, Rosa's attentive care was that of the gentlest nurse. She took such attention removing Nathalie's dressing, dabbing on lotion, and reapplying the bandage that the invalid could never complain of any pain. When Rosa's students sent word that her guidance was needed back in Paris, she refused to cut her trip short; she could not leave Nathalie. To her relief, a move to a superior bedroom precipitated a heartening improvement in her companion's condition.

'Nathalie has got over her attack,' Rosa assured Mme Micas. She went on:

> I could never leave her alone, she is so weak and has so much need of someone to love her and make up for the physical pain she has gone through. [...] As for myself, I am better and hope these waters will give me back my strength. Then I will paint some fine pictures and earn a good deal of money, so as not to be always a burden to you, as I am at present.[25]

Her health sufficiently recovered, Nathalie was only too willing to repay Rosa's kindness. 'You know what funny tastes dear Rosa has,' Nathalie wrote teasingly to her mother, 'for instance, for some days she has been clamouring for maize gruel; so I have made her some. I don't know whether she will go into ecstasies over my attempt, but I do know that I myself find it a very nasty mixture.'[26]

As two women, living together, sharing a room, dressing as men and, in Rosa's case, publicly championed by Théophile Gautier, author of the controversial *Mademoiselle de Maupin* (1835) (in which the anti-heroine dresses as a man and enjoys an intimate relationship with another woman), it was perhaps inevitable that people should start to speculate as to the nature of Rosa and Nathalie's relationship.

The terms *lesbienne* and *lesbianisme* in their primarily sexual sense were not yet common currency in France. Neither appeared in Napoléon Landais's *Petit Dictionnaire Français* of words approved by the Académie in 1850. Nonetheless, the concept of female homosexuality was by no means novel. The great poet Sappho had long been a figure of interest and in 1850, a new play by Philoxène Boyer revisited the classic theme. Indeed, female love was sometimes referred to as *saphisme* and it had become an area of fascination in the fiction of the 1820s and 30s.[27] George Sand had made a powerful impression on the public at this time. With her masculine attire, close relationships with women and outspoken remarks on the female condition, she came to embody popular fears about women who refused to conform and resisted categorisation.

Part of the controversy lay in the judicial opacity over lesbianism. The Napoleonic Code of 1804 had made no legal provision for penalising private acts of female homosexuality; the unseen went unchecked.[28] Lesbianism was thus socially taboo but legally plausible. Novelists' minds were set racing.

From Gautier's *Mademoiselle de Maupin* to Balzac's *The Girl with the Golden Eyes* (1835), love – or more accurately, sex – between women had become a subject of titillation and fetishism by the mid-19th century. Concomitantly, Parisians' attention had been drawn more seriously to the practice of lesbianism in 1836, when hygienist Alexandre Parent-Duchâtelet published his landmark text *Prostitution in the City of Paris*.[29] The more outwardly conservative tranche of society placed unwavering faith in the author and drew what seemed a logical conclusion: lesbianism was the enemy of man's human legacy, a depraved and monstrous vice common to prostitutes.

At the time Rosa and Nathalie made their trip to the Pyrenees, that dualistic view held firm, stimulating the imagination of novelists, exciting their readers and horrifying partisans of the traditional gender templates across society. The theme was at once food for male fetishism and an inflammatory source of debate.

That Rosa and Nathalie each represented the other's closest relationship, there could be no doubt. Their affection and tender care for each other was that of a married couple. Their closeness excluded all other romantic attachments (and complicated many platonic ones). Nathalie in particular was inclined to become wildly envious of people who took an interest in Rosa.

'She showed herself jealous of certain persons Rosa Bonheur numbered among her friends,' recalled one of Rosa's close acquaintances, the theatrically trained Valérie Simonin.[30]

'Nathalie Micas literally worshipped Rosa Bonheur,' agreed Rosa Mathieu, Rosa's goddaughter. 'The latter had her painting as well as having Nathalie; but Nathalie had only Rosa, which will explain why she was sometimes jealous of Rosa Bonheur's other friendships.'[31]

But those who knew Rosa maintained that the women's 'long companionship' was 'more than beneficial to both'.[32]

'Rosa Bonheur could never have remained the celebrated artist she was without someone beside her, at each instant,' Valérie Simonin explained.

Thanks to Nathalie, Rosa never had to give a moment's thought to keeping house or cooking meals. Because of Nathalie, she could work in peace, shielded from interruption from the outside world. Due to Nathalie, Rosa never wanted for companionship or care. Rosa and her art were Nathalie's own delicate sapling; her whole raison d'être was found in encouraging this precious specimen to flourish. In short, 'Nathalie made herself small, ungrudgingly, so that Rosa might become greater.'[33]

Rosa made no secret of her love for Nathalie, whom she affectionately called her 'old Inès', after the Spanish beauty Inès de las Sierras in Charles Nodier's 1837 novel. Indeed, the peculiar Hispanic wardrobe for which Nathalie had a penchant struck many observers.

'Nothing was more comical than seeing this couple together,' recalled another of Rosa's contacts, the politician, geologist and botanist Antoine François Passy, 'Rosa Bonheur, who, in her blouse, looked like a lad, and that tall, lank, pale woman, with her head crowned by a big hat with black and red plumes.'[34]

'She was my equal in everything, and my superior in many things,' Rosa defended. 'She preserved me from being spotted by the mud that was thrown at me.'[35]

Rosa never failed to speak her mind when a passion excited her. More than once, she was asked why she had not married.

Rosa Bonheur, *Portrait of Nathalie Micas*,
c. 1850, graphite on paper, 62 x 49 cm.

Photo © RMN-Grand Palais
(Château de Fontainebleau)/Gérard Blot

'Nobody ever fell in love with me,' she usually answered dismissively.[36] Then on another occasion: 'It is not because I am an enemy of marriage; but I assure you I have never had the time to consider the subject.'[37]

In an interview given in the 1850s, Rosa expanded: 'I am not fit to be a wife in the common acceptation of that term. Men must marry women who have no absorbent, no idol.'[38] Nathalie Micas would accept her with both.

'She alone knew me,' Rosa said of Nathalie many years later, 'and I, her only friend, knew what she was worth. We both of us made ourselves humble, so as not to hurt the feelings of other people, while we were too proud to seek the confidence of idiots who doubted us.'[39]

No human would ever witness what occurred between Rosa and Nathalie once their door had been pushed closed and they were alone.

Nor would Rosa's cryptic explanations of their bond be satisfactorily resolved. The closest, most intimate love relationships can exist without sex; whether they can thrive could be debated.

᛫

For the remainder of their time in the Pyrenees, Rosa and Nathalie explored, travelled, took the waters and revelled in each other's company. They went on horseback to the famous Cirque de Gavarnie (a circular form excavated in the mountain and surrounded by precipices). ('I warrant you it is a son you have at present,' Rosa told Mme Micas.)[40] They saw great mountains, passed over the gushing, crystal-clear Gave de Pau River, marvelled at hamlets nestling in the rocks, studied the famous breach, a gap of some hundred metres tall and 40 metres wide, said to have been made by Charlemagne's Roland. They were rendered awestruck by the Marboré mountain, then took an excursion on the backs of donkeys to the Pic de Bergons above Luz, from where they could see the mountains descending into Spain. Their chosen means of transport 'cost quite as dear as horses', Nathalie exclaimed.[41] But Rosa insisted; this was a research necessity. 'One of the best ways to get acquainted with a beast is to get on his back,' she affirmed.[42]

Finally, they finished their sojourn in the elevated Barèges, noted by guidebooks for 'the efficacy of its waters', but also for its throng of 'miserable invalids' and 'inferior accommodation'.[43] Nathalie found it especially depressing.

It was an unfortunate note on which to end the voyage. And perhaps because of this, when the girls returned to Paris that autumn, the doctor consulted declared himself unsatisfied with their progress. They were advised not to settle in Paris, but to take another trip. In little time, Rosa and Nathalie found themselves preparing to leave for Germany.

'Ems is situated in one of the most picturesque spots of the Lahn Valley,' announced Dr Pressat in his study of the German baths published in the 1850s. With its 'stretch of magnificent hotels facing the Midi and backing onto the mountain which shields them from the

North winds,' the area had much to commend it to the leisured traveller. The doctor continued:

> The pure balsamic air that one breathes there, the
> mild temperature, [...] the elegance and comfort of
> the hotels, the luxury of the establishments catering
> to bathers, the gentle and well-maintained walks, all
> make Ems an attractive and pleasant destination [...]
> Consequently, it is one of the most fashionable resorts
> in the whole of Germany.[44]

As soon as the pair arrived, Rosa seized pen and paper and rushed outside. Settling herself beneath some trees, she began a letter to Juliette.

'Here I am at last,' she told her younger sibling, 'and I can assure
you I am not sorry to get to the end of the journey.'[45]

Rosa told Juliette, with some indignation, how their baggage was
searched both when they left France and on reaching Cologne. There,
they found the hotel acceptable, but the dinner 'quite dear and very
bad', and the wine expensive.[46] From Cologne, Rosa and Nathalie had
departed early in the morning for Bonn, where they boarded a boat
to Coblenz, and then an omnibus for Ems.

'Here at Ems the only thing we cannot stand is the cooking,' Rosa
informed Juliette, 'with its devilish sauces. These Germans concoct dis-
gusting mixtures. For instance, you are served strawberries along with
fat meat, oil, potatoes, and pears, and then, to crown all, you are given
water to drink.'[47] Rosa was partial to a glass of something stronger.

But for all her complaints, she conceded that they were 'compensated by the pretty scenery'.[48]

'I am told the waters have wonderful medicinal properties,' Rosa
admitted to her sister. 'The physician has ordered me to take it, though
I should very much like to disobey the command.'[49]

Fellow tourists at least offered a source of amusement.

'There are flirts here as everywhere, and lots of sentimentalists,
especially among the English,' Rosa joked.[50]

With persistent rain having pursued them from the Pyrenees, Rosa and Nathalie were relieved when the time came for them to return to Paris. Rosa had not collated the quantity of sketches she had hoped, nor had the trip left them in a healthy financial situation. But it had brought one happy outcome, perhaps the most important.

'I shall bring back to Paris nothing but an unbounded desire to begin my great picture,' Rosa told Mme Micas shortly before they left.[51] For indeed, time away from the French capital had sparked an idea. And now, she returned home fired with creative zeal.

CR

Rosa had seen pictures of the great friezes depicting horses in the Parthenon, a fragment of which had been acquired by the Louvre in the early 1800s.[52] In addition, a lithograph of Théodore Géricault's 1821 composition *Horses Going to a Fair* had been widely circulated in France. The piece depicted five heavy workhorses making their way up a rocky incline, and had allowed Géricault to flaunt his skill by showing the creatures in different positions.[53] When the contents of Géricault's atelier went to auction at the Hôtel Bullion in 1824 after the artist's death, Rosa's friend Mêne had acquired some of the pieces. Then some years ago, the Republican cavalier turned vet, doctor and founder of an agricultural college, Antoine Richard, had given Rosa one of his equine studies which she had pored over voraciously.[54] Now after her recent communion with horses and donkeys in the Pyrenees, suddenly, all the pieces fell into place and other concerns melted away. Rosa could suddenly see her next important composition with unwavering clarity.

She began visiting Paris's horse market on the Boulevard de l'Hôpital near the Asylum of Salpêtrière. The market took place in the afternoon on Wednesdays and Saturdays, finishing at 4.00 in the winter and running on until dusk in the summer. There, buyers found the ground arranged into avenues for exercising the horses. At the sides of these were stalls and on one side was a contraption known as an *essai.* This artificial hill with a steep ascent and descent was designed for testing the strength of draft horses by harnessing them to a cart with clogged wheels.[55]

'It is necessary to be very careful in the purchase of horses,' warned a contemporary guidebook discussing the market. 'Dealers only warrant them for nine days. It is for the buyer to discover any vices in the animal.'[56] The market was consequently as much a noisy crucible of bartering and testosterone as it was a showcase of equine prowess. Rosa took in everything she saw.

She made other research trips, too. The director of the Paris Omnibus Company gave her permission to visit their stables and even allowed Rosa to take models back to her studio.[57] But she did not confine herself to the city centre.

'I received your letter on my return from Ivry,' Rosa informed her father's Saint-Simonian friend Gustave d'Eichthal in October 1850, 'where I went for two or three days to make some studies of horses which I needed.'[58]

Rosa immersed herself in her project. Like Géricault, she had decided to show the noble Percheron horse, and on an enormous rectangular canvas of 5 × 2.5 m. Her horses would be wild, frenzied, pulling, rearing, galloping as their handlers strained to control and command them. Rosa was intent on conveying the power and magnificence of the creatures. Just as the burly buyers tested the steeds' physicality at the market, so Rosa now explored the creatures' musculature with no less tenacity. Pencil studies, charcoal drawings, watercolours accumulated, capturing movement, energy and heat. And as the work came together, the composition grew strong, virile and intense – and all this from a woman not yet 30. Rosa was determined that the viewer should experience the surge of adrenaline generated by the horse market, and feel the reverberation of thundering hooves in their chests.

The work had Rosa utterly absorbed. And while she was engrossed, her existing canvases were acting as her ambassadors, both in France and abroad. That summer, her *Charcoal Burners Crossing a Moor in*

Auvergne was sent to the Exhibition of the Painters of All Nations at Lichfield House in London, where the evening private view was 'brilliantly lighted by gas'.[59] The *Daily News* declared Rosa's offering equal to the painting of Paulus Potter and 'one of the most charming works of the exhibition', while the founder of the Pre-Raphaelite brotherhood, Dante Gabriel Rossetti, publicly proclaimed Rosa's *Charcoal Burners* to be '*the* best work in the place'.[60] In July, *Le Palais de Cristal* announced her presence in the Album de la Société des gens de lettres at the Great Exhibition of 1851 in London.[61] Then, the following month, *Le Nouvelliste* reported her participation in a corollary show held in Brussels. Rosa's work was circulating her name on an international scale.[62]

But 1851 brought other, personal changes that were harder to accept.

Rosa was not the only Bonheur to have become enthralled by the Auvergne. Auguste too had now visited the area, and that year he and Rosa celebrated their shared passion in a co-authored landscape entitled *The Cère Valley and Puy Griou*. From his forays to the region, Auguste had brought back countless sketches – and some new acquaintances. Marguerite Picard's mission to strengthen the ties between her own family and the Bonheurs and her fondness for matchmaking had steered Auguste into the path of a young woman named Marie Fauché, his stepmother's niece. A romance blossomed and that year, Auguste announced his intention to marry. By the end of the summer, Auguste and Mlle Fauché were husband and wife.[63]

However affable her new sister-in-law, Rosa disliked the manner in which her stepmother obtained spouses for the younger generation. Juliette and Hippolyte's attachment was growing, too; Rosa vowed never to satisfy any aspirations her stepmother might entertain on her account.

Meanwhile, as Rosa wrestled with her personal misgivings, France was experiencing an internal conflict of her own.

Louis-Napoleon's tenure as president was due to expire in 1852, when the term of the existing Legislative Assembly (elected in May

1849) would also run out. The threat of looming anarchy instilled panic. Determined to remain in office and see his reforms implemented, the President decided that the time had come to act. On the night of 1–2 December, he put the coup he had been covertly planning into action. Principal party leaders were arrested and troops sent in to occupy the Chamber. Then, he reinstated universal male suffrage. Resistance in the capital was swiftly thwarted, with the first signs of bloodshed sufficing to silence Parisians who had witnessed the revolutions of 1830 and 1848. Meanwhile, objections in the provinces were also answered with repression which, in many cases, took the form of deportation. In a matter of hours, Paris had fallen back into Bonapartist hands.[64]

Rosa watched the events unfold with a mix of horror and political ambivalence. She had found much to commend in the principle of a republic. However, the perceived failure of the current government had left many who had entertained Saint-Simonian beliefs jaded. Louis-Napoleon seemed to promise so much – and for many, his empathy with the main tenets of Saint-Simonianism was all too apparent.[65]

'Up to a certain point, her intelligence had received the impression of her father's ideas,' Rosa's friend Valérie Simonin explained of the artist's politics. 'She all her life preserved the most lively sympathy for democratic and socialistic aspirations. But [...] she recognised and acknowledged Napoleon's efforts to increase the prosperity of France and to improve the lot of the working classes.'[66]

However equivocal her opinion, shortly after the coup, Rosa had a chance to judge the new administration for herself – and at closer quarters than she had anticipated.

One day, Rosa was working in the studio when she was interrupted by the arrival of a message. Mlle Rosa Bonheur had been summoned to a meeting with the newly appointed head of the Ministry of the Interior, who supervised the Division of Fine Arts. And under Louis-Napoleon's new regime, the man fulfilling this role was none other than Charles de Morny, the illegitimate half-brother of the Emperor himself.

Nearly four years younger than the Emperor, Charles de Morny already had thinner hair, but with the same slim face, intense, narrowed eyes and majestic moustache, he clearly shared genes with Emperor Louis-Napoleon. The men's mother was Hortense de Beauharnais, but while the new Emperor's birth certificate identified his father as Louis Bonaparte, younger brother of the great Napoleon, Morny was the product of an illicit affair between Hortense and Charles Joseph, Comte de Flahaut – which also happened to make him the grandson of the redoubtable orator and diplomat, Charles-Maurice de Talleyrand.[67]

Brilliantly educated, Morny had entered the army before he was twenty; there, his actions in the Algerian campaigns earned him a Légion d'Honneur. But it was on his return to Paris and following his entry into the world of business that he truly made his mark. That he took as his mistress Fanny le Hon, daughter of the rich banker François-Dominique Mosselman, was a considerable advantage. Shrewd in business, a determined speculator, Morny made his first acquisition a sugar refinery. It proved a spectacular success and from there on, his business portfolio grew exponentially.

Though he was elected to parliament in the 1840s, Morny took a backseat in party politics, contenting himself with offering his wise counsel on business and financial matters. The revolution of 1848 nearly precipitated his ruin, since he lost both his seat in parliament and his financial security. But Morny would not admit defeat; he was a social strategist, a man who identified opportunity and encouraged it to knock. He utilised his connections with his half-brother to claw back a place in parliament and his affair with Fanny le Hon to relaunch his investments. Before long, Morny was back at the forefront of the capital's business world and circulating through Paris's fashionable salons as though he had never done any differently.

If he harboured reservations about his half-brother's political strategy, Morny was savvy enough to gauge Louis-Napoleon's clemency to be vital to his private affairs. His love of order and authoritarianism made him an invaluable asset to the team who had engineered the President's coup. Louis-Napoleon could be flat-footed and socially

awkward; he had repeatedly shown himself unable to strike that delicate – yet critical – balance between steel and tact. Morny veiled
steadfast determination in a personable exterior; Napoleon needed
Morny – in fact, Morny counted on it.[68]

His new role as head of the Ministry of the Interior offered gratifying reward for his pains. Now, he was perfectly placed to indulge his
love of the arts, good living and elegant society.

Morny's reputation as a fast-living, cultured tycoon preceded him.
Then he was the man who had stage-managed the coup. As she read-
ied herself for their meeting, Rosa prepared to encounter a predator.
But her presumption, she told friends, was quite wrong; Morny was
distinguished, courteous and supremely eloquent. He immediately had
Rosa's attention.[69]

The new administration, Morny began, wished to commission
Mlle Bonheur to produce a painting. As for the subject, the patrons
were open to discussion. And there would be a substantial remunerative reward if she agreed.

Maintaining her composure, Rosa assured him that she would.

So it was that not long afterwards, Rosa found herself arriving to
meet M. de Morny again, clutching a portfolio of drawings. She had
been sure to include preparatory studies for her horse fair and had also
brought sketches for a haymaking scene. Her folder was ceremoniously
opened before the Minister. Leafing through, Morny explained the
dimensions sought. He also disclosed the payment: the government
were offering no less than 20,000 francs, more than six times what
Rosa had been paid for *Ploughing in the Nivernais* (1849). It was a tremendous amount of money.

Morny was a renowned horse fanatic, and her own mind being
given entirely to the big painting she was preparing, Rosa was keen that
he should consider those studies first. But Morny was unconvinced;
Rosa was not known for her pictures of horses. The administration
wished to be sure of its investment. *Haymaking in the Auvergne* would
do very nicely.

Rosa was perplexed. Her every waking moment was currently

consumed by *The Horse Fair* and she was not afraid to say so: the Minister must excuse her, but if that piece did not fulfil the brief, then she would be unable to satisfy his request until it was complete. Incredibly, her condition was accepted: Morny agreed that she could take her time to finish *The Horse Fair* and the government would be happy to receive *Haymaking in the Auvergne* afterwards.

Louis-Napoleon might have conquered Paris – but Rosa had tamed his administration.

Even so, as Rosa left the meeting, she could be in no doubt that she had taken on a monumental task. If the deadline for next year's Salon were not sufficient pressure, she now had the government waiting expectantly to see the results of its sizeable investment.

⁂

The remainder of the year was spent working furiously. Nathalie had announced that she would like to show work of her own at the Salon, so Rosa good-naturedly coached, critiqued and counselled the enthusiastic pupil – all the while attempting to fulfil her own responsibilities to the drawing school – as she prepared two still lifes. Rosa did not send a painting to the Salon that year. The load was beginning to encumber her. She sorely needed someone to share her burden.

Now a practising artist in her early twenties, Juliette Bonheur seemed the ideal candidate. The young woman was blossoming and 1852 was already proving an extraordinary year. She made her first appearance at the Salon with a still life. She also changed her status – for in August, Juliette married her stepbrother and became Mme Hippolyte Peyrol. The ties between the Bonheurs and their stepmother's family tightened.

For Rosa, Juliette's marriage was just another signpost heralding the relentless march of time. France's changing political situation merely reiterated that sense.

On 2 December 1852, Louis-Napoleon accomplished the final step in his campaign to secure power, by making himself emperor. France's new sovereign gave the people his word that he would repair the damage occasioned by the Second Republic, a promise he intended to fulfil by restoring the authoritarian order of the Bonapartist regime. When the Second Republic had disillusioned so many, Napoleon's stated mission to boost internal prosperity found widespread support and diverted attention from the loss of liberty many of his reforms entailed. The Empire cloaked its structural shortcomings in a mood of optimism and possibility, of gaiety and frivolous living. In a country wracked by disenchantment, such euphoria was contagious. All at once, prosperity ceased to be a utopian dream – now, it seemed an achievable goal.

The Salon of 1853 would thus open to a new political dawn. Already at the Salon of 1852, artists had lost their right to elect the jury.[70] Shortly before that exhibition's inauguration, it had also been decided that a Palais de l'Industrie should be created on the Champs-Élysées to provide a more suitable exhibition forum. In the meantime, the show would be deposed to the Hôtel des Menus-Plaisirs, away from the city centre.[71] The decision was at once controversial and symbolic; it placed even greater distance between the artists and that prestigious temple of fine art, the Louvre. If Louis-Napoleon was unsure of himself in the field of art and initially reluctant to impose his personal tastes (which were, broadly speaking, traditional and conservative), he recognised the propaganda potential of the visual image. Though he was no connoisseur of art, power was a concept he did understand – and he could see the correlation between the two. As for the intricacies on matters art-related, he could defer to his advisers (and to Morny). In the organisation of that year's Salon, the Emperor's new administration and the official bodies were demonstrably flexing their muscles.[72]

As an artist honoured with a commission, Rosa had every reason to feel apprehensive. She had stood her ground by prioritising her *Horse Fair* over the regime's own canvas. She could only hope that the Salon audience and the press would vindicate her resolve.

Rosa was not the only person with a vested interest in her fate at the Salon that year. Someone else had a beady eye fixed on painters who had demonstrated promise.

Slim-faced with an imperial beard and small, determined eyes that never missed a detail, Ernest Gambart was a mogul of the Victorian art world. Single-minded, energetic and persistent, the Belgian had been a resident of Queen Victoria's London since 1846, where he had gone into business as a publisher and importer of foreign prints. Gambart had entered the trade at a fortuitous time; sales of prints were taking off. With the profits he made from publishing, Gambart began investing in pictures by living artists. It quickly became clear that he had found his niche. By the early 1850s, Gambart had become a powerful mediator between painters and their public, and as foreign pictures grew more popular in England, he glided through Paris's galleries like a hawk waiting to strike.[73]

Gambart had had multiple opportunities to cross paths with the Bonheurs. Years later, he claimed to have first met Rosa in 1852.[74] But already in the spring of 1849, he had staged a show – his first – which featured bronzes by Rosa's friend Mêne. He was abreast of the critical responses roused by the Lichfield House exhibition. Meanwhile, his was a familiar face in Paris's ateliers, auction houses and exhibitions that year. There was scarcely a piece of art news that escaped Gambart's pricked up ears.[75]

If a painter caught his attention and showed talent, Ernest Gambart had the power to make a man – and perhaps even a woman – rich.

The stage was set. The audience gathered. Then, on 15 May, the Salon opened its doors.

10

---•••---

A Woman's Work

'May the innovators be in no doubt, more often than not, their so-called originality is merely an imitation of another school or master.'[1]

It was a damning introduction that Simon Horsin-Déon gave to his report of that year's Salon. As conservationist for the Imperial Museums and secretary for the Société Libre des Beaux-Arts, Horsin-Déon's was a voice which carried weight.

These days, too many of France's young artists were content to simply copy. 'That,' Horsin-Déon opined disdainfully, 'is not progress.'[2]

The rumination on the criteria defining excellence typified the kind of review on which painters hung all their hopes. In an era where the Salon's offerings remained inaccessible to many and where reproductions (when they appeared at all) were often limited to small black-and-white lithographs or engravings, the descriptions and judgements of reviews were tremendously important. Having toiled over their work for months – sometimes years – an artist's success rested entirely on its reception. And that was greatly influenced by the critics. In a moment, a reputation could be made – or it could be crushed. Then with the limitation imposed on submissions that year, positive reviews had become imperative.

Rosa's position was rendered especially fraught. Before she even had a chance to gauge the public response to her canvas, she learned that someone had deviously informed the Directeur des Musées, the

Comte de Nieuwerkerke, that she was claiming *The Horse Fair* (1853) to be a State commission and that she had reneged on the ostensible agreement by refusing to give the administration their painting in favour of a more affluent buyer.

The sculptor-turned-Imperial attaché Émilien de Nieuwerkerke was a prominent figure on the cultural scene. At over six feet tall and stocky with a thick, fair beard, his towering, bear-like physique had become a redoubtable omnipresence in the art world since his appointment as Directeur des Musées in 1849. The doubtful nature of his qualifications to fulfil the role – and the certainty of his affair with Napoleon III's cousin, the Princess Mathilde – had provided Paris's gossips with an endless source of material.[3]

The rumour about *The Horse Fair* threatened more than Rosa's pride; it jeopardised her relationship with the administration. Therefore, the day before Horsin-Déon delivered his discourse, Rosa had penned a hasty letter to Nieuwerkerke, impressing her honourable character and denying the tale. Rosa was starting to realise that celebrity was not without its complications.

Horsin-Déon's report was delivered at a fractious moment. But one artist's misery was to be quickly dispelled:

'Mlle Rosa Bonheur is an original painter […] her beautiful picture of *The Horse Fair* [is] the jewel of the Salon!'[4]

It was a triumph. Such early approbation was cause for overwhelming relief. And this review was just the start.

'Mademoiselle Rosa Bonheur has kept the promises she made with her [*Ploughing in the Nivernais*],' *La Mode* seconded. '*The Paris Horse Fair* is a masterpiece of movement, truth and naturalness [….] Mademoiselle Rosa Bonheur […] is incontestably one of the best artists of the day,' the reviewer went on, and her canvas, '*the* work' of the show.[5]

By mid-June, the praise was flooding in.

'Mme Rosa Bonheur has proved that she is a true artist,' declared N. Berthon in *L'Eventail*. 'Her painting is unquestionably the best in the Salon, and will make an epoch in the annals of the 19th-century school.'[6]

If the stark Realism critics identified in Gustave Courbet's frank, unidealised interpretations of subjects drawn from everyday life had its adversaries, Rosa offered a more palatable and picturesque alternative. Writing for the culturally focused *Revue des Deux Mondes*, even the staunch opponent of Realism Henri Delaborde praised the work, insisting it would be a mistake to bracket Rosa together with the Realists.

Soon, commendations were arriving from across the Channel, too.

'The French exhibition which has been looked forward to with great hopes and expectations, is excessively feeble,' arraigned the *Art Journal* in London. But a concession was made: 'Mademoiselle Rosa Bonheur has executed *The Horse Market at Paris*; it is large, seventeen feet long, and is a most splendid production.'[7]

The Horse Fair had catapulted Rosa to celebrity status. Suddenly, the art world buzzed with her name, so much so that she made the front page of *Le Nouvelliste* in early August when the paper recounted how one Salon-goer had been rendered starstruck simply by talking to a man who had met the great Rosa Bonheur.[8]

It seemed iniquitous, then, that Rosa could not receive a medal. Having already been presented with a first-class prize in 1848, Rosa was barred from accepting another; an artist could not be awarded the same prize twice. This frustrating element of Salon pedantry exasperated the painter Eugène Delacroix, who complained about the injustice in his journal: 'This year, Mlle Rosa Bonheur has made a superior effort to any previous year; and yet we can only salute and show her verbal encouragement.'[9]

It was not just the quality of Rosa's work which impressed: the unlikeliness of its author was causing a stir.

'Never before has a woman excelled in the difficult genre of animal painting; never before has a canvas of 5 m long like *The Horse Fair*, offered lessons to the even most expert in the field,' gushed the reviewer Courtois in *Le Nouvelliste*.[10]

Théophile Gautier enthused liberally in a similar vein:

This work [...] is astonishing in its vigour and its energy, particularly when one thinks that it is a feminine hand which has painted these robust working horses. [...] We do not know where Mlle Rosa Bonheur will stand when it comes to the distribution of prizes (she has already received a first-class medal). (If she were a man instead of a woman, she would almost certainly receive the cross, and in our opinion, she should be given it) [...] Mlle Rosa Bonheur has more right to a red ribbon than the majority of her bearded counterparts.[11]

The critic Henri Delaborde shared Gautier's awe:

When one thinks that it is the hand of a woman which has determined these profiles and accentuated these contours so vigorously, one may rightly be astonished at both the character of such a talent and the resolve with which it is employed. [...] Only a few women painters have made a name for themselves in the history of French art [...] Mlle Rosa Bonheur is the first among them to distinguish herself by a touch which is completely virile.[12]

Rosa's appeal was fanned, at least in part, by an emerging feminist consciousness in 19th-century France. The word *féminisme* had come into use only in the late 1830s and was attributed to the utopian socialist Charles Fourier. By the mid-19th century, multiple factors had combined to bring the delicate matter of women's rights (or their lack thereof) to the fore. An important contributor was the growth of the middle classes in France, whose female members – unlike women hailing from the other social extremes – were not obliged to contract marriages to secure estates and titles or to stave off poverty. Another driving force was the ideal of liberation fostered by the Revolution of 1789. This laid the foundations for socialist movements like Saint-Simonianism, which encouraged people to review the female condition with publications such as *La Femme Libre* (later *La Femme de l'Avenir* and then *La Femme Nouvelle*). Then with general expansion of a women's press, which saw the launch of publications like *La Gazette des Femmes* (in 1836), as well as increased leisure time nurturing friendships between middle-class women, the notion of feminism had taken hold and was being actively promulgated.[13]

Such ideas were set against France's long history of male privilege and a deeply ingrained gender hierarchy to which conservatives and traditionalists still clung. In the middle to upper classes, it was felt that a woman should aspire to be 'accomplished', not gifted. A good pianist, a lovely singer or a fine watercolourist was an amusing diversion, akin to an after-dinner entertainment in polite drawing rooms. To make a career of a creative pursuit demanded a drive and stamina which were quite at odds with the sweet, submissive model of femininity society promoted. It also called into question the status of a woman's husband or family; a respectable girl should have no need to work. She would only do so if she were forced.

In such a climate, the novelty of a woman tackling a subject as ambitious as *The Horse Fair* and then presenting it in the fiercely competitive context of the Salon, was either titillating or inspiring (depending on one's standpoint). Even the most laudatory reviews couched their praise in condescension. The common response was incredulity that such a work could have been produced by a woman. Many critics equated any praise Rosa might receive with 'gallantry', immediately undermining the notion that she could possess a talent comparable with men's. But the disjuncture between society's feminine model and Rosa's style had clearly piqued the Salon-goers' interest. Incredibly, it was proving to be a promotional tool.

The acclaim was thrilling. But Rosa had been exhibiting long enough to have seen that no work was immune to criticism. The handling of her horses' legs was felt to be wanting and several critics declared the beasts to have been painted at the expense of the people.[14] Meanwhile, the cartoonist Cham sketched a witty caricature in which

Rosa was seen riding on horseback (significantly, sidesaddle) in a furious steeplechase against the sculptor Emmanuel Frémiet, in a bid to be crowned the best artist representing animals.

While the critics weeded out flaws, Rosa had her own grounds for discontent. The Salon catalogue erroneously accorded both her father and the artist Léon Cogniet the joint honour of being her tutor. Still, this was a trifling irritation; *The Horse Fair* was a magnificent success. The crowd massing around the painting was sufficient testimony of public approval while among the critics, it was agreed that the gamble Rosa had taken in shifting from sheep to steeds had paid dividends.

⳽

After all the exhilaration, Rosa was in need of some respite. She and Nathalie could think of nothing they would enjoy more that summer than to revisit the Pyrenees. Buoyed by the euphoria of Rosa's Salon success, the pair set off.

This time, they wanted to take in Cauterets, which a contemporary guidebook described as 'a neat little mountain town, in an upland valley surrounded by colossal peaks'.[15] Cauterets was renowned for its sulphurous waters, which came particularly recommended to anyone suffering from bronchitis or rheumatism. There were also ample excursions to be had and, emboldened by her recent reception in Paris, Rosa quickly lapsed into a recreational mood. In little time, she had found the next addition to her menagerie.

'I may tell you that I have an otter which was caught in one of the lakes hereabouts,' she wrote to the Bonheur family's good friend Mme Verdier (whose son Joseph René was currently being tutored by Auguste) on 18 August 1853. 'You can't imagine how intelligent the little creature is. I am trying to train it to bring me what it catches in fishing.'[16]

'I am making some rough sketches of Spanish people,' Rosa told Juliette in early September. 'You would so like the men's manly faces. How I should enjoy admiring, in your company, my own Juju, the fine landscape here. But it is only a pleasure deferred I hope. I mean to earn a good deal of the "filthy lucre",' she assured her sister, affectionately quoting their father's favourite catchphrase, 'for it is only with that that you can do what you like.'[17]

On that count at least, Rosa's mounting international popularity boded well; while she enjoyed her break in the Pyrenees, *The Horse Fair* was receiving a warm welcome in Ghent at the Exposition Nationale et Triennale, where the picture earned Rosa a gift of a cameo by way of thanks.[18] But Rosa was discovering that commercial success came with a price.

'Fame is not without its inconveniences as well as its agreeable side,' she conceded writing to Juliette. 'Up to now I had succeeded in keeping my incognito; but at present I am receiving cards from all quarters, and my hotel landlord [...] is so proud to have me in his house that he walks about the streets singing my praises.'[19]

Still, quietly, Rosa was coming to enjoy the 'agreeable side' of celebrity. Growing up, her eccentricity had always made her a social outcast. Life had taught her self-reliance, and accepting, even flaunting her own idiosyncrasies had become a survival mechanism. Now, her quirkiness was actually attracting positive attention, and not just from her family, but from outside, too. It was a terrific confidence-builder. Never before had Rosa experienced such approval simply for being what she was. And that was just as well – she had no intention of changing to fit society's rigid expectations.

'I have been making a rough sketch of some smugglers,' she wrote excitedly to Isidore, 'and have managed also to get you a few Havana cigars – smuggled ones. This time they will not do you any harm, old boy. I can smoke them myself and enjoy them.'[20] Indeed, Rosa had now become an inveterate smoker, although more used to rolling cigarettes than to puffing on cigars. Her habit flew in the face of 19th-century codes of propriety. In respectable society, men could smoke; women who did so invited all manner of aspersions. Smoking was felt to undermine a woman's femininity, her class, and even her chastity. For many, the habit was associated with prostitutes.[21]

A few days after her acquisition of the Havana cigars, Rosa had to report to Isidore that she had been unwell. 'This has prevented me from getting on with my work, which makes me fume,' Rosa grumbled. But once she was able to go out again, Rosa could barely contain her enthusiasm as she recounted her zoological findings to her younger brother.[22]

'There is here a big mountain with lots of animals on top,' she exclaimed breathlessly, 'where the cows do wonderful things when the fancy takes them. For instance, they will set off and gallop like mad, executing twists and turns, and carrying their tails high in the air when they have a fly behind them. The sheep of this country have a more lively way of working their caudal appendage than those I have seen elsewhere.'[23]

Surrounded by animals, Rosa wrestled constantly with her desire to collect more furry friends to add to her menagerie.

'My dog is getting enormous,' she updated Isidore in another letter. 'I don't know how I shall manage to convey him from here, for he will be as big as a donkey. Dear me! What an unfortunate hobby mine is. What would you say if I were to confess what efforts I have made to resist the desire to bring back a sheep and a goat?'[24]

Rosa had earned the right to indulge her weakness that autumn. Following the success of *The Horse Fair*, it had been agreed that she should henceforward be exempt from assessment by the Salon jury, as was her fellow female artist, Mme Herbelin. The *Art Journal* felt the need to explain the concession: 'ladies not receiving the Croix d'honneur'.[25]

Nonetheless, Rosa's landmark picture had yet to tempt an admirer to reach into their pocket. The exhibition in Ghent had resulted in favourable reviews, but still no buyer. When the Société des Amis des Arts in Bordeaux called for submissions to their end-of-year exhibition, Rosa seized the opportunity to rekindle connections with her native town. In previous years, successful artists had had work sent straight to the Musée de Bordeaux after the show, and Rosa could conceive of no fate more fitting for her epic canvas.[26] But her hopes were quickly dashed; the museum would not fund the acquisition of such a piece and it did not appear in the show.

'Rosa has only been able to show a bronze, her great *Horse Fair* not having given her the chance to honour her native town more substantially.' The report in *L'Illustration* betrayed latent friction.[27] 'We nevertheless salute the Bonheur family for not having entirely forgotten their native city,' conceded the *Gazette des Beaux-Arts*. 'No doubt next year they will treat us to a brilliant exhibition.'[28]

While the fate of *The Horse Fair* remained undecided, Rosa had much to attend to. In May 1854, three of her pictures appeared at the First Annual Exhibition of the French School of Fine Arts in London. Meanwhile, back in Paris, her work, her male clothing and her menagerie had turned her into the talk of the capital's art world. Such was her renown that now, other artists were requesting loans of animals.

'I don't know M. Bellangé's address,' Rosa explained to Mme Mêne in June 1854, referring to the popular painter of battle scenes, 'so I can't send him my eagle direct, which, however, I will be happy to lend him. Please tell him so and send him it by your servant.'[29]

As her professional profile soared, a move to a new, purpose-built studio helped foster an environment even more conducive to work. Scarcely any distance from the studio she had occupied in the Rue de l'Ouest, the new space between the Rue Notre-Dame-des-Champs and the Rue d'Assas was specially built for her by the art connoisseur Georges Meusnier, father of the sculptor Mathieu Meusnier.[30] It was one of three studios the art-loving Meusniers had constructed, one being for their son, another for Adolphe Yvon and the final one for Rosa.[31]

The sparkling new workspace was exceptionally well appointed. Adjoining the studio was a garden, one area of which functioned as a courtyard with stables, which a vast window enabled Rosa to gaze out on as she worked. Scratching around in the yard, goats, heifers, horses and a mule – whom Rosa named Margot – turned the space into a veritable urban farmyard.[32]

The composition of the menagerie changed constantly, as new members arrived and others sadly departed. Years later, Rosa could still list the residents of the small zoo she kept at one time in the Rue d'Assas: 'One horse, one he goat, one otter, one monkey, one sheep, one donkey, two dogs, and my neighbour Mme Foucault, mother of the famous physicist, who used to get on the wall to see me practise mounting on my mare Margot.'[33]

As Rosa was enjoying her new studio and planning her next creative move, an encouraging proposition presented itself. In 1854, Bordeaux agreed to welcome *The Horse Fair* to the fourth exhibition of the Société des Amis des Arts. Rosa still nursed the hope that the museum might purchase her painting after the exhibition's close, and the first wave of reviews seemed to endorse her optimism.

'Needless to say that the famous *Horse Fair* by Rosa Bonheur, the masterly painting from the Paris exhibition of 1853 and the Brussels show [...] occupies the place of honour [...] This painting is a masterpiece.'[34]

But while *The Horse Fair* was away and Rosa waited to discover how the Musée de Bordeaux might respond, she received a noteworthy caller. The visitor was none other than the mastermind behind the recent exhibition of the French School in London and renowned picture dealer, Ernest Gambart.

Those who had done business with Ernest Gambart were invariably struck by his presence. The quintessential European, Gambart was articulate, methodical and alert. Tireless and constantly interested, Gambart seemed to be everywhere, to know everything. There was seldom a scenario which he had not anticipated. He thought ahead, about and around every deal he made, and that began with establishing a solid rapport with the artist. In this, Gambart excelled. His sharp wit and eloquence had won him many an attentive listener. And once he had engaged a painter's attention, he was a tenacious salesman.[35]

Gambart wasted no time in clarifying the purpose of his visit: he wanted to buy *The Horse Fair*.

Ernest Gambart.
Collection Atelier Rosa Bonheur

This was the first serious offer for the painting that Rosa had received. And Ernest Gambart had a proven reputation. But Rosa still harboured a lingering desire; she would dearly love to see her painting in Bordeaux. Even so, she knew not to take such an offer lightly. Thinking quickly, Rosa proposed to leave the painting where it was in Bordeaux and if it did not find a buyer after the show, Gambart could take it with him to England. However, with Nathalie overseeing Rosa's financial affairs, the agreement quickly acquired a condition: if the painting were unsold after the show, he could indeed have it – but not for the price offered to Bordeaux. If the picture were to leave France, the price demanded was 40,000 francs, nearly three times the figure mooted for Bordeaux.[36]

Gambart was impressed. For women, Rosa and Nathalie certainly drove a hard bargain. And Rosa's eccentricity excited his salesman's nose. Gambart sensed a covetable commercial product. He made no hesitation: Rosa could have her deal.

The exchange was universally gratifying. But before either Gambart or the Musée de Bordeaux could celebrate a victory, something unexpected happened.

Not long after Gambart's call, Rosa received another surprising visit. In one account, Rosa affirmed it was the Marquis de Chennevières, the man now charged with overseeing exhibitions, who addressed her; the Bonheur family claimed it to have been his coeval the Comte de Nieuwerkerke who acted as spokesman. Irrespective, the mission of the official party which arrived one day at Rosa's studio was to relate that the administration wished to make an amendment to their existing agreement. Rather than taking *Haymaking in the Auvergne* as planned, the administration wanted *The Horse Fair*; it would make a superb present for the Emperor.[37]

It was an incredible turn of events. Rosa had concentrated all her energies into *The Horse Fair*, but while admirers were many, sensible offers had been non-existent. Now, two powerful male parties suddenly coveted her equine scene. Rosa's response to the administration's change of heart was terse.

'It is the *Haymaking* which was ordered and it is the *Haymaking* which will be delivered in due season as agreed. It is quite natural that you should wish to make the Emperor a present, but not at my expense,' she retorted. Then, as though to impress her independence of mind: 'If I should decide to offer His Majesty a gift, you may rest assured that I will act myself without any intermediary.'[38]

It was a bold response. And when word came that the Musée de Bordeaux had declined *The Horse Fair*, there was reason to doubt the wisdom of her actions. But once Gambart returned to Rosa's studio shortly afterwards, events suddenly assumed a positive spin. Gambart was delighted – he would take the painting immediately.

Now, Gambart enthused freely about his plans for *The Horse Fair*. It would be put on show in Pall Mall where all London would be able to see it. He should also like to have it engraved. Thomas Landseer, brother of the great painter Edwin, would do a fine job. Rosa was overjoyed. But whatever Nathalie said, she still felt uncomfortable about the excessive price they had demanded. It seemed greedy.

'I don't mean to take undue advantage of your liberality,' she ventured. 'The picture is very large and it will be difficult to find a place for it in an engraver's studio. [...] Wouldn't it be better for me to paint you a smaller copy? [...] I will give you this copy into the bargain, and so my conscience will be clear.'[39]

Gambart could hardly have hoped for more. By the spring of 1855, the *Revue des Beaux-Arts* could report: '*The Horse Fair*, by Mlle Rosa Bonheur, that famous canvas which has appeared and been remarked in so many exhibitions, has just been sold by its creator for 40,000 francs.'[40] Gambart began to prepare for the painting's unveiling in London.

෴

As Rosa began her 33rd year, her star was shining brightly. She enjoyed regular correspondence with her siblings, she boasted numerous friends and although they bickered like husband and wife, her bond with Nathalie was growing stronger with each new experience they shared. *Haymaking in the Auvergne* was completed in time to satisfy the public (and more importantly, the administration) at the Salon of 1855. And with sales of her paintings accumulating, Rosa could even afford to employ a domestic help, a young girl named Céline Willaume, who had come to Paris from the *département* of the Vosges with her sister in search of work. Meanwhile, the studio in the Rue d'Assas was arranged just to Rosa's taste, while she also now rented an old barn at Chevilly a little to the south of Paris, which she repurposed as a second studio. There, she could store work in progress and house additional animals, including sheep and goats, with her mule, Margot, providing an efficient means of shuttling herself between the two workspaces.[41]

Above all, the public were in raptures over Rosa's paintings and fascinated by her peculiar appearance. She had now grown a little stouter and she wore her hair short. But her bright eyes remained vivacious and her hands and feet were still exquisitely delicate.

'Her hair was short and curly,' reflected Valérie Simonin, 'her eyes were black, keen, and merry; merry, too, her mouth, which was rather large, with well-formed lips and dazzling white teeth. Her stature was small, and she wore trousers, surmounted by a woman's short jacket.'[42]

'Her studio costume helped the illusion that she might be of the male sex,' added Rosa's friend Paul Chardin, 'it being invariably a blue peasant's smock and a man's trousers. When she received company or when she went to Paris, she resumed her woman's dress, a black skirt and a sort of black velvet cloak, half cassock, with a rather masculine cut, beneath which showed a kind of waistcoat which was buttoned straight up.'[43]

Ernest Gambart was only too conscious of Rosa's appeal. *The Horse Fair* had proved a wild success in Paris and he felt certain that the English would be enthralled not just by the painting, but also by its unconventional female author. A personal appearance from Rosa could only increase the British public's interest in the picture – and thus sales of the engraving. A brilliant project began to take shape in Gambart's mind. He saw *The Horse Fair* and he saw Rosa – and he saw success greater than she could ever have imagined. His mind was soon made up: Rosa Bonheur must come to England.

II

Beyond the Sea

'England is one endless pastoral poem,' eulogised the introduction to an 1850s guide for French travellers. 'The landscape is charming [...] The aspect of this landscape is that of a fine park.'[1]

But however bucolic England's pastures, Gambart would need stronger arguments if he were to convince Rosa to come on tour with her painting.

Rosa was always loath to quit her studio when absorbed in work. 'Social duties are a great loss of time,' she was once heard to grumble, 'for when we [artists] have begun any part of a picture, we want to do it as quickly as possible.'[2]

A short working break to the Pyrenees or the Auvergne, from where she could be sure of returning with a bulging portfolio, was acceptable. But crossing the sea to an unfamiliar country, of whose language she knew scarcely a word, was quite a different matter.

Yet Ernest Gambart was undeterred. Their conversation thus far had apprised him of Rosa's love of both unspoiled nature and the writing of Walter Scott. Those nuggets of information now became ammunition. And to these Gambart added the tantalising prospect of being able to study the work of Edwin Landseer at close hand, not to mention supervising his brother as he engraved her painting.

The final obstacle Rosa advanced was the linguistic barrier. This Gambart found the easiest argument to counter: why, he would accompany Rosa and Nathalie on their tour and act as their guide and interpreter. They need only bring themselves and their hunger to discover England's magnificent, rolling hills.

Rosa had run out of excuses. Her trunk was opened and she prepared to set sail.

☙

Cross-Channel travel was not a new phenomenon when Gambart invited Rosa to England, but over the last half a century, the advent of steam power had increased both the speed and the dependability of sea vessels. Meanwhile, steam's application on land in the form of railways had facilitated access to the coast, extending to the masses a privilege which had once been the virtually exclusive prerogative of soldiers and sailors. In 1821, the pioneering 90-ton wooden paddle steamer *Rob Roy* was launched on the Dover Strait, and was then purchased by the French postal administration two years later. After undergoing a year of repairs, the ship was relaunched as the *Henri Quatre*. Regarded as the first cross-Channel passenger steamer, the vessel heralded a new dawn for travel and the birth of an intimate relationship between passengers and post. Opening the services to people proved a useful source of additional revenue for operators, and henceforward, men and mail became travelling companions as they were ferried across the Channel in what came to be known as 'packet boats'.[3]

Paddle steamers were particularly well-suited to this task, since they could operate effectively in ports which were still undeveloped and shallow. In the early 19th century, Dover, where Rosa was bound, was a notoriously problematic port in which to land. The entrance was extremely difficult to navigate and if a ship missed the tide and there was not enough water, passengers had to wait or be landed by a small rowing boat. This made it virtually impossible to keep regular timetables. Though even paddle steamers were not without their disadvantages; paddle floats were prone to damage and the early steamers were small with wooden hulls, meaning that they were constantly at the mercy of the elements. Passengers frequently reached their port of destination wrestling with nausea. 'The steamer was packed with nearly 300 passengers,' one traveller recorded after a trip taken in the mid-1850s, 'and the deck looked, in a few minutes, like a battlefield of sick and groaning.'[4] Nevertheless, the service was constantly improving and already by 1852, the *New Guide to Paris* could boast that 'splendid packets leave from London-bridge for Calais, Boulogne and Havre, almost every day, particularly during the summer months. Packets start daily from Dover and Folkestone; others two or three times a week from Brighton to Dieppe, and from Southampton to Havre.'[5] At the time Rosa made her trip, crossing the Channel had become the standard prelude to the increasingly common European sojourn.

It had been agreed that Rosa should come to England first for just a few days and that this would be followed by a second, longer trip during which Rosa and Nathalie would visit the Highlands.

July had been a clement month that year, and Ernest Gambart could feel hopeful that his guest's first impressions of England would be favourable. But when Rosa arrived on Monday 16 July 1855, the temperature dropped, the sky clouded over and from mid-morning, rain drizzled down persistently.[6] This, she was told, was England. And there was no time to rest – for that very evening, Gambart had accepted an invitation to a grand dinner in the country's capital.

⁘

1850s London was a grey, clunking engine of smoke, politics and industry, for much of the time smothered in a yellowish, acrid fog – that London particular to which Charles Dickens had recently alluded in his serialised novel *Bleak House* (1853).[7] Its infrastructure was expanding, its population swelling and as overall wealth increased, for many people poverty and sanitation deteriorated pitifully. Cholera had swept mercilessly through the city in the first half of the century. Nevertheless, with the Great Exhibition of 1851, London had presented a triumphant front, showcasing its Imperial dominance to the world. Foreign visitors were frequently struck by the city's immensity. Approaching on the

Thames, French guidebook writer Louis Énault was overcome by the looming silhouette of the metropolis: 'Soon a great shadow fell over the river; the thickening atmosphere turned gloomy; we were sailing into a cloud, breathing in a fine carbon dust. We had arrived in London.'[8]

Disembarking and advancing into the city, the traveller was met with no less intimidating a sight:

> on the pavements, which are as wide as the roads, streams of people move along; carriages with rich tack and frisky horses, driven by coachmen with sparkling livery, brush against businessmen's cabs and heavy omnibuses which hawk members of the bourgeoisie around from one place to the other. There is noise, tumult and a constant sense of coming and going before which the foreigner is brought up short, troubled, dumbfounded. It takes several hours, often several days, to acclimatise to this sense of vertigo, before starting a more fruitful exploration.[9]

London, Énault went on, 'is no longer just a city – it is a world. An immense world, of multiple facets'.[10]

For Rosa, whose assent to come to Britain had been largely swayed by the irresistible temptation of the wild and breathtaking landscape of Scotland, London was an unnatural habitat. But as Nathalie was constantly at pains to impress, public relations were vital. And even Rosa had to admit that Gambart had choreographed some invaluable meetings that week. The first of these was the dinner held to honour her arrival which was presided over by none other than the President of the Royal Academy, Sir Charles Eastlake.

With his light features and earnest expression, the sexagenarian Charles Eastlake was learned, creative and exceedingly influential. Born in Plymouth and educated at the Royal Academy, by the 1830s, Eastlake's pictures of bandits, landscapes and female portraits were earning him plaudits. From the 1840s, much of his time had been given to writing about art. His honourable professional nominations accrued, culminating in his election to the post of President of the Royal Academy and a knighthood in 1850. Along with the art critic John Ruskin and Gambart himself, Eastlake was one of the most important figures of London's art world. Above all, he was eminently powerful and well connected. And for Rosa, those attributes were to prove momentous when, that evening, Eastlake introduced her to one of her long-standing heroes: Sir Edwin Landseer.[11]

Gruff-looking and sturdy with a mass of fair curls and sideburns, Edwin Landseer was heralded as the tortured genius of the Victorian art world. He was now in his mid-50s, but his artistic talents had been discovered young. In his teens, he was already exhibiting at the Royal Academy, where he was made an academician in the 1830s. Landseer's anatomically precise depictions of animals had earned him a prodigious reputation. Like Rosa, he had carried out dissections as a means of informing himself and his meticulous industry had won him acclaim across a sweep of social classes. Landseer found admirers in households ranging from middle-class villas to Buckingham Palace (where he was a particular favourite). For all his success, the artist was prone to severe bouts of melancholy and depression. Notwithstanding, professionally, he remained unrivalled. In his animals, Victorians saw expressions of the virtues they held dear: nobility, pride, courage and the sexes performing gender-appropriate roles. Landseer had illustrated Walter Scott, he had worked extensively in Scotland and thanks to his brother's engravings of his work, he had established himself as the reigning sovereign of Britain's answer to the *animalier* genre. Now standing before this master of the brush, Rosa was profoundly humbled.[12]

Once they had been introduced, it took little further mediation on Eastlake's part for Rosa and Landseer to relax into mutual, if verbally restricted, appreciation (with Lady Eastlake and other French speakers being called on to act as interpreters). As the rain hammered down outside and thunder rumbled, as in the room around them, voices hummed and glasses chinked, Rosa and Landseer became engrossed in each other's presence.[13] Indeed, so assured did Landseer apparently feel in Rosa's company – and so quickly – that it led him to make an unfortunate joke: there were many bachelors present at the dinner, he quipped, a deputation of marriage should surely be put to Mlle Bonheur. For his part, he would be delighted to become Sir Edwin Bonheur. Lady Eastlake never forgot the awkward hush which followed. Word that Landseer, a determined bachelor, had made a proposal of marriage to that peculiar French lady artist Rosa Bonheur spread rapidly among the guests and subsequently on the artistic circuit. William Powell Frith, the painter of intricately detailed scenes of Victorian life, thought it outrageously funny, and hastened to offer Landseer his hearty congratulations.[14]

The visit Rosa made with Lady Eastlake to Landseer's studio the next day did nothing to dispel the rumours, and nor did her enthusiasm. With Rosa lost in silent reverence, Landseer presented one picture or sketch after another, and at the end of the visit, offered her two of his brother's engravings of his *Night* (c. 1853) and *Morning* (c. 1853), on which he inscribed her name with his. Lady Eastlake remembered Rosa being overcome with emotion. As their carriage pulled away, the Englishwoman noticed that 'the little head was turned from me, her face streaming with tears'.[15] Rosa, Lady Eastlake concluded was 'only a man in her unflagging work, and renunciation of all a woman's usual sources of happiness [...] She was a real, and truly interesting, simple woman – quite above all the compliments and flattery; and I found her very tired of it, though taking all in the most modest way [...] She is one of those earnest, true creatures, whom one can meet but very seldom in this world, and whom one never forgets.'[16]

Rosa was not sufficiently perturbed by the gossip to conceal her admiration of Landseer afterwards: 'I consider him the greatest painter of animals and I believe that he will remain the greatest of his kind,' she maintained unashamedly some years later.[17]

Though Rosa's first visit to England was brief, Gambart also managed to engineer an invitation to the home of the Irish-born editor of the *Art Journal*, Samuel Carter Hall, where guests were entertained by a Chinese mandarin, who honoured them with a song in his native tongue. The sounds of this strange language struck virtually everyone gathered as deeply comical, and having failed to stifle her laughter with a handkerchief, Rosa herself was obliged to run from the room. An American interpreter had to be utilised to convey the offended mandarin's objection that the song was actually deeply tragic.[18]

Despite a few such cultural faux pas, Rosa and Gambart could congratulate themselves on a productive trip. When Rosa returned to Paris to prepare for her now-annual visit to the Pyrenees, she could do so with a light and contented heart. *The Horse Fair* (1853) was earning her international acclaim, while, having enchanted audiences at the Paris Salon, *Haymaking in the Auvergne* was now pleasing the public at the 1855 Exposition Universelle, where the guide to the show declared the canvas to have placed Rosa 'in the same ranks as our greatest painters'.[19]

'My dear Everybody,' Rosa wrote to her family from the town of Borce on the French–Spanish border on 28 July 1855.

> As I promised, I send you a few lines to announce my safe arrival. The journey was long [...] This place is quite wild and there are neither bathers nor tourists [...] Tomorrow being Sunday, we are going up to the frontier, at the top of the Pyrenees, whence we shall see Spain and France [...] I am with some very nice people, so simple and hospitable [...] I thought such types were to be found only in novels.[20]

When she penned a letter to Gustave d'Eichthal a few days afterwards, Rosa had to admit that accommodation in the Pyrenees had scarcely improved since her last visit. Still, 'I lack nothing in the way of material for painting,' she assured her late father's friend, 'and I intend to profit by the opportunity.'[21]

Ten days later, Rosa had arrived in Saint Sauveur. Her trip was drawing to a close, but she still felt compelled to send a detailed letter home to Juliette. The youngest Bonheur sister was a particular focus of family interest at present; she had given birth to her first son early in June, and the baby had been named Hippolyte, like his father.

'I hope, my dearest Juju, that, notwithstanding my fiery-red complexion, I will not seem to you to have grown too thin. As you anticipated, the sight of Spain has not done me any harm.'[22]

Rosa recounted her adventures in an affectionate and light-hearted tone, though deferral of some payment due led her to lament: 'I have financial anxieties at present.'[23]

Rosa adored her sister, but she had long struggled to comprehend Juliette's contentment with a more conventional female role. The new mother was talented. 'I noticed a little hare which one would have believed to be painted by Rosa Bonheur herself,' a critic had commended when Juliette showed work in Bordeaux in 1853.[24] Rosa was frustrated to see such ability relegated to a subsidiary position, and in favour of what she felt to be an unambitious – if more socially acceptable – way of life. She constantly strove to encourage her sister's painting.

'Hippolyte tells me you are painting something,' she pushed. 'I long to see your little cottage, where I shall have time to make a sketch for a hunting picture which I have in mind.'[25]

Rosa tried hard to accept that her sister simply had different priorities.

'Circumstances do not allow all women to combine the various elements of happiness,' Rosa's fellow female painter, Virginie Demont-Breton, remembered the artist once sharing candidly. 'In my case, art alone has absorbed my whole being,' Rosa explained. 'To be an artist as well as a wife and mother must be complete bliss,' she mused.[26] Yet nothing in her conversation or conduct confirmed that she believed such a dual role to be possible. To Rosa's mind, a woman who was creative had a choice; she had made hers.

❦

While Rosa travelled about the Pyrenees, in London, *The Horse Fair* was proving the toast of Pall Mall.

'To-day (Saturday) closes the French exhibition in Pall Mall,' recorded the *Athenaeum* on 8 September 1855, 'which, since the arrival of Mdlle Rosa Bonheur's great picture of *The Horse Fair in Paris*, has been the chief subject of art interest in London.'[27]

Echoes of the warm British welcome had reached American ears, too:

'Rosa Bonheur is the pretty name of a French woman who is just now charming the connoisseurs of the British metropolis,' the *New York Times* told its readers. 'She has taken London by storm by her skill and happy talent in depicting what Englishmen can understand and appreciate better than any other people.' The novelty of female talent particularly struck the American correspondent: 'Why should there not be more Rosa Bonheurs? Art is open to women as much as men, but up to the time of Rosa Bonheur there has never been a female painter worth remembering [...] It is rare to find a woman with sufficient artistic talent to make a design for a cap-ribbon [...] Rosa Bonheur is an example for artists.'[28]

Gambart's British campaign was having powerful repercussions. And when the London show closed, the dealer arranged for the picture to tour the rest of the country. But before that, a supremely important admirer had requested a private viewing.

'Majesty commanded a first appearance of Mdlle Rosa Bonheur's picture of *The Horse Fair at Paris*,' announced the *Athenaeum*. 'Her Majesty, we hear, has caused a letter to be written to Mdlle Bonheur expressive of her admiration, – a rather exceptional, and therefore very complimentary, manner of announcing royal gratification.'[29]

However, back in the gallery, the absence of the painting visitors had come expressly to see was cause for general dismay: 'One country dame declared that she had come up by railway to see this new lion of London; and was obliged to leave again next day [*sic*] by nine o'clock. She was ultimately reconciled to her disappointment on hearing that the Queen had to leave town at half-past seven!'

Reports of foreign acclaim were immensely reaffirming, while the news that *Haymaking in the Auvergne* had been awarded a gold medal gave additional cause for celebration. Rosa knew that she could not allow her industry to lag, but she was now in such demand that she could be more discerning about the requests she gratified.

'Some art amateur wants me to make him a drawing,' Rosa wrote to Mme Mêne as the year drew to a close. 'But it will be impossible for me to undertake any new work between now and New Year's day. My head is full of subjects which I want to give birth to and which the devil keeps preventing me from bringing into the world.'[30]

Rosa refused to compromise on quality. Her heart had to be committed to what she was painting or she would not proceed. Thus far, that approach was bearing fruit – and it was becoming increasingly sought after. Now, the moment had come to test her international popularity with a second trip to the British Isles. At last, it was time to visit Scotland.

12

The Lady of the Lakes

Scotland, 'land of brown heath and shaggy wood, land of the mountain and the flood'– thanks to Walter Scott, Rosa could see only rugged Highland vistas and cool, deep lochs.[1] Her open suitcase could call for little besides paints, pencils and brushes.

But Nathalie was more percipient of Gambart's intentions. Wisely gauging that the dealer was not about to convey them to Britain for the sole pleasure of painting, Rosa's companion readied all manner of outfits and accessories which the artist might need for the inevitable public appearances. Silk skirts, broad-brimmed hats, elegant dresses with delicate lace trim, were all prepared and defiantly packed. The headstrong Nathalie would hear of no compromise, even when Mme Micas objected that they were taking far too much. However, once the boat dropped anchor at Dover, the old woman's anxieties were immediately validated.

When ships arrived in England, duties owed were assessed by officers who boarded the vessel and investigated passengers' luggage. Hence the women's first challenge was convincing the authorities to allow their baggage through.

Finally stepping off the boat at Dover to be whipped by the sea breeze and mocked by the chattering gulls overhead, Rosa set foot into a land now even more receptive to French visitors than when she made her first trip.

The British government had initially been wary of Napoleon III, but when his intentions were shown to be peaceful, had presented an amiable front. Britain had learned – through bitter experience – that France was best kept in check by cooperating with her. And just a year after the French Empire was established, the strength of that alliance had been put to the test.[2]

In 1853, Latin and Orthodox monks had entered into a dispute over the guardianship of the Holy Places of Jerusalem. Napoleon acted to promote – and thereby gain support from – the Roman Catholics, while Russia intervened on behalf of the Orthodox Church and demanded that the Turks grant her virtual protectorate over Orthodox Christians within their Empire. Britain had long regarded Russia with a distrustful eye, while Napoleon harboured personal misgivings about the Tsar. War was declared on and around the Crimean Peninsula and from 1854, France and Britain found themselves united as they battled to keep territory out of Russian hands. The prolonged episode of butchery had only officially concluded with the signing of the Treaty of Paris early in 1856, and as Rosa and Nathalie now left the port of Dover, the freshness of this bloody episode impressed itself; there, camping out on the South Downs, were troops returning from the Crimean Peninsula.

While it did little to increase France's territories, the conflict occasioned an Allied victory and a rekindling of France's relationship with Britain. Napoleon III had made an official visit to London shortly before Rosa's own in April 1855, and the following August, Queen Victoria had returned the honour. The British no longer looked on the French as foes but as allies, while Francophilia was steering interests and ideas. This state of affairs had not escaped Ernest Gambart.[3]

Gambart conveyed his guests first of all to the house he had leased that spring in the small hamlet of George Green in the parish of Wexham. Just north of the River Thames and a short carriage ride from Windsor, the pink-bricked Old House was a fine, 17th-century former rectory with a generously planted garden shaded by majestic

trees and surrounded by fields and pastures. This retreat from the bustling metropolis was to serve as their base while Gambart made the
final preparations for their trip to Scotland. And as Rosa and Nathalie
quickly realised, their sojourn in Wexham would be anything but dull.

Gambart and his lovely wife Annie (a pretty, cherubic brunette
less than half his age), embraced socialising as a requisite of the dealer's
career. This 'duty' they accomplished with panache and evident relish.
Seldom did a week pass when there was not a dinner, musical soirée
or gathering in the Gambart house, and the guests included the cream
of Europe's art world and its literati. The artist William Powell Frith
and his family were regular visitors, while the French painter Constant
Troyon was no stranger to the warm welcome offered at Wexham.
Since the Gambarts' arrival, Old House had frothed into a lively hub of
sociability and culture. The sound of laughter and lofty artistic debate
echoed through its rooms and hallways. And the intense conviviality
was invariably accompanied by a mouth-watering spread.[4]

'In this country people are always eating,' Nathalie exclaimed in
one of the first letters to her mother.[5]

Gastronomic pleasures were something Rosa rarely tired of. But
enforced mingling she found far less palatable. Unfortunately, with
Gambart conducting her tour, society was to be compulsory.

Since Rosa's first trip to England the previous summer, Gambart
had been fanning a mounting publicity campaign and working tirelessly
to generate press interest. By the time Rosa arrived, the English had
been whipped up into a veritable frenzy of anticipation.

'We hear from Paris that a new character portrait of Mdlle Rosa
Bonheur, by M. Dubufe, is exciting much interest,' the *Athenaeum* had
reported in March. 'The artist is represented as leaning, pencil in hand,
on the neck of a favourite heifer – one of those fine young bulls which
she loves so well to paint.'[6]

Now, the movements of the woman the *Manchester Times* called
'the talented lady' were being watched closely.[7] If Rosa's submissions to the French Exhibition that summer had not been felt to rival
The Horse Fair –'a picture of a century'– her name instantly attracted

attention, while her participation reiterated her central place on the British art scene.[8] Added to which, an English translation of F. Lepelle de Bois-Gallais's recent biography of her had been shrewdly timed (by its publisher, Ernest Gambart) to appear just before Rosa arrived. The reviewer for the *Athenaeum* saw through the publicity ruse, but nonetheless described Rosa as 'one of the most remarkable women who ever attacked easel [*sic*]'.[9] By the time Rosa arrived in Wexham, Gambart had laid the ground for success.

Social duties aside, Gambart's grounds at Wexham gave Rosa a highly favourable impression of the British flora and fauna.

'England is really a fine country,' Rosa wrote home to Juliette, 'though rather trim. The vegetation is admirable, with magnificent trees. The oaks are almost black, which gives an imposing character to the landscape.' But she added darkly: 'it seems that it often rains in this country, and especially in Scotland.'[10]

Wexham's proximity to Windsor meant that on one of Rosa and Nathalie's first excursions, they happened upon a herd of some 200 deer. Rosa called to the driver to stop the carriage, and her joy was magnified when the beasts did not take flight but instinctively formed themselves into a kind of battalion, with the male deer in front as though protecting the females. Transfixed by their behaviour, Rosa immediately began sketching.

Though Windsor provided a happy diversion, having heard and read such laudatory accounts of Scotland, Rosa was impatient to begin their expedition to the north. 'I am longing for Gambart to have finished his preparations and to be off on our way to Scotland,' she moaned to Mme Micas.[11] Still, before they could leave for the Highlands, there was one further trip Rosa knew to be imperative:

'We are going to London to-day,' she told Mme Micas, 'for I want to see what they are doing with the engraving of my *Horse Fair*.'[12]

The foray into the capital complete, at last, Rosa could experience for herself the peace and undulating hills of Scotland.

During the early part of the 19th century, a surge of publications had appeared in France promoting the charms of Scotland, with works such as Amédée Pichot's *Historic and Literary Journey through England and Scotland* (1825) and the Bonheurs' friend Saint-Germain-Leduc's *England, Scotland and Ireland: An Account of a Recent Journey in the Three Kingdoms* (1838) sensitising the French to the scenery so evocatively captured by Walter Scott. Rosa was now restive with anticipation.

'We shall take three days to get there,' she laid out the expected itinerary to Mme Micas, 'as we are to visit three English towns on the way.'[13]

Rosa would have preferred to arrive sooner, but Gambart had warned against fatiguing themselves. That their route would take them through Birmingham, which was currently playing host to *The Horse Fair*, as well as Manchester and Liverpool, where it had also excited interest in recent months, was simply a happy advantage.[14] It would be foolish not to stop in these delightful locations. Nathalie was quietly thrilled; Gambart's crafty route planning was sure to increase Rosa's professional prestige – and ultimately, the women's material comforts.[15]

The party set off by train from Slough.

'Gambart is the best travelling companion imaginable,' Rosa gushed in a letter to Juliette. 'He looks after everything, so that his little wife is the most spoilt of females. He is always running about and coming to tell us something about the journey, so that he generally seems as if he were about to fly away by the edge of the skirts of his frock-coat, which go ever floating in the wind behind him.'[16]

On 13 August, they arrived in Birmingham, where Rosa's appearance caused a furore. When their train pulled into the station, they were met by crowds and whoops of delight. Flags and banners flapped in the breeze, schoolchildren pushed and elbowed each other out of the way to see the curious lady painter, while bouquets were thrust into Rosa's hands and the air crackled with applause.

Gambart had arranged for them to take lunch with the coal mine owner, ironmaster and picture collector, Charles Birch, at which appointment they also met the landscape artist David Cox. Cox had been afflicted by a stroke a few years before which had left him with deteriorated eyesight, but notwithstanding, he took the time to give Rosa and Nathalie a tour of his studio. Then with no chance to repose, the women were whisked off to the home of the iron founder and art collector Edwin Bullock, who had purchased one of Rosa's pictures from Gambart – and there they were met by an unexpected reception: 'All the most eminent artists and men of letters in Birmingham had assembled to pay their respects to Rosa,' Nathalie proudly reported in a letter to her mother.[17] There was a personal triumph for Nathalie, too, when she learned shortly afterwards that two of the four paintings she herself had exhibited in Gambart's show in Birmingham had been sold.[18]

The next day, there was scarcely time to visit the pen factory of Gambart and Bullock's mutual acquaintance, the art patron Joseph Gillott, before the dealer was ushering them back onto the train and off towards Liverpool. En route, they stopped in Manchester, where they were joined by the painter Frederick Goodall, another of Gambart's protégés.

In his mid-30s (like Rosa), the round-faced and corpulent Goodall was famed for his anecdotal genre scenes. He had been an associate member of the Royal Academy since the early 1850s and when he was introduced to the French *animalier*, he immediately warmed to her:

> It was the opinion of many people who had never seen her that she was a masculine woman. I can say with truth that she was quite the reverse. Her hands and feet were *petites*; her face was not strictly beautiful or fine, or handsome; but her expression was so vivacious and intelligent that I thought her charming.[19]

Once the augmented party of travellers arrived in Liverpool, they boarded the steamer which would ferry them to Greenock.

When Gambart recounted their trip, he insisted that Rosa travelled the next day to the wild and picturesque locations of Loch Eck, where she sketched a herd of oxen, to the waterfront town of Oban, not far from Glencoe with its dramatic mountain vistas, and then to Ballachulish on the pretty shores of Loch Leven (a village Nathalie and Rosa loved but whose name they found impossible to pronounce). For Gambart, even the midges proved Rosa's exceptional character, for she 'bore their bites with a resignation which astonished me,' he affirmed, adding that numerous insects were caught and trapped forever – poetically – in the wet paint of Rosa's studies. He highlighted locations which inspired future paintings, and conveniently skirted over the more banal stops mentioned by Nathalie in her letters home (many of which Rosa embellished with an illustration). In fact, Nathalie recorded them heading almost immediately for a far less bucolic corner of Scotland – the industrial city of Glasgow.[20]

By the mid-19th century, Glasgow was a place of radical contrasts. The burgeoning engineering, shipbuilding and cotton industries had created a prosperous middle class. But for the poor, overcrowded dwellings, long working hours, physical hardship and ill-health were an everyday reality. In Glasgow's most destitute areas, sanitation was primitive, space at a premium and poverty painfully visible in the malnourished, bow-legged children who shuffled along the pavements. But the arts had a place and there was a new acquaintance to be made in Glasgow, too.[21]

Arriving in the thronging city, the travelling companions crossed paths with the Irish painter Daniel Maclise, with whom Gambart was well acquainted. Big boned and balding, the 50-year-old Maclise had begun his career sketching portraits, leaving Ireland in the 1820s to join the Royal Academy, where he received the highest honours. He had made a name for himself with a series of lithograph portraits of famous celebrities in the 1830s, as well as two large frescoes, one showing the meeting of the Duke of Wellington and Gebhard Leberecht von Blücher, and the other entitled *The Death of Nelson*. Motivated and possessing an astounding visual memory, Maclise had been present when Queen Victoria visited Gambart's French exhibition in 1855. The addition of his company injected new interest into the remainder of the expedition, and together, the group visited an iron foundry which Nathalie, who always found machines and gadgets fascinating, particularly enjoyed.[22]

Indeed, the trip was proving an inspiring one for Nathalie on multiple levels.

'We have got to thinking that I should learn to copy Rosa so as to earn more money,' she confided to her mother, explaining:

> one of Gambart's schemes as a way of her making a fortune more quickly, and of me earning a little too. You must not tell anyone about this. Here, all the paint-ers are copied, this is how they are able to enjoy quite a comfortable existence. They retouch and sign the works. I do not want to get carried away too early. But my health permitting, I will manage it and then I will help you, that is my dream.[23]

CR

It was September when the group reached Edinburgh. Now surpassed by Glasgow in terms of size and industrial development, Edinburgh nevertheless remained an important financial centre and a commercial hub into which investment had been poured from the mid-18th century to create a new town, as a way of coaxing back from London wealthy former residents who would encourage luxury industries to thrive. The city was also a vibrant locus of culture, with superb libraries, beautiful architecture and an important figurehead in the person of Rosa's hero, Walter Scott, who was born and educated in the city and who had tri-umphantly stage-managed King George IV's visit to Scotland in 1822.[24]

One of the days of Rosa and Nathalie's stay fell on a Sunday – and that, the companions agreed as the rain drizzled down on the mourn-ful landscape outside, was their most peculiar Scottish experience yet.

'In this country the Lord's day is sanctified to such good purpose that there is not a cat in the street and you can't visit the castle, either.

We are in the big drawing room engaged in dozing or studying the tips of each other's noses,' Rosa told Mme Micas.[25]

After such tedium, a trip out to the island of Bass Rock was eagerly anticipated and a copious picnic optimistically packed. Gannets nested on the island in the spring and summer months, and there was always the hope that there might still be some wildlife to be found in September. But the waves crashed so violently on the outbound voyage that the very thought of food made stomachs retch, with Maclise being particularly afflicted, and they had to return with empty bellies.[26]

At the very least, Rosa could now boast more boat travel than many 19th-century women would take in their lives. 'Nathalie and I are becoming perfect sailors – real feminine jack-tars,' she joked.[27]

Rosa's mood lifted still further when a visit to Falkirk was proposed. The large lowland town in the Forth Valley was the site of a renowned livestock fair, and being virtually equidistant from Edinburgh and Glasgow, a trip there seemed natural. Every day in the run-up to the fair, herds of oxen were driven across the Firth, closely supervised to ensure that they did not drown. The spectacle made a profound impression on Rosa and she busied herself sketching.

Gambart had arranged for them to be put up in the nearby village of Banknock in the home of the colliery owner and art enthusiast William Wilson, who had purchased Rosa's recently exhibited *Chalk Wagonners in the Limousin* and was described by the *Morning Post* as a 'spirited picture collector'.[28]

The sale of cattle and horses commenced on Tuesday 9 September. The weather had been dull and wet over the last three days, but as Gambart and his party awoke on the morning of the fair, clearer skies promised an agreeable day.[29] When Wilson's carriage pulled up at the fair carrying not only Rosa, but also Goodall and Maclise, both members of the Royal Academy, excitement rippled through the crowds.

From Rosa's perspective, the British enthusiasm for her was beginning to lose its appeal. 'The Inquisition', as she and Nathalie had rebaptised it, was in no way quelled by the fact that the press had got wind of her stay in Scotland and an article was being shared among the leading newspapers.

'Rosa Bonheur [...] is at present in Scotland,' the report announced.

> Mademoiselle Bonheur is earnest and honest in her study of art [...] She is thoroughly fearless in the presence of animals, and, in some instances exercises a peculiar power over them, which arises partly from fearlessness and partly from that sympathy with other orders of creation.

The writer solemnly assured readers that Mlle Bonheur was one of those extraordinary people who could exert 'a kind of mesmeric power upon the objects upon whom it is exercised', and that her companion Mlle Micas, 'exercises this power in a remarkable manner'. The report went on: 'She lives like a hermit [...] she is unassuming and, although thoroughly at her ease, retiring [...] She is no ordinary person.' Attention was now entirely unavoidable and Nathalie became fixed in the public's minds as an unearthly hypnotist who followed Rosa wherever she went.[30]

As Gambart remembered, Rosa had not even stepped down from the carriage at Falkirk when she spied a bull and a group of oxen which she declared she simply must buy. In a market judged to be particularly 'stiff', the seller was so jubilant to do business with a celebrity that his haste to hurry the beasts along caused some loitering sheep to be crushed.[31] Swept away in the visual impact of the Scottish cattle with their long coats, Rosa was oblivious to the logistical complications of such a purchase. Gambart indulged her whim, and immediately paid to have the creatures sent back to Wexham.

The trip to Scotland and the Highlands would not have been complete without a visit to the Trossachs and while in the area, the group also took in Glen Falloch. So contented was Rosa by the scenery that one evening as they ambled by the water's edge, she spontaneously broke into song. Gambart was struck.

'Her voice was really very fine and she used it to great effect,' he remembered.[32]

Coincidentally, the party's stay in the Trossachs brought them close to where a sensational artistic drama had played out just a few years before.

Seeking repose after a period of intense work, the renowned art critic John Ruskin had arranged to holiday near Glenfinlas with his wife Effie. There, the couple were joined by their great friends, the painter and founder of the Pre-Raphaelite brotherhood, John Everett Millais and his elder brother, William. Grouped together in close quarters, Effie agreed to pose for the younger Millais brother – and as he worked, the pair had fallen deeply in love. Effie and Ruskin's marriage crumbled, and she glided into the waiting arms of Millais, whom she married not long afterwards.

Millais and his new wife were staying in the area that summer, and as Gambart and his party were driving past a church one Sunday during their visit, they spied a man the dealer recognised: it was the elder Millais brother, William. To Gambart's delight, he was wearing a kilt. (As a woman who dressed in men's clothing, Rosa had been eager to see a man who did the reverse.)[33]

Learning the younger Millais brother to be nearby, Gambart proposed that they all lunch together at the hotel where he and Rosa were staying.

Having dined with one of the foremost members of the Pre-Raphaelite movement, the final leg of the journey took the group to the Island of Arran, the jewel of the Highlands, famed for encapsulating the full array of Scotland's varied landscape. There, Rosa and Nathalie were entranced by the mountain peaks and the play of light on the water. 'Such beautiful sea tints and skies,' Rosa marvelled, 'I enjoyed myself immensely.'[34]

All the while, as Rosa's eyes devoured the scenery, Gambart obligingly loaded himself up with her painting equipment so that she need never miss an aesthetic subject.

Ten-year-old Marion Hamilton (who later took up the pen and married the artist John Adams-Acton) remembered meeting Gambart's party during their stay at the hotel in Brodick. 'We were all invited to dinner with the Gambarts, and I remember the enthusiastic admiration of the celebrated Rosa for the grandeur of the island scenery,' Miss Hamilton recalled. 'She expatiated loudly, and with much gesticulation, on its wonderful beauty.'[35] Rosa also ventured a few of the English expressions she had heard Annie Gambart uttering:

'Oh magnificent! Oh beautiful! Oh grand! *Oh very well!* ...'[36]

'Rosa was of commanding presence, and looked essentially a being above the common herd,' Miss Hamilton remarked. 'Her dress was a compromise between that of a man and a woman; she wore her hair in a brown, curly crop, and she rode on horseback astride, to the horror of all kirk-going folk.'[37]

This was the last Scottish marvel on the itinerary. From Arran, the group returned by sea the nineteen-hour voyage to Liverpool and then finally back to Gambart's house at Wexham.

'I am not sorry to be back from my trip,' Rosa admitted in a letter to Auguste. The visit had been inspiring, but business in Paris did not stand still. Rosa's presence at the drawing school's annual prize-giving was imperative. Besides, with recent publications like Anatole de La Forge's *Contemporary Painting in France* (1856) (which dedicated an entire chapter to her) and Eugène de Mirecourt's *Contemporaries: Rosa Bonheur* (1856), she was more in demand than ever. Satiated with new experiences, Rosa and Nathalie boarded the boat for France, but on the understanding that Rosa would return to collect her animals, whose entry into France was complicated by the dictates of customs.

Never a woman to renege on her word, Rosa was back in England a few weeks later. She was dismayed when she ultimately had to resign herself to reselling her herd in England (customs having proved more dogmatic than she had hoped). But Rosa's enforced return was otherwise fortuitous. During their trip through the Highlands, Frederick Goodall had been gathering material from which to paint a study of Rosa at work (Gambart 'gave me permission', he said).[38] Not yet departed from Wexham after their Scottish tour, Goodall decided that he would stay a little longer so that he might begin the final painting of

Frederick Goodall, *Rosa Bonheur Painting in the Scottish Highlands*, 1856–1858, oil on panel, 39.7 x 58.4 cm.

Morton and Marie Bradley Memorial Collection, Eskenazi Museum of Art, Indiana University; photograph by Kevin Montague 98.170

Rosa working in the countryside, a piece which would further bolster Gambart's publicity campaign.

Goodall studied Rosa intently. One Sunday, the pair went out for a stroll, having first promised Gambart not to paint (a stipulation made so as not to offend local sensibilities on the Sabbath). Rosa kept her word, though Goodall could see that it near tortured her to do so.

Still, Gambart was not an unmitigated killjoy. Before Rosa left England again, he had one last surprise. A very important person had expressed a desire to meet her. This man was intelligent, influential and one of the most important spokesmen for French art in England. There, arriving to dinner one evening and causing a flurry of excitement in the tiny village of Wexham, was the world-famous art critic, John Ruskin – the man recently cuckolded by Rosa's new acquaintance John Everett Millais.

With his pale, even features, dignified mien and air of self-assurance, the Victorian sage Ruskin was a commanding presence. Born into a middle-class family, his academic and religious education had fostered in him a love of culture and an exquisitely refined taste. He had begun publishing short pieces of prose and verse in magazines in the 1830s and after completing his Oxford education, he turned his attention more seriously to art criticism. Ruskin became one of the most ardent defenders, first of J.M.W. Turner, and then of the Pre-Raphaelites, developing a style which employed words with adroitness to simulate the visual effects of paintings for those unable to access galleries. The ultimate polymath, a gifted painter, writer, critic and theorist, and a committed interdisciplinarian, Ruskin was convinced that art had the power to transform lives and enlighten mankind. To his mind, the public needed to learn – and he was determined to educate. As the newly wealthy commercial and professional classes found themselves in a position to buy and collect art, Ruskin's voice came to authorise good taste and by the 1850s, he had risen to a position of extraordinary prowess. Few people wielded Ruskin's power to shape viewpoints. Sharp, bright, discerning in his praise and generous with his opinion, John Ruskin could command words like a general did his troops. The result was a lyrical defence – or a devastating destruction. Ruskin's imminent arrival was the talk of Wexham.[39]

A few days before, a servant was sent to hire rooms for him, and when the furniture was found to be wanting, better was promptly shipped down from Windsor. A cook was expedited so that Mr Ruskin would have his breakfast prepared just the way he liked it, and a whole procession of domestic staff was seen arriving to attend to him. Everything was readied so that the critic's slightest whim should be catered for.[40]

Finally on 20 October, John Ruskin's carriage pulled into Wexham (the critic disdained the railway). This, Gambart knew, would be a meeting of art-historical magnitude.

Pleasantries were exchanged over a meticulously choreographed dinner. And then, Ruskin could begin the debate he had come for.

'Why don't you work in watercolours?' he enquired abruptly.[41]

'I could not,' Rosa responded quickly. 'It would be impossible to put in every hair.'

'If you come and dine with me some day, I will show you a watercolour drawing – made in Scotland – in which I put in every leaf of a tree in the foreground.' He persisted: 'I do not see that you use purple in your shades.'

'I never see shade two days alike, and I never see it in purple.'

'I always see it purple.'

The tension was palpable.

'I don't yield,' the critic shot. 'To vanquish me, you would have to crush me.'[42]

Rosa was unfazed: 'I wouldn't go so far as that,' she said.[43]

Once the sparring was over and Ruskin had left, Gambart turned to Rosa, burning to know her thoughts: what did she think of the eminent critic?

'He is a gentleman,' Rosa allowed, 'an educated gentleman; but he is a theorist. He sees nature with a little eye – just like a bird,' she concluded.[44] That told Gambart enough.

'Drive down to Slough to Mr Gambart's,' read Ruskin's diary entry for the day. 'Pleasant evening with Rosa Bonheur.'[45]

Years later, Ruskin expanded on his impressions of Rosa. 'Her feelings for animals,' he decided, were 'more akin to the menagerie keeper's love.'[46] He was right. And to Rosa's mind, that was no flaw: it was the key to her success.

CB

Rosa's last trip to England was drawing to a close. As she bid farewell to her host, it was a pertinent time to turn her attention to her career. The English enthusiasm had been gratifying. There was even a horse named after her running at Newmarket that autumn, and Nathalie had conjectured that they no longer need worry if French interest waned.[47] Though Rosa was mindful of complacency, it certainly looked as though the Salon might not be the only forum for finding success. The sole reservation expressed in the English press was that Rosa might never be able to rival *The Horse Fair*. But to Rosa, that simply represented a challenge.

To withdraw from the Salon would be a dangerous step. Yet Rosa now had proof that there was a market for her work abroad.[48]

To produce the best pictures, Rosa needed quiet and she needed peace. That was difficult to come by in Paris. She returned home that autumn with two gnawing questions: firstly, was she brave enough to concentrate her energies on the international market? And secondly, could she create the right working conditions to be able to satisfy it?

Answers began to present themselves almost immediately. As Rosa's boat docked in Calais, a radical change was brewing; her working environment, her home life with Nathalie and her reputation were about to transform in ways she could scarcely have imagined.

13

Such Stuff as Dreams

It was not the first time that Mme Micas had peeled back the coverlets of her bed to find that the otter had got there first.

She had grown exasperated with the little creature, which persisted in sliding out of its tank and coming to find her bed, then wriggling down so that the sheets, and sometimes even the mattress, were soaked through.[1]

Irrespective of impracticalities, Rosa's passion for collecting animals was unstoppable; it bordered on addiction. Besides the otter, other permanent residents at the Rue d'Assas still included birds, a horse, a donkey, a monkey and sheep, and that was to say nothing of the 'visitors' whom she borrowed from time to time. The space Rosa shared with Nathalie and her mother was quickly shrinking – and cleaning had become Mme Micas's full-time occupation.

But after the phenomenal success of *The Horse Fair* (1853) in France and England, Rosa's presence in central Paris seemed primordial.

While Thomas Landseer had been working on his engraving of the great painting, the English art patron Jacob Bell happened to see the diminutive version. Struck by its potency, Bell penned Gambart a letter, asking if he could purchase it so that it could join his collection of Landseer pictures. Gambart agreed, accepting 25,000 francs. Then, as his triumphant parade of *The Horse Fair* around England was nearing its end, Gambart finally found a buyer for the original work, too – and one even more catalytic than he could have hoped. William P. Wright, an American collector from New Jersey, had come forward offering 30,000 francs. It was less than Gambart had paid, but Mr Wright's proposal came with a sweetener: Gambart could keep the work for the next two or three years and continue exhibiting in England and America, provided he share the proceeds of these shows with the painting's new owner. The deal worked in Mr Wright's favour; takings from the exhibitions were soon flowing in, and it looked as though they could virtually offset the cost of the painting. The agreement also suited Gambart. If the picture itself had not commanded a substantial profit, sales of the engraving were generating a small fortune. More importantly, Mr Wright had unblocked a threshold which could be difficult to cross: the doorway to the American art market. Meanwhile, as exhibitions of *The Horse Fair* accrued, the more secure Rosa's reputation became – and that boded well for the prices Gambart could ask for subsequent paintings.[2]

However, Rosa's family were evidencing misgivings about her arrangement with the Micases. Rosa later gave friends to understand that their reaction stemmed from monetary pique. Although Rosa had made her own, new family with Nathalie and her mother, she continued to nurture the mutually supportive relationship she had always shared with her siblings. She also assisted her stepmother, giving Marguerite Picard money towards the education of her eight-year-old half-brother, Germain. Moreover, as Rosa's work schedule intensified, not only Nathalie, but also Auguste and Juliette were at times called in to help completing canvases and Rosa made a point of sharing the profits of any such work with them. Juliette's husband and Rosa's stepbrother, Hippolyte, maintained a particularly close working relationship with the artist. He had begun casting her animal sculptures in bronze, the royalties for which Rosa was happy for him to keep. To Rosa's advantage, Hippolyte was also an astute businessman. She sometimes used him as an unofficial agent when there was a painting to sell; in a still gender-biased art world, it paid to be represented by the authoritative presence of a man, particularly one with Bonheur interests at heart. Besides, Rosa abhorred dealing with the commercial

Rosa Bonheur, *A Grazing Sheep*, bronze, 14.6 x 21.6 cm.
Dahesh Museum of Art, New York, USA/Bridgeman Images

side of painting. 'Do you know,' she once told the aspiring young artist Léonide Bourges, 'even now I cannot quote a price for a picture ordered, without blushing?'[3]

French, English and a growing number of American viewers were eager to purchase engravings of Rosa's work, while collectors were clamouring to own an original. And virtually every day, people were turning up at her studio in the Rue d'Assas, some who had been invited, but many who had not.

'During the early years of her career,' explained one of Rosa's students, Mlle Keller, 'she lived in continual contact with several of the great painters and sculptors of modern France. I recall, especially, the frequency of the presence of the famous David d'Angers [the acclaimed sculptor] in her studio in the Rue d'Assas.'[4]

To accommodate these visitors, Rosa had fallen into the pattern of giving a reception on a Friday to which some of the art world's greatest luminaries would travel. It was even said that M. de Morny himself appeared from time to time.

But whether people were coming to see a star or a spectacle was not always clear. The chance it could be the latter played on Rosa's mind incessantly. She was always ready to welcome family and she positively blossomed among her close friends, becoming lively, quick-witted and humorous. Nor was she afraid to crack a bawdy joke when she judged her listener man enough (though she insisted that everyone else refrain from lewd humour). But Rosa was equally prone to dark moods and could survive isolated from society for weeks if she were absorbed in a picture, with only Nathalie and Mme Micas for company and her witty letters to friends for interaction with the outside world. These missives were frequently illustrated with an impromptu sketch or supplemented by a light-hearted verse. Indulging in ludicrous wordplay was one of Rosa's favourite pastimes.

She accepted invitations only occasionally, episodes infrequent enough for friends to remember them distinctly.

The former actress née Valérie Simonin recalled a ball which Rosa and Nathalie attended dressed respectively as a black African and a clown. Then at one of the Mênes' gatherings where fancy dress was required, Rosa appeared as a gypsy and Nathalie as Pierrot, whom she played most convincingly. On each occasion, Rosa too threw herself into her role with gusto, explaining drily that as a black African and a clown, she and Nathalie had come as 'an arrangement in black and white'.[5]

Rosa was also passionate about music and the theatre, and more than once, a good stage show had been known to lure her out of her studio. The evening when Rosa had arrived at the Opéra Comique in Paris dressed in her painting smock was still talked about long after the event and referenced as proof of her eccentricity. A friend attributed the oversight to Rosa's absorption in the anticipation of the approaching show. However, Rosa later clarified that she had simply not had time to change. Once again, her love of the arts took precedence over social mores.[6]

Whenever Rosa received friends at home (where she was infinitely more comfortable), it was common for her to sketch or sculpt as she talked. Visitors were astounded that she could multitask so efficiently that neither the artwork nor the discussion was in the least bit affected.

By 1857, Rosa Bonheur was indisputably the unlikely artistic star of the moment.

However, when the Salon opened its doors that summer, there was a shock in store for the audience. As expectant eyes scoured the walls, Rosa's work was nowhere to be seen. Most were surprised; her admirers were horrified.

'In the absence of Mlle Rosa Bonheur, who has not exhibited [...] the most remarkable *animalier* to whom we must draw attention is M. Albert Brendel,' exclaimed the reviewer Maxime du Camp, 'a German.'[7]

To some, it seemed as though Rosa was turning her back on the country which had parented her. With the burgeoning international interest and a schedule now straining to satisfy it, Rosa had taken the bold decision not to exhibit a canvas under her name that year. But through a crafty sleight of hand, her continued sovereignty was affirmed.

'M. Dubufe has become *the* fashionable portrait artist,' announced the *Revue des Beaux-Arts*.[8] And there among his six portraits was the picture of Rosa which had caused such a stir while she was in England. The piece had been masterminded by Ernest Gambart.

Of all his submissions, 'we prefer the portrait of mademoiselle Rosa Bonheur and her favourite cow,' proclaimed the same reviewer, 'which is painted with greater vigour and is closer to serious art.'[9]

Serious it was. Against a sombre, brooding landscape, Rosa stood confidently, wearing a dark green dress in a three-quarter length portrait. Her wavy, chestnut hair was side-parted, while under her left arm, she clutched a folder (presumably of drawings), and in the other, she gripped a pencil or paintbrush, her arm resting absentmindedly on the neck of a bull. With the highlighted patch of cloud behind her gently haloing her head and giving a semi-religious nuance to the piece, Rosa's gaze was fixed on an unidentified point to her left. Meanwhile, it was not the human subject but the bull who adhered to the pictorial conventions common to portraiture by looking directly out of the canvas at the viewer. Rosa's bodice and skirts, though dark, were rich and sumptuous, and she wore a delicate lace collar with a silk bow tied loosely at her neck – utterly feminine, perfectly in keeping with contemporary ladies' fashion. The figure depicted was undoubtedly a woman, but one who emerged strong, determined and assured.

What a pity, critics regretted, that Rosa herself had not shown a canvas this year. Still, it was a fine portrait and the bull – particularly the bull – stood out.

'The famous artist, who has not exhibited anything this year, is shown with her arm resting on the neck of a superb bull,' explained Louis Auvray. [10]

That 'superb bull' had seduced the viewers – and silently, Rosa had triumphed again. For the bull was not part of Dubufe's original plan; when the work had been started by the artist (who had had ample opportunity to encounter Rosa at the home of their mutual friend, Mêne), Rosa quickly became alarmed that the piece was growing too sickly and sentimental. Could it not be adapted, she implored, so that her hand rested on one of the animals she loved rather than an irrelevant item of furniture? Why, she would even paint the creature herself if he preferred. Dubufe could hardly refuse. To have such an acclaimed artist collaborating in his piece was an honour.

In the catalogue, Rosa's contribution went uncredited. Yet without even submitting a canvas, her presence had been asserted and her skill tacitly showcased.

CB

The next eighteen months passed in an eddy of tireless industry: planning, painting and perfecting private commissions from all over the world, liaising with the likes of Gambart, Tedesco and the house of Goupil (the printer, publisher and subsequently painting dealer with whom Rosa had been associating since the early 1850s) and approving – or declining – the sale of paintings and/or reproduction rights.

With technological advancements, notably the invention of photography, the reproduction industry was democratising art by making it more accessible. From the 1850s, publishers were able to offer their customers photographic reproductions in addition to lithographs and engravings, meaning that artworks could now be disseminated widely, affordably and in a multiplicity of forms. Copies of Rosa's timeless and nostalgic scenes of idyllic rural life were among the most desirable pictures available.[11]

The commercialisation of art was making many shrewd speculators rich. It was also provoking heated debates. When a Mme Hudel asked to paint a copy of *Ploughing in the Nivernais* onto porcelain (the latest fashion in the 1850s), a fierce dispute erupted between the lady artist and M. Goupil, who objected on the grounds that he held exclusive rights to the work. Reproductions were big business; there was money to be made for the smart and the canny.[12]

Meanwhile, with Rosa an established household name in France, *The Horse Fair* was now causing a sensation in the United States.

'Among the freight of the steamer *Persia*, which arrived on Tuesday last, was the celebrated painting of the *Horse Fair*, by Rosa Bonheur,' the *New York Times* reported enthusiastically on 17 September 1857.[13]

The Horse Fair did not disappoint. The work met with rhapsodic reviews when it was shown at the Stevens and Williams gallery in New York in October 1857, where its power was greatly enhanced by the ingenious placement of a mirror. As the reviewer for the *New York Times* explained, this device emphasised 'the admirable perspective of the composition with singular force'. The writer was enchanted by the work of this 'wonderful little lady' and compared Rosa with Charlotte Brontë. Once again, the perceived disparity between the virility of the painting and the gender of its author was a common source of astonishment: 'That a woman should be able to paint the horse and the dog as well as she could love them – and should rival with delicate fingers the boldest sweeping pencil of the most adventurous artists of the "stronger" sex, this did provoke wonder even from little-wondering Paris,' the *New York Times* review went on, concluding that Rosa could rightly call for her painting be treated as 'high art'.[14]

Such praise offered ample reward for Rosa's industry. Her gruelling work schedule was also punctuated by correspondence and time spent with her siblings, which frequently served to revitalise her, all the while reminding her of the remarkable trajectory her life had taken. Then with the birth of Auguste's third daughter that summer, the Bonheur dynasty could celebrate its durability.

Financially, Rosa was now more secure than she could ever have dreamed possible in her youth. The days of economising, of agonising over which of the necessary items to do without, were over. Her lifestyle was hardly extravagant, but she found that all her needs were comfortably met.

Yet all too often, the price of material freedom seemed very dear.

That year, Rosa was visiting her friends, the Passy family, at their home in Gisors in Normandy when she found herself impelled to encounter the renowned brothers and masters of a merciless pen, Jules and Edmond de Goncourt.

When their mother died in 1848 bequeathing them a respectable fortune, Edmond (who was the same age as Rosa) and his younger brother Jules found that they were able to survive without exerting themselves unduly. Fanatical about aesthetics, they settled into an existence centred on the arts and on scrupulous, often acerbic observation. Obsessive in their attention to detail, fastidious in the order in which they kept their home, the brothers espoused the notion that literature should offer a faithful picture of everyday life. Writing as one, the Goncourts turned their hand to plays and subsequently fiction; all proved unsuccessful. However, in the 1850s, they began publishing a series of social histories which met with a more favourable reception. But by 1851, their attention was primarily absorbed in another interest, one which would become a lifelong project and a compulsion; it was then that they started recording their anecdotal critique and judgements on contemporary society in a journal. Meticulous and scabrous, each of nervous disposition, the diary keepers lived together, worked together and were virtually never seen out in Paris separately. Neither was known to entertain any serious marital prospect. Their approach was precious and their working arrangement unique.[15]

Incorrigibly curious, the brothers' thinly veiled attempts to ferret information out of Rosa instantly put her on her guard. She had no desire to find herself the subject of a novel, so was careful not to betray anything which might be used as material. Rosa formed an immediate dislike of the pair, and the brothers were no more enamoured with her.

'Meeting with Rosa Bonheur at a dinner at the Passys',' read their diary entry for their first counter with the artist. 'She has the head of a little, hunchbacked Polish Jew. She was flanked by her eternal friend Nathalie, who has the head of a worn out Pierrot, an old Deburau, who is missing only a skullcap.'[16] The entry was written on 16 March – Rosa's birthday.

As befitted scrupulous social observers, the brothers were undeterred by Rosa's studied evasiveness. A subsequent encounter the following year at the home of Hippolyte de Villemessant, the press tycoon responsible for *Le Figaro*, provided the occasion to resume their analysis.

'There is nothing womanly about her,' they declared. 'Nothing of the artist in her; nor does she have a man's way of thinking; she talks like all women.' Then came the coup de grace: 'and then, in truth, she wears dresses which are too common.'[17]

Still the brothers felt they had not yet seen enough.

'My friends, the de Goncourt brothers, whom you don't much care for, I believe, are living at present not far from you, and they ask me for a word of introduction to you,' begged Louis Passy in June 1859.[18]

Rosa did not conceal her aversion: 'though I don't at all like to receive the Goncourts, I will do it [...] I know too well the ways of the world, and what I owe myself, to let them perceive my real feelings for them.'[19]

While such unpalatable social duties accumulated, space was inversely telescoping. Rosa's celebrity had reached international proportions. In 1859, the British publication the *Gardeners' Chronicle* had even advertised a plant named after her (a red, variegated perpetual rose), while in the same year, her work was warmly received by viewers across Europe and in the States.[20] Rosa could now see that the art world was by no means confined to the French capital. By the end of 1859, she had reached a pivotal decision: it was time to leave Paris.

ℭ

As France's capital continued to swell and the railway crept further and further out into the provinces, the countryside was assuming new importance in Parisian eyes. The upper classes had long been dividing their year into two parts, the winter being spent in the city and the summer at a country residence. Now, a favourable economic trajectory had taken hold, spawning a leisure-hungry upper and middle class, and what had once been the exclusive privilege of just a small, aristocratic elite was being extended to a wider social bracket. More and more city dwellers were following the upper classes' example and turning towards France's rural suburbs as a fashionable antidote to an increasingly fast-paced city life. Popular guidebooks both informed and encouraged the trend. So established was the summer exodus that already in August 1854, journalist Auguste Villemot could observe in *Le Figaro*: 'Decidedly, everyone is leaving and we are commencing that period where the only people left in Paris are porters and intellectuals.'[21] Though many purses could only stretch to a day trip, for some, a rented estate – or even a holiday home – in one of the quaint little villages around Paris became an achievable dream. It was now the conviction of fashionable society that a second home was simply the only way to savour the uncomplicated charms of the countryside.

Conforming with the voguish elite had never been Rosa's aspiration. But she yearned for somewhere she could work and breathe and live, a place where she would not be disturbed without warning, scrutinised without sensitivity or criticised without remorse. In short, Rosa longed for somewhere she could be herself.

Yet at the same time, the accessibility of Paris remained imperative. It was an ambitious request. But early in 1859, Rosa's wish was granted.

cߧ

Comte Louis Albert Marie de la Forest d'Armaillé was of noble descent. His résumé included roles as an officer in the cavalry and administrator for the Compagnie du Chemin de fer d'Orléans. He was also a passionate art connoisseur, while his wife Marie Céléstine Amélie de Ségur gravitated towards literary pursuits. A good friend of Rosa's, it was the Comte d'Armaillé, the artist later told people, who having learned of her desire to escape Paris, came to her one day with exciting news: he believed he had found her the perfect property.[22]

The Comte d'Armaillé's father-in-law lived in the village of Thomery on the eastern edge of the Forest of Fontainebleau, southeast of Paris. And that spring, an advertisement had appeared in the Paris press:

'Country house known as the Château of By, near the Forest of Fontainebleau,' read the notice in *La Presse*. 'Parkland of 4 hectares. Price, 60,000 francs.'[23] The Comte d'Armaillé was well placed to provide Rosa with further details.[24]

Thomery was a pretty area. The *Indicateur Officiel des environs de Paris* recorded only 800 residents to be living in the village and surrounding hamlets in 1859, making it one of Paris's smaller outlying communities. Notwithstanding, Thomery's economy was flourishing and by the end of the 1850s, its grapes had become world-famous.

'This little village, which has an Italian feel, is well worth visiting,' urged the *Indicateur Officiel des environs de Paris*, 'not only because it produces the best dessert grapes in the world, which are known by the name of Chasselas de Fontainebleau, but also to see the vines with which the houses are covered.'[25]

Much had been written about the bountiful grape harvest and the Forest of Fontainebleau. In addition, Thomery had been made accessible by train in 1849 and passengers who took the line run by the Chemin de fer de Lyon had little more than 70 km to travel before they reached their destination. The journey took approximately two hours at the end of the 1850s, less than 90 minutes if the traveller were fortunate enough to catch an express. Then, stepping off the train onto the short platform, a visitor could be forgiven for thinking they had been transported into a fairy tale; the train line ran right into the forest and with the absence of virtually any landmark besides trees, the spot felt both timeless and fantastical. If Rosa sought seclusion with access to Paris, there could hardly be a better location.[26]

A short carriage ride from the station was the Château de By.

The house itself was dramatic. Set behind a tall metal fence, the whole property exuded a grand, somewhat austere air of regal importance. Though advertised as a château, 'stately manor house' would have been a more accurate description. The ground floor comprised an entranceway, a vestibule, an expansive sitting room, a bathroom, a dining room, an office and a kitchen. On the first floor were six bedrooms, while the second floor boasted further bedrooms and a billiard room. With its great windows, high ceilings and wall space, the billiard room could immediately be repurposed as a workspace. It benefited from an enormous fireplace, so Rosa would be able to paint there when the thick stone walls transferred the icy chill of winter from outside.

In an adjoining wing was further accommodation. There were lofts, a shelter for carriages, stables and a tack room, while outside, Rosa found an orangery, an orchard and a wood store. Water was pumped directly to the house from a well and from the main courtyard, a person could admire banks, bushes and flowers. The house came with additional plots, woodland, vegetable patches and, if Rosa wished, all the furniture.

Rosa was instantly beguiled. Sixty thousand francs were being asked; she offered 50,000 francs, to include the furniture. Her proposal was accepted. On 9 August 1859, accompanied by two old friends from the Luxembourg quarter, the financial controller Léon Augustin Chazel and the architect Louis Jules Saulnier, Rosa signed for the property.[27]

The Château de By, Thomery.
Image courtesy of the Archives Départementales de Seine-et-Marne, cote AD 772 Fi 7956

That Mme and Nathalie Micas would join her, Rosa had taken for granted. But fiercely proud, Mme Micas refused to move into the château unless permitted the dignity of paying rent. Though incredulous, Rosa respected her wish. However, she insisted on a lease which would run until the old woman's death, after which point the agreement would automatically transfer to Nathalie. Rosa was anxious to safeguard their bond.

The details finalised, Rosa prepared to move as soon as possible. She decided to retain her domestic help, the 21-year-old Céline, who had lately married a young man named Étienne Rey, to whom Rosa gladly offered the position of coachman. Keeping a pied-à-terre in Paris at number 7, Rue Gay-Lussac and subletting her studio in the Rue d'Assas, she arranged for her animals, her affairs and her art materials to be transported to Fontainebleau.[28]

Quite how daily life would change and her art be affected, Rosa could not yet say. But one thing was certain: a new chapter of her life was beginning. All that remained was to discover what adventures lay before her.

14

•••

Pure Invention

Rosa was in raptures over her new home – and she had not been resident long before By's rich character began to reveal itself.

With parts dating back to the 1400s, the building was steeped in history. Thomery lore held that the royal beekeeper, a man named M. Bigre, had been lodged there in the 15th century. Over time, his name had evolved into By and was subsequently conferred on the property. The pertinence of this connection struck Rosa when, not long after she had moved in, she was plagued with an infestation of bees. In the 18th century, the property had passed from Jean-Maximilien Leleu and his wife Anne (who had a chapel built on the grounds) into the hands of one of the Leleu nephews, then the grandmother of Louis Jules Michel Fabre, from whom Rosa had purchased her new home.[1]

Once installed, Rosa was impatient to begin modifications. She had already envisaged a brand-new, light and spacious studio, for which purpose she planned to have the wing of the house augmented. The workspace would be built above the gardener's accommodation, next to the carriage port. Rosa approached her architect friend, Jules Saulnier, to design the extension. However, to her frustration, she had to wait just a little longer, legal intricacies meaning that full ownership would not commence until the following year.

But this was a minor setback. Rosa was blissfully happy. She was immediately captivated by the ancient beauty of the surrounding Forest of Fontainebleau. Like an adolescent falling in love for the very first time, as she discovered all the walks and drives, she allowed the woods to claim more and more of her heart. In the restless hubbub of Paris, this was exactly what she had thirsted for. The forest brought her a profound sense of peace.

'One of Rosa Bonheur's greatest delights was to walk through the Fontainebleau Forest,' remembered the dramatist and librettist Henri Cain, grandson of her old friend Pierre-Jules Mêne. 'She would start out early in the morning and would stop to sketch when she noticed a spot which took her fancy because of the coloration.'[2]

'Walking and driving among the trees was an endless source of delight to her,' confirmed Rosa's cousin, Mme Lagrolet. 'It always seemed to put her in a sunny mood.'[3]

Gradually, Rosa came to know every species of tree – the oaks, the beeches, the elm – and as time passed, she grew intimately acquainted with each and every corner of the forest. It was here that she was at her happiest. Fontainebleau became as vital to her as air and water – and art.

Rosa Bonheur's atelier at By, Thomery.
Image courtesy of the Archives Départementales de Seine-et-Marne, cote AD 772 Fi 16599

With Mme Micas and Nathalie running the kitchen and tending to the animals, Rosa could divide her time between art and nature. And with letters arriving buzzing with news from Paris, she scarcely noticed any disadvantage to her change of situation. Besides, she could now invite visitors of her choosing, and crucially, only when it suited her.

'You must come out to see me some Sunday, otherwise you are no friends of mine,' she threatened Mme Mêne back in Paris. 'If the weather is good, we will go a-fishing or for a drive in Fontainebleau. We will try and have a good time and I'll do my best to give you one or two rabbits shot by my own hand.'[4]

Hunting had now become a favourite pastime. Rosa applied for a permit to shoot rabbits in Fontainebleau and was irked when it was not immediately granted.

'Rosa Bonheur had a passion for shooting,' remembered Juliette's son Hippolyte. Rosa's student Mlle Keller could add that she was 'a remarkably good shot', while another friend affirmed that she was regarded locally as 'the Diana of Fontainebleau'.[5]

Indeed, Rosa's enthusiasm for hunting betrayed one of the curious discrepancies of her character, for while she could care for an animal as though it were the child she had never had, she derived immeasurable pleasure from hunting and relished sitting down to a table quaking with joints of meat and game. Equally, if an animal were sick or injured, she adopted a stoical approach.

'When she saw them suffer or getting old, she had them killed,' clarified her friend the Romanian Prince Georges Stirbey.[6]

Rosa would not prolong a creature's suffering, nor would she keep an animal if it had exhausted its useful life. Thus she could write to M. Verdier:

'Could you find me a small dog, male or female, for coursing rabbits? My dogs are no good and I want to get rid of them.'[7]

As Rosa gradually acclimatised to her living quarters, news from outside kept her updated. In July 1860, Juliette had given birth to another son, whom she named René. Rosa's letters reflected a growing affection for her nephews, but she nonetheless felt increasingly rooted to By. There, she could work and inhale the intoxicating perfume of nature. Rosa gladly voiced her support for the cause championed by military veteran Claude François Denecourt, whose conviction that Fontainebleau should be seen as a living museum of ecological and artistic import had prompted him to publish guides and lay out pathways for visitors.[8] Trips back to Paris were a professional necessity, but Rosa had no desire to resume permanent residency in the capital. During the course of 1860, she decided to renounce her directorship of the drawing school. Rosa became emeritus, while Juliette agreed to uphold the Bonheur presence and Mme Marandon de Montyel was named the new director.[9]

The sense of well-being and contentment Rosa derived from By did not prevent occasional bouts of despondency with her new dominion. Nor were her episodes of melancholy eliminated when she left Paris.

'You know how often I get sick of everything, even while animated with the best intentions,' Rosa disencumbered herself to Juliette in 1861, when the business of hiring domestic staff was beginning to exasperate her. 'You know, too, that my temper is none of the best,' she admitted, continuing: 'I am really sick at heart in my little kingdom. How much sovereigns are to be pitied! [...] You haven't much luxury; but, at least, you are happy.'[10]

But Rosa knew her own temperament well enough to be able to assure her sister: 'Bah! my dear Juju; the fit will pass.'[11] And it did. Rosa never seriously entertained reappropriating her status as a Parisienne.

Rosa recognised how easy it was to lose one's footing in the capital, where the constant buzz of activity could distort a person's view. Living at By afforded her the distance to indulge her natural tendency towards philosophising, and with gossip filtering back from the capital, there was ample material to which she could apply it.

'I hear that simpleton, M. Gérôme, has nearly got himself winged for the sake of a light-o'-love,' Rosa exclaimed to the Mênes in 1861.[12] In fact, the academic artist had been seriously injured in a duel fought against the Belgian picture dealer, Arthur Stevens. People whispered

Nathalie Micas and Rosa Bonheur, c. 1860.
Collection Atelier Rosa Bonheur

that there had been turbulence between Gérôme and Stevens's wife, Mathilde, an important cultural figure who wrote art criticism and was known for her scathing reviews. As to the precise nature of the provocation, the papers remained elusive, all the parties having agreed to keep the details secret. But Rosa's letter hinted at a complex situation. 'It would have been a fine thing if he had deprived the arts of one of its first champions. Happily he is all right again. May it be a lesson to him and may he in future prefer paintings to women. It's much wiser and less deceitful.'[13]

Rosa was happy to be able to hold Paris and all its foibles at arm's length. She was among the celebrants when, in 1861, Emperor Napoleon III answered the appeal of Théodore Rousseau by decreeing

that part of the Forest of Fontainebleau should become a nature preserve. Between Fontainebleau and Paris, there was no contest in Rosa's
heart.[14]

'You couldn't get her to come to Paris if she was in the midst of a
study,' observed Henri Cain.[15]

'What bored her most was going to Paris,' seconded one of her
new neighbours, M. Grivot, 'for it meant the discarding of trousers,
smock, and felt hat, as well as the putting away of cigarettes, which
she constantly smoked.'[16]

Rosa could now wait for Paris to come to her. She had the where-
withal to employ staff, not to mention accommodation to lodge them.
And with Nathalie and Mme Micas overseeing the housekeeping
and commandeering the kitchen, By was ripe for receiving carefully
selected guests. Weekends were frequently given to lunching with
friends or family.

'We are counting on you for Saturday evening,' Rosa instructed
Juliette in a letter dated 1861. 'I say we, because Mother Soup
[Mme Micas] is grieved to the soul when she prepares a meal and
the visitor does not turn up. On the other hand, she's in a rage when
the visitor does not announce his arrival beforehand, considering it a
dishonour to have nothing but cheese to offer in a house that respects
itself.'[17]

The painter Paul Chardin, whose acquaintance Rosa had made at
the Passys' in Gisors and whom she affectionately called her *rapin* or
'art student', remembered the meals to which he was invited at By. He
knew always to expect a hearty welcome.

'Rest assured of how happy the general will be to greet her Rapin
as warmly as can be whenever he wishes to come,' Rosa had told him
early on in their relationship, using the soubriquets it would henceforward amuse her to employ.[18] 'The general will not be formal,' she
assured him, and in another letter: 'Please come as often as you like
to show me your studies and don't ever worry about disturbing me.'[19]

'Mme Micas especially prided herself on her cooking and you had
to be careful never to ruffle her in this domain,' Chardin recalled.[20]

On one occasion when he arrived to dine, his appetite had been roused by a long ride on horseback, and he unwisely made his hunger known. When the main course appeared, he instantly regretted his declaration.

'Just before the fish was brought in, my nostrils were assailed by a sickly odour, and in proportion as it approached the table my stomach began to rise.'[21]

His hasty volte-face visibly offended Mme Micas.

'The good lady's menus sometimes comprised the most unusual mixtures,' Chardin explained. When one day pigeon appeared on a dish of sorrel, the young painter imprudently expressed surprise at the pairing. The big-bosomed and matronly Mme Micas peered over her spectacles at him with an expression which hovered between disdain and disbelief.[22]

'I, sir, have never seen pigeons served otherwise than on sorrel.'

While her mother attended to By's culinary offerings, Nathalie was incubating projects of her own. Now in her mid-30s, Nathalie's eccentricity showed no signs of abating, nor was her imagination any less vivid. She remained energetic, game and utterly confident in her diverse abilities. Nathalie persisted with her painting and also claimed to possess elementary medical knowledge. If one of the animals at By fell ill, Nathalie was immediately on the scene with her supply of medicines and instruments. Perfectly sanguine, she set to work with unwavering faith that she could restore the creature to health. Nor did she consider human medicine beyond her remit, and if one of the locals incurred an injury, Nathalie appeared with her first-aid kit and a firm resolve to use it.

But amateur paramedics were just one string to Nathalie's many-stranded bow. Fascinated by gadgets and machinery, she amused herself devising assorted inventions. Not long after Rosa purchased By, Nathalie's attention became absorbed with a project especially close to her heart. She had drawn up plans for a railway brake which she was convinced would save lives. All she needed were a few successful trials and a well-placed investor.

From the very first, Nathalie encountered difficulties. In her efforts to find a company willing to construct the brake, she turned to the Belgian company, the Société du Chemin de fer de l'Entre-Sambre-et-Meuse.

The invention itself was remarkably simple, but, Nathalie insisted, supremely effective. When a lever was operated, a wedge moved into contact with each carriage wheel, thus slowing and ultimately stopping the vehicle. A small tramway with platform cars was erected outside the house. And there, the trials of the invention could commence.

As soon as a prototype was ready, Nathalie appealed to the Compagnie des Chemins de fer de Paris à Lyon et à la Méditerranée to send one of their engineers to endorse her invention and was elated when her invitation was accepted. In a frenzy of excitement, she penned a letter to the Mênes:

'How the thing will go off, I cannot say [...] As I don't want my friends to run the risk of a disappointment, I haven't asked them to come and see the first experiments.'[23]

On Wednesday 23 July 1862, the nervously awaited visitation took place. The official was eagerly welcomed and ushered outside to view the contraption. To Nathalie's delight, the brake performed perfectly and even the engineer had to agree that the experiment had been a success.

The Micas brake.

Collection Atelier Rosa Bonheur

'But,' he warned in his report, 'I do not think that it should be concluded therefrom that in actual practice the result will be the same [...] If the Micas brake were applied to a real train, the experiment would simply bring out its mechanical defects, it cost and its problematical resistance.'[24]

Nathalie was disappointed but not defeated. Determined that her friends should witness her endeavour, the inventor summoned a group of human guinea pigs to By. Mme Mêne, Mme Cain and one or two others were instructed to board the tram cars. Once the passengers were settled one behind the other, the train began its descent down the hill. Onlookers watched with bated breath as the convoy picked up speed, going faster and faster. The bottom of the track approached – and gradually, a ghastly realisation hit the spectators: the train was not going to stop.

Whether it worked too suddenly or not at all was unclear. But Rosa's nephew Hippolyte remembered that all at once, half a dozen ladies were thrown into the air, before landing on the grass, offering the spectators 'a copious display of white nether garments'.[25]

Nathalie considered the episode unfortunate but not fatal to her project. Afterwards, she wrote to useful contacts, called in favours and even hoped that Rosa might be able to use her Saint-Simonian connections to gain her support. But Rosa's visit to the financier, Émile Pereire, proved unsuccessful.

'They didn't take the trouble to answer her request,' Nathalie fumed bitterly in a letter to Antoine Passy, 'though they seemed happy to see her again, these people who drew her father into Saint-Simonianism.'[26]

Early in 1863, a report from the Société du Chemin de fer de l'Entre-Sambre-et-Meuse confirming that further trials had proved 'very satisfactory' went some way to buoying Nathalie spirits. She continued to tinker with her invention, while Rosa, who found her absurdity endearing, offered constant support. Nathalie's determination was inspiring and if nothing else, her outlandish experiments provided Rosa with a novel focus to break her relentless work schedule.

Such interludes were invaluable. The year 1863 also brought hard work and challenges. Auguste's wife had given birth to their first son early in 1861, and in 1863, the toddler Raymond fell worryingly ill. Rosa had intended to take her brother to Scotland, but the infant's illness forced her to abort her plans. Then between Tedesco and Gambart contacting her incessantly with new commissions, and shows promoting her work worldwide, Rosa's timetable was full, despite her continued abstention from the Paris Salon.[27]

'Yesterday was the opening day at the Salon,' she wrote to Juliette on 2 May 1864, 'and yet here I am in By! My word! how I have stuck to my work!'[28]

At long last, Rosa had broken free of Paris's vice-like grip. But notwithstanding her seclusion, she still managed to accommodate a trip to Belgium in May that year. She confided her project with M. Mène:

'I am going to accompany Nathalie to Belgium to see about her affair. She is not well and I can't let her go alone. If you see any of my family, say nothing about my going to Brussels, for, as you know, I am always between two stools.'[29]

The friction between the Micases and the Bonheurs showed no signs of easing. Rosa could never fully relax and talk freely when discussing either party with the other. Still, that did not prevent her inviting family members to By.

One day, Rosa's brother-in-law Hippolyte had joined her for lunch. After the meal, the pair settled themselves into the studio to smoke their cigarettes, Rosa at ease in her painting smock.

Presently, the unmistakable sound of bells and horses' hooves could be heard outside. As the noise grew louder, Rosa realised that the thing she disliked most, an unexpected visitor, was about to disturb their leisure. Certain it could be no one she wished to see, she urged Hippolyte to hurry to Félicité, the maid, so that she would know to instruct the intruder that the mistress was out.

But before he could do so, the studio door was flung open, and in burst Rosa's servant Olive in a state of breathless urgency.

'Mademoiselle, Mademoiselle,' she gasped, 'it's the Court, the Empress!'[30]

15

All That Glitters

With no time to think, Rosa and Hippolyte sprang from their seats. Empress Eugénie was perhaps the foremost woman in France. Her fashion sense was imitated, her decoration style copied and her taste widely proclaimed to be the most elegant in all of Paris. Since her marriage to Louis-Napoleon in 1853, Eugénie had been living out her life on the Imperial stage, where behaviour, customs and clothing were all strictly codified. And now, Rosa was about to meet her Imperial Majesty – dressed in a peasant's smock and reeking of tobacco, the Empress's pet hate.[1]

Rosa's instant reflex was to tear off her blue painting overall. She pulled it hastily over her head, but there it got stuck. With mounting panic and unable to see for fabric, Rosa battled to extricate herself, thrashing blindly this way and that. Footsteps approached. Frantically, Rosa spun round, pulling and tugging, and Hippolyte rushed to her aid. All at once, Rosa's head popped through the neck hole, and the smock was cast aside. She grabbed an indoor jacket – and seconds later, the door opened. The Empress wafted into the room in an emanation of skirts and stateliness and surrounded by an entourage of some twelve male and female courtiers.

Empress Eugénie was a perplexing figure. With clear blue eyes, even features and a porcelain-white complexion, the Spanish daughter of Count and Countess Montijo was hailed as a beauty. She wore her red-brown hair centre-parted in a neat chignon and invariably appeared with her already tiny waist accentuated by an enormous crinoline, the dress style she had popularised in the mid-1850s (to the distaste of many aesthetes and health professionals).[2]

'She was distinguished-looking, though she had a very pronounced foreign air,' recalled Louis-Napoleon's cousin, the Princess Mathilde. 'She was also free in manner, with a decisive tone in conversation, full of spirit, like a woman well accustomed to homage from men.'[3]

But for all her dignity and self-assured mien, the Empress had her enemies. The Royal Bonapartists (including Princess Mathilde herself) largely considered the Bonaparte–Montijo union to be a disastrous alliance, and a vicious smear campaign had preceded Eugénie's marriage to Napoleon. Sounds of discontent in the provinces had left no doubt: the people of France would have preferred a princess, or at the very least, a Frenchwoman of some standing. For many, Eugénie would always be the Spanish intruder. Those close to her could vouch for her pain.

'I who used to be so obsessed with my liberty am in chains for the rest of my life: never by myself, never free, amid all that court etiquette, of which I'm going to be the principal victim,' the new Empress opened her heart to her sister.[4]

Still, however, Emperor Napoleon had assured his people that with Eugénie would return something of the morality and goodness embodied by Empress Josephine. And when Eugénie was offered an exquisite diamond necklace as a wedding gift from the municipality, she endeared Parisians to her by refusing the jewellery and asking instead for the money to be donated to a girls' orphanage.[5] Added to which, in 1856, she had finally provided France with a Bonaparte successor, a baby boy, who was duly named Napoléon Eugène Louis Jean Joseph.

Having recovered her composure sufficiently, Rosa now greeted her guest with due reverence, bringing out for her Imperial Majesty's contemplation a selection of sketches and drawings.

Examining the pieces, Eugénie seemed pleased. Turning her attention to the artist, she enquired: would Mlle Bonheur paint a picture for her? Rosa was staggered but quickly assented.

Rosa's sense of pride swelled still further when the Empress expressed admiration for Auguste's paintings and Isidore's fine craftsmanship.

Finally, the Imperial party announced that it was time to leave, and Rosa accompanied the Empress out to her carriage. Before turning to board the vehicle, Eugénie held out her hand. Instinctively, Rosa drew it to her lips.

'Thereupon,' Rosa reported the next day in a letter to Auguste and Juliette, 'with the greatest of kindness, this sovereign, whose simplicity and affability are her distinction, did me the honour to embrace me.'[6]

Before the Empress's carriage pulled away, she issued an invitation, too: Rosa should come and dine at the palace in Fontainebleau. Furthermore, she should prepare herself for a visit from the Emperor. Of one thing, Rosa was adamant: this time, prepared she would be.

Frédéric Théodore Lix (after Auguste Victor Deroy), *Her Majesty the Empress Visiting Mademoiselle Rosa Bonheur in her Studio in Thomery*, 1865, engraving on wood, 16 x 22 cm.
The Picture Art Collection/Alamy Stock Photo

☙

Throughout the following week, Rosa waited in expectantly. The Emperor did not arrive. And as the days passed and still the Imperial carriage did not appear, Rosa began to grow restive. Enforced confinement sat ill with her temperament.

'I have been cooped up all this while, and you know how little I like to be tethered,' she vented to Juliette.[7]

And imprisonment was not the only hardship inflicted. 'I have to endure the trying on of a dress with a train and to be on the alert lest I am surprised in trousers and blouse,' Rosa grumbled.[8]

As a woman, Rosa's approach to fashion was notoriously atypical. 'She cared nothing about jewels and would have given all the finery in the world for an animal that she wanted,' affirmed her stepbrother and brother-in-law, Hippolyte.[9] However, examining her wardrobe more closely, the keen-eyed observer would find jackets and capes neatly finished with rich gold brocade, ornate buttons and carefully stitched lining; in her own way, Rosa was acutely self-aware. But she knew how far her everyday attire diverged from the gendered norm. Sensitive to the comedy inherent in daily life and never afraid to tell a joke against herself, she continued her letter to Juliette: 'You can imagine, my rogue of a sister, how fine I must be in harness. Tell Tatan that her niece is even pretty! And if I go to court, I am likely to take the Emperor's fancy!'[10]

At long last, the tension was broken when Rosa received, not a visit, but a formal summons to the palace at Fontainebleau. This would be the grandest reception she had ever attended.

☙

The Château de Fontainebleau was an awe-inspiring monument. Dating from the Middle Ages, the castle had firmly established itself as a favourite residence of the kings of France on account of its well-stocked hunting ground. As monarchs succeeded each other, the building had been extended and elaborated, with Henry IV making the most significant alterations in the 1600s when pavilions, a new courtyard, galleries and an indoor tennis court were constructed and the park and gardens generously planted. What was once merely a fortified castle had now become a magnificent exercise in architectural ostentation, a palace which epitomised the sense of pomp and ceremony and bygone splendour that Napoleon III sought to resurrect.[11]

Rosa now had to draw on everything she had heard or read about the protocol observed at court. It was common knowledge that guests summoned to the Tuileries were told to arrive in private carriages, not the small, single horse-drawn hired cabs.[12] On the day of the reception, a specially appointed vehicle was sent to collect Rosa.

Stepping down from the carriage, Rosa beheld the resplendent palace before her. It was difficult for a guest not to be overcome with trepidation. Rosa approached the main entrance, but her appearance clearly failed to indicate that she had arrived in the capacity of a guest. She was redirected to another entrance, where she was turned away again. It took a third, closer inspection of her invitation and the chivalrous intervention of the senator and fellow Bordelais, Jean-François Mocquard, for Rosa to finally be allowed to pass.[13]

Describing the court of Napoleon III, the Emperor's American dentist Dr Thomas W. Evans affirmed it to be 'less rigid in its etiquette than most European courts, and at the same time more splendid.'[14] But that splendour nonetheless fostered an ambience far grander than anything Rosa had experienced to date. Napoleon III had reinstated knee breeches and court dress, male guests knew to wear evening attire when they dined, household staff appeared in uniform, and at formal dinners, a footman would stand behind each chair while meals were served on gilt silver and fine Sèvres porcelain. Court life under the Second Empire may have been less prim, but for a newcomer, such decadence was profoundly intimidating.[15]

The Galerie Francis I to which Rosa was led was no less daunting. What had originally been a high-ceilinged passageway had been absorbed into the private apartments of Francis I in the 1500s. Rich,

golden and finished with frescoes and stucco in a fine example of
Renaissance decorative finesse, the room was already full of well-heeled
guests when Rosa entered.

She had eventually settled on a black velvet dress with gold buttons and narrow sleeves – an outfit indistinguishable from her usual
attire and markedly different from the hooped crinoline skirts worn
by the fashion-conscious ladies at court. Such flagrant disregard for
clothing trends was apt to make a neophyte the attention of all eyes
– and one of the first unashamed stares Rosa attracted belonged to
Mme de Metternich, wife of the Austrian ambassador and a renowned
member of the Imperial court.[16]

Scrawny with dull brown hair, dark, bulging eyes and a nose and
mouth which looked just a little too big for her face, the Viennese-born
Pauline de Metternich may not have been the prettiest lady at court,
but she was undoubtedly the most eccentric. She had married her
half-uncle, Prince Richard von Metternich, in 1856, and since her
arrival at the French court at the end of the 1850s, she had galvanised
her reputation as a socialite, patron of the arts and one of the most
determined gossips who had ever set foot in the Tuileries. Princess
Pauline drank, smoked and swore, while her passion for music had
been known to inspire impromptu renditions of rather vulgar songs.
Pauline had acquired the curious soubriquet of Cocoa Monkey. Still,
outfitted as she was by the acclaimed couturier Charles Worth, she
insisted that she had to be 'the best dressed monkey in Paris'.[17] Despite
her unorthodox manner, Pauline was fiercely intelligent. She and the
Empress had become desperately fond of each other.[18]

Rosa later remembered that not one of the group huddled
around Mme de Metternich paid her the least bit of attention. She
took a seat on her own. But before long, one of the young men of
Mme de Metternich's entourage approached her. Bowing, he explained
that he had come to offer some friendly advice, since Mlle Bonheur
was no doubt unfamiliar with court etiquette. In a few moments, the
Emperor and Empress would enter the room – and on no account
should Rosa rise. Rather, she should remain seated until told otherwise.

Sensing a spiteful trick designed to humiliate her, Rosa politely refused. Crestfallen, the man returned to his comrades to report that their ruse had been guessed.[19]

At last, the sovereigns arrived. (Everyone rose to their feet.) Once Rosa had been formally presented, she was stunned when the Emperor gave her his arm and insisted that she sat next to him during lunch. Whatever the criticisms commonly laid at the Emperor Napoleon's feet, Rosa found him to be courteous, attentive and interested.

A determined gastronome, Rosa had been especially looking forward to a delectable spread, and felt rather disillusioned when she was served an egg which was far from fresh. But this was a trifling complaint.

After the meal, Eugénie invited Rosa to join her aboard a little rowing boat on the serene, mirror-like surface of the Carp Pool and at the end of the ride, the Prince Imperial was introduced.

When his mother explained that Mlle Bonheur owned a menagerie, the eight-year-old Prince begged to see it, so before she left the Château de Fontainebleau, Rosa assured his Imperial Highness that he would be welcome to come whenever he chose.

The Prince was accordingly brought to By a few days later. Rosa had been described as a woman who dressed as a man, and finding such a social anomaly perfectly marvellous, the Prince was disappointed to see that she had changed into a skirt. Learning of the child's dashed hope, Rosa made sure to wear trousers the next time they met.

For a woman reluctant to leave her workspace, it was a relief to have concluded the episode at Fontainebleau. The remainder of the year was given to work and punctuated with less stately social exchanges.

In November, Rosa was able to award one of her prize students, Mlle Keller, her diploma.[20] More sobering was the news that the Bonheurs' old friend Justin Mathieu had passed away, a loss which placed even more weight on Rosa's duty as a godmother to Mathieu's daughter. Still, visits from friends and family brought relief at such times of trauma. During one more jovial evening spent by the fireside in the company of Paul Chardin, Rosa had the idea of designing a cravat for their friend Antoine Passy. They began that night, with Isidore and Nathalie joining in on subsequent evenings, adding to various corners of a section of fabric amusing pictures of themselves engaged in characteristic activities.[21]

But despite such frolics, neither home life nor business always ran smoothly.

That February, Rosa found herself in a legal dispute, when her refusal to supply a picture ordered in 1860 spurred the Lyon-based collector M. Pourchet to take her to court. Rosa would never allow a painting to leave the studio until she felt entirely happy with the outcome, and she could be obstinate when she had decided a work fell short of perfection. Pourchet's case resulted in her being issued a fine, which she grudgingly paid, complaining bitterly about the injustice. Notwithstanding, she saw no need to review her decision to withhold the canvas.[22]

Even the very closest personal relationships brought their trials. Rosa could be grouchy and was prone to mood swings, while Nathalie was highly strung – and both women were passionate characters. Sometimes their bickering intensified and a row would erupt, whereupon Mme Micas naturally sided with her daughter. At such times, Rosa felt the absence of her siblings most keenly.

'You may imagine how I long for a little diversion, and the sight of a smiling face like yours, little Sis,' Rosa opened up in a letter to Juliette. 'Now, on Monday, I think of going over to meet you all, including Auguste and the children [...] As Tatan will be one of us, I beg Mammy to provide at my expense a truffled foul, together with a Quillé cake.'[23]

Auguste had lately established his family in the commune of Magny-les-Hameaux, south-west of Paris. The former presbytery he had acquired had previously been owned by the painter Robert-Fleury and subsequently by the *animalier* Jacques Raymond Brascassat, to whom Rosa had often been compared. The Bonheur children were all settling in their respective corners of northern France, Juliette and Auguste with growing families. Independence felt more like isolation when storms raged at home.[24]

Rosa Bonheur and her siblings,
André-Adolphe-Eugène Disdéri, c. 1860–1870.

Photo © RMN-Grand Palais (Musée
d'Orsay)/Hervé Lewandowski

Nonetheless, Rosa and Nathalie usually managed to resolve their differences and by the summer of 1865, a more hospitable atmosphere had re-established itself at By. That stability was now needed; the following months brought a disorientating chain of events.

☙

Empress Eugénie's interest had firmly fixed Rosa as the artist of the moment; now, *le tout Paris* wanted to say that they had visited Mlle Bonheur. Even Mme de Metternich presented herself at By on one occasion, giving Rosa the chance to exact revenge for the slight issued at Fontainebleau. When the ambassador's wife requested a canvas she particularly coveted, Rosa refused and instructed her to address her interest to Gambart or Tedesco – just like everyone else. Mme de Metternich never returned.[25]

That May, Rosa also received a visit from the politician Prince Lucien Murat, son of Napoleon Bonaparte's sister Caroline, accompanied by his American-born wife, also called Caroline.

The obese cousin of Emperor Napoleon III had ruffled feathers more than once in the Imperial nest by proclaiming his rights to the throne of Naples. But arriving at By, he demonstrated his passion for the arts and with his wife's Scottish heritage, there were ample topics of conversation. Rosa found them most agreeable.

'They were nicer than ever,' she wrote to Juliette while she was playing hostess to their stepmother and her nephew, René. 'I promised to go and see them at the castle. The Prince is intending to lend me some very handsome hunting hounds.'[26]

The visitation provided a valuable refresher on royal protocol; just a few weeks later, Rosa was to receive a priceless gift – and it was delivered by a very eminent messenger.

Early in June, word reached Rosa that the Empress Eugénie might call on her again. With Napoleon currently on tour in Algeria, Eugénie had been appointed regent and given complete power (to the dismay of many statesmen). A female regent could only be of benefit to women working in creative professions. Hippolyte Peyrol maintained that Rosa was advised the mooted visit would take place imminently, since the Empress planned to come to Fontainebleau to meet her husband when he returned from his tour. The whole household was immediately thrown into a frenzy as they readied themselves to receive their illustrious guest.[27]

There was no way of predicting precisely when the Empress would arrive, but Nathalie judged it as well to be prepared, so she called for a bath to be filled. While Rosa busied herself in the studio next door, Nathalie unbuttoned her bodice, stripped off her skirts and discarded her undergarments before lowering herself into the water.

And at that very moment, the sound of carriage wheels and horses' hooves could be heard on the gravel outside. The alarmed face of a servant appeared at the studio door: the Empress was here.

Panicking, Nathalie hoisted herself to her feet, scrambled out of the bath, and dripping with water, dived for clothing.

She appeared 'with a slipper on one foot and a buskin on the other', Rosa reported gleefully to Paul Chardin, struggling to remain solemn as she reasoned: 'In moments of embarrassment, it is a case of putting on whatever is handy. A white dressing-gown, together with a feather-trimmed hat, completed her attire in this instance!'[28]

The Empress and a swarm of courtiers swept into the studio. Greetings were paid, work admired and compliments offered. Then the Empress did something unexpected: taking a little box, she opened it to reveal a glinting, golden cross with a red ribbon attached. Eugénie explained the purpose for her visit: Mlle Rosa Bonheur was to be awarded the title of Chevalier de la Légion d'Honneur, the first level of the prestigious order created by Napoleon Bonaparte in 1802 and awarded for military or civil merit.

It was a historic moment; no woman had ever been made Chevalier de la Légion d'Honneur for the arts.

Taking the cross from its box and a pin from one of her entourage, the Empress leaned forward to attach it to the disbelieving Rosa's bodice.

As Eugénie spoke, explaining the decision and bestowing congratulations, one powerful phrase particularly struck Rosa: 'Genius has no sex.'[29] Rosa had encountered that sentence before; it had been the closing line to Eugène de Mirecourt's 1856 biography of her. It was also de Mirecourt who had issued another call: 'nuns and sutlers are decorated with the Légion d'Honneur: why should women artists be denied the same recompense? [...] May the powers that be think on and act consistently.'[30] Apparently they had. The Empress had consummated de Mirecourt's prophetic statement.

On 11 June 1865, an announcement appeared on the front page of *Le Moniteur Universel*: 'According to the proposal of the Minister of the Imperial House and of Fine Arts it has been decreed that the decoration of Chevalier de la Légion d'Honneur should be conferred upon Mlle Rosa Bonheur, painter of landscapes and animals.' It was signed Eugénie, Empress Regent.[31]

'She is the first female artist to have been thus decorated,' enthused the *Journal des Arts*.[32] 'Until now, women *artistes* have not been called on to partake in the Légion d'Honneur,' *Le Monde Illustré* reminded its readers. 'Only a few women, nuns, like Sister Marthe [a nun who helped prisoners during the Revolution and the 1814 campaign], and a camp follower like Breton-Double [a courageous voluntary female soldier] have been made an exception.'[33]

'It fell to a sovereign to crown a sovereign,' triumphed D'Aubarède in the publication *La Salle à Manger*, 'it fell to a woman to elevate a woman in this way, a woman who works and thinks like a man.'[34]

Rosa's decoration marked a turning point in the history of gender equality. She was now well placed to offer counsel to the younger generation.

'One does not come into the world, my child, solely for one's own pleasure,' Rosa sermoned the nine-year-old Georges Cain, Pierre-Jules Mêne's grandson, later that month. 'You will find that out when you are big.'[35]

Letters of congratulations began arriving at By by the sack load. One was even signed the Mayor of Bordeaux. And that summer's excitement was far from over.

In the middle of August, Rosa learned that she had also been awarded the Imperial Order of San Carlos of Mexico, while not long after receiving her title of Chevalier de la Légion d'Honneur, she was finally granted year-round hunting rights in the Forest of Fontainebleau. 'You see, I have no grounds for complaint on the score of honours,' Rosa joked in a letter to Mêne.[36]

Luminaries and aspirants now all begged an audience with the first woman artist to hold a Légion d'Honneur. At a friend's house, Rosa had made the acquaintance of the emerging composer Georges Bizet (who would make a name for himself posthumously with the opera *Carmen*). She was honoured when the impresario put to music one of Mêne's laudatory little verses ('inspired,' Rosa reminded the recipient of her letter, 'by your kind friendship').[37] The news that Isidore had been awarded a medal at the Salon of 1865 completed her happiness that summer.

By the mid–1860s, Rosa's star was in its zenith. She was at the centre of a turning point in the history of women's rights and was being written about and pictured more than ever before. Thrust into the spotlight, not even Rosa was immune to anxiety over her appearance; one of the official photographs offended her self-esteem to such an extent that she implored Hippolyte to ensure it was not printed.[38]

Amid the honours and attention, Rosa attempted to remain focused on her commissions. However, friends had noticed that a particular woman's name had begun appearing in Rosa's correspondence. The lady in question was spirited, celebrated, and supremely talented – and because of her, Rosa's relationship with Nathalie was careering straight into the eye of a tumultuous storm.

16

Gathering Storms

Mme Caroline Carvalho was a musical sensation. Sturdy with a lustrous mane of thick brown hair and an indisputable air of confidence, at nearly 40, Caroline had Paris's opera-going public in the palm of her hand.

She had begun her musical career studying with her father, François Félix-Miolan, a military bandmaster, oboist and music teacher. After then receiving more formal training at the Conservatoire, she made her stage debut in the late 1840s, and as early as 1849 was commended as possessing 'a rare talent and a sympathetic expression which is rarer still'.[1] In 1850, Caroline was hired by the Opéra Comique, where she enchanted listeners with her clear, soprano tones and her versatility. While appearing there, the singer also formed an attachment to Léon Carvalho, the director of the Théâtre Lyrique. They married in 1853 and by the late 1850s, Caroline Carvalho ruled the stage at the Théâtre Lyrique.[2] Parisian audiences conquered, the singer next set her sights on the British public. Her performance at the Royal Opera House in London in 1860 quickly turned English opera enthusiasts into Carvalho converts. Mme Carvalho was, the *Athenaeum* declared, 'to our judgement, one of the most remarkable vocalists whom we have ever heard'.[3] Now, after nearly twenty years in opera, Caroline knew just the type of composition and arrangement which best showcased her voice – and she was not afraid to tell composers so.

Rosa was passionate about music. Then with their mutual love of

Mozart and Charles-François Gounod and their shared understanding of what it meant to be a woman negotiating the hazardous world of celebrity, Rosa and Caroline Carvalho found common cause. Rosa was always delighted when an invitation to the Mêne-Cain household was appended by the happy news that Mme Carvalho was on the guest list. On such occasions, Rosa's aversion to social engagements was forgotten – and Nathalie became wild with envy.[4]

'When Mme Carvalho made a visit to By,' remembered Rosa's domestic help Céline Rey, 'Mlle Micas went out of one door as Mme Carvalho came in the other, and remained in Fontainebleau throughout the visit.'[5]

From 1865, Rosa's correspondence was peppered with joyful references to her dear friend Caroline.

'I had the pleasure of seeing Mme Carvalho for a moment last evening,' she informed Mêne. 'But as I was afraid of disturbing her, I wasn't able to learn positively her day and hour. M. Carvalho said a few words to me that made me almost despair of having her with us. It appears that there are rehearsals for a first performance soon to come off. If she can't come, I shall be very sorry.'[6]

On another occasion, Rosa spoke fondly of a recent 'evening passed so pleasantly, thanks to the grace and kindness of Mme Carvalho, to whom I want to send a little sign of my gratitude and some mark of my fraternal admiration, to speak artistically,' and she concluded enthusiastically: 'I have managed to finish the little drawing for Mme Carvalho.'[7]

Nathalie fumed and vituperated, but she was powerless to frustrate the budding friendship; instead, she was grudgingly forced to tolerate it.

'If you see Mme Carvalho, there is no necessity of your hiding from her that I was in the capital,' Rosa told Mme Mêne following a visit she had tried to keep secret in May 1866. 'To her,' she added weightily, 'I always tell the truth.'[8]

When pressed to explain her attachment to Caroline Carvalho, Rosa admitted that the sound of the beautiful voice reminded her of her mother. Whenever she heard it, she was transported back to her childhood in Bordeaux, when she would sit on her mother's knee and lose herself in the soothing timbre of the song.

Mme Carvalho remained a serious bone of contention and Nathalie's temper flared whenever a visit presented itself. To compound matters, Rosa's affection for Caroline's artistically inclined brother, M. Miolan, did nothing to curtail the frequency of the women's tête-à-têtes. Nevertheless, once Nathalie had raged and vented, Rosa was usually able to pacify her companion. Besides, Nathalie could see that it was work, not social engagements, which monopolised Rosa's thinking as the year 1866 unfolded. And in the spring, her attention was caught by a terrible catastrophe.

That May, Ernest Gambart had planned to host an elaborate fancy dress ball to mark Derby Day at his current home 'Rosenstead' at 62, Avenue Road in north London. However, on the morning of the ball, the temporary wide lead gas pipes which had been laid specially for the occasion had leaked. Members of the household had awoken in the early hours of Wednesday 16 May to the ominous smell of gas. Soon after, a massive explosion was heard. The result was grievous human injuries and unimaginable destruction. The artist G.A. Storey remembered that 'the portrait of Rosa Bonheur with a bull' was found a few days later in the garden, pitifully damaged.

Rosa's empathy for her dealer's misfortune was profound. She was only too willing to repair the damaged canvas, though she scoffed at the cheque Gambart proffered as payment, returning the money with the restored painting. Gambart was obliged to purchase a Scottish bull, a form of remuneration he knew full well Rosa would be unable to resist.[9]

Rosa was now in her early 40s, and not for a moment did she take her achievements for granted. Her only complaint was that her siblings had not enjoyed the same degree of success.

'I have just written to Auguste, because you told me he was in the dumps, and that troubled me,' Rosa wrote to Isidore on 9 August 1866. 'I have been wanting each week to go and see both him and you. But I am so busy and the time is so short. […] I have good hopes that Auguste will receive his cross. This time, I shall be cut up, if he doesn't get it.'[10]

But Rosa was to be disappointed; Auguste did not receive the Légion d'Honneur.

Still, there was little time to wallow in regret. The Exposition Universelle was approaching and Rosa had decided it was time for her to demonstrate her patriotism. As always, she shared her pre-exhibition hopes and fears with her siblings.

Portrait of Rosa Bonheur, André-Adolphe-Eugène Disdéri, c. 1860–1870.

Private Collection/Prismatic Pictures/Bridgeman Images

'I am so busy! Just now I am fetching back some of my pictures from England,' Rosa updated Isidore in February 1867.

Two days later, another letter was dispatched:

'Peg away, peg away, my dear Dodore! You must produce something fine in two months! As for your Sis, why, she is a body that hesitates at nothing.'[11]

Yet despite that relentless drive, Rosa remained her own harshest critic. Occasionally, her confidence wavered:

'At times,' she confessed to Hippolyte, 'I am afraid I have thoroughly diddled many sincere amateurs in art.'[12]

On 1 April, the Exposition Universelle opened and the amateurs could judge for themselves.

The Champ-de-Mars had been chosen as the site of the show and the huge, rectangular exhibition ground was widely agreed the pride of the city. In its centre was a garden, while around this ran rings of galleries, where all manner of aesthetic wonders and feats of engineering dexterity could be beheld. Outside, visitors could amble along the pathways in the carefully planned garden area, itself dotted with smaller buildings and further pavilions. As ticket holders strolled through the grounds, their senses were assailed by every temptation imaginable. There were restaurants and cafés purveying exotic international treats, theatres and boutiques selling extraordinary goods, not to mention demonstrations of photography. Visitors could see horses and elephants, aquariums and orchestras, farm machines and steam generators. And with Greek porticos, Swedish log cabins and Chinese pagodas, the exposition held up one source of amazement after another. Then when dusk fell and the galleries closed, bedazzled spectators could meander outside where the twilit park took on a new character. Opalescent globes gave the impression of filtered daylight, memorable music reached susceptible ears, while taste buds were enticed by mouth-watering refreshments from across the world and noses inhaled the intoxicating perfumes from the horticultural garden.[13]

'Every day, the railways are ferrying coachloads of visitors to Paris,' commented C. Speranza in *L'Indépendance dramatique*, 'so that from morning to night, the vast galleries of the Palais du Champ-de-Mars are overflowing with people.' The effect was that of being 'transported into a fantasy world'.[14] For seven months, Paris became a dazzling carnival, an incandescent pageant, to which the whole world was invited and where social problems and politics were pigeonholed (at least for now).

In room 5, Rosa delighted the public with nine canvases, including the painting she had produced for Empress Eugénie, *Sheep by the Sea*. Even the otherwise critical review in the *Journal des Arts* proclaimed the French school to be 'remarkable', and Rosa was identified as one of its figureheads.[15]

But among the praise were misgivings; Rosa's sudden, very public reappearance on the Paris exhibition scene sparked resentment and accusations that she had been neglecting her country.

'All those people who made a fashion out of the author of *The Horse Fair* must be very disappointed with the herds she has brought us back from Scotland,' sneered Alphonse de Calonne in the *Revue Contemporaine*.[16]

The reviewer M. de Saint-Saintin neatly résuméd the prevailing critical stance after the event:

> since the Exposition Universelle of 1855 [...] Mlle Bonheur has only enjoyed the honour and profit of working for the English. But to better satisfy her new clients, she forgot France [...] Her painting, once so French before her voluntary exile from our Salons, has today assumed an unpleasant and clumsy cross-Channel accent [...] We only find the Rosa Bonheur of yesteryear in her sheep.[17]

However, as the reviewer for *Les Curiosités de l'Exposition universelle* reminded readers, the critics were not the public – and the opinions of these two parties frequently diverged:

Some critics have been suspicious of the official distinctions which have repeatedly been bestowed upon
[Rosa]; they fear her reputation has been overrated.
But the public always contends this reservation. These
landscapes, these herds, these shepherds, these sheep are
familiar to us. They provide a nostalgic vista onto our
holiday or travel souvenirs.[18]

Rosa knew always to expect criticism from exhibitions. But there were
further, more personal attacks that spring which were less easily ignored.

In May, she found herself compelled to write to a number of leading papers refuting claims made in a defamatory article printed in the
journal *L'Europe* that the artist many people already considered to be
eccentric was not of sound mind.[19]

Seeing past such malicious aspersions was made easier when she
was awarded a second-class medal at the Exposition Universelle. Then
a few months later, Rosa received the happy news that Auguste was to
be made Chevalier de la Légion d'Honneur.

'At last,' Rosa exclaimed to Juliette. 'He has it. Hurrah! [...] I shall
be at Magny on Sunday, where we can all meet and drink to the health
of the newly-made chevalier.'[20]

For all that she enjoyed such cheerful family gatherings, as the
summer neared its end, Rosa was more than ever inclined towards
seclusion. Life's ups and downs persisted, and Rosa took the opportunity of a letter to Paul Chardin to philosophise.

'One finally becomes so enervated and worn out by the things of
this life,' she sighed, 'one has to become, if not hard, if not selfish, at
least tough.' She continued: 'I shut my door in the face of all that is
commonplace and keep only three or four sincere affections.'[21]

The hermit-like status quo was still in force in November 1867,
when Isidore was asked if his sister might grant an audience to a
potential customer.

'Tell this gentleman that I cannot receive him,' Rosa snapped. 'I
am at work [...] It disturbs me to receive people.'[22]

Rosa was now in the luxurious position of being able to choose the commissions she accepted. Gambart alone could ensure that her paintings and prints found a constant stream of buyers. Besides, with his separation from his wife Annie at the end of the year, absorption in the careers of 'his' artists became a convenient curative for listlessness. If Rosa felt disinclined to gratify a request, she could afford to do so – and frequently did.[23]

A visit from her half-brother, Germain, provided a pleasant distraction in July 1868. The twenty-year-old had planned a trip to the Auvergne and afterwards, Spain and Portugal. In recent years, Germain had delighted (but not surprised) his family by showing a proclivity for painting, and he was duly enrolled to study under the illustrious Gérôme at the École des Beaux-Arts. He was not an especially robust youngster, but he showed promise and Rosa was deeply fond of him. Pleasure with family continued after Germain's departure, when Rosa proposed a short trip to the sea to Isidore and Juliette, assuring them not to worry about the cost: 'the ex's are my affair.'[24] Indeed, Rosa still helped various members of her family financially, and she always ensured that her aunt Elisabeth – Tatan – received her monthly allowance.

Rosa's commitment to her friends was equally titanic. Once she had decided she liked someone, she was fiercely loyal, and old friends frequently benefited from her generosity. But at 47 years old, Rosa especially enjoyed the company of the younger generation, and with her growing list of decorations and commendations (which now included membership to the Académie des Beaux-Arts in Antwerp), she was well qualified to impart her wisdom.[25] In April 1869, she agreed to give some art coaching to the Verdiers' son, Jean Louis Joseph, whom she was pleased to find a receptive and talented pupil. 'What especially gives me hope,' Rosa told the parents, 'is that he is very simple and well understands that he must study nature ingeniously and honestly without stuffing his noddle with a heap of conventional ideas.'[26]

It was in a similarly mentorial capacity that Rosa wrote soon afterwards to congratulate Isidore, who had been awarded a second medal for his sculpture at the Salon of 1869 and so was henceforward exempt from jury scrutiny.

'That's what comes of being good and working,' the older sister commended her brother, 'I am all the more pleased as I think you deserve it [...] While you are in the humour, peg away, my dear old Dodore [...] We have got to live; and to live well, the best thing is to work.'[27]

Rosa's counsel was worth heeding. Her professional star was twinkling brightly. Now, admiring fans could even purchase a collectible Rosa Bonheur doll dressed in characteristic clothing. 'Fashion dolls' had soared to popularity in France in the 1850s, when they were used primarily to showcase French clothing trends to the world. However, as magazines and journals were gradually usurping the dolls' role as fashion arbiters, their function was evolving. They were now becoming both a toy and a cherished collectible. Dolls modelled on celebrities were especially popular, and a 19⅝ inch Parian doll of the Empress Eugénie with moulded hair and a leather body, hand-finished with rosebud lips and clear blue eyes, had been charming its owners since the mid-1860s. The head and cropped hair of the 20 inch model of Rosa were cast in fine porcelain, while the makers had taken care to capture her blue eyes and rosy lips. Such porcelain heads were often made in Germany, and by association, the Rosa Bonheur figurine became widely known as the 'German gentleman'. The clothing worn by the diminutive Rosa varied, but while some dolls were sold wearing a black velvet dress with back beading, at least one American child remembered her doll being adorned in an outfit modelled on the one Rosa wore for Dubufe's portrait.[28]

Still, for all Rosa's prestige and philosophising, the year 1870 began unsteadily. In February, Nathalie's health took another downward turn and this time, the malady seemed serious. Fraught with anxiety, Rosa did all she could to nurse her companion back to health, declining an invitation to the wedding of Gambart's Paris representative, M. Surville. The news that her stepmother had also been taken unwell did nothing to lift Rosa's spirits, especially when a painting she was working on

The Rosa Bonheur doll, *c.* 1865.

Image courtesy of the Doll Museum at The Old
Rectory, Worthington Historical Society, Ohio

would not come together as she hoped. 'You know yourself what it is to be tempted to kick a hole through the canvas,' Rosa fumed in a letter to Juliette on 25 February.[29] Ill-health and artistic blocks were closely connected in Rosa's mind, and she often referred to problematic pictures as her 'infirmities'.[30]

Once Nathalie recovered, so did Rosa's state of mind. But the news that Gambart's estranged wife Annie had died of liver disease aged only 35 provided a chastening reminder of life's fragility. And as the spring unfolded, further problems were brewing, both for the residents of By and for France more generally.

Ever since Otto von Bismarck, the Prussian Prime Minister, had formed the North German Confederation in the wake of the

Austro-Prussian War in 1866, Prussia's swelling dominion had been a source of unease. Bismarck was fixed on extending German unification and establishing Prussia as its core. Napoleon had cautiously agreed to let him organise Germany, though in return for his cooperation, he asked that the states south of the Main river retain some independence and that France be given territory, specifically – and preferably – Luxembourg, to secure her position. Bismarck dismissed the request. Time was his most powerful weapon against the French (and he had ensured that there was ample of it to put in an appearance at the Exposition Universelle in 1867, as though to offer France a forceful reminder of his pre-eminence). Meanwhile, Bismarck's dogmatic mission to secure Prussian supremacy continued. Any cynical strategist could see that provoking a conflict with France now would likely arouse nationalism in the southern German states, thus pushing them to join the North German Confederation. But the possibility of a united Germany under Prussian control was too fearful a threat to ignore. A showdown was surely imminent. In France, the papers were full of apprehensive accounts of Bismarck's activities.[31]

'These war rumours disturb me,' Rosa admitted to Juliette in March, when an unusual lack of rainfall was adding to Parisians' worries, 'and I have no time to lose considering the work I have on hand; for the drought and the impending conflict, which won't be favourable to art, urge me not to lose my time.'[32]

Rosa was right; the clock was ticking. Finally, in the summer of 1870 it stopped. Time had run out.

17

•••

Knowing the Enemy

'I have stopped taking my meals with the Micases.'[1]
Rosa's letter to her aunt on 7 July 1870 delivered a bombshell.
'Without falling out,' she continued, 'we have settled so as to be free reciprocally.'

Rosa and Nathalie had always shared a tempestuous relationship. Both women were sensitive and each could be volatile when she felt cornered. But this episode marked a new level of domestic malaise. To Rosa, mealtimes were sacred. In the Bonheur household, the evening meal had been the moment when the family routinely came together to share their grievances and their glories. Spending mealtimes apart from the Micases reflected a seismic mental shift. Henceforward, Rosa would be quite alone as she sat down to a meal for one in her vast, reverberating château.

But as usual, Rosa attempted to give a light-hearted spin to the adversity: 'If my servants wish to poison me, it will be easy for them to do so at present.'[2] (None took advantage of the opportunity.)

The discord at By turned the château into a microcosm of broader political conflict, too – for at that very moment, France had been thrown into uproar.

Just a few days before Rosa penned her letter to Tatan, a prince of Prussian descent, Leopold of Hohenzollern-Sigmaringen, had been nominated as a candidate for the vacant Spanish throne following the overthrow of Queen Isabella II. The proposal heralded terrifying possibilities. A Prussian ruler in Spain would place France's southern frontiers under immediate threat. France would be virtually surrounded, a thought apt to send an icy chill coursing through patriotic French veins. Prussia was closing in.[3]

The reaction in the press was cataclysmic. France had not even been consulted on the question of the Spanish crown. National outrage triggered the swift dispatch of a series of telegrams, calling for the candidacy to be withdrawn. On 12 July, the French demand was gratified. But for many – including the all-important Corps Législatif – that was not enough: how could France be sure that a second attempt to seize power would not be made? Prussia must be made to promise that the move would not be repeated.

Eventually, a telegram was issued – thereafter known as the Ems telegram – and significantly, passed via Bismarck, stating that King Wilhelm of Prussia had declared that the Prince had withdrawn his candidacy and that no more would be said on the matter. By the time the memo reached Paris, its style had become curt, its message provocative and its implication defiant: France was being goaded to fight. The country started preparing for war.

⁂

Rosa regularly took *Le Figaro*. The front page on the 18 July 1870 issued a stirring rallying cry:

'Paris has been struck by a fever,' the journalist proclaimed, 'the magnanimous fever of patriotism. Over the last few days, the citizen body has abandoned the thousand little trifles [...] which had constituted its daily recreation. It now has but one thought: the safeguard of national honour [...]. One objective: the Rhine. One preoccupation: the triumph of our armies. In a word, the Parisian mindset is no longer in Paris – it is at the front.'[4]

Rosa and Nathalie's dispute was suddenly thrown into sobering perspective.

'I certainly won't prevent your husband renting a room in the country and making a kitchen of it,' Rosa informed Juliette on 18 July 1870, responding to Hippolyte's suggestion that some space from Nathalie might be beneficial to both parties. 'I have calculated that this would give me two – one for days of storm,' she continued.[5] But Rosa quickly updated her sister:

'I have gone back to my friend's table […] I was born with a spirit of contradiction, and as the newspapers are very bellicose at present, I, on the contrary, am inclining toward peace […] I offer to your eyes the appearance of equilibrium within my household.'[6]

Rosa concluded by asking Juliette to thank their stepmother's sister (who lived in Portugal) for the generous gift of a pineapple. Pineapples had only been enjoyed in France since the 1700s and still in the 19th century, the fruit was costly and widely considered an uncommon luxury.[7] Both the fragrant treat and Rosa's truce with Nathalie were timely; the very next day, daily life in France was turned on its head. All at once, friends, families, neighbours, lovers, were called on to pull together, while exotic foodstuffs like pineapple were to become a distant memory. On 19 July 1870, war was officially declared on Prussia.

War now became a lens through which all other experiences were filtered. Just how long it might last was a matter of conjecture. Some were so confident of a French victory that a few days, weeks at the most, was thought all that would be needed. To others, it seemed as though daily life had been mercilessly blown apart and that this precarious state was the new norm to which they must simply become accustomed.

'Please don't buy those books I asked for,' Rosa implored Paul Chardin on the day the news broke. 'We must all think only of how to economise […] pray God that the conflict will soon be over.'[8] Rosa's prayer was left unanswered.

On 26 July, Empress Eugénie resumed her role as regent and two days later, his health devastated by a large gallstone, the Emperor left for Metz with the fourteen-year-old Prince Imperial.

Rosa had now pushed her differences with Nathalie firmly to one side. Juliette had written, diplomatically explaining how she had not discussed Rosa's domestic fracas with any other family members; she had always known it would not last. Rosa was grateful for her sister's caution, but she assured her: 'I don't like people meddling with my business in my own home, and I don't care a fig about what may be thought of my private affairs, into which no one has the right to poke his nose [...] it is quite indifferent to me what people think.'[9]

Besides, if France was going to war, there were more pressing matters to attend to.

'I intend to make sacrifices,' Rosa informed Juliette. 'In other words, I mean to economise.'[10]

Rosa's wartime mentality had now set in, and to Paul Chardin, she could speak more frankly about what she understood 'economising' to mean:

'Before winter comes, the animals that ministered to my pleasure and professional wants will have to hop off,' Rosa declared. She would rather have her animals killed, 'one after the other,' than hand them over to the Prussians.[11]

Her fighting spirit ignited, soon, Rosa, Nathalie and Mme Micas were hard at work squirrelling out of view any valuables which might be looted. Rosa even told Paul Chardin how she planned to fill cavities of the château with explosives so as to outsmart Prussian intruders.

A desperate need to gather her friends and family close consumed her. But the assembly of her loved ones evaded her. Now in her nineties, Rosa's aunt Elisabeth, her Tatan, was in no fit state to travel. Then the news that her younger half-brother Germain had been dispatched to the front as part of Marshall Mac-Mahon's army reiterated Rosa's sense of powerlessness in the face of war.

'As there is nothing better to do, I have quietly and philosophically returned to my labours,' Rosa told Juliette on 16 August. 'Alone, I could not save my country, even were I able to defend her in arms. If I had been a young male, I should have left for the front long since.'[12]

Nonetheless, Rosa remained defiantly optimistic: 'I have great confidence in the affair not being so serious as some people imagine,' she assured Juliette, adding how she was certain that 'we shall gain a few little victories, which will put everything to rights.'[13]

But the 'little victories' did not materialise. When the French arrived at Metz, they were both unprepared and grossly underequipped. With little more than half the troops Napoleon had been promised, the situation was desperate.

'I would go to the front, if I believed I could make myself useful picking up the poor wounded,' Rosa volunteered to Juliette. If the Prussians came to By and Rosa was forced to flee, she vowed that she would destroy the contents of the château, kill the animals and as far as the enemy were concerned, ensure that she had 'polished one or two of them off' with her own hand. 'I am persuaded this sad war will soon be over, if we give these rascally Prussians a good drubbing,' Rosa reasoned.[14]

Her hopes were in vain. Communications were hampered and unreliable, and at the time of her letter, Rosa still had no idea what had become of Auguste. Being closer to Paris, Juliette now became a vital source of information.

By the end of August, Rosa could report to her sister how she was busy fortifying her château. To her mind, the conflict with Prussia had placed her nest under threat – and that meant that her primary objective must be securing her property. Until that was done, painting would have to take second place.

'I should not like to abandon the Micases and I could do no good in Paris,' Rosa attempted to justify her refusal to leave By.[15] 'It isn't the Micases who are keeping me here,' Rosa wrote defensively to Juliette three days later, contradicting her earlier claim. 'It's the calculation I make of what is likely to happen.'[16]

But that was only part of the story. The truth was, war had deeply unsettled Rosa. She suddenly felt acutely conscious of her own vulnerability.

Rosa had always viewed the concept of God with a mixture of curiosity and circumspection; she did not attend church regularly. But now, her assurances to family were repeatedly couched in her professed faith in divine intervention: 'God must punish the wrong acts of those who would inflict such evils on this poor earth. I have faith that this will happen, because I firmly believe in the justice of God, although I don't go to mass and don't believe in all the stupid inventions of men.'[17]

Heavenly intercession or no, as a woman, Rosa's indignation towards the Prussians could not be substantiated by meaningful action. 'We poor women,' Rosa commiserated with her sister on 1 September, 'should do no good in trying to defend ourselves […] This task must be performed by men who run the risk but who also reap the glory. Alas! What else can we do except submit to the inevitable?'[18]

But to Paul Chardin, her Rapin, Rosa showed herself less resigned to the gendered nature of war. What most excited her anger was the fate her animals might suffer at the hands of the Prussians. And on that matter, Rosa was unflinching: 'I had rather die than abandon to them a single creature!'[19] In the event of a Prussian siege, Rosa had formulated two plans. The first involved her assuming leadership of a battalion in the local area. The second was to flee.

The first plan had demanded rather more strategic groundwork, and Rosa even contemplated approaching the local mayor with her proposition. Indeed, a friend later reported that she had done just this, whereupon the mayor humoured his visitor sufficiently to point out that her sex made her virtually useless on the battlefield. She might instead make herself helpful by rolling bandages. Rosa returned home, at once enraged and bitterly disappointed.[20]

Meanwhile, bleak reports trickled back from the front. French defensive efforts were proving pitifully ineffectual. On 1 September 1870, Napoleon III was defeated close to the Belgian border at the battle of Sedan. Giving himself up, the Emperor was escorted to captivity in Prussia.

Having fizzed and dazzled for nearly twenty years, the Empire had spectacularly fallen. Rosa was aghast.

'I am as sad as it is possible to be over the dishonour of our poor country,' she exclaimed to Paul Chardin on 5 September 1870, the day

Rosa Bonheur, *Ploughing in the Nivernais*, 1849, oil on canvas, 133 × 260 cm, Musée d'Orsay, Paris.

Auguste Bonheur, *Portrait of Rosa Bonheur*, 1848, oil on canvas, 130.5 × 98.3 cm, Musée des Beaux-Arts-Mairie de Bordeaux.

Photo: F. Deval. No. d'inventaire: Bx E 1169

Édouard Dubufe, *Portrait of Rosa Bonheur*, 1857, oil on canvas, 130.5 × 97 cm, Château de Versailles.

Photo by Heritage Images/Hulton Fine Art Collection via Getty Images

Rosa Bonheur, *The Horse Fair*, 1853, oil on canvas, 244.5 × 506.7 cm, Metropolitan Museum of Art, New York (accession no. 87.25).

Rosa Bonheur,
Brizo, a Shepherd's Dog,
1864, oil on canvas,
46.1 × 38.4 cm.

Wallace Collection,
London, UK/
Bridgeman Images

Rosa Bonheur,
King of the Forest, 1878,
oil on canvas,
244.8 × 175 cm,
private collection.

Rosa Bonheur, *Stalking Tiger, c.* 1876, oil on canvas, size unknown.
Private Collection/Photo © Gavin Graham Gallery, London, UK/Bridgeman Images

Rosa Bonheur, *The Lion*,
1879, oil on canvas,
95 × 76 cm,
Museo del Prado, Spain.
NMUIM/Alamy Stock Photo

Rosa Bonheur, *Portrait of William F. Cody (Buffalo Bill)*, 1889,
oil on canvas, 47 × 38.7 cm, Buffalo Bill Center of the West, Cody, USA.

Rosa Bonheur, *The Duel*, 1895, oil on canvas, 149.9 × 243.8 cm,
Warner Collection of Gulf States Paper Corporation, Tuscaloosa, Alabama.

Georges Achille-Fould, *Rosa Bonheur in her Studio*, 1893,
oil on canvas, 91 × 124 cm, Musée des Beaux–Arts, Bordeaux.

Consuélo Fould,
Rosa Bonheur, 1893,
oil on canvas,
130.7 × 94.7 cm.

Leeds Museums and Galleries (Leeds Art Gallery) UK/Bridgeman Images

Anna Klumpke,
Portrait of Rosa Bonheur,
1898, oil on canvas,
117.2 × 98.1 cm,
The Metropolitan Museum
of Art, New York
(accession no. 22.222).

Historic Images/Alamy Stock Photo

after a republic been declared in Paris. Ernest Gambart had written the day before, attempting to persuade Rosa that her best course of action now was to remain safely ensconced at By.[21] But Rosa's mind was made up: 'I intend to leave France,' she told Paul Chardin firmly. 'France is lost, and, in my opinion, she is disgraced forever: for public favour has changed too often, and I can no more swallow this cardboard republic than I could the earlier one of 1848.'[22]

The outburst reflected, if not a burgeoning conservatism, at least a more sceptical approach to the ebb and flow of politics and social doctrines. The days of unquestioning acceptance of Saint-Simonianism and the Templars were gone. A week later, Rosa's resolve had scarcely wavered:

'I want to stay here until the war is nearly ended, when it is my fixed intention to go and settle in Belgium,' Rosa informed Paul Chardin. 'If France becomes Prussian, I will never live in it; but if she should be a durable republic or empire, I might come back later. I am quietly awaiting the Prussians.' And to greet them, Rosa vowed she would appear in full evening dress with her cross of the Légion d'Honneur prominently displayed.[23]

The opportunity was closer than Rosa expected. The Republic had renewed its declaration of war – and now, the enemy was heading straight for Paris. On 15 September, Prussian forces reached the outskirts of the city. Five days later, the capital had been surrounded and a full-scale siege set in.

'I am still without any news from you,' Rosa scrawled frantically to Juliette. With bridges having been blown up in the vicinity, the Prussians had not yet imposed themselves at By. But Rosa and her manservant had seen them from a distance. The Prussian troops appeared haggard, famished and clearly suffering the effects of war.[24]

Rosa had more personal concerns, too. Mme Micas was unwell and aunt Elisabeth even more poorly. With little choice but to hunker down at By, the sense of paralysis was unbearable. 'Poor old aunt,' Rosa moaned to Juliette, 'who knows whether I shall see her again! [...] I none the less hope she won't die before I can get to Paris.'[25]

Rosa sealed her envelope and dispatched the letter expectantly. It disappeared; Juliette only received her sister's correspondence six months later.

☙

For the remainder of the autumn and the winter, daily life in Paris and the provinces was in chaos. The provisional government established itself at Tours, and French forces continued to fight, but their efforts were having little effect. Communications were cut off and food shortages bordered on famine. Rosa was not alone in regarding her animals with a revised agenda. In upper-class households, sewer rats were proudly turned into patés, while poorer homes abated gnawing hunger devouring cats and dogs. All the brilliance had been sapped out of the formerly glamorous capital. What remained was an empty carcass ravaged by starvation and despair.

A few kilometres away at By, Rosa and Nathalie struggled to keep their household afloat. Mme Carvalho's brother, M. Miolan, had given Rosa a small caravan, which she had repurposed as a modest outdoor studio. As Rosa remembered, it was here that she was working when, at the end of September, an officer arrived at the château with a very special document.

The man presented his paper. It was a safe conduct pass, issued on behalf of Prince Frederick Charles of Prussia, who wished to demonstrate his respect. The pass stated that Mlle Rosa Bonheur should be left untroubled and undisturbed and that a very dim view would be taken of any officer contravening that order.[26]

Rosa was incensed. The preferential treatment disgusted her. She was furious that the enemy should think she would deign to accept a favour from them and a rumour spread that she had even torn up the paper on the spot. In reality, a degree of foresight (which Nathalie could always be trusted to supply) prevented such a hot-headed reaction. And those efforts soon proved worth the trouble; by November, Prussians had been sighted around Fontainebleau.

246

So long as the enemy left By undisturbed, Rosa vowed that no animal kept there would suffer. But as her fodder supplies dwindled, she could see that there was no place for pride – and she knew just the sharp-witted dealer to turn to for help.

⁂

Like many well-to-do city dwellers, Ernest Gambart had taken refuge outside the capital, settling in the fashionable seaside city of Nice. With its expanding rail links and its annexation to France in 1860, in recent years, Nice had firmly established itself as a voguish winter holiday retreat for well-heeled Parisians and European sovereigns. Feeling the effects of nearly 60 years and looking to reduce his workload, Gambart had lately joined the throng of socialites and travelled to Nice to view a villa to the west of the city. As soon as he beheld the Villa Gastaud, he was smitten. Despite the proximity of the railway line, the uninterrupted sea views, balmy winter climate and gentle breeze off the Mediterranean were profoundly restorative. The property offered a secluded haven when Gambart wished to withdraw from the hurly-burly. Then whenever he craved an injection of cosmopolitan society and entertainment, Nice's gluttonous spread of operas, theatres, restaurants and parties were all close at hand. Henceforward, Gambart would divide his time between Spa in Belgium and Nice, taking a few months each year to travel.

The outbreak of war merely reiterated the sagacity of Gambart's choice. Though demonstrations had momentarily broken the city's calm when the Republic was first declared, by 20 September, the British Consul in Nice had been able to report that 'both the towns of Nice and Mentone have continued in a state of perfect tranquillity'.[27] In Nice, Parisian high life found fertile ground in which to supplant itself, with the result that, at times, a visitor to Nice could almost forget that the country was at war at all.

Rosa penned Gambart a letter requesting that he send some sacks of grain so that she might keep her animals alive while she could – though that, it seemed, might not be long.

Rosa was fully committed to the war effort. She served on an unofficial home guard which had been organised in the area and also helped Nathalie and Mme Micas dish out soup to needy locals. Food distribution to the poor and ailing was a vital, if un-glorious, feminine occupation during the war.

Supplies were now critically low. By mid-December, even horse-meat had been rationed.[28] In the New Year, bread, that timeless and symbolic dietary staple, was also restricted, while any foodstuff not subject to rationing became virtually unaffordable. Milk was four times its normal price, while the cost of potatoes increased tenfold. Cheese, butter, beef and lamb gradually disappeared from the Parisian table. Cooks and housewives had to dig deep in their culinary know-how to put even the simplest meal on the table. Across the city, opportunistic cat and dog butchers conducted flourishing trade. The Christmas sky that year was grey and heavy and the mood scarcely brighter.[29]

At the end of January 1871, with Parisians desolated by hunger and the country's provincial armies failing, France finally accepted that she must ask Bismarck for an armistice.[30] Firing ceased and the intricate process of negotiating a peace agreement was set in motion.

Rosa immediately began putting together a parcel for Juliette, containing a little money and – always of utmost importance to Rosa – some food.

'I am contriving to send you a basket in which you will find a leg of mutton, a chicken and a bit of cheese,' Rosa wrote insistently. 'You have no idea of the crowds of people everywhere who are trying to express packages.'[31]

Times remained perilous, and as Rosa herself pointed out, 'we are at the Prussians' mercy'.[32] But now, at least, Rosa felt able to consider the practical implications for art.

'I am very much afraid the arts won't flourish for long months to come,' Rosa shared her concerns with her sister.[33]

Over the following weeks, a combination of uncertainty and hampered communications kept Rosa on high alert. She wrote regularly to Juliette, begging her to head for By at the first opportunity. Prussians remained stationed nearby, the postal service had stopped and it was impossible to send money, which, in any case, was sorely lacking.

Rosa was relieved to learn that Auguste had shepherded his family and Juliette's two children to safety in La Vandée, more than 300 km away from Paris. It was now Juliette about whom Rosa was most concerned.

'I am going to try and send you a haunch of deer,' she announced to her sister on 18 February 1871. 'For three days before the deer was killed, I was making sketches of him.'[34]

Since moving to By, agricultural livestock had become less prevalent in Rosa's work and woodland creatures had begun to take their place. Rosa's canvas was increasingly populated by deer, boar and more occasionally, birds, like the *Wounded Eagle* (c. 1870), which she painted around this time. The grey and tawny bird of prey was shown as though surprised mid-flight, its open beak evoking the dreadful cry which the viewer would never hear, its left-wing lowered, its right raised in a frantic effort to arrest its plummet. The metaphorical potential of the message was hard to ignore: even the most eminent power was ultimately mortal.

Rosa could not bear to see an animal suffer unnecessarily, but she was inherently philosophical. Death was a part of life. On one sheet of studies of a boar produced during that post-war period, Rosa inscribed stoically at the bottom: 'Born in June. Killed in December.'[35] Animals were to be drawn and loved and eaten. Most in Rosa's care fulfilled at least two of those briefs. Provided the species were preserved and suffering minimised, Rosa was satisfied. Hence Paul Chardin once received a stern reprimand when he killed a female game bird: 'I respect and love but one thing in nature, that's the mother. Kill all the males you want to, there will always be enough left.'[36] Rosa had a profound respect for animals – in all their states.

Rosa Bonheur, *Wounded Eagle*, c. 1870,
oil on canvas, 147.6 x 114.6 cm.
Los Angeles County Museum of Art, CA, USA/Bridgeman Images

'I hope you will find the haunch a good one,' Rosa persisted in her note to Juliette. 'A piece that I dined on was excellent, splendid meat and covered with fat.'[37]

Just days after Rosa sent the venison, the newly elected leader of the republican assembly, the septuagenarian Adolphe Thiers, signed a preliminary agreement with Prussia. But peace came at a crippling cost. Bismarck demanded Alsace and the north-eastern part of Lorraine (including Metz), and a 50 billion franc war indemnity did nothing to cushion the blow. After all the country had suffered, the surrender struck the French as the very worst kind of humiliation.

Throughout February and March, Rosa's correspondence to Juliette overflowed with lyrical effusions about the humiliation her beloved country had suffered at the hands of the Prussians. And to Rosa's exasperation, the armistice did not precipitate the immediate departure of enemy troops – far from it.

'Prince Frederick Charles has been appointed to the command of the German troops to remain in France until the indemnity is paid,' the *Indianapolis News* reported on 6 March 1871.[38] More cruelly, France was expected to pay for those soldiers' upkeep.

'Rosa Bonheur' now became an open sesame which repeatedly proved the value of the safe conduct pass. The mention of Rosa's name ensured the prompt return of one of her wagons which was requisitioned when her servants went to buy provisions, while the coachman succeeded in forestalling an inquisition by announcing that he was the person responsible for 'Rosa Bonheur's' horse.[39]

Eventually, a handful of German officers arrived at By with a view to camping out. There was no choice but to receive them. Rosa later told a friend that, notwithstanding, Nathalie would not eat in the same room as the officers, a rebuff which she claimed sparked wry asides about the implacability of French women. But Rosa's servant Céline Rey corrected her mistress's version of the story, swearing that it was Rosa who refused to cooperate with the troops, insisting on eating in her studio. And to that, Rosa irrefutably forbade the Prussians access.[40]

The studio was clearly a source of fascination to the enemy. One day, a group of officers arrived with the intention of inspecting it. Years later, Céline still maintained that one of the men was Prince Frederick Charles himself. To Rosa's mind, it made no difference who the intruders claimed to be. They found that the studio doors had been firmly bolted. Undeterred, they persisted on a tour of Rosa's grounds, whereupon the soldiers' eyes alighted on the stag Rosa kept enclosed in a paddock. Dismissing the cautions they received, the officers went inside to inspect it at close range. To Rosa's amusement, the stag rushed at them, splashing up muddy water from the ground and ruining their smart uniforms.[41]

On another occasion, an even larger number of soldiers appeared at the gates. Rosa hastened outside to confront them.

'Moutons,' the men ordered, in abrupt, heavily accented French.

'I have no sheep, or anything else to give you,' Rosa barked. 'You may have a drink, and then you had better be off.'[42] The soldiers were stunned, but impressed by the fierce little artist of uncertain gender. To Rosa's delight, they scurried off, having taken nothing.

In the town of Thomery, stories of Rosa's dealings with the enemy were eagerly recounted; she had attempted to rally a group of locals to march with her and prevent the Prussians crossing the Seine at By, one story ran. Another neighbour was reportedly coaxed into camping out with Rosa all night and firing at an enemy sentinel. Countless examples of Rosa's patriotic fervour soon became woven into the fabric of Thomery folklore.[43]

Though Rosa's personal dealings with the Prussians remained largely innocuous, Auguste was less fortunate. His house at Magny was ransacked during the events, and when he was finally able to return, he found that the interior had been converted into a stable and the furniture used for firewood.[44]

Auguste was not the only Frenchman with grounds for enmity. In the terrible aftermath of war, the rest of France simmered with resentment. Parisians were already enraged at the defeat when Thiers' republican assembly proved itself sorely wanting. The people were told that the National Assembly was to sit at Versailles, not that iconic heart of France, Paris, while the National Guards' pay was to be docked. When the government then demanded the return of some 200 guns which had been funded by public subscription, the request was angrily rebuffed. Detachments of the National Guard moved to seize the guns, while loyal French Army troops attempted to reclaim them, and in the resulting skirmish, two elderly generals were shot. That sparked the final fuse. The Franco-Prussian War had fostered national unity. Now, in a ghastly epilogue to a catastrophic volume of history, the people of Paris turned on each other.[45]

A rival regime formed in Paris which assumed the title of the Commune de Paris and the mission of taking on the government. Revolutionaries established their headquarters in the Hôtel de Ville, while in Versailles, Thiers' party began planning the reconquest of the capital. And then, Paris became the centre of a ruthless and bloody civil war.

Before they could properly assimilate the aftermath of the Prussian siege, citizens of Paris were forced to watch as once more, their streets were transformed into a sprawling battlefield of carnage and destruction. Thiers' private house was demolished, the Vendôme column (erected by Napoleon Bonaparte to celebrate the victories of 1805) was pulled down. Fireballs were hurled through bourgeois windows, barricades littered the streets and buildings were torched as Parisian blood sullied Parisian hands.

Thiers' army eventually succeeded in entering the capital, and for a week which would become branded *la semaine sanglante* (the bloody week), a terrifying confrontation unfolded. One evening in May, a blushed sky in the city centre signalled catastrophe: the Tuileries Palace had been set on fire. Then, in one of the Communards' most barbaric acts, the Archbishop of Paris, who was being held hostage, was brutally murdered.

Out at Thomery, word of the commotion induced terror. Rosa was panic-stricken when she learned her old friend Mêne to be in the capital. 'What the devil can you be doing in the Paris of *Père Duchesne*?' she demanded, alluding to the name of a radical newspaper from the Revolutionary period. 'Can it be that you are caught up in the Commune, my old Mêne? I could not swallow that even if you told me so.'[46] For those outside Paris, certainty remained an elusive concept.

At last, Thiers' army managed to suppress the remaining Communards and by the end of May, the conflict was over. But Paris and its people had been scarred beyond recognition; some 20,000 citizens were killed and the capital's streets reduced to a crumbling, blood-stained reminder of a week of savagery.

_CR_

France's position and status in Europe had radically changed since the days of the Empire. The events of 1870–71 had upset the balance of power in Europe and France now found herself isolated and humiliated. The ambitious foreign expeditions of yesteryear were no longer a priority. Instead, the country turned its attention towards repairing the war damage, fulfilling the demands of the repressive Treaty of Frankfurt and grappling to establish a stable government. The sight of German troops patrolling the country would be a necessary evil until the indemnity was paid. But what the majority of France craved now was peace and stability and quiet.

As the country struggled to rebuild morale and material well-being, Rosa too could reassess her career. Though Nathalie maintained that art had been Rosa's solace throughout the war and the Commune, Rosa had repeatedly told friends and family how her heart was not in her work. To her mind, what she produced during the conflict she did so ill. The tumultuous period now over, there was much to reflect on – and much to do.

Ernest Gambart had announced that he would be retiring that spring. His nephew Léon Lefèvre had agreed to take over the firm, but there was no denying that the charismatic Gambart would leave a chasm in the art world which could not easily be filled. 'St John's Wood never ceased to lament his loss,' recalled writer and artist's wife Jeanie Adams-Acton when the dealer emigrated to the continent; 'the whole neighbourhood seemed changed after his departure.'[47] For Rosa, however, who had found multiple international outlets for her work, the financial implications of Gambart's retirement were not so perilous – but a reduction in opportunities to enjoy his company would be quite another matter.

For now, at least, it looked as though Rosa's dealings with Gambart would not abruptly cease. Though resolutely retired, in a final spasm of professional zeal, Gambart attempted to buy back _The Horse Fair_ (1853) that year (a bid which ultimately proved unsuccessful). He also helped

Rosa assist a good friend. Since her befriending Caroline Carvalho, the singer's brother, M. Miolan, had gone into business trading pictures, and his stock naturally included a number of works by Rosa. However, when his affairs left him financially chagrined, Rosa went straight to Gambart with some sketches, proposing to sell them to bail out her friend's brother. Gambart obligingly made a large sum of money available and passed the pictures on to his nephew for sale at auction. M. Miolan was overwhelmed by Rosa's gesture, but he protested that he could not possibly accept her offer.[48]

That post-war period brought some revitalising pleasures, too. Happily returned from fighting, Germain arrived at By in July 1872, giving Rosa the opportunity both to admire her half-brother's artistic progress and to entrust him with a letter to be delivered discreetly and by hand to her stepmother.

'My dear Mammy,' she enthused, 'I intend to spend a week at Mme Carvalho's.' Rosa stipulated that should her half-brother return to By, 'tell him to say nothing to the Micases about my staying with Mme Carvalho. If he were to, Nathalie would very likely go into a state of rage that might be dangerous to her. I intend to stuff her up with a story of my being with Auguste and Marie, for I don't want to give her an attack of apoplexy.'[49]

As planned, Rosa left By for Caroline Carvalho's property in the little hamlet of Puys in Normandy, just 2 km from Dieppe. As soon as she arrived, the excellence of the project became clear. The rugged coastline and lush green pastures of Normandy had long been attracting artists and in the company of her friend, Rosa was sublimely happy. At Caroline's request, she eagerly wrote to both Isidore and Juliette apprising them of the brilliant idea that she and her hostess had concocted of their coming to Normandy to join them. Juliette's refusal was not well received.

'It won't be kind if neither you nor Auguste is willing to give her the pleasure of seeing you,' Rosa accused, 'especially as she shows us such a friendly feeling. As for me, little Sis, you know how much I love her and esteem her. If only you were to spend five or six days with her as I have, you would see how good and sincere she is, as well as intelligent [...] I intend to stay as long as possible.'[50]

Time away in such scintillating company prompted Rosa to meditate on Nathalie's dislike of Caroline Carvalho – and all at once, anger surged through her. It would serve Nathalie right, Rosa snapped to Juliette, if she were made to join them there.

Rosa had turned 50 that year. She felt she had earned her right to a little pleasure. Henceforward, she would work only on projects which truly excited her.

'I possess the nature of old boars and more and more I want to be alone,' she had explained to Paul Chardin only a few months earlier. 'Now and again I work with passion; for, when I am not in the humour, I can't force myself.[51]

'I am working for my own satisfaction,' she reiterated defiantly to Isidore at the end of 1872. 'My aim is to paint a few pictures toward the end of my career. I, too, dream of glory!'[52]

That was not to say that Rosa resisted innovation. Young people surrounded her, and while she imparted her wisdom, they in turn exposed her to nascent artistic tendencies. Then students could be enormous fun. The trainee architect Alexandre Jacob often visited his family's country home at Fontainebleau, which was not far from Rosa's. He distinctly remembered a jovial Shrove Tuesday at By in 1873, where M. Miolan supervised a merry, if rather chaotic pancake-making session.[53]

The swing towards what Rosa called 'photographic intensity' at the Salon of 1873 particularly caught her attention. She did not explicitly denounce it. Indeed, she believed photography to be one of the century's most fascinating advances. In time, Rosa set up a small darkroom adjoining the studio at By where she could develop her own prints, not to dictate her compositions, but rather to inform her research.[54]

But while Rosa's mind welcomed new technology, her body was beginning to quake under the strain of her years. In July 1873, she grudgingly had to concede that another trip to Puys was out of the question that summer. Rosa had injured her calf (trying to rid herself of cramp with her riding whip, she confessed to Juliette). Then the general aches and pains that came with age were curtailing her sporadic desire for adventures. Still, having to content herself with By was never a chore. By contrast, not being agile enough to go out or move around her canvas as she would like was positively torturous.

As the year unfolded, Rosa's faltering health began to affect her character, too. Friends started to notice. For a period, 'she became taciturn, almost unapproachable, seeking solitude and receiving no one, not even those she called her friends,' remembered Paul Chardin.[55]

If Rosa reduced her socialising that year, by contrast, her work was taking a new course and proliferating. A fresh interest had come to fill her thinking and desensitise her to the absence of society. The war, the siege, the Commune, perhaps the sense of powerlessness against it all, had led Rosa to start thinking about more ferocious predators. Lions and tigers began to obsess her. Their regal appearance, sleek movements, total command of their powerful physique and that inherent potential to destroy – these creatures were the true masters of nature.

In 1872, she had produced a painted sketch entitled *Couching Lion*. The piece showed a majestic cat reclining against a mountainous backdrop, its head raised, its gaze directed to the right, out of the canvas. Seemingly motile shades of ochre, ivory and burnt sienna were applied in harmony to evoke the velvety sheen of its coat in the sunlight and suggest the folds of skin beneath it as the animal sat at rest, its limbs gathered neatly underneath its large frame and its soft paws resting in front of it. Rosa's brush gently traced the beast's powerful musculature to create a silent ode to the subject's apparent docility and latent force. Big cats now became Rosa's raison d'être.

By the mid-1870s, the metamorphosis of Mlle Rosa Bonheur's creative oeuvre was a source of widespread – and very public – interest. Aware of her specialism and her proclivity, it occurred to the recently retired circus entrepreneur M. Louis Dejean (the mastermind behind the wildly popular Cirque d'été and the lately renamed Cirque d'hiver) that the great animal artist might like to sketch one of the lions he allowed to roam freely around his property, the Château de Saint-Leu

Rosa Bonheur, *Couching Lion*, 1872, oil on canvas, 45.72 x 60.96 cm.
Courtesy of Rehs Galleries, Inc., NYC

near Melun. The prospect of studying his tame lioness Pierrette at close hand would surely appeal to the animal lover – and the association of Rosa's name would do no harm to his business legacy or his reputation.[56]

Rosa was instinctively wary. A number of lions had been brought back to France after the Algerian campaign in 1830. Though comfortable with farm and forest creatures, big cats were a new and unfamiliar species. Rosa knew she could calm a raging bull and pacify a startled pony. But she had no experience which would allow her to predict how a lion might react to being studied and that made her unusually nervous. Besides, models could be readily observed – if only from a distance – in purpose-built enclosures like the Jardin des Plantes. But in her heart, Rosa could not settle with such a facile approach to research when she could gain a more intimate knowledge of a beast. So with

Nathalie's encouragement, Rosa surmounted her nerves and arranged to visit the animal.

When the ladies arrived at the Château de Saint-Leu, Nathalie's courage did not waver. She marched straight up to the lioness and ran her hand along the creature's back; the animal did not object. Rosa was awestruck.

From that day, a series of trips to Saint-Leu permitted Rosa to study the lioness's unique physical and temperamental blueprint. And the more her eye followed the beast and her pencil grew accustomed to its curves, the more Rosa's respect for big cats mounted. As she worked, the lioness grew increasingly easy in her company too, and, Rosa later recalled, would stand guard over her materials protectively whenever she took a rest from painting.[57]

Pierrette had been bottle-fed from birth and so had grown accustomed to human contact. She was tame to the point where a cat could sit and eat between her paws, not to mention amiable, for she gleefully played with the horse and donkey which were kept near her. To Rosa's amazement, the lioness even took herself from view when nature called.

Professionally, lions marked a new departure for Rosa, and her studies were soon amassing. But at the end of 1873, an upset came to shake her out of her creative reverie: her aunt Elisabeth died.

The loss was not wholly unexpected, but Tatan was the closest remaining link to Rosa's father. Having always enjoyed a fond relationship with the wily, headstrong aunt whom she had supported financially, it was a chastening blow.

Health, Rosa knew only too well, was the critical ingredient without which the rest of life came to a standstill. Though medicine had made impressive advances in the 19th century, in many areas, knowledge remained fragmentary. In an era where basic treatment could still be primitive and doctors unaffordable to many, maintaining good health was a major preoccupation. Rosa was consequently encouraging when she wrote to Nathalie the following spring at Gambart's property in Belgium, where it had been agreed that the amateur inventor might benefit from a curative break. Nathalie had set off, leaving Rosa in charge of 68-year-old Mme Micas.

Rosa had previously mooted the possibility of taking Caroline Carvalho to Gambart's property in the summer, a plan which threatened to spark another explosive row with Nathalie. Rosa was now careful to keep her letter light and positive. She recounted a bet she had made with Nathalie's mother the previous evening that the latter could not get into Rosa's trousers. Never a woman to shrink from a challenge, old Mme Micas had set to, with only her rolls of belly fat preventing an impressively neat fit. Rosa concluded her letter sending love from herself, Mme Micas and Gamine, the little lapdog whom Nathalie adored.[58]

Rosa ultimately resolved that the likely upset occasioned by taking Caroline Carvalho to Gambart's outweighed the pleasure she might derive from the experience. However, she grumbled bitterly that affection should not be measured as a grocer did his sugar; her feelings for the two women should not be compared. But though Rosa was prepared to make compromises, she refused to terminate her intimate friendship with the opera singer. In a letter written to Juliette on 1 August 1874, Rosa remarked that she was 'not quite up to the mark' at present and that a stay with Mme Carvalho might be in order.[59]

But pleasure trips could not arrest the relentless march of time. Nor could they impede tragedy.

In the following months, death was to pay two more calls – first, it would strike in Rosa's extended family. And then, one day, it arrived at By.

18

···

Standing Out from the Pack

Auguste Bonheur would never be the same again. Though he lavished affection on all five of his children, none inspired his tenderness more readily than his second daughter, nineteen-year-old Françoise. When she died suddenly at the end of October 1874, Auguste was inconsolable.

For a girl to die in late adolescence was especially shocking. Average life expectancy for a French woman at the time was at least her early 40s. Infancy was always a perilous stage, and even afterwards, outbreaks of typhoid, smallpox, venereal disease and that ubiquitous and indomitable curse, tuberculosis, continued to devastate households. Nonetheless, the severity of epidemic diseases was declining, and throughout the century, mortality rates outside the city centres remained lower than those in built-up, urban areas. To compound Auguste's sense of grief and injustice, conceptions of childhood and adolescence were changing. With life expectancy on the rise, increasingly in the 19th century, offspring were being accorded greater importance, with children being viewed less as subordinate pawns who merely bolstered family numbers and secured property ownership, and more as little people to be known and nurtured and loved. Then with Raymond Bonheur's socialist leanings, the Bonheurs were, by default, more family-minded than many households. The death of one of their youngsters was a life-altering tragedy. And for Auguste, the blow came at an especially difficult time.[1]

The traumatic experience of war and his personal loss at the hands of the Prussians had grievously upset Auguste's health. The well-being of body and soul had yet to be re-established. Now, it looked as though that state might never be attained.

Aching for her brother's loss, Rosa offered what support she could. Isidore too proved a vital prop, joining his brother as witness at the young girl's death. But everyone could see that Auguste's heart was unlikely to mend. Added to which, Rosa and Nathalie had anxieties of their own at home.

Since the early 1870s, Mme Micas's eyesight had been deteriorating. In 1874, Nathalie took her mother to Paris to receive specialist treatment. Rosa wrote to them while they were away, in one of the upbeat moods which she was inclined to adopt in times of crisis, updating them on the state of the household: Céline's cooking was causing her belly to swell, Nathalie's donkey had been moving coal with the draft horse, Roland, while the turkey and the other birds were thriving and Nathalie's little dog Gamine missed her owner profusely.[2]

Rosa attempted to buoy her companion with cheerful spurs not to give up hope. But when Nathalie and Mme Micas returned to By, it soon became clear that the trip to Paris had not brought about the desired improvement. Rosa and Nathalie watched with deflating spirits as Mme Micas continue to fumble her way around the kitchen and blindly negotiate the rest of the château. Rosa later remembered that a servant was tasked with looking after the old lady while she and Nathalie worked. When the girl exhibited the unfortunate habit of falling into a profound slumber, Nathalie was called on to tap her inventive streak. A cord was attached to the girl's leg at night so that a sharp tug on Mme Micas's part would immediately summon assistance. The old lady found this system highly amusing. Still, her failing vision proved merely a precursor to a more generalised and rapid decline in her health.

Nor was Rosa enjoying her usual level of vitality. Early in March 1875, she was obliged to excuse a tardy reply to Juliette on account of having been unwell. Anticipating her sister's alarm, Rosa assured her that she would not be following in the footsteps of the recently deceased painter Camille Corot – at least, not yet. Juliette should come and stay soon – at the same time as Caroline Carvalho, for example, which would be easier while Mme Micas was not well enough to attend to guests. Juliette did not have to study her letter closely to realise that all at By was not well.[3]

With home life fraught, Rosa struggled more than usual to keep abreast of professional challenges. But at the end of March, her temper was sufficiently riled to prompt her to seize a pen and compose a strongly worded letter to the editor of *The Times*. It was written – and printed – in uncompromising French.[4]

Rosa objected that the publisher Louis Brall had unlawfully printed an engraving taken from her painting *Coming from the Fair* (1875), for which she had not been shown proofs and on which a facsimile of her signature had been superimposed. The publicly shamed Brall was compelled to write a letter of defence, in which he nonetheless admitted that while he was not personally responsible for the false signature, the accusation was justified.[5]

Meanwhile, when Ernest Gambart learned of the universal ill-health at By, he was worried. He wrote to Rosa, instructing her that her physical well-being, not her career, should be her priority now. Nathalie would always be at the mercy of her delicate constitution, but she possessed a fiercely resilient character and for now, she soldiered on, while Rosa too was soon able to return to her usual activities. Mme Micas never did; she died on 11 May 1875.

If Rosa was grieved, Nathalie Micas was utterly disconsolate. Rosa enveloped her heartbroken companion with as much love and empathy as she could. The two friends had now faced the loss of all their parents, and the reduction of their 'family' from three to two consolidated their mutual attachment. Now in their early 50s, both women tacitly understood the implications of Mme Micas's death: all that remained of their unit was each other. This realisation injected a heightened sense of anxiety, vulnerability and dependency into their relationship.

Under the circumstances, that year's Salon brought a welcome distraction.

Though she had absented herself from the Salon for many years, Rosa always kept a close eye on each year's artistic offerings. There was rarely a Salon when a Bonheur or a Peyrol did not exhibit and it was fascinating to track the progress of the painters she had tutored over the years. Less than a week after Mme Micas's passing, the Salon provided a more upbeat topic of conversation in a letter to Juliette.

'I hear your picture looks very well at the Salon, which gives me much pleasure, as you will quite understand,' Rosa enthused.[6]

A few weeks later, *Les Gauloises*, a publication dedicated to the literary and artistic achievements of women, also recognised Juliette's skill. Having declared the work worthy of a first-class prize, the reviewer observed that 'we no longer have to stress the merits of these vigorous studies after nature, carried out under the instruction of Rosa Bonheur.'[7] The connection with Rosa was presented briefly, as though that alone was felt sufficient explanation for the work's excellence.

For the older sister, it was profoundly gratifying to see her sibling's work flourishing in spite of her commitment to motherhood. At the same time, Juliette provided a vital channel to the Paris art world, and she occasionally represented Rosa at official functions. That capacity proved invaluable the following summer, when Rosa fell off her horse and injured her arm.

'I cannot tell you how grateful I feel to you for being willing to represent me in the Delaroche hemicycle at the School of Fine Arts,' Rosa effused appreciatively. The thought that the sisters, so very different in type and temperament, might be confused tickled her. 'Now people will go and believe I am a charming little lady, fair-complexioned and shy.'[8]

Such playful asides were a typical feature of Rosa's correspondence. Despite her patchy education, she was a voracious letter writer, amusing friends and family with her bizarre pet names, witty verses, slang, impromptu sketches and her abundant use of animal terminology; she had always 'trotted' rather than walked somewhere, she might complain of an injured 'paw', while she habitually finished her letters with 'your old donkey of a sister' or something similar.[9] Every now

Handwriting and signature of Rosa Bonheur, 18 June 1863 (pen and ink on paper).
Private Collection/Bridgeman Images

and then, there were philosophical digressions. But provided there was not a more serious matter to address, her letters positively danced with her lively style and energetic, frequently illegible, handwriting. Many began with an apology for a delayed response and often incorporated a joke against herself. Her correspondence invariably gave the impression that she was leading a lively existence. But the letters set up a convenient smokescreen.

Behind the facade, Rosa was growing increasingly averse to face-to-face contact, especially if it compromised her workspace. When her successor at the drawing school, Mme Marandon, proposed coming to By with some students to present Rosa with a casket which had been made as a gift, the recipient hastily stalled her plan; Rosa would come to Paris instead. That way, she could determine the length of the interview.

As the months passed, Mme Micas's absence impressed itself. She had been a vital cog in the domestic machine at By, keeping house, tending to the animals, overseeing the running of the château and commanding the kitchen. With her loss, there was suddenly a great deal more to attend to at home, even employing servants (of whom there were nine at one point).[10] Notwithstanding, Rosa guarded her working time jealously, particularly in the winter, when it seemed

265

as though the hours of daylight were being spitefully snatched away from the moment she woke. Capturing animals in paint remained her life. And when she was not leaning over her canvas, she read widely, choosing texts on natural history and absorbing as much as she could.

CS

On 20 August 1876, Rosa's regular paper, *Le Figaro*, published an article entitled 'The Last Tiger', in which the author Méry advanced a protracted eulogy on the physique, beauty and stamina of the Bengal tiger. Venerating the beast as 'the gentleman of the highest rank of felines', the author offered proof of the animal's ferocity by recounting a horrific massacre which had taken place at a London zoo when two tigers were let into an enclosure with a lion. 'Seeing this marvellous animal, one regrets not being able to introduce him into domestic life and make a fuss of him,' the author mused.[11]

The long, front-page article was almost impossible for the animal-loving reader to ignore. Just a few months later, a tiger arrived at the Château de By.

'When you come over, you mustn't be too much afraid of the tame tiger I have got from Marseille,' Rosa forewarned her sister.[12]

The appearance of a tiger in Fontainebleau was a major event – not to mention a source of considerable alarm among Rosa's neighbours. The thought of keeping a big cat at By was not a prospect she had seriously entertained before now. But her experience with M. Dejean's lioness Pierrette had reiterated the importance of close observation, irrespective of the animal's size and spirit. Nothing surpassed studying such a creature in her own studio or on the grounds at By, where time constraints were less inhibitive. This was a professional necessity. Besides, Rosa did not intend to keep the tiger, merely to rent it.

Nonetheless, keeping a big cat at By, even temporarily, was an enormous undertaking. A small female might grow to 200 cm long, but an adult male could attain nearly 4 m in length and weigh 300 kg. The tail alone stretched to 1 m. Mucking out, enabling exercise and feeding – everything had to be done on a huge scale, and each task required careful planning in anticipation of the multiple risks. The largest of these animals needed up to 15 lbs of flesh and as much as 6,000 calories every day just to meet their basic nutritional requirements. Their privacy had to be respected, their enclosure reinforced and their unpredictability accepted. For Rosa's staff, the tiger represented a massive task to add to their already ponderous list of duties.[13]

That winter, Rosa studied the tiger intensely. She could not house the creature indefinitely so only had a limited time before it would have to be returned. Then with the added pressure of a study of some boars which urgently needed completing for Gambart, that Christmas, Rosa shut herself away, telling Juliette with regard to her porcine subjects: 'I don't allow myself even the time to go out at present and shan't go to Paris before they are done.'[14]

As was often the case, Rosa was far less tolerant when she noticed others inflicting the same kind of self-imposed toil.

'Poor Sis, I know how you love your painting and how hard you work; but you must get a little fresh air now and then,' Rosa instructed Juliette two months later, apparently oblivious to the hypocrisy of her own counsel.[15]

After a gruelling winter, Rosa was jollied that spring by the forthcoming marriage of 27-year-old Germain to Marie-Joséphine-Renée Besnard, the daughter of the esteemed porcelain painter from Blois, Jean Jude Ulysse-Besnard. Like Auguste, Germain, who had never been a pinion of strength, had been badly shaken by the war and had not yet recovered even his usual, hesitant degree of health. Rosa was greatly cheered by the news of the nuptials, which would no doubt be remedial to her half-brother.[16]

Rosa also made two very brief trips to Paris that spring, one to view an exhibition of paintings which were for sale and a second for a hasty perusal of the Salon. But on neither occasion did she spend long in the capital and promptly returned to work. Soon, Rosa was feeling the strain of her relentless industry. By April, she had begun fantasising about what the summer might hold.

It had been agreed that Nathalie would benefit from another visit to a spa town, and Rosa had in mind a return to their beloved Pyrenees. She extended an invitation to Juliette, outlining the proposed itinerary, which included an irresistible detour via Bordeaux. Rosa felt certain that the mention of Quinsac would tempt her sister to leave her family for a few weeks, and she was right. However, in the event, it was Rosa who had to alter their plans. A scant day exploring the Salon had not begun to satisfy her need to formulate an opinion of the year's talent, and then she still owed Gambart the painting of the boars. As the day of departure approached, Rosa could see that leaving now would mean settling for imperfection.

Her frustration at having to delay the holiday was somewhat alleviated by absorbing herself supervising some landscape work which she wished to have carried out in the wood adjoining By, where she had envisioned a small pond and an enclosure for a stag, surrounded by a gravel pathway. As for Juliette and Nathalie, they would simply have to be patient if they wished to holiday with her.

They did not have long to wait; by July, the expedition was underway.

The women spent five days in Bordeaux and as soon as they arrived in Bayonne, Rosa stole herself away to pen a letter to Auguste, in the hope that her lively account might lift his spirits.

'We found time to go to Quinsac,' Rosa exclaimed. 'I succeeded in finding my fig-tree and the tree under which mama tried to make me read [...] I insisted on taking some soup with barley-bread in it, as in my childhood [...] There were peasants of my own age with whom I perhaps played as a girl [...] I abandoned myself to all my childish reminiscences.'[17]

The trip certainly served the intended purpose: 'We are taking life easily and enjoying ourselves so far,' Rosa reported. 'We all three tuck in alarmingly.'[18]

The restorative interlude was needed. When Rosa returned to By, her job list had grown no shorter. Painting was her life, but it was also her livelihood. Any work undertaken on the château or the grounds must be paid for and her fortune was by no means limitless. Rosa was not averse to accepting a loan from Gambart whenever funds were running low. She always reimbursed him, but repayment usually took the form of pictures which he could pass on for sale or auction, so a cash injection invariably cost her even more of that most precious commodity – time.

With his long-standing friendship and his continued and repeated intervention on Rosa's part, Gambart's relationship with her had scarcely altered since his retirement. He knew that Rosa's works would always sell and she was profoundly trustworthy. It was no gamble for Gambart. Then Rosa was a celebrity; cultivating her good favour meant that she might be coaxed into attending one of his social receptions and ensuring that his guests returned home with an indelible memory of the brilliant evening hosted by M. Ernest Gambart.

It was accordingly to Gambart's residence, the Château d'Alsa in Spa, that the Belgian press reported Rosa to have travelled in August 1877, a trip conveniently timed to coincide with the celebration of Rubens which had consumed the city of Antwerp. But that was not Gambart's primary motivation for inviting Rosa to Belgium: he also had in mind an enormous group portrait of the artists felt to be the most prominent and influential during the 19th century. The prospective masterpiece would hang in his villa in Nice and he had asked the Director of the Académie des Beaux-Arts in Antwerp and acclaimed painter of history scenes and portraits, Nicaise de Keyser, to undertake the work. The selection of subjects was telling: all the greats were men. But there was to be one exception – Rosa. And her visit to Belgium was organised expressly to enable Keyser to undertake the necessary sketches.

On her previous visit, Rosa had been dismayed by the lack of good quality wine in Belgium, but accounts of the lavish evening reception Gambart laid on in her honour hinted that he might have changed her opinion. Readers of *L'Echo du Parlement* were told how the grounds of the château had been lit up by Bengal lights and complemented by a torchlit serenade courtesy of the Société des Montagnards, while

Gambart's old friend, the energetic *chansonnier* Gustave Nadaud, had even sung a six-verse composition which had been written specially for Rosa. The press observed that Mlle Bonheur, who proved herself full of 'charm and simplicity', appeared to be 'extremely touched' by the occasion.[19]

It was true; secretly, such ceremonies and circumstance flattered Rosa's ego and she could present a sociable front when required. But that was not to say she found these occasions relaxing. Once honour had been served, she was soon back in France, having spent barely four days in Belgium. There was much calling her home.

œ

The Exposition Universelle of 1878 had a lot to live up to. From the very outset, the unspoken benchmark was the magnificent Exposition Universelle of 1867, which hindsight had aggrandised as the Empire's spectacular finale. After the undignified episodes of the Franco–Prussian War and the Commune, the show would provide France with a much-needed opportunity to reassert herself and rebuild her reputation in the eyes of the world. The exposition was laid out at the Champ-de-Mars, where France dominated the exhibition space, while Germany was notable for its unsurprising absence. When the day of opening arrived, Parisians looked out onto a grey and drizzling sky. As the whole world watched the French capital with bated breath, citizens hoped rather than knew that the show would be the triumphant renaissance the organisers had visualised.[20]

Officially, the pièce de resistance was the Trocadéro, a grand congress centre and concert hall of a staggering 5,200 seating capacity with an aquarium beneath it. However, Thomas Edison's more developed version of Alexander Graham Bell's telephone and an impressive show of electric light bulbs proudly demonstrated that technology and industry were thriving. The principal streets and public buildings had been illuminated, coloured lanterns were everywhere to be seen and before long, excited crowds were pushing their way through the exhibition entrance, desperate to be able to say that they too had seen the marvels on show. The tension was broken: 'The exhibition may so far be considered a success,' reported *The Times* on 2 May.[21]

But for the Bonheur family, the show had but one centrepiece: Isidore's sculptural offering. His tremendous, life-sized bulls towered on a plinth above craned-necked, open-mouthed observers in the exhibition grounds. With over 16 million people visiting the show between June and November (far more than the previous exposition hosted in Paris), Isidore's work was on view to a maximum amount of spectators. Rosa, who had not participated this time, could not have been more pleased.

The Exposition Universelle brought other highlights and diversions, too.

Among the foreigners flocking to the capital were the British painters John Everett Millais and William Powell Frith. Always at home in the role of tour guide, Ernest Gambart welcomed his old acquaintances and led them on an expertly commentated visit of some of Paris's key ateliers, including the workspaces of the painters of battle scenes, Edouard Detaille and Ernest Meissonier. Gambart also used their visit as an opportunity to have their portraits painted by Keyser, to add to the group portrait for which he had already captured Rosa.

The picture was now taking shape. Arranged in rows, one seated and one standing, were some of the most celebrated luminaries the 19th-century art world had to offer – painters such as Jean-Auguste-Dominique Ingres, Eugène Delacroix, Paul Delaroche and J.M.W. Turner. And there on the left, in the front row of the picture, seated next to Sir Edwin Landseer, was Rosa. Keyser depicted her with a manuscript on her lap, her sideways gaze fixing the viewer in knowing complicity, the flicker of a wry smile playing on her lips. She appeared poised, assured and undaunted by the great men who both surrounded and outnumbered her. The message was clear: a woman could be great too.[22]

Millais and Frith were eager to meet with Rosa while in Paris. Rarely in need of an invitation to act as social mediator, Gambart had soon choreographed a lunch date at By.[23]

Nicaise de Keyser, *Schools of the 19th Century*, 1878, oil on canvas, 285 x 400 cm, Musée des Beaux-Arts, Nice.
(Seated from left to right: J.M.W. Turner, Sir Edwin Landseer, Rosa Bonheur, Ernest Meissonier, Peter Cornelius, Ary Scheffer, Jean-Auguste-Dominique Ingres, Horace Vernet. Standing: Hiram Powers, John Everett Millais, Lawrence Alma-Tadema, Jean-Léon Gérôme, William Powell Frith, Ludwig Knaus, Antonio Canova, Albert Thorwaldsen, Henri Leys, Eugène Delacroix, Paul Delaroche, Louis Gallait, Ernest Gambart, Hans Makart and Joseph-Nicolas Robert-Fleury.)
Copyright Musée des Beaux-Arts Jules Chéret, Nice – photo Muriel Anssens

On the appointed morning, the men stepped off the train at Fontainebleau station, where Frith noticed an attending carriage. Its driver had white hair and was dressed in a broad-brimmed hat and a long black coat and looked, Frith remembered, like 'a French *abbé*'. However, a flash of scarlet on the chauffeur's breast bewildered the artist, who was sufficiently versed in French decorations to understand its significance. He quizzed Gambart:

'Do priests wear the Legion of Honour?'

'What priest? That is Mademoiselle Bonheur. She is one of the very few ladies in France who is *décorée*. You can speak French; get onto the box beside her.'[24]

Besides the professional engagements, there were more personal enthusiasms Rosa could satisfy over the course of the Exposition Universelle. In September, a selection of the world's finest steeds were put through their paces just outside Paris at Maisons-Laffites, culminating in a parade two days later before the President of the Republic, Patrice Mac-Mahon, and the Minister of Agriculture. The chance to admire horses in action never failed to arrest Rosa's attention; indeed, she told Germain that she had come to Paris specifically 'to see the horse-show'.[25]

Meanwhile, Ernest Gambart was indulging passions of his own. While in Spa, he had struck up a friendship with Manuel Silvela, the Spanish Foreign Minister and grandson of Raymond Bonheur's old friend of the same name from Bordeaux. Spain needed allies in prominent foreign locations, and Gambart had assured Silvela that he could establish a small Spanish colony near his Belgian home. Gambart proved as good as his word, and with his connections and international profile, he was the natural choice when Silvela needed help finding a suitable candidate to appoint as Spanish Consul in Nice. Eventually (and not without some delicate footwork on Gambart's part), the post was conferred upon Gambart himself in September 1878. Gambart was now one of the most prominent and powerful men in Nice. And from there, he could flex his sociopolitical muscles to Rosa's advantage.

The following summer brought the death of the Bonheurs' old family friend, the sculptor Pierre-Jules Mêne. But otherwise, Rosa had every cause to feel confident as the decade neared its close. 'Good luck in your work, my young brother,' Rosa wrote encouragingly to Germain on 5 July 1879. 'You can succeed, if you try. You are still young enough to secure a distinctive and honourable position in our field of art. Mark what I tell you,' she concluded earnestly. 'There will be more Bonheurs still.'[26]

Such reserves of spirited mettle were soon to prove indispensable – for Rosa was about to embark on her wildest adventure yet.

19

The Call of the Wild

'Has the great artist got her sights set on the Cross of Isabella the Catholic?' the journal *Les Gauloises* speculated provocatively in September 1879.[1]

Given Rosa's connections with Bordeaux's Spanish colony and Gambart's appointment as Spanish Consul, people were naturally suspicious when a painting of a lion from Gambart's collection was offered to the Museo Nacional del Prado at the end of the year.

But even when she got wind of them, idle aspersions seldom worried Rosa. Painting was all that mattered. And that autumn, big cats remained her obsession.

Sufficient time had now elapsed since the tiger's stay for the memory of the complexities involved in keeping such a creature to have dissipated. The lions Rosa hired for a short time from the famous animal tamer François Bidel failed to satiate her creative appetite and Ernest Gambart, always eager to watch Rosa turn nature into masterpieces, was keen to feed the artist's growing hunger. By October, he believed he had found the perfect specimens to join her menagerie.

The beasts were currently being held in captivity in the Jardin Zoologique de Marseille, a generously stocked zoo whose management were no strangers to financial turbulence. Gambart had spotted a male lion named Néro and his female companion, Sarah, and he wrote to Rosa apprising her of his discovery: she should come and see these magnificent animals. A trip to his villa in Nice would provide a perfect opportunity.

But before Rosa could consider such a visit, something sensational happened.

'I write to you at once the news I have just received and which will be made public in a few days,' Rosa exclaimed breathlessly to Juliette on 21 January 1880. 'The King of Spain has just conferred on me the title of Major of the Royal Order of Isabella the Catholic.'[2]

Rosa suspected the Silvela family to have had something to do with the commendation. Either way, she was thrilled. But as she told Auguste, if the Spanish thought this would inspire her conversion to Catholicism, they were sorely mistaken.

℅

An additional medal was not the only novelty to greet Rosa that spring. The beginning of 1880 also ushered in new acquaintances. One of those was the vet who had served with the 5th squadron, Major Anatole François Placide Rousseau, to whom Rosa's coachman Étienne was sent one day when one of her dogs fell ill.

As a military vet, Major Rousseau considered domestic animals to be outside his remit. But the chance to meet the great painter of *The Horse Fair* was irresistible. He had heard the talk – and the whispers – and he was excited, if a little apprehensive, to make her acquaintance.

When Major Rousseau brought his horse to stop outside the heavy metal gates at By, Nathalie was there to greet him. Her warmth immediately struck him as, without further ado, she shepherded him inside and upstairs to meet the redoubtable châtelaine. The studio door creaked open to reveal a stout, middle-aged woman toiling over a canvas. The Major never forgot his first impressions:

> She was dressed in a blue jacket with white embroi-
> dery, which had beautiful emeralds at the fastening. Her

expression was open and frank, and her head topped with abundant, greying hair which was a little untamed and cropped at about ear level [...] But all I saw were her eyes; they were clear and looked straight ahead. It seemed as though a person could see right into her soul. One felt she was incapable of telling a lie.[3]

Little conversation sufficed for Rosa and Rousseau to see that they were going to get along famously. Rousseau was charmed by the celebrity's genuine character, while his expertise in the field of animal husbandry fostered Rosa's profound respect. Henceforward, the sight of Major Rousseau arriving on horseback at the gates of By became a regular feature in the château's social calendar. The vet's company and conversation enlivened many a pleasant lunch, while his medical nous brought Rosa reassurance whenever a member of her menagerie was taken ill. As the friendship blossomed, Rousseau extended an invitation to Rosa to return his visit and was delighted when she quickly fell into a warm friendship with his wife.

But the doctor could be counted on for more than veterinary advice and scintillating conversation. He became privy to much more sensitive, personal information of which admirers of Rosa's work had no inkling. Her true state of health was one such matter. In her letters, Rosa was selective about what she shared – and with whom. But Major Rousseau knew more than most. Shortly after Rosa and the doctor met, she was taken unwell. In her letters to family and friends, she did not divulge explicit detail (though it was no secret that she was overworked). Still, the malady was serious enough to seek a doctor's opinion and for the trip she had planned to Gambart's property in Nice to be thrown into jeopardy.

'Don't be anxious about my health,' she assured Juliette on 11 April 1880 after the worst of the crisis had passed. 'I have good news to give you. The doctors tell me I can start for Nice as soon as I like.'[4]

Rosa and Nathalie had arranged to meet the unassailable 'Messire Gambiche' (as Rosa now delighted in calling him) in Marseille, where he would show them the lions he had found. From there, they would travel together to Nice, where they would stay for a week.

'The annoying part will be the two or three visits and dinners which I shall have to swallow,' Rosa grumbled.[5] But the incentive of the lions and the break her doctors actively prescribed made the discomfort bearable. Within a few days, Rosa and Nathalie had set off.

'The sea air seems already to have benefited me, and the change has calmed my mind,' Rosa told Auguste. 'I found my lion and lioness, who looked quite handsome,' she continued eagerly.[6]

Her appetite whetted in anticipation of bringing the lions back to By, Rosa's next stop was Gambart's luxurious Niçoise villa.

Nice in the early springtime was a technicoloured explosion of activity. 'It is a paradise,' journalist Maxime Gérard had observed just a few months earlier in *Le Gaulois*. 'The city's coastline is fringed with rows of white, princely houses [...] Before you is the sea and beyond ... Africa. In your imagination that is. Don't laugh; when you see this blue sea beneath this blue sky, you can think only of Africa. [...] This azure water and sky have been so talked about and celebrated that a person no longer believes they could be real.'[7]

But they were. And now, weary of the dismal winter weather and the sluggish social calendar which accompanied it, fashion-conscious, sun-seeking Parisians were leading a seasonal migration of well-heeled socialites from all corners of France and Europe.

According to *Le Gaulois*, the 'season' had begun early that year in mid-November. The world-famous carnival was now over, but the promise of sunshine and entertainment ensured that fashionable society lingered. Such was the popularity of Nice as a winter tourist destination among the Parisian elite that national publications like *Le Figaro* and *Le Gaulois* dedicated lengthy columns to Mediterranean gossip and reports on the high life, relocated for the season from Paris to Nice. 'The emigration of Parisian fashions is more marked by the day in these enchanted surroundings,' *Le Constitutionnel* had noted shortly before Rosa's trip.[8] Meanwhile, regional papers such as *La Vie Mondaine* kept holidaying socialites updated on protocol and people – and parties. And whether she liked it or not, the latter was something Rosa would have to get used to if she wished to stay with Ernest Gambart.

ℂ

Ernest Gambart's Rivieran kingdom was renowned. Since its grand opening on 29 December 1875, sovereigns, artists, actresses and politicians had all made appearances on the glittering guest list. In 1877, Gambart had hosted the Prince of Wales, the following year, Queen Victoria's son, Prince Leopold and in 1879, General Ulysses S. Grant, veteran of the American Civil War and former US president. Then in 1873, he had sold the Château de Fabron which had come with his estate to the promiscuous Duke Ernest II of Saxe-Coburg-Gotha, who thus became a neighbour and a regular guest at Gambart's soirées along with his wife, the Duchess, Alexandrine. And with Gambart's connections in Spain, the villa had become the unofficial social club of the well-to-do Spaniards now congregating in Nice.[9]

It was not hard for Rosa and Nathalie to understand Les Palmiers's appeal. The two-storey, neoclassical, marble-fronted villa was widely agreed to be 'one of the most beautiful in Nice'.[10] The entrance was guarded by statues of lions and Corinthian columns flanked the door-way, while the vast space within included a large vestibule, a capacious library, a salon and a dining room. Meanwhile, outside, a veritable Eden awaited the visitor, in the form of acre upon acre of meticulously landscaped garden.

'Through its position on the Mount Saint-Hélène which overlooks the sea, M. Gambart's splendid villa offers an exceptional setting for a daytime party,' *L'Indépendance Belge* had reported in 1877. 'There is such a profusion of roses in the garden that one begs for mercy; these are not just gardens, this is an olfactory laboratory.'[11]

From the very first, Gambart had been anxious to ingratiate himself with the elegant and affluent Niçoise society. With his deter-mined congeniality, people soon came to associate an invitation to Les Palmiers with brilliant company, good taste and apparently effortless hospitality. Whether to attend a musical, literary or artistic evening, a children's party or a charity ball (like the one hosted to help victims of the 1879 flood in the Spanish city of Murcia), a guest could be sure of a splendid reception.[12]

When they beheld Gambart's exotic paradise, Rosa and Nathalie were overcome.

'At last, I am in Nice and it feels as though I am dreaming,' Rosa marvelled the day after she arrived.[13]

'As for this home of Mr Gambart's, it's a superb palace. Everything is trim and neat, with palms, aloes and all sorts of tropical plants growing in the open air. As a background, there is the Gulf of Nice,' Rosa effervesced.[14]

Ernest Gambart, Rosa Bonheur and Nathalie Micas.
Collection Atelier Rosa Bonheur

Gambart's 'gallery' was sheer indulgence for the art enthusiast, 'a veritable museum', *Le Constitutionnel* had noted admiringly. Journals dedicated whole articles to describing Gambart's embellished halls and corridors. There were works by modern masters, including Rosa's friend Jean-Léon Gérôme, as well as Ernest Meissonier, Lawrence Alma-Tadema, Jules Breton and even sculpture by Gambart's new acquaintance, the actress Sarah Bernhardt, not to mention studies by Rosa herself.[15]

With such delights on offer, Rosa's week in Nice passed quickly and she returned to By, her mind overflowing with new experiences. And just a few weeks later, the lions who had prompted her trip arrived in Fontainebleau.

Rosa's household now had to reimplement the system employed with the tiger. Years later, Rosa remembered her servants tentatively offering the creatures as much as 20 lbs of raw beef through the bars of their cage using pitchforks. The lions were difficult to lodge, hard to keep and expensive to feed. Rosa was in her element.[16]

Neighbours and visitors were alarmed. One fellow Thomery resident, the acclaimed tenor M. Grivot (who had made his name at the Opéra Comique and now spent the summer months in Fontainebleau), was unable to conceal his terror. Rosa could not help laughing.[17]

She now understood big cats intimately and had become highly attuned to their needs. As she worked, a profound and unspoken affection gradually formed between artist and subject. Of the two animals, it was Néro, the male lion, who captured a particularly special place in Rosa's heart. Contrary to the warnings she had received, she found him to be gentle and obliging. In time, she could get close enough to stroke and pet him, and the sensation of her touch made him rear up and wriggle with pleasure. Whenever the sound of Rosa's chatter alerted him to her approach, he lifted his great head expectantly, recognising his owner by her voice.

Néro was kept in a shuttered cage mounted on wheels and whenever Rosa wanted to start a drawing session, her staff would lead the wagon out and set it down on the lawn at By. Rosa maintained that as soon as the shutters were removed, Néro routinely lifted his gaze towards the château windows. Rosa felt certain he was trying to ascertain if his mistress was up and required him to pose that day. When she was ready, Rosa came down into the garden and took up her place on a small covered platform which had been erected to protect her from the elements.

Rosa worked assiduously, watching, recording, checking again and reworking in a continual, multistage process. From time to time, the lion moved and the whole practice had to be started again. But Rosa's determination was soon bearing fruit, resulting in pieces like *Lion in a Mountainous Landscape* (1880). The work showed a male lion sideways on, his back leg stretched out behind him, indicating that this was only a temporary pause from motion. The animal held his head upright, while he gazed out of the canvas to the left, as though fixing on some unidentified activity outside the frame. The sapphire sky and dramatic mountain vista bore the influence of Rosa's stays in Nice and the Pyrenees, while the dramatic tonal variations applied to the beast himself brought him virtually springing out of the canvas. Shades from darkest brown to the most dazzling gold worked in perfect harmony to convey the velvety sheen of his coat and the contrasting thick, bushy texture of his mane. The piece shamelessly subverted the usual power distribution common to portraiture. Here, the artist, traditionally the empowered party, had resigned herself to the role of reverent vassal as she worked to immortalise her regal sitter. In Rosa's painting, the model was king and through her brush, she became the venerating courtier.

Rosa now produced many such pictures every year, each one the result of countless more studies and sketches, the fruit of an ever-expanding knowledge of the assorted species represented.

Rosa was utterly absorbed in her work when that June, she received a sudden shock. Having battled with his health since the war, her frail half-brother Germain had been diagnosed with heart disease. At the end of the month, he died in Blois where he now lived. He had only just turned 33 years old.

'I was painfully affected by the sad news arriving just when he seemed a little better,' Rosa mourned with Juliette. 'He has finished like a poor lamp that has no more oil; and his life could never have been very happy, like that of a man who is able to accomplish something.'[18]

Press obituaries acknowledged Germain's artistic talent, but one feature eclipsed his professional achievements: he was the half-brother of the great Rosa Bonheur.[19]

Rosa chose not to attend the funeral. The truth was, she sensed that she herself was far from well. She could not compromise her own strength; too much depended on her. Besides, she failed to see how she could be of any help now. The best support she could offer her family going forwards was financial – and that meant she had to work.

'I think it my duty to preserve my health,' she attempted to explain to Juliette.[20] Her family was only part of the reason; there was also Nathalie to think of. But the duty Rosa spoke of was as much to art. She acknowledged her role in developing her skills, but she took no credit for her talent. To her, the ability to paint was a gift which she felt obligated to nurture. She could not leave this earth now; there was too much to do.

As the autumn approached, Rosa remained focused on her work and her animals. The purchase of two new horses in November gave her and Major Rousseau a fresh topic of conversation. Then, as the year before, in the New Year, family and friends started receiving letters bearing a postmark from Nice.

Rosa had fallen in love with the winter retreat. She had no desire to imitate the fashionable elite; rather, the climate seemed beneficial to Nathalie, and, she had to admit, to herself. Ever percipient, Ernest Gambart seized the opportunity to make a seductive proposition. When he acquired the Villa Gastaud, its 24 hectares had come with a handful of other properties, including an oil mill. On this land, he had built the fine Villa Africaine; what if Rosa were to take it for her winter stays? She was famously loath to leave By, but in her own villa, she could set up a studio and continue working, spending months at a time there if she chose. And if she insisted on payment, she could supply Gambart with paintings up to the value of 5,000 francs a year. All parties agreed it to be a splendid suggestion.[21]

Villa Africaine was a delightful building, surrounded by palm trees and close to the sea – an exquisitely comfortable winter haven which Rosa would be able to furnish just as she pleased. There, she could work and revitalise herself at the same time, while letters home kept her in touch with any matters concerning the animals.

'My servant, Céline, has written to me about the trouble given by my little bitch Bellotte,' she told Major Rousseau on 11 March 1881. 'I think she is going to have pups, the father being Charbonnier. I am not displeased about this, as the little ones will be a good mixture, and may turn out good hunting dogs, with keen scent.'[22]

But Rosa currently had another, more serious gynaecological concern to deal with. This one concerned herself – and it was becoming more acute.

For some time now, Rosa had been experiencing episodes of unusually heavy, menstrual-like bleeding. She had just turned 60.

'I have had another attack,' she admitted to Major Rousseau that spring, 'I consider myself fortunate to have a capable young man as my doctor.'[23]

When the crises hit, she was reduced to a pale, weak, often bed-ridden shadow of her usual self. Work became unthinkable. The mysterious affliction had become a veritable handicap and was starting to rule her life. Surely, so much blood could not be right. The episodes were not only distressing for herself, but also for Céline who assisted her and most especially, for Nathalie. Still, they always passed, and when they had, Rosa fell on her work like a starved man would a meal, absorbing herself and drowning out any anxieties. Rosa simply endured the attacks while they lasted. Besides, in the moments of respite, there was always something more pressing to attend to. One dramatic event of this kind occurred early in 1881.

Rosa was resting in the villa one Saturday evening in March when Nathalie burst into the room, frantic. Rosa must come quickly; something terrible had happened.[24]

Getting up and hurrying with her companion to the window, Rosa immediately understood Nathalie's panic. Outside on the horizon, the two women could see flames licking the sky. They were coming from the Théâtre Italien. An explosion had been heard and as Rosa and Nathalie watched the building crackle and roar, suddenly, the whole structure appeared to cave in on itself. It was like a scene from a nightmare.

And that was not all – because for anyone acquainted with his social calendar, Ernest Gambart was meant to be inside.

20

Mastering the Moon

The gala evening at the Théâtre Italien was set to be spectacular. Internationally renowned soprano Mlle Bianca Donadio's last performance in *Lucia di Lammermoor* had brought theatregoers clamouring to the box office and ticket holders were soon pushing through the theatre's narrow access ways to take their seats. As the auditorium filled up, the sense of anticipation mounted. At last, the curtain began to rise, encouraging the hum of chattering voices to peter out.[1]

Suddenly, an almighty explosion erupted from above the stage. Flames began leaping out of the border, and in seconds, fire had consumed the stage.

Gasps of disbelief followed by cries of panic rippled out through the audience as flames swept from the stage towards the auditorium. Men, women and children bolted for the exits, falling over each other in a frantic effort to escape. The tight stairwells and passageways were soon congested and filling up with smoke. Weaker members of the public began passing out from the fumes.[2]

Outside, horrified onlookers watched as people could be seen leaning out of windows, gesticulating in terror before being overcome by smoke and falling to the ground.

Firemen, soldiers and naval officers were rushed to the scene, and by 10.00 pm, they had assumed control of the blaze. Bodies were soon being extricated from the wreckage. The charred cadavers of a father, mother and child were pulled out, their blackened forms clinging onto each other, the infant still gripping an orange in its free hand. The next day, the body of an elegant lady was discovered. Her torched and shrunken head made it impossible to identify her, but her beautiful arms remained intact. She was still wearing her long, modish gloves with their twenty buttons neatly fastened up to her elbows.[3]

As more and more information was released and the death toll crept up to nearly 200, Rosa knew she must reassure her family back in Paris.

'I write in haste to tell you that I was resting quietly at home,' Rosa told Auguste. 'We are in consternation at the heartrending accounts of what took place.' She added: 'Mr Gambart had a narrow escape. He was on his way to the theatre but had not got there when the fire broke out.'[4]

The catastrophe so close to home served as a chilling reminder of life's inherent fragility. The renewed vigour with which Rosa now approached her painting reflected a heightened sense of urgency, as though she felt time was running out.

Rosa's haemorrhaging continued. In a letter to Juliette written shortly after the incident at the Théâtre Italien, she alluded to the encumbrance of what she now called her 'attacks'. The affliction aroused as much Rosa's anger as it did her anxiety. Had it not been for these episodes, she would have finished the picture of the lions she was struggling to complete.[5]

At least the beauty of her surroundings offered some solace. The weather in Nice heralded the approach of summer, with balmy days, mild nights and the gentle breeze off the Mediterranean brushing thankful skin as it carried delicate floral perfumes on the air. There were natural wonders to be discovered in every corner of this Gallic paradise. One evening, Rosa and Nathalie were taking a stroll in the garden when they suddenly found themselves surrounded by a swarm of tiny, flickering lights. The fairylike apparition filled Rosa with wonder and brought flooding back a long-forgotten memory. As a little girl, she remembered having seen what she thought to be shooting stars gathering in a cluster near the ground. Now, she realised her error: they were actually fireflies. The disavowal of such long-held convictions was symptomatic of a more generalised mood of reassess-ment which permeated Rosa's life at present.[6]

Rosa could not deny the very deep level on which the Mediterranean environment affected her. In the spring and early sum-mer, Nice was at its finest. With each breath, the sea breeze filled the lungs with vitality, while on mountaintops, flocks of goats and sheep were herded by shepherds in visually appealing costumes. Everywhere, Rosa spotted splendid backgrounds just calling out to be captured in paint, frozen in time, transformed into picturesque settings for her animal friends.

Though Rosa resented the social engagements imposed on her by Gambart, there were a handful of new acquaintances whose friendship she was pleased to cultivate. One such companion was Alexandrine, the Duchess of Saxe-Coburg-Gotha, who, wintering as she did at the Château Fabron, was now a neighbour.

The Duchess was the eldest of the eight children of Leopold I, Grand Duke of Baden and Princess Sophie of Sweden. Formerly a porcelain-complexioned beauty, by her mid-60s, Alexandrine had grown agreeably sturdy. Her light brown hair was immaculately set, typically gathered on her head with an impeccable centre-parting and a crown of neat curls or carefully pinned braids around it. Indeed, she might have appeared intimidating were it not for the gentle smile which lit up her pale blue eyes. Her amiability was admirable; her life had been one of suffering and subservience.[7]

While still in her early twenties, Alexandrine had been briefly considered as a potential fiancée by the future Tsar Alexander II of Russia before being hastily discarded in favour of Princess Marie of Hesse. Not long afterwards, her path crossed with that of the man who would become her husband, Prince Ernest of Saxe-Coburg-Gotha, whose brother Albert (Queen Victoria's consort since 1840) had urged him to wed in the desperate hope that marriage might subdue Ernest's promiscuous behaviour. A wanton youth had left the Prince suffering from venereal disease, and a postponement of the marriage with Alexandrine was proposed in order to potentiate a full recovery.

When the marriage was finally contracted, the libertine Prince quickly demonstrated that he had not the slightest intention of changing his lifestyle. The marriage was said to be of the most turbulent nature, and people whispered that Alexandrine's loyalty was repaid by repeated infidelities on Ernest's part. The couple's failure to produce an heir seemed to confirm what everyone suspected – that Ernest had been made infertile through his countless affairs. Incredibly, it was said that Alexandrine not only accepted the situation, but that she even held herself responsible. Queen Victoria was appalled at her brother-in-law's disrespect for Alexandrine, whom she declared 'really a most dear aimiable [sic] character whom one must love dearly'.[8] A person need only consider Alexandrine's charitable works, not least assisting the Red Cross during the Franco-Prussian War, to appreciate her good-ness. Virtually everywhere she went, Alexandrine inspired warmth, affection and above all, heartfelt pity.

Whether Rosa genuinely disbelieved the accounts of Ernest's immoral conduct or whether she chose to ignore them remained unclear. She always maintained that Alexandrine and Ernest's love was as strong as the day they married and that Ernest was an intelligent, cultured sovereign with a politically sound strategy for restructuring Germany.

Whenever their winter visits coincided, Alexandrine and Rosa took advantage of their homes' proximity to call on each other. Alexandrine was fascinated by Rosa's work and could sit for hours in the studio, absorbing the captivating scenes the artist created. Rosa, the Duchess affirmed, was 'kind' and 'indulgent', 'so warmhearted, so affectionate, often so merry'. Her Highness was deeply moved by Rosa's 'generosity, touching simplicity, and tireless labour'.[9]

But for all the friends and the picturesque surroundings in Nice, no workspace could rival the one Rosa had now perfected at By – and no city feed a person's appetite for art so well as Paris.

'If I see that I can't finish my picture here, we will pack up and be off in a few days,' Rosa informed Juliette. Two weeks later, the fate of the lions Rosa was painting was decided: 'I am bringing them back to By with me […] I begin to want to see a little painting.'[10]

Rosa Bonheur, c. 1880.
Photo by adoc-photos/Corbis Historical via Getty Images

Besides creating and consuming art, there were also the animals impelling her return. She enjoyed unique, affectionate relationships with the full cast of diverse characters who populated her menagerie. Friends had lost count of the beasts Rosa had welcomed through her doors over the years. The stables had been home to her mare, Margot, numerous horses, including Roland the draft horse, and donkeys. There was the deer, Jacques, Ratata the monkey, and dogs in their tens, among them Rosa's beloved Cairn terrier, Wasp (whom she painted in 1856), as well as her long-haired canine friends Charlie and Daisy (who could impress visitors performing tricks). Nathalie was particularly fond of the tiny shorthaired Gamine, while Niniche, the female basset Bellotte, Pastour, Charbonnier and the strapping Danish dog Ulm ensured that the house was always full.[11] Meanwhile, sheep and goats succeeded each other and a flock of assorted birds was a permanent feature of the château.

The guest list was always changing, in an ever-shifting zoological kaleidoscope. One addition to the family that year was a chamois (a small, horned species of goatlike mammal with a rich brown or light grey coat and striking black-and-white markings up the side of its face). Rosa acquired the animal from M. Mauger, head of the journal *La Basse-Cour*.[12] However, the ravaged health of the first specimen which arrived was the cause of universal dismay and its replacement consequently subjected to an exhaustive veterinary examination before Rosa handed over the 416 francs being asked. She insisted that any animal arriving at the château be in good physical condition. It was hard enough when one of her long-standing residents fell ill.

That year, the need to put one of the horses down was an event of such solemn magnitude at By that it was photographed. On such occasions, Rosa did not balk at the prospect of performing the grim act herself. It was the only way she could be certain that the creature had not suffered. 'Though she was strong and brave at the moment of performing the unpleasant duty, it unnerved her afterward, and I have known her to feel the effects of this during three or four days,' Rosa's student Mlle Keller recalled.[13]

'They are friends, don't you see?' Rosa entreated her fellow female artist, the recently married Virginie Demont-Breton, to understand, 'they have worked with me. I owe them half of what people are pleased to admire in my pictures. So they have to grow dangerous before I can bring myself to kill them.'[14]

The older she got, the more such harrowing occurrences turned Rosa's mind to the bigger questions of life and death. She had always been inclined towards philosophising, and this tendency now became more pronounced.

From the end of June that year, a comet was visible over France, captivating a public who, ordinarily indifferent to the expanse of space above them, were now routinely hurrying outside at dusk to gaze up in wonder at the night-time spectacle. The reason, the journal *La Science Populaire* speculated, was that 'it is interesting to see one of those stars that, in times gone by, people took as a sign from above'.[15]

'Last night I saw the comet for the first time,' Rosa recorded during the uncomfortably hot summer of 1881, writing to her sister, whom she had affectionately taken to calling 'mother Jub'. 'I have also much observed the moon of late.'[16]

The vast sky above her seemed to hold a myriad of secrets. These days, Rosa often found herself gazing upwards reverentially, as though there might lie the answers to the questions with which she wrestled.

⤞

It was to be a different Christmas that year. Rosa had invited her step-mother to join her and Nathalie in Nice, and once Marguerite Picard was safely installed, Rosa was pleased to report to Juliette that the sea air appeared to be suiting the old woman (who was now approaching 70). Given the friction which had historically agitated the relation-ship between Nathalie and the Bonheurs, it was cheering to see her stepmother and her companion getting along.

The Christmas and New Year festivities inevitably took in a num-ber of invitations to Ernest Gambart's home. One evening soirée in January gave Marguerite Picard a chance to bask contentedly in parental pride when Rosa appeared with her decorations pinned to her breast. Rosa's own pleasure was more dilute; besides the music, she found the occasion indescribably dull. There were no amusing characters, merely 'pretty women [...] fine dresses galore, decorations, and orders', while Nathalie's Spanish mantilla was stolen. 'Such things please me about as much as twenty kicks in the back-side!' she grumbled afterwards.[17]

Still, when she did not have to endure socialising, work was prov-ing deeply satisfying. The Tedescos were still conducting a roaring trade in Bonheur pictures, and with a constant flow of other commis-sions, it was difficult to keep up with the demand. Having recovered from a bout of flu and momentarily experiencing a respite from her gynaecological troubles, Rosa was enjoying a period of vitality. Her painting was showing the effects.

'As for my art, the older I grow, the more I love it,' she shared candidly with Auguste. 'Were I to paint only daubs, it would make no difference.'[18]

Rosa's overarching philosophical mood now even nudged her to make peace with the faults that her ill-health had caused her to perceive in her relationships. The news that Paul Chardin's wife had passed away spurred Rosa to cast trivial irritations aside. Reaching for pen and paper, she composed an empathetic letter to her Rapin and the recipient was deeply moved. It was as though no time had passed since their last correspondence and it had the happy effect of reigniting their friendship.

In sickness and in health, whether in Nice or at By, ensuring the well-being of her menagerie remained paramount to Rosa. And with her extensive knowledge of animal behaviour, she was well placed to advise others when the need arose.

'Change nothing in your horses,' she ordered Isidore that year in relation to a piece he was working on. 'The hack always starts from the right, for the simple reason that, like us, the right side of horses is always the stronger.'[19]

But the price of constantly shuttling between Fontainebleau and Nice was now starting to take its toll. Donating some of the land she owned at By to the local commune for the construction of a school was a pleasing way of reducing the burden of maintenance, while benefiting the locality. However, a more complex problem concerned Rosa's menagerie. Though her staff were supremely capable, it was difficult to provide the animals she had tamed herself with ongoing personal attention. And some were harder to care for than others, particularly when they became infirm. With heavy heart, Rosa realised that the time had come to part with her lions.

The day Rosa watched Néro's wagon-cage trundle out of the gates of By was a deeply unhappy one. On 7 August 1882, *La Presse* reported new additions to the menagerie at the Jardin des Plantes, which included 'the lion Néron [sic] [...] donated by Rosa Bonheur'.[20] After Néro's partner Sarah died of a spinal complaint, Rosa sometimes went to see the solitary lion at the Jardin des Plantes. One day, she was saddened to learn that Néro's vision was deteriorating. Before long, he had become virtually blind. During one of her most distressing visits to see the fading creature, Rosa went to the cage bars and called his name. The lion recognised her voice immediately. Hoisting his heavy frame to its feet, he stumbled towards the sound, staggering and sway-ing confusedly, trying to locate her. The trauma was too much to bear. Rosa never went back and Néro died not long afterwards.[21]

∽

The Mediterranean air had always helped dispel any upsets and as usual, Rosa and Nathalie wintered in Nice that year. The weather was deliciously mild for the season and Rosa was hopeful that Nathalie, who had been unwell, would soon be able to join her on her ambles in the surrounding countryside. But the New Year 1883 had barely begun when Rosa herself was crippled by another of her attacks – and this time, it was severe.

A doctor Cusco was summoned as a matter of urgency, but an initial consultation confirmed only the need for further investigation. What was required was a full assessment – and very probably, surgical intervention.[22]

Rosa was now faced with a life-changing decision.

In the early 1880s, gynaecology was a developing specialism. Women's health remained a contentious realm, where tradition and innovation, folklore and science, met and frequently clashed. Historically, the hysterectomy (one of the possible treatments for heavy postmenopausal bleeding) had been synonymous with certain death.[23] Only at the beginning of the 19th century could measurable advances be recorded, the use of anaesthetic being one of the chief milestones of progress. But in many cases, the patient's death was the ultimate consequence. The chances of success remained uncertain and the hazards multiple. Sepsis, peritonitis (inflammation of the layer of tissue covering the inside of the abdomen), 'terrible neural complications' and fatal haemorrhaging were just some of the very plausible outcomes.[24] In the year Rosa faced the possibility of surgery, a full hysterectomy remained a controversial procedure. 'It is only advisable to perform a hysterectomy when one has exhausted all other measures,' it was noted in a report on the use of hysterectomies to extract tumours in *La France Médicale* that year.[25]

However, Rosa's attacks had become incapacitating. As she recuperated from yet another, she started seriously considering the next step.

'I can write only pencil, my doctor forbidding me to sit up,' Rosa explained feebly to Juliette on 5 March 1883.[26]

It was impossible to go on like this. But the outcome of surgery could not be guaranteed. Then there was the question of dignity. Few interventions demanded greater intrusion. And that was to say nothing of the deeper, psychological implications. For despite her rejection of the trappings of a gendered society, Rosa was still proud to call herself a woman. She might have dressed like a man, but she nonetheless exhibited a wealth of womanly traits. From her empathy with animals and people to her creative sensibilities and even her weakness for pretty fastenings and embellishments on her clothes, she was not devoid of femininity. Rosa had never denied the fundamental differences between men and women, but as she told the writer Theodore Stanton, 'in all that is moral and intellectual, she contributes as well as he to the security and happiness of the family. Consequently, there is no reason why her judgement, thought, in a word, her moral strength, should be inferior. Is not intelligence, especially as regards the artistic sense, to be found first of all in the heart?'[27] Rosa did not reject her biology, but rather demanded that it should not curb the opportunities available to her. She neither yearned to be a man nor resented being a woman; she was first and foremost an artist, asking only the liberty to be herself.

With her pragmatism guiding her, Rosa decided to consult a very unique kind of specialist.

Dr Georges Apostoli was a former military physician and a pioneer in the application of electricity in gynaecology. In 1881, he had authored *On a New Application of Electricity After Parturition* and he even ran a course at Paris's École Pratique on the medical, surgical and obstetrical application of electricity.[28] In Dr Apostoli's opinion, uterine complications were 'the dominant chronic malady of the day'.[29] Accordingly, since the early 1880s, he had been experimenting with the galvanic treatment of uterine fibroids and metritis, either of which could cause abnormal haemorrhaging. The doctor was now moving towards systematising a cure for uterine ailments. His method involved treating the uterus with low-intensity voltage without having to enter as far as the womb itself. The procedure was still in its early stages and thus not widely practised, but Dr Apostoli had clearly proved that it was possible to alleviate the kind of heavy bleeding Rosa was experiencing using electricity. He could counter opposition with a catalogue of successful stories, while his approach was far less invasive than a hysterectomy and probably safer. But it might require more than one treatment and as a medical procedure, electrical therapy remained experimental.

By April, Rosa had made her decision: she would keep her womb. Major Rousseau was one of the first to know.

'I know how glad you will be to hear that I hope I shall soon be finally rid of the miserable ailment which has been upsetting my life for several years,' she told him. 'At last, I will be as I was in my youth [...] I no longer have as much energy as I did at 30, but I hope I will still have enough to work and move around as I choose.'[30]

It was a sanguine approach. The question was: would the procedure resolve the condition or aggravate it? For now, all Rosa could do was hope.

While she did, there was much to occupy her. The winter season over, Rosa waited for her strength to be sufficiently restored to return to By. Impatient to test her capabilities, she set herself the target of completing a picture of a vixen and her cubs before she left Nice. The painting was to form part of the rent she insisted on paying Gambart (despite his protestations). Though celebrity had accustomed her to idle gossip, Rosa's pride received a crushing blow when she learned of stories circulating regarding the purported favours she was receiving from Gambart, not least free accommodation at the Villa Africaine. For his part, Gambart failed to see why Rosa did not dismiss the aspersions. But Rosa was determined that the slanderous tales should be disproved. Whether in coin or in kind, she was proud to say that she always paid her way.

A happy surprise momentarily unwrinkled her furrowed brow in May, when a Corsican mouflon arrived at the Villa Africaine, courtesy of Mme Borriglione, wife of Alfred Borriglione, the Deputy of the Alpes-Maritimes, whom Rosa had met through Gambart. Rosa was elated, not least because she quickly spotted that the small, dark brown, wild sheep was pregnant.[31]

'You have caused me great pleasure in sending me this animal, which I have so long desired to have,' she thanked her benefactress. 'It is such a charming animal to paint, perched up on its rocks.'[32]

With the mouflon exciting her creative juices, Rosa prepared to set off for By. She and Nathalie would break their journey in Marseille, ostensibly to ensure that Rosa did not tire herself, but also to satisfy her longing to carry out more studies of the lions held in the Jardin Zoologique.

The artist attempted to justify the detour to her sister: 'As the animals are in the open air, one gets very different shades of colour than if they were caged.'[33]

Before leaving, Rosa sent word ahead to Major Rousseau to ensure that he was on hand to receive her horse and the mouflon, who would arrive a few days earlier. However, when the mouflon's crate was opened, the animal leapt out and fell, injuring itself badly and obliging Rousseau to perform a hasty operation. To Rosa's delight, it recovered and she returned to By just in time to see the animal give birth to a little male mouflon.

It was a pertinent homecoming; in just a few short months, Rosa was to face her own gynaecological ordeal. The year had been punctuated by further attacks – and that winter, one of them proved to be critical.

Rosa had travelled into Paris with the intention of spending a few days at the pied-à-terre she still kept in the Rue Gay-Lussac. Though she was at her happiest flitting between By and Nice, every now and then, the artist in her craved an injection of the capital's culture. Besides exhibitions, Paris boasted some of the most polished theatrical productions and music recitals in Europe; Rosa was partial to both. But while in the capital, she suddenly suffered a haemorrhage of unprecedented severity. Her doctor was summoned, and friends and family rushed to her bedside. When Major Rousseau and his wife arrived, they were horrified.[34]

'The blood loss was considerable and her face was drained of all colour,' Rousseau observed. 'We thought she was going to die.'[35]

Seeing such a vigorous, charismatic fount of creative energy reduced to a pale, lifeless ghost, Mme Rousseau could not hold back her tears.

Had Rosa's turn taken place at By or in Nice, it might have passed unnoticed. But Paris was no place to keep secrets. In a short time, news of the incident had been leaked to the press. And now, every fluctuation in her condition, the arrival of each close friend or family member at the Rue Gay-Lussac, was being watched, scrutinised, evaluated and interpreted for the public's delectation.

'She is still very ill, but she is able to take some nourishment and hopes of a recovery are entertained, provided her strength can be maintained,' reported the *Athenaeum* on 24 November 1883.[36]

On 8 December 1883, the journal updated its readers: 'the health of Mlle Rosa Bonheur is reported to be improving, although she gains strength but slowly.'[37]

Accounts of Rosa's state varied considerably, alternating between convalescence and catastrophe.

On 10 December 1883, *Le Figaro* was delighted to announce 'a slight improvement in her general state' and that 'the doctors now consider her to be out of danger'.[38]

But two days later, *Le Radical* painted a far bleaker – if more sensational – picture:

> One of our sources tells us that there is bad news concerning the health of Mme Rosa Bonheur. [...] last month [...] Rosa Bonheur was taken ill with severe pain and her usual physician, Dr Hubin, advised that she should be taken to Paris where the scientific care is more readily available.[39]

Le Gaulois judged this a pertinent time to review Rosa's career and popularity.

'Rosa Bonheur no longer belongs to herself,' journalist Frédéric Gilbert proclaimed. 'Gambart absorbs everything, and the artist can hardly keep up, particularly since she is attentive in her art and works with uncommon sincerity, not churning works out as though on some kind of production line as do so many of her coevals.'[40]

The comment was designed to flatter, but already living on her nerves, Nathalie was enraged when her eyes scanned the page. The public must not be allowed to think of Rosa as a mere marionette. Nathalie seized her pen and addressed a terse letter to the paper's editor.

'It was said that Mlle Rosa Bonheur was absorbed by M. Gambart,' she recapitulated sharply. 'Although the relations between Mlle Bonheur and M. Gambart have always been most genteel, she has never allowed herself be absorbed by anyone, and her talent, like her individuality, have always retained the greatest independence.'[41]

Nathalie's heightened neurosis was exacerbated by the latest medical prognosis: Rosa's operation was now imperative. There was not a moment to lose. Dr Apostoli prepared to act.

The doctor was a staunch advocate of maximising patient awareness; he maintained that it made his job easier and the therapy more effective. Nonetheless, having seen Rosa so poorly, Nathalie and the

Bonheurs could only wait anxiously to learn what the outcome of the procedure would be.

 cᖆ

By 17 December, Ernest Gambart was buoyant with relief; he had received word that Rosa was recovering and he informed Nathalie and the convalescent of his hope that the intervention had proved successful.[42] Less than a week later, he was thrilled to be thanking Rosa for a letter written in her own hand.

The press too were jubilant. From the *Athenaeum* on 22 December 1883 came the reassurance: 'we hear from Paris, with a pleasure that all readers will share, that the improvement in the health of Mlle Rosa Bonheur causes her friends to be hopeful of better things.' Rosa was quoted as having declared herself to be 'in a fair way of convalescence'.[43]

Those who knew her were relieved, though not surprised. Indeed, accelerated recuperation time was one of Dr Apostoli's proudest contentions.[44] Still, in Rosa's case, Major Rousseau attributed the prompt post-operative recovery as much to her astounding resilience and titanic will.

'Within a month, she had almost forgotten about it and she was back to drinking her glass of wine (or rather, several of them), her coffee and her dram of liqueur,' the vet noted with disbelief but not disregard.[45]

And with Rosa apparently recovered, Gambart felt able to broach what he knew would be a sensitive issue. It concerned his villa in Nice.

Rosa should know that she was welcome to stay at the Villa Africaine as often as she wished, he told her. He owed a large part of his fortune to her; it seemed the least he could offer. But if the cost of upkeep was becoming a concern, he would see to it that certain expenses, such as garden maintenance, were met.

Though Rosa was recovering well, she was still working to restore her pre-surgery level of health and attending follow-up appointments with Dr Apostoli. Such a letter was as exasperating as it was exhausting.

Gambart clearly failed to understand the expense incurred spending so much time in Nice, while still running her château and paying staff in Fontainebleau. But above all, it was the malicious rumours that she was being cosseted that were gradually convincing her to quit the place.

Gambart was astonished. That Rosa could be swayed by such petty fabrications was, to his mind, ridiculous and he told her as much.

By the time the New Year arrived, the dealer and the artist had reached a stand-off. Rosa was annoyed. She would go to Nice that year, for she needed a break. Nonetheless, as she turned her attention to her schedule for the next twelve months, she was already contemplating alternative arrangements.

But in the middle of March, Rosa's planning was brought to a shuddering halt. Before she could undertake a journey of any kind, something terrible happened.

21

A Question of Pride

It was a drizzly Friday morning in February when Auguste Bonheur, his wife Marie and one of their daughters boarded a train in the commune of Trappes on the outskirts of Paris, a short carriage ride from their Magny home. The locomotive chugged along its usual route and was just approaching Bellevue station when Auguste's body abruptly stiffened before collapsing in the seat. Panicking, his travelling companions rushed to assist him. A nearby doctor named Groussin was hastily fetched, but the verdict was unequivocal: Auguste Bonheur was dead.[1]

The artist had suffered a fatal aortic aneurysm. He would have turned 60 that winter.

'We are only three now, my dear sister,' Rosa lamented to Juliette in the days following the incident. 'It is only in the grief of losing a brother that one realises what is the intensity of fraternal love [...] I will go to Magny as soon as I can.'[2]

Auguste's death could scarcely have come at a worse time. The stress occasioned by Rosa's gynaecological ordeal had ricocheted, obliging Nathalie to take to her bed. Meanwhile, though improved, Rosa herself had yet to regain her optimum vitality. All at once, life's inexorable cruelty overwhelmed her. It was as though a dark, heavy shadow had settled at her shoulder. It followed her everywhere, inflecting on each experience and saturating it with a bitter aftertaste.

'Without the belief in another life, our present one, having no aim, would be infamy,' Rosa wrote wistfully to Paul Chardin. Man's earthly campaign was, she proposed, 'a field of battle on which courage is necessary.'[3]

As Rosa attempted to summon that courage, letters of condolence flooded in. She was especially touched by the words of her father's old friend Gustave d'Eichthal, as she was by those of Alexandrine of Saxe-Coburg-Gotha.

Such empathy cut through her melancholy. And as the weeks passed, Rosa grew more pragmatic. She knew that in times of trial, one thing could be counted on to sustain her: painting. Work now became her solace and her salvation. The public watched admiringly as Rosa Bonheur underwent a triumphant renaissance.

On 21 March 1884, *Le Figaro* reported that 'Mlle Bonheur, whose health is completely recovered' had visited the girls' drawing school.[4] Less than two weeks later, Rosa drew a crowd when she appeared at a sale exhibition of paintings by an acquaintance of hers, Eugène Lavieille, at the Hôtel Drouot. To Lavieille's delight, punters took Rosa's interest to authorise artistic merit and were soon fighting over pieces.[5] Meanwhile, in May, *Le Figaro* recapitulated critics' interpretations of 25 modern masterpieces. All the creators were men – apart from one. *Ploughing in the Nivernais* (1849) firmly staked Rosa's place among the masters.[6]

'I ask your pardon for being so late in replying, my good old Sis, but I am in the conception period of painting, and the days pass like lightning,' Rosa excused herself breathlessly in May.[7]

Her workload was increased still further when she was asked to provide artwork for the publication *Stud-Book*, the organ of the recently formed Société Hippique Percheronne. The commission would include producing a study of that summer's prize-winner, Voltaire, who had impressed spectators at the races held at Nogent-le-Rotrou. A devout admirer of Percheron horses (the breed she had depicted in *The Horse Fair* [1853]), Rosa could hardly refuse such an assignment.[8] Little by little, art was restoring her spirit.

'I am very well,' Rosa updated Dr Apostoli at the end of June when she wrote to settle his fee. The doctor had taken a couple to court in 1880 over an unpaid bill, and Rosa was keen that he should have no cause to complain on her account. 'I think I am cured, thanks to you, dear Doctor. It seems to me that I had more than my share of misery. I am so happy to be able to take up my art again and to begin life anew,' Rosa expressed her gratitude frankly. 'You have given me back my life,' she proclaimed.[9]

'Rosa Bonheur has entirely recovered from the cruel affliction which kept her in bed for a year [sic],' Le Gaulois announced on 14 December 1884. 'She left yesterday evening for Nice.'

'I have begun a new life,' Rosa was quoted as saying.[10]

It was true. And a new life demanded a change of setting. Rosa had now firmly decided that this would be her last stay at the Villa Africaine. Because of one thing she was determined: no one should be able to accuse her of being dependent, least of all on a man.

With her heightened awareness of the importance – and the fragility – of family bonds, Rosa invited Isidore to join her and Nathalie for their last Christmas at the Villa Africaine. After months of confinement due to illness and grieving due to loss, being able to stomp about freely in her trousers and explore the landscape around Nice was both invigorating and liberating.

'I don't know what I should do if I had to lift up my skirts,' Rosa joked to Juliette. 'It amuses me to see how puzzled the people are. They wonder to which sex I belong.'[11]

Striding out with Isidore and discovering pretty little nooks and breathtaking vistas to paint was profoundly therapeutic. The scenes would form marvellous backgrounds onto which she later planned to paint lions. With the mild weather, the Mediterranean winter felt more like May in Paris. But neither the climate, the countryside nor the company could reverse her decision to leave Gambart's villa.

'We are here till the end of April, when we shall leave Nice for good, unless we decide to rent somewhere else; which means that we are to change our villa,' Rosa informed Paul Chardin.[12]

Rosa Bonheur and Nathalie Micas.
Collection Atelier Rosa Bonheur

Isidore would return to Paris beforehand in February, when his place at the Villa Africaine was to be taken by Rosa's usual doctor, Xavier Hubin, and his wife. The doctor's stay provided an opportunity for Rosa to repay his kindness, while his medical nous was also reassuring whenever a small setback presented itself. Rosa never took her restored health for granted.

She remained in Nice long enough to visit the city's Salon that spring, where a piece by Juliette was on show (though Rosa was annoyed for her sister that it was so disadvantageously hung). During her last few months at the Villa Africaine, Rosa was also honoured when the Duchess of Saxe-Coburg-Gotha requested a copy of her photograph for her nephew, the Prince of Wales, who was a great admirer. Rosa was flattered when his Highness's note of thanks arrived accompanied by a photograph of himself. But however memorable her stay in Nice that season, returning to By merely strengthened Rosa's resolve to quit the Villa Africaine.

Nathalie had been unwell again at the start of the year and with her own recent traumas, Rosa was conscious that stability should never be undervalued. But she could not depart without regrets; as she told Juliette, 'every one here is so kind to me that I should be extremely sorry to leave Nice altogether.'[13]

In fact, the more Rosa reflected on the matter, the clearer the solution became: she must acquire her very own Niçoise residence.

Such an acquisition would entail great expense, not to mention considerable patience. If she rejected Gambart's hospitality and did not rent somewhere else in the meantime, Rosa's absence from Nice might be extensive. But to Rosa's mind, no sacrifice was too great where the preservation of pride was concerned.

While she finalised her plans, there was much to coordinate at By. Several of the projects which came Rosa's way that year involved one of her favourite animals, the horse.

Towards the end of the spring, Rosa received a visit from an American named Samuel D. Thompson. He had been sent on behalf of the importer and breeder of Percheron horses, Mark W. Dunham, who wanted to commission Rosa to paint several of the prized horses he kept at Oaklawn farm in Illinois, since he wished to offer prospective buyers a visual guide to his stock. Among the proposed models was the star of Oaklawn, the magnificent sixteen-hand stallion, Brilliant.

By way of enticement, Thompson came armed with a copy of the second volume of the Société Hippique Percheronne's *Stud-Book* which he had had specially inscribed by society officials with a personal dedication to Rosa. Even so, Rosa was initially wary of overcommitting herself. But Thompson, a master of persuasion, was undeterred and Rosa eventually gave in.

'In the face of such arguments, I feel I cannot refuse Mr Thompson his request,' she relented.[14]

Thompson's assurance that he could have some wild mustangs sent to By soon reassured Rosa that she had been wise to cooperate. She had in mind a picture depicting the Great Plains of America, and she was so excited to have found her models that she happily agreed when Thompson asked if he could alter the original brief to include more horses.[15]

To further swell Rosa's equine portfolio, she had been offered a superb black stallion named Solferino by a prominent local man, M. de Montgomery, and though declining the gift, Rosa was pleased to make studies of the magnificent steed.[16] There was also the provision of a horse-shaped trophy to oversee, an object intended to be awarded to the winner of a nearby steeplechase (originally called the 'Prix Rosa Bonheur', but Rosa agreed with Major Rousseau that the 'Prix By' sounded less conceited).[17] Then her longing to make studies of her two mouflons provided further competition for her time.

Meanwhile, Rosa had not lost sight of her desire to possess her own little slice of paradise. While she worked, she now began actively searching for her Mediterranean retreat. But this task always had to be fitted around the countless others vying for her attention at By – and some demanded immediate action.

One of the most pressing matters was deposited one day in a basket at the Gare d'Orléans. Its delivery was brought to her attention via a note which arrived courtesy of the animal tamer Bidel. The usual greetings paid, the tamer informed her that he had sent her a very special package. It would be waiting for her at the station and she must take excellent care of the contents – for inside, Rosa would find two tiny, wild lion cubs.[18]

Like schoolgirls chancing on the location of untold treasure, Rosa and Nathalie could hardly get to the central Paris station fast enough. Having claimed the basket and peered furtively inside, Rosa found two, velvety-soft and deceptively cuddly-looking baby lions, a brother and a sister. They were barely the size of small lapdogs.

Overjoyed, the women scurried home with their controversial booty and Rosa set to work taming and painting Bidel's gift.

That year, she produced a watercolour entitled *Royalty at Home* (1885). On a parched mountainside, a lion and lioness were shown resting radiantly in the sun. Their front paws were stretched out before them, and the male stared directly out of the canvas, fixing the viewer with a stony stare, while his companion turned her head reverently towards her partner, as though inviting spectators to follow suit. Rosa carefully positioned the viewer directly opposite the male and a little further down the landscape's incline, thus instantly establishing the lion's superiority in the encounter.

Such works had Rosa utterly absorbed.[19]

'This year we will spend but a little while in Nice, for the bringing up of two lions takes much of our time,' Rosa informed Major Rousseau on 4 January 1886. 'We find them more frank, more grateful – these wild beasts – than are most humans.'[20] If she and Nathalie did go to Nice for an extended stay that winter, Rosa vowed that the lions would travel with them on the train.

But as ever, absorption in her menagerie was punctuated by human interruptions. Rosa was alarmed at the start of 1886 when news reached her that Dr Apostoli was himself unwell.[21] Keen to reiterate her gratitude and anxious to be of service, Rosa set to work on a picture of some stags, from which she hoped the doctor would derive some pleasure.

Rosa was eventually forced to renege on her earlier promise to Major Rousseau, when she made a short visit to Nice later in the year and had to accept that a train was not a natural habitat for a lion. Besides, she needed the freedom to be able to view potential candidates for her second home. Notwithstanding her sacrifice, as her letter of 8 April to Mme Rousseau after one particular viewing revealed, the search so far was not proving fruitful. 'The grounds are very handsome and very big – one might even say too big,' she updated the vet's wife. 'As for the house, we could make good use of it, but I think it needs too much spending on it.'[22]

Finally, on 11 May, *Gil Blas* could report Rosa's success: Mlle Bonheur had just purchased a property at Sainte-Hélène, close to Ernest Gambart's home. The journalist explained that the plot boasted an existing villa. In fact, Rosa's purchase reflected a longer view: if she could not find a villa which met her requirements, she would simply have to build one.

Rosa's architect friend, Alexandre Jacob, was privy to her project. As he remembered, it was in the wake of a particularly heated dispute with Gambart that Rosa arrived before him precipitately one day with an earnest request: could he supply the plans for a villa of her very own?[23]

The area she had settled on was set back from the seafront but within walking distance of the fashionable, palm-lined Promenade des Anglais. And while she awaited construction of her dream home, her lions gave her ample incentive to return to By.

'My good lions welcomed me and Nathalie home again from Nice, and here I am amidst all my animals once more,' Rosa purred contentedly to Major Rousseau in May.[24]

By the autumn, there were some new arrivals at By, too. The horses Rosa had been promised from America were finally delivered. There were three wild mustangs in total, and Rosa was quick to write and express her gratitude.

Rosa Bonheur, *Lions at Rest*, 1892, oil on panel, 21.6 x 32.4 cm.
Courtesy of Rehs Galleries, Inc., NYC

'I write to thank you with all my heart for the very great pleasure you have given me – so courteously and generously – by the gift of the three wild horses of the prairies which were brought to me,' she wrote to Mr Dunham.[25] The animals were just the kind Rosa had seen Indians riding in pictures of the prairies, a setting to which she was finding herself increasingly drawn.

Once home, Rosa could dedicate more time to her lions too. She was still in raptures over the animals, especially the female, Fathma, who followed her around like a loyal dog. Fathma would let herself be stroked and petted and anyone who presumed to question the creature's docility could be quickly silenced by a photograph taken that year. Céline was seen kneeling on a blanket outside the château with Fathma reclining next to her, happily stretched out, allowing herself to be caressed like a domestic cat. Another photo showed Rosa lying on her side with Fathma dozing beside her. The artist appeared utterly at ease, her tousled hair and ungainly pose flying in the face of accepted codes of feminine propriety, while her defiant gaze fixed the viewer with assurance, as though daring the onlooker to challenge her conduct.

Rosa Bonheur and her lion Fathma, c. 1886.
Collection Atelier Rosa Bonheur

Rosa's dedication to taming her models was unimpeachable. Major Rousseau remembered how she would routinely take her newspaper outside to her deer park after lunch and sit for hours reading so that her stag would grow accustomed to her presence. Devoting the time to forming an intimate bond with her models was no less an intrinsic part of Rosa's working method than mixing her paints. 'I find it monstrous when people say that animals do not have a soul,' Rosa spoke plainly to her friend Virginie Demont-Breton.[26] To her, every animal was unique, individual, a character to be known. Her commitment to her lions was characteristically affectionate and zealous. It grieved her considerably when the male lion became paraplegic and died before he had even been at the château a year.

As much as it harrowed her to see an animal in pain, so Rosa was deeply upset by human suffering. Benjamin Tedesco distinctly remembered driving out with her one winter when they passed a group of paupers shivering with cold. Rosa immediately thrust a wad of banknotes into Tedesco's hand and ordered him to share them between the unfortunate souls and a selection of other charitable institutions. Examining the money, Tedesco saw in disbelief that he had been given no less than 1,000 francs, more than a postman might earn in an entire year at the end of the 19th century.[27]

Joseph Verdier also witnessed a remarkable event at a dinner party. A newly married young woman was explaining that she and her husband lacked the money to finish furnishing their house. As soon as the diners had left the table, Rosa asked for some paper and, puffing on a cigarette, sketched a rapid hunting scene while the guests were talking. When finished, she signed it and presented the drawing to the young woman with explicit instructions: she should take the picture straight to M. Tedesco in Paris who would pay her at least 1,500 francs for it. Then, she should waste no further time: she must complete that drawing room.[28]

Rosa was now approaching 70. With accounts of similarly charitable gestures accumulating and her staggering professional portfolio, few could dispute that she had earned her right to a little luxury. Finally at the end of 1886, her wish was granted.

'Rosa Bonheur is in Nice at her villa in Sainte-Hélène which she has only just had built,' *Le XIX Siècle* informed Parisian readers on 18 November 1886.[29]

Le Gaulois was able to supplement the snippet: 'Anyone strolling around Nice might well wonder who the unusual-looking woman of a certain age and wearing a red ribbon in her buttonhole might be. It is Rosa Bonheur who, in her recently constructed villa at Sainte-Hélène, is working on a painting which has been commissioned by an American.'[30] The identity of the patron was not disclosed, but he was tipped to be a multimillionaire.

⬡

Despite the series of minor earthquakes which came to disrupt daily life and communications in Nice at the end of February, Rosa was still in ecstasies on 8 March 1887 when she wrote to Major Rousseau as the proud proprietor of a building which exceeded all her expectations. She gleefully introduced her second home to visitors as the Villa Bornala, taking its name from a nearby spring.[31]

'Nathalie is so happy to be here and so enjoys the villa that she already looks better,' Rosa enthused. 'As regards myself, I am as well as possible, and I also look upon myself with pleasure as a landlord. The truth is we really have a very pretty villa, and what a staircase!'[32]

But if the staircase pleased her, the crowning glory was the doorbell which she had installed. Her protégé, the aspiring painter Consuélo Fould, daughter of Rosa's friend Valérie Simonin, remembered how the cord was weighted, but not attached to any bell. The opportunistic passer-by hoping to surprise the celebrity would thus be left utterly perplexed as they stood on the doorstep waiting indefinitely for someone to answer. Friends alone were made privy to the location of a secret button to announce their arrival. Rosa was exultant. Henceforward, she would not be interrupted by unscheduled callers and would receive only guests of her choosing.

'What do you expect?' she laughed with friends, 'I had to do something to protect myself from the hordes of English coming by their coachloads to see my animals as they do at By.'[33]

As it happened, Rosa's efforts to sequester herself were not entirely successful – far from it. The most prominent foreign figure she had ever encountered was already preparing to travel more than 8,800 km to get to France.[34]

But even before that, there was a professional surprise in store – for Rosa was about to become front-page news across the world.

22

The Price of Fame

On 25 March 1887, an auction room on the other side of the world began filling up with ravenous art connoisseurs and collectors. This was tipped to be a most extraordinary auction.

The sense of expectation was almost palpable as 'New-York aristocratic, New-York artistic, and New-York commercial' all 'melted together incongruously', spilling over into every spare corner of Chickoring Hall that Friday evening to witness the sale of the collection of the late Alexander T. Stewart, the Irish-born entrepreneur.[1] When the lots were announced, two works had indisputably stolen the show. One was Ernest Meissonier's painting, *Friedland – 1807* (c. 1861–1875). The other was *The Horse Fair* (1853).

It took nine men to lift Rosa's 5-m-long canvas into place. And as soon as the curtains were drawn back, before the auctioneer had even opened the sale, bids were being put forward. $20,000 quickly became $30,000 and then $40,000. 'That painting should stay in the city,' the auctioneer ventured when the stream of offers finally began to dwindle. $50,000 was advanced. Finally, the dealer Samuel P. Avery emerged victorious with his bid of $53,000, placed on behalf of a mysterious buyer.

As spectators filtered out of the auction room, New York was abuzz with speculation: who could possess the nerve – and the notes – to make off with such a prize? The city's burning curiosity was soon satisfied: *The Horse Fair* had been purchased by none other than the wealthy businessman and socialite Cornelius Vanderbilt. And on 26 March 1887, he wrote to the Metropolitan Museum of Art to make an outstanding offer: he wished to donate his new painting to the city.

'It seems to me to be a work of art which should be in a position where it can be permanently accessible to the public,' Vanderbilt reasoned.

So it would be. And *The Horse Fair*'s triumphant return to the public arena sparked a powerful resurgence of interest in Rosa and her painting.

But back at By, the rejoicing was cut short early in April 1887, when a letter arrived from Juliette. Their stepmother had fallen gravely ill. The decline was rapid and Marguerite Picard died less than a week later, obliging Rosa to rush back to Paris for the funeral.

'It seems to me, as to you, that I have been having a painful dream,' Rosa wrote to Juliette once she had returned to Nice. 'I keep thinking of you all and of the aching void you will now feel [...] I shall often be with you in spirit, and with her, too. However, I am resuming the work which I had begun before going to Paris, and in a month we shall see each other again.'[2]

Though personal upsets persisted, Rosa could hardly deny that life in Nice was every bit as blissful as she could have dreamed. With its acres of land and a purpose-built studio under construction, the Villa Bornala catered perfectly to Rosa's needs. Nathalie too relished the novelty of owning a second home, and she quickly fell into a pattern of ceremoniously packing up for their extended stays. Her luggage included boxes of what she considered to be sacred soil from the Forest of Fontainebleau, her intention being to grow assorted plants while they were away, for it had occurred to her that they might prove profitable. What she was unable to grow in Nice in the way of produce for personal consumption, she insisted on having sent down from By by the crate load. Shipments of fruit, vegetables and poultry were duly dispatched in a seemingly never-ending succession.[3] Rosa worried at the unnecessary surplus, but her protests made little effect. Besides, she did not have the heart to insist; Nathalie was happier than Rosa had seen her in a long time.

Nonetheless, the world outside the villa remained an uncharted minefield of opposition. On one research trip that summer, Rosa and Nathalie set off with their manservant, Auguste, intending to photograph the evergreen mastic trees near the Italian border, not far from the peaceful and wooded Cap Ferrat, with its peninsular views out over the ocean's glinting surface. Rosa was busily recording the scenery when a shepherd in the most eye-catching costume crossed their path with his flock of goats. An improvised mime and the flash of a coin overcame the linguistic barrier and Rosa was soon capturing her unsuspecting model in a range of striking poses. But just as she was doing so, angry voices could be heard from behind her. Rosa and Nathalie spun round to see a pair of artillerymen marching towards them. The men demanded that she hand over the camera; photographing the newly constructed fort would not be tolerated.[4]

Impulsively, Rosa's hotly refused. Her masculine garb did nothing to proclaim her innocence, and now certain that they were dealing with a German spy, the soldiers demanded that she open the camera so they could see inside. Exasperated with their ignorance, Rosa protested that the film would be ruined. Tempers flaring, the soldiers ordered Rosa to follow them to the fortress; her presenting her Légion d'Honneur did nothing to hasten an armistice. Eventually, Rosa volunteered her manservant to go in her stead, provided the soldiers send their superior to speak to her (a human sacrifice which made Nathalie very cross). The women were guarded and when the prisoner and his captor returned, they brought a message: the superior would not be pursuing the matter. But Rosa must seek permission if she wanted to photograph in the environs in future.

Misrecognition was seldom a problem for Rosa nowadays though. Fascination with her paintings and her persona never ceased, and people flocked from all over the world to visit her.

By the late 1880s, Nice was more than ever a magnet to the stars and sovereigns. Some came for an isolated dose of the Mediterranean high life, others were regular visitors with second homes and a penchant for sun-drenched repose. All arrived with a determined aim to enjoy themselves. And when Rosa took up residence, great names were not long in requesting an interview with her.

From July that year, Paris was taken up with the arrival of Dom Pedro II, Emperor of Brazil, who had stepped onto French soil with his wife, the Empress Teresa Cristina, in a bid to improve his health.

At over six feet tall and wearing a majestic white beard, the Emperor was a commanding presence. His blue eyes remained serious and pensive, while he appeared 'open and full of candid loyalty', yet as Maxime Serpeille remarked in *Le Gaulois*, 'somewhat weary and altered since his last trip to Paris'.[5]

The fatigue was not surprising. After nearly 62 years, all but the first fourteen of them on the throne with full power, Pedro was exhausted. From birth, he had been groomed for sovereignty, having the precedence of duty instilled in him as a child. As Pedro's tenure unfolded, the timid boy grew into a self-assured and measured man who demonstrated supreme mastery over his emotions. Though initially disappointed with the wife who was selected for him, in time, Pedro became profoundly attached to Teresa Cristina (originally of the Two Sicilies). He had steered Brazil through some of the most delicate diplomatic encounters and bloodthirsty conflicts, notably the Paraguayan War. Controversially, Pedro espoused the movement to abolish slavery. Culturally too, his erudition was remarkable, with the sciences, humanities and the arts all receiving his keen attention, while he was passionate about photography.[6]

But if his approach to learning was enlightened, Pedro's gender politics remained staunchly conservative. Grieved by the premature death of his two sons, Alphonso and Pedro, the Emperor's faith in the monarchy had plummeted. He failed to see how, as a woman, his daughter Isabel could successfully lead the people of Brazil when he had gone. By 1887 Pedro's health was deteriorating and his drive all but lost. Nonetheless, his passion for art held strong and accordingly, one of his first stops when he arrived in Nice was Ernest Gambart's picture collection. Among the works he most enjoyed were those by Rosa.

'The Emperor would have liked to greet the great artist in person,' *Le Figaro* told its readers, but 'unfortunately, Rosa Bonheur will not arrive in Nice until next Tuesday.'[7] For the Emperor, next Tuesday was soon enough.

Pedro's wish made known, the Villa Bornala was immediately thrown into a frenzy of panic and excitement. Nathalie was recovering from one of her winter afflictions and still suffering from a persistent cough. Meanwhile, the studio was not yet complete. With scarcely any notice before his Imperial Highness arrived and insufficient time to employ the necessary labourers, Rosa was left with no choice but to get down on all fours and wax the floor herself.[8] Her pains soon proved worth the effort.

'I can confess I was well repaid yesterday,' Rosa gushed in a letter to her neighbour M. Grivot back in Fontainebleau. 'I was very happy to once more meet with a proof of the great and noble simplicity of sovereigns so misunderstood by fools and ingrates.'[9] The Emperor was 'a fine sovereign *par excellence* […] a man distinguished for his learning, artistic tastes, and elevated mind', Rosa opined in a similar vein to Dr Hubin.[10] Apparently, Dom Pedro's views on gender had not been expressed emphatically enough to impair their mutual respect.

The following week, Antoine d'Orléans, alias the Duc de Montpensier, King Louis-Philippe's youngest son, also arrived in Nice. The Duc de Montpensier's nephew, the military-minded Prince Gaston d'Orléans, had married Dom Pedro's daughter Princess Isabel in the 1860s and become the Comte d'Eu. Having learned of Dom Pedro's visit to Rosa's newly finished studio, the Duc de Montpensier was eager that he too should be granted an audience with the artist. After tantalising his creative taste buds with a visit to Ernest Gambart's collection, the duke proceeded to Rosa's studio along with his wife and the pretty, erudite 23-year-old who had recently become his daughter-in-law, the Infanta Eulalia (daughter of Isabella II, the former Queen of Spain).[11]

Such prominent admirers were now regularly appearing at Rosa's door. Before long, she could also count Princess Isabel and Prince Gaston among her recent acquaintance.[12]

Ernest Gambart was at the centre of all these encounters. Having asserted her independence, Rosa now felt more inclined to lay her differences with the dealer aside. After all, they had gone through so much together, and a painter could hardly expect to navigate the art scene in Nice without deferring to Gambart's agency. Whenever he learned of an eminent holidaymaker's arrival on the Riviera, Gambart rushed around gathering paintings which he could loan for the duration of their stay. It was a crafty tactic, one from which an artist like Rosa stood to benefit.

In the meantime, life at By did not stand still. While Rosa was busy receiving royalty, an extraordinary story was circulating.

Visitors to Thomery should not be alarmed, a journalist writing for *Le Figaro* advised, if they happened to spot three large polar bears pacing up and down behind the heavy gates of the Château de By. The animals were a gift from the Grand Duke Nicholas Mikhailovich, a towering and eccentric Russian aristocrat with a neat beard, liberal views and such pronounced Francophilia that he was widely agreed to fit more comfortably into French society than he did Russian. The bears were the consequence of an incident which had taken place over a year ago and which Rosa had virtually forgotten.

She and the Grand Duke had both been guests at a dinner party where they found themselves placed next to each other for the meal. During the course of the evening, Rosa beat the Grand Duke at the German game of 'philippine' (where a double almond is found and players must compete to say 'bonjour philippine' before their opponent by an agreed time or day, whereupon the loser must present the winner with a prize or receive a forfeit). Accepting defeat, the Grand Duke invited Rosa to issue whatever penalty she felt appropriate.

'Send me a nice little animal of some kind which I can use as a model,' she said lightheartedly, upholding the spirit of the game.[13]

So it was that on one of her returns to By, Rosa was amazed to find three large polar bears, so impeccably trained that they would pose on demand.

Not all of the four-legged presents Rosa received made quite such menacing additions to the menagerie, but even some of the more standard specimens could present a challenge. *The Horse Fair* (1853) had fixed Rosa in people's minds as a woman who could handle an unruly creature and even relished the task. Nor had Rosa made a secret of her passion for wild horses. But one of the American steeds she had been sent proved exceptionally wilful. Despite her most committed attempts, the horse jumped and spooked and reared and remained utterly unapproachable.[14]

A decision would ultimately have to be made on the fate of the horse. For now, Rosa had her hands full establishing her second home in Nice.

But when Rosa returned to Paris after one of her trips, Céline informed her that during her absence, the wild stallion had received two unexpected callers.

One day, a man had arrived at the gates of the château, accompanied by a young woman. The stocky, Scottish-born Mr John Arbuckle was a successful coffee magnate in the United States, where a penchant for Percheron horses had won him the role of President of the Wyoming Post Percheron Company. Meanwhile, his female companion cut a curious figure. With chestnut hair and blue eyes, she could scarcely have been more than 30 years old, and yet she walked with a stick which was clearly designed to mitigate the effects of a pronounced limp. The man spoke in fast, incomprehensible sentences and seemed to understand very little French. By contrast, the woman explained fluently to Céline how they had come to verify that Rosa had received the equine gift which she had been sent a few months previously. Disappointed to learn that the châtelaine was away (and, Céline surmised, unnerved to find her dominion guarded by a lion), the American and his interpreter soon left.[15]

There seemed little that could be done now that the Americans had departed. But it struck Rosa as odd, for she had already thanked the sender of the horses she had received. Still, she had soon dismissed the episode and resumed her work. With two homes, there were now hefty expenses to meet.

'I have been working like a horse,' Rosa proudly announced to Major Rousseau early in March 1888, explaining: 'I have substantial outgoings on account of furnishing our villa.'[16] Then acquainting herself with the male and female monkeys she had just acquired, Rosa was left with scarcely any time to keep up with her correspondence.

Though she never lost sight of where she had come from, Rosa was not immune to irritation with both her surroundings and her staff.

'I am awfully bored in these fine apartments,' an exasperated Rosa wrote to the sculptor Auguste Cain's wife in early May 1888. 'I can't make any excursions or do any sketching, being obliged to stay at home, as we have had to send away our servants twice running. You may judge, therefore, what sort of a government this household enjoys just now […] We have a temporary woman cook, who would surely poison us if Nathalie didn't keep her eyes open.' Rosa could not wait 'to quit this luxurious and boring spot'.[17]

But returning to By, Rosa was soon reminded of her life's priorities. When her monkey Ratata bounded in to groom her hair or to tease Nathalie's diminutive dog Gamine, and when this spirited little creature brought a smile to everyone's faces with her attempts to boss Bellotte and Ulm about, or equally when her parrot let slip a particularly ripe expletive in Spanish, Rosa could not remain uptight for long.[18] Besides, there were more serious bestial matters to attend to. Before the year was out, Le Figaro could report that Rosa had been lent three large panthers, courtesy of the renowned German animal dealer and trainer, Carl Hagenbeck, a man whose opposition to traditional, often crueller methods of taming resonated with Rosa's ethos. The panthers had come with their very own keeper and the promise of similarly fascinating loans whenever Rosa desired.[19]

However, life in the menagerie continued to present its tragedies. That year, Rosa's beloved lion Fathma developed the same debilitating condition as her deceased brother and within a few months, had become paraplegic. Rosa nursed her as tenderly as a human mother might her child. Major Rousseau recalled that, as though to demonstrate her gratitude, the lioness would draw close to her mistress and lick Rosa's face.

Fathma had now grown so docile and loyal that Céline did not object when Rosa let her roam around the house. A cage was built for the animal to sleep in at night, but otherwise she was allowed to wander freely. However, one day, Rosa was struck by the animal's particular anxiety to be left alone. Fathma was no longer able to climb the stairs to assume her usual post in the atelier, and unable to defer her work, Rosa promised the mournful lion that she would return, before mounting to her studio. A short while later, a muffled sound was heard. Returning to the stairwell, Rosa found the lion having attempted to drag herself up the steps. All at once, the reason became clear: Fathma was about to die. Heartbroken, Rosa rushed down to the animal and wrapping her arms about the expiring body, caressed her as she slipped away. In little time, Fathma lay motionless in her mistress's arms.[20]

CR

As the New Year 1889 began, the human occupants of By were also giving cause for concern. Nathalie was recovering from yet another bout of ill-health. Indeed, lately, she seemed to rebound from one ailment or illness to the next, while the periods of vitality between were becoming shorter. She was susceptible to everything, from colds and flu to stomach complaints and migraines. Rosa had conditioned herself to enjoying the good times and enduring the bad. After a difficult winter, Nathalie's improvement put Rosa in a jovial frame of mind. The sculptor Auguste Cain had sent some of his homemade pâté, and Rosa assured him that it would be central to their day's enjoyment. 'When one's heart is contented, your mouth is disposed to gormandise,' Rosa conceded happily.[21]

But Cain's culinary offering had come with a thinly veiled proviso: Rosa simply must enter the Exposition Universelle that year.

Reading the request, Rosa was filled with disinclination. Her reputation was assured and she had a list of good-paying commissions pressing to be fulfilled. Nonetheless, Cain was an old friend whom Rosa respected. Nor was he the only person to have urged her to exhibit. Reluctantly, she sent word to Gambart, asking if he might be able to lend a few pictures from his collection. Gambart agreed, but characteristically, set his own condition: he must be allowed to oversee their hanging. His request was rebuffed and it fell to *Ploughing in the Nivernais*, which the government had put forward, to uphold Rosa's position among France's modern masters.[22]

Under normal circumstances, Rosa's participation in an Exposition Universelle would have caused Nathalie to bubble over with pride. And indeed, spiritually, her loyalty and attachment remained titanic.

But over the course of the spring, Nathalie's body was protesting more vociferously to all that was being asked. The fleeting improvement Rosa and Céline had celebrated in January had been short-lived. Nathalie had grown melancholy, introspective and resigned. In short, she had given up. It was as though she sensed that this time, recovery was beyond her grasp. Her letters to Céline while she and Rosa were away were both depressive and depressing. She could think only of her fading vitality; she could not go out, she was weak, losing weight and, as she put it, struggling to fly with only one wing – like Rosa's *Wounded Eagle* of *c.* 1870. The doctor was summoned and friends sent their well wishes. Ernest Gambart urged Rosa to convey Nathalie to Aix-les-Bains where the waters would surely benefit her; he would see to all the arrangements. It was an enlightened suggestion. Rosa herself had eulogised the waters of Aix-les-Bains only two years previously when Dr Hubin was taken ill.[23] But Nathalie remained despondent. How she would travel anywhere was beyond her.

Rosa was becoming desperate. If she was Nathalie's life, Nathalie was at the centre of her every project, formed the soul of each trip, represented the heart of all the canvases that Rosa painted. Rosa's god-daughter, Rosa Mathieu, remembered one occasion when the artist was putting the finishing touches to a painting and Nathalie appeared at the studio door with a biscuit. Not liking to interrupt the master at work, she gently set the snack down on top of the canvas frame. Crumbs and sugar immediately tumbled onto the still-wet canvas, so that only a prolonged amount of time would be able to restore the near-finished work. Nathalie was full of self-reproach, but Rosa remained sanguine. It did not matter, she assured her friend; in their twilight years, no painting was more important than their relationship.[24]

'Their affections, well-being, and occupations were one,' remembered the dramatist and librettist Henri Cain some years later. Those

Rosa Bonheur and Nathalie Micas.

Collection Atelier Rosa Bonheur

close to Rosa knew how central Nathalie was to her existence. Few could imagine either one coping without the other.

And so at the age of 67, Rosa was about to face her greatest test yet. On 22 June 1889, Nathalie Micas died of stomach cancer.

23

The Final Awakening

'Do you believe in a future life?'[1]

Rosa pressed her friend and admirer of her work, Georges Stirbey, for an answer.

The question had been coursing through her mind obsessively since Nathalie Micas's body was pronounced dead.

With her pragmatic, frequently ironical stance on life, Rosa had always tended towards an objective view of those more existential questions. She had never denied that she and Nathalie were ageing, nor had she resisted time's relentless march. But waking up in the morning without her soulmate was a gasp-inducing pain for which she was utterly unprepared.

'It was as if she had been struck by a thunderbolt,' Stirbey recalled.[2]

Every stage in her daily routine now defined itself by its ghastly difference; on awakening, that split second before she remembered the cause of the nausea and unease in the pit of her stomach; her thoughts wandering errantly with no sounding board to tame them; instead of a caring enquiry to discover whether the trifling ache she had mentioned yesterday had improved overnight, there came only silence.

Le Figaro informed Paris of Rosa's grief on 23 June:

> Mlle Rosa Bonheur has just been cruelly affected by the death of one of her most loyal friends, Mlle Micas. Mlle Micas, herself a talented artist, had made a cult

of Mlle Rosa Bonheur, whose life she had shared for a number of years.[3]

However ambivalent her own spiritual convictions, Rosa felt it only right that Nathalie's funeral conform precisely to the ecclesiastical model. It would take place in Thomery and the interment, later that day at Père Lachaise in Paris. There was much to organise.

'My dear Monsieur and friend,' Rosa wrote to Major Rousseau on 27 June. 'Would you mind having some cards with a black decorative rule printed for me? I will need 300, as well as letters announcing the death; as few as possible of the latter, since I do not intend to send many outside Paris.'[4]

On the day of the funeral, Rosa's old friend Valérie Simonin did not leave her side. The artist's deep, choking sobs were heartbreaking. Every now and then, Rosa's quivering voice would ask a question, always the same:

'What will become of me?'[5]

Not one of the mourners could provide a satisfactory answer.

⁂

In the following weeks, friends became a vital source of strength and support.

Rosa's correspondence with Valérie Simonin had petered out until only recently, due at least in part to Valérie's itinerant existence and her colourful personal life.

After dazzling the Second Empire's theatre audiences, Valérie had abandoned her stage career at the end of the 1850s when she became involved with the politician Gustave Fould, youngest son of the Empire's Minister of Finance, Achille Fould. When the young man announced his intention to marry an actress, the Foulds were outraged. Gustave was emphatically warned that if he did, he would forfeit his right to the family's fortune. The lovers' determination resulted in a move to London, then Germany, a marriage and two daughters.

Unfulfilled with the traditional roles of wife and mother, Valérie satisfied her creative appetite through work as a book and manuscript restorer and subsequently as a sculptor, boasting first Mathieu Meusnier then the eminent Jean-Baptiste Carpeaux as her tutors. When they returned to France, M. and Mme Fould proved themselves spirited hosts, with a whole tranche of *Paris élégant* regularly arriving at their tastefully furnished apartment to attend their erudite soirées. Assuming the pseudonym of Gustave Haller, the multitalented Valérie now turned her hand to playwriting before penning novels.

In the early 1870s, the couple had separated, albeit amicably (rumour had it Fould had been having an affair). Valérie had remained on good terms with her former husband, so much so that when she learned Fould to be suffering from paralysis, she took him into her home and nursed him until he died in 1884, an act of charity which bewildered the press. Following Fould's demise, his acquaintance, the Wallachian-born Romanian aristocrat and politician Prince Georges Stirbey, had provided Valérie with an emotional and creative bedrock; with their shared love of the arts, their already-close friendship grew even deeper. So invested was Stirbey in the lives of the widow and her children that in 1888, he adopted the girls (the youngest of whom had even been named after him). Henceforward, he played an instrumental role in supervising their education. Paris's gossips indulged themselves on the feast of material.[6]

Repatriated in France and with grown-up daughters showing artistic promise, Valérie had remembered herself to her friend. Rosa asked Valérie to bring her girls to By, and there, the three women received the usual warm reception extended to invited guests.

'What touches me most in your last letter is the vivid recollection which you retain of my friend Nathalie,' Rosa thanked Mme Fould on 28 July. 'I am not so fortunate as you. I can see her only in my memory. So my thoughts on life are not very gay.'[7]

'My health is very good,' Rosa responded to an equally empathetic letter from Auguste Cain's wife the same month. 'I am like iron in that respect. As for my mind, my dear friend, you can very well understand how hard it is to be separated from a friend like my Nathalie, whom I loved more and more as we advanced in life [...] I desire to be a little quiet and to remain at home.'[8]

But if Rosa longed for quiet, the citizens of Paris had other ideas.

The Exposition Universelle of 1889 was now in full sway and by the summer, it had monopolised Parisian thinking.

From the very outset, this world fair was going to be special. The year 1889 marked the hundredth anniversary of the French Revolution, a milestone which sparked alarm among those European countries still headed by monarchs and consequently reduced the expected number of participants. Notwithstanding, Paris was determined to stage an extravaganza. And from the moment the show opened in May, the capital had transformed into a glittering fairground, with Parisian skill shining as the undisputed star.

Fine arts and industrial exhibits could be admired at the Trocadéro and the Champ-de-Mars, while a colonial exhibit and state-sponsored pavilions captivated visitors at the Esplanade des Invalides. There was artistic skill to bedazzle, architectural dexterity to impress and techno-logical innovation to astound. But by far the city's proudest offering was the Eiffel Tower.

At over 300 m high, the Eiffel Tower was the tallest metal structure in the world to date, a bold architectural statement which inevit-ably aroused controversy. But when its mastermind, the Burgundian engineer Gustave Eiffel, climbed on foot to its summit and hoisted an enormous Tricolore flag to mark its inauguration, few cynics could remain apathetic. From the poorest street urchin to the wealthiest duke, a sea of wide eyes looked to the sky transfixed, as over 20,000 gaslights turned the great iron skeleton into a dazzling beacon of progress.

Millions rushed to admire the breathtaking views over Paris. Celebrities were as entranced as commoners – and among the famous faces was an American legend.

Born in Iowa, USA, William Frederick Cody had been around horses since infancy and had perfected his equine skills working for the freight company Russell, Majors and Waddell. Legend had it that he was only eleven when he killed a Native American in defence, making him the youngest Indian fighter on the Great Plains. He had subsequently begun riding for the Pony Express, conveying messages across the perilous plains of America. During the American Civil War, Cody served as a union scout before enlisting with the Seventh Kansas Cavalry, and afterwards, he was employed by the army as a civilian scout and dispatch bearer. A temporary role providing railroad construction workers with meat fixed his renown as one of the most skilled buffalo killers on the Great Plains, and earned him the nickname Buffalo Bill. With his precision, spatial memory, knowledge of Indian customs, and bravery, the young cowboy had won respect and hearts across America. It was only a matter of time before his adventures found their way into popular culture.[9]

Cody's escapades were soon furnishing dime novelists with lucrative material and in 1872, he agreed to star in the stage production *The Scouts of the Prairie.* His acting was mediocre, but his showmanship magnificent. A new career was launched.

Forming his own troupe, the Buffalo Bill Combination, Cody fell into a pattern of performing during the winter and scouting in the summer. The public response was exhilarating; America adored him. But of all Buffalo Bill's achievements, by far the most talked about occurred in 1876, when he was reported to have killed and scalped the great Cheyenne warrior, Yellow Hair.

In 1883, Cody organised his own Wild West show, a kind of outdoor circus or contemporary living museum. There was shooting and chasing, cowboys and Indians and above all, drama and excitement beyond a spectator's wildest dreams. People could visit a buffalo enclosure and horse stables, there was a pony race and bronco riding. Cowboys raced, lassoed and fired, Indian attacks were re-enacted, while Native Americans in feathered headdresses and vibrant costumes stamped their feet in heart-pounding tribal dances. The show was fast and colourful, wild but slick, a cacophony of thundering hooves, shouting, gunshot and whip-cracking. It provided a visual explosion, a surge of adrenaline and a performance like nothing the public had ever witnessed before.

Cody had struck lucky. He was delivering exactly what the public craved, at just the right time. *Buffalo Bill's Wild West* was declared a sensation, and by the end of the 1880s, the show had begun touring Europe, even performing at Queen Victoria's Golden Jubilee in 1887.

Arriving in Paris in May 1889, the troupe of over 100 American Indians set up camp at Neuilly. In little time, the charismatic Cody had people flocking to the western suburb in their thousands, with some 20,000 spectators being counted at the very first performance.[10] Cody brought the stuff of novels kicking and whooping off the page with all its danger and excitement. One paper classed it 'the greatest attraction in the world'.[11] The whole city had been infected with cowboy fever.

And because of – or perhaps thanks to – Buffalo Bill, 'quiet' was the last thing Rosa would experience that autumn.

Rosa had long harboured an interest in America and the Wild West. Living in Paris during the 1840s, it had been hard to ignore the arrival of George Catlin. The Pennsylvanian-born traveller, painter, author and zealot had turned heads – and raised eyebrows – when he brought his Indian exhibition to the Salle Valentino in Paris in 1845. Captivated by the indigenous peoples of America, Catlin had made it his mission to document the natives, their environment and their customs. Besides his own paintings, his collection included fascinating artefacts, such as costumes, musical instruments, weapons and scalping knives. He would speak animatedly on Indian anthropology and his exhibition had been the talk of Paris, not least because he had arrived with twelve real-life Indians in tow.[12]

'Never has a curiosity seemed more deserving of our interest,' *La France Théâtrale* had eulogised in May 1845.[13] Visiting the show was declared 'almost like making a trip to America'. The *Journal des Femmes* noted that the writer George Sand had been making daily visits to see the troupe, adding that these savages deepened a person's appreciation for the writing of James Fenimore Cooper, America's answer to Rosa's hero, Walter Scott.[14]

Rosa still possessed copies of Catlin's engraved plates. But now, over 40 years later, Buffalo Bill offered more. His show did not just mount an exhibition – he gave audiences an experience.

Though Rosa was consumed with grief and, as she told Mme Fould early in September, had 'not felt in a mood to paint' since Nathalie's death, Buffalo Bill piqued her interest.[15] She shared more than just a passion for horses with the cowboy. Buffalo Bill was a staunch advocate of gender equality. He employed a number of women and ensured that, provided their work matched the standard of the men's, they all received equal pay. It was an enlightened approach which harmonised with Rosa's ethos.

Buffalo Bill's arrival in Paris had turned postcards of the rancher and cowboy hats into indispensable commodities, while the Wild West had cast its favourable economic spell on the art world, too. M. Tedesco had won a commission for a picture of Buffalo Bill and his troupe, and it took little intervention on his and art dealer M. Knoedler's parts for Rosa to be invited to come and sketch at the camp.

Rosa found the native peoples enthralling. In little time, powerful pictures were being produced, images quite unlike anything she had ever painted before.

In the oil study *Indian Encampment* (1889), Rosa showed a diagonal line of tepees with clusters of swarthy Indians standing or seated on the parched grass before them. There were men in vibrant costumes and women tending to children; all but one infant were shown staring straight at the viewer. Rosa may have been welcomed into the camp, but the sense of otherness roused in her audience was overwhelming. In her work, the spectator became the spectacle. It was almost as though she was trying to subvert the unspoken roles of coloniser and colonised. And incredibly, there was not a single animal in the picture.

Refining her skills with watercolour was providing an absorbing creative challenge after Nathalie's death, and it was in this medium that she produced another small, loosely painted study entitled *Indian on Horseback* (1889). The work showed a Native American in a colourful feathered costume, a bright contrast to his stony, determined expression as he sat astride his muscular steed. The composition left no doubt: here was a man full of purpose, ready to act.

Finally, Rosa could not allow the troupe to return to America without capturing their leader himself. Upright and proud, Buffalo Bill was depicted in his trademark cowboy hat and buckskin fringed jacket, mounted on a dapple grey horse. His steed was shown lifting its legs and swishing its tail as though in motion, while Buffalo Bill sat erect and dignified, towering above the deferential viewer. The cowboy looked out of the canvas to the right, anticipating action, keenly alert, fully prepared. The affinity with Anthony van Dyck's *Equestrian Portrait of Charles I* (1637–1638) was striking.

Rosa's appearance at the camp did not pass unnoticed.

'Mlle Rosa Bonheur has been going every morning to Buffalo Bill's camp to make studies of the Indians in his troupe,' reported *Le Matin* on 13 September.[16] Rosa was even treated to a performance of a tribal

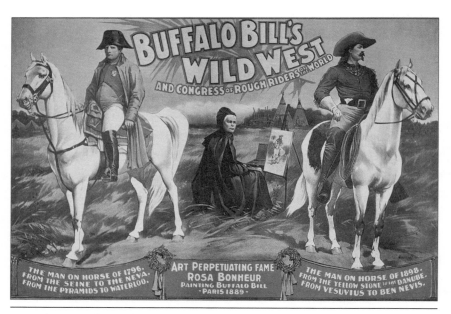

American School (19th century), poster for Buffalo Bill's Wild West Show, featuring Napoleon and Rosa Bonheur, 1898, colour lithograph.
Private Collection/Peter Newark Western Americana/Bridgeman Images

dance, for which she and M. Tedesco were invited to sit in Buffalo Bill's own private box.

Having been welcomed so warmly, Rosa felt it only polite to reciprocate.

So it was that on Tuesday 24 September, the little commune of Thomery was buzzing with excitement. Early that morning, the star of the Exposition Universelle was seen stepping off a train at Moret station with three other men and M. Tedesco. Rosa's carriage was there to meet them.[17]

Rosa later told friends how the cowboy's tight schedule prevented them from returning to By to dine, so they contented themselves with the nearby Hôtel de France. Major Rousseau joined them. He remembered both the meal and the company as having been most agreeable and he was particularly struck by Buffalo Bill's self-restraint; the cowboy drank only mineral water apart from a token sip of champagne to toast Rosa's health. (Regrettably, his interpreter demonstrated no such abstinence.) For Rosa, the whole experience was surreal. Buffalo Bill spoke passionately about horses and the Great Plains and Rosa happily lost herself in his tales, soaking up the images he painted in her mind. In her turn, she could add colour to the American's knowledge of the monarchs and notable personalities of France.

All too quickly, it was time for Buffalo Bill to return to Paris. But as he was leaving, it occurred to Rosa that the cowboy might like to take the wildest of the American horses she had been offered. She could think of no one more capable of taming the unruly creature, and to her great satisfaction, Buffalo Bill accepted the gift. He then presented her with a broken mustang for use as a model.[18]

But the very next day, a letter arrived which gave Rosa cause to feel nauseous with regret.

The correspondence was written on behalf of Mr Arbuckle, the American coffee merchant who had come to By two years previously. It was his female interpreter who was writing now, having located Juliette in Paris to discover the best way of approaching the creator of *The Horse Fair*.

Mr Arbuckle had arranged to come to Paris for the Exposition Universelle and he wondered if he might call at By to visit Rosa – and of course, to check on the progress of the sprightly young stallion he had sent her. All at once, Rosa realised her terrible mistake: she had understood all the American horses to have been sent by the same person, whom she had thanked accordingly. Not only had she failed to acknowledge Mr Arbuckle's gift – she had just given it away to the most famous cowboy in the West. She could hardly write and renege on her offer to the great Buffalo Bill. But now, Mr Arbuckle was on his way, expecting to see the horse.

Thinking quickly, Rosa seized a pen.

In an apologetic but mildly defensive tone, she explained her error and excused herself. If Mr Arbuckle and his interpreter could forgive the simplicity of the spread, they were welcome to join her for lunch at By in a week's time. Mr Arbuckle asked for nothing more.

In the meantime, a pair of cowboys arrived at By equipped with lassos, gusto and the fixed intention of capturing Rosa's frisky animal, as well as one other horse which she had offered. Despite the misunderstanding over the beast, Rosa succumbed to her instinctive admiration as she watched them capture then pacify the unruly creature. But once the men and the horses had left, her mind soon returned to the uncomfortable task which lay before her. Now, she would have to justify what she had just done to Mr Arbuckle.[19]

On Saturday 5 October, the sound of carriage wheels could be heard coming to a stop outside the gates of By. Rosa hurried to the entrance to meet her guests, with Gamine tucked under her arm. Sensing that the occasion demanded the attire for which she was famous, she had dressed in her trousers and painting smock. As the American and his companion stepped down from the carriage, a look of surprise could be detected momentarily passing across their faces. But quickly remembering themselves, formal acquaintances were soon being made.[20]

Mr Arbuckle greeted his hostess. And then Rosa was introduced to his interpreter, Miss Anna Klumpke.

Rosa beheld the much younger lady before her. She was slim and exquisitely graceful, while her blue eyes, though pale, were at once lively and clear. The oval face in which they were set was finished with a well-defined nose and a sizeable mouth and her head was topped with an elegant chignon into which unruly locks of wavy, nut-brown hair had been resolutely tamed. Though she could only claim some 30 years, her cane, composure and comportment gave the impression of a woman decidedly older – one who had experienced life and weathered its storms. She was polite and well spoken, eloquent and thoughtful. And her name was not unfamiliar to Rosa.

Anyone with an interest in the plight of aspirational women would have read about the Klumpkes.

Anna was the eldest of seven children born to a couple of German descent living in San Francisco. Her father was a cobbler who subsequently turned to real estate, while her mother Dorothea was a capable and bright woman who had devoted herself to motherhood. While still a toddler, Anna had fallen from a chair severely injuring her knee. When she was nine, Anna's mother had consequently taken her, along with her three younger sisters, Augusta, Dorothea and Mathilda, to Berlin and afterwards to Switzerland, seeking treatment for her eldest daughter's tragic lameness. After two years in Europe and innumerable consultations, Mrs Klumpke was forced to return to San Francisco in 1867 with little to show for her efforts.[21]

Twins John Wilhelm and John Gerald (who died in infancy) as well as another sister, Julia, arrived in the next five years. But in 1872, marital tensions spurred Mrs Klumpke to seek a divorce from her husband. The mother shepherded her brood of six to Europe, where she felt certain superior educational opportunities would afford her children brighter futures. Anna attended a German boarding school for three years before joining her mother in Switzerland. There, she began using a leg brace and her perseverance eventually helped her transition from the crutches she had depended on since infancy to a more discreet cane. Her vocational well-being also began to flourish. A short visit to Italy galvanised a growing passion for painting, and by the time she was nineteen, Anna's brushwork had become so proficient that she was selling pictures to tourists.

In the mid-1870s, the family settled in Paris. The move was primarily designed to benefit Augusta, since Paris would provide the opportunity to pursue her medical aspirations. But the change of environment was equally propitious to the budding artist Anna. She entered the forward-thinking Académie Julian, an art school which not only accepted women (the prestigious École des Beaux-Arts famously did not), but permitted them to draw from an undraped model and gave them the freedom to pose the model themselves. Anna studied hard, made her Salon debut in 1882 and was soon specialising in the commercially sagacious domain of portraiture.[22]

Anna Klumpke in her studio, c. 1890.
Axis Images/Alamy Stock Photo

Meanwhile, Augusta Klumpke's star had been rising in the world of medicine. Her success in the competitive medical exams at the Sorbonne had made the papers, and then in 1886, the third Klumpke daughter, Dorothea, had become the first woman to graduate from the Sorbonne with a degree in mathematics. But the Klumpkes' most high-profile achievement to date had occurred the following year when Augusta became the first woman ever to be granted an intern post at the Hôpital Lourcine, which treated sufferers of venereal disease. On 3 February, *Le Figaro* had run a long article on Augusta's accomplishment. Classing the feat as 'a minor revolution' and observing that Augusta wore not so much as a ribbon in her hair nor a jewel to make her sparkle, the journalist had concluded that the only feminine attribute she had retained was her devotion.[23] Augusta's response to the attention had been self-effacing; she asked only that she cease to be treated as exceptional and be allowed to get on with her job.

Such a reaction had not assuaged the press. Detailing the horrific, stomach-turning condition of Augusta's female patients, the journalist had posed a provocative question: 'Is this really the role of a woman? Does a person not need a will of iron to tolerate the life of an intern in this grim environment?'[24] Based on those criteria, all the Klumpke sisters met the brief.

Since Augusta's triumph, the eldest Klumpke sisters' names had featured regularly in the papers, while the two youngest sisters, Mathilda and Julia, were now proving music to be their forte. From Augusta's marriage in 1888 to her fellow medical student Dr Déjerine (a neurology specialist), to Anna's plaudits at the Exposition Universelle and her mounting profile at the Salon, where the portrait she painted of her mother that year had been pronounced 'excellent' – the Klumpke women were a united force to be reckoned with.[25]

The charms and challenges of belonging to a talented dynasty were things Rosa could relate to. Over lunch, she was able to find out more about her visitor. She could also explain to Mr Arbuckle why he would not find his horse grazing outside. To her relief, the coffee tycoon was most understanding. Once he had complimented Rosa on the famous Thomery grapes she served, she suggested that the guests follow her to the studio.

As they walked, Rosa studied Anna Klumpke intently. Presently, she revealed that she knew of Miss Klumpke's Salon success and reputation, as well as the achievements of her siblings. The American bashfully dismissed the compliment, deflecting flattery back onto Rosa herself. But Rosa was determined; she commended the American approach to women and their enlightened ideas about freedom and equality.

The key turned in the studio door and the guests were shown inside. Miss Klumpke stood dumbfounded. Her eyes devoured the

Rosa Bonheur at 67 years old, 1889.

French photographer (19th century), Private Collection/
Archives Charmet/Bridgeman Images

high-ceilinged space before her, noting the titles of the books on the shelves, the number and quality of the studies on show, the furniture and all the furnishings. It was the realisation of a childhood dream.

When a conversation about photography evolved, Mr Arbuckle proposed that he send Rosa some pictures of horses and in return, Rosa offered him the drawing she had made of his horse. To his interpreter, she gave a photograph of herself wearing her Légion d'Honneur, which she signed with a dedication. Anna Klumpke seemed pleased. At length, the visitors and their hostess bid each other farewell. But not one of the three forgot the encounter.

With the departure of Rosa's new American contacts, the distraction from her solitude vanished as well. M. Knoedler's gift of an Indian chief's costume was a delightful souvenir, but it was no substitute for a human exchange. A state of melancholy crept back into the Château de By. Before the year was out, Rosa had resolved to sell her villa in Nice.

'It would be too painful for me to go there alone,' she told Valérie Fould.[26]

Over the next eighteen months, Rosa's letters to friends echoed with the hollow ring of loneliness and a growing consciousness of her age.

'Since I have lost my friend, I care for being nowhere else than here alone in my corner, where nearly all our life has been spent,' Rosa wrote to Paul Chardin on 19 January 1890. 'I live on the souvenirs that surround me, just as if she were here, and I find it difficult to quit them.'[27]

'Nothing makes an impression on me,' she told Mme Fould flatly.[28]

However, just a few months later, that claim was to be put to the test.

In September, Major Rousseau arrived before Rosa one day with a request. He had been visited by a presidential aide-de-camp. President Sadi Carnot was currently in residence at the Château de Fontainebleau, and he wished to pay the revered artist a visit. Unsure how his solicitation would be received, the President had thought it wise to approach Rosa through Major Rousseau.[29]

Rosa became flustered.

'This is inconvenient,' she snapped. 'My studio is untidy. I have work to do. I ask nothing. I want nothing. Why can I not be left in peace?'[30]

Major Rousseau was taken aback. Eventually, and after some gentle coaxing, the cause of Rosa's resistance was revealed; she was nervous. She feared the President might be intending to bring her some kind of decoration and she wanted nothing to dilute her memory of the day Empress Eugénie had come to By.

Major Rousseau assured her that the President had no intention of decorating her, and he begged her to reconsider. Rosa tentatively agreed and she wrote to M. and Mme Carnot extending a formal invitation. The staff at By immediately set to work preparing.

This would not be the usual encounter with a notable political personality. Though not close acquaintances, Sadi Carnot and Rosa shared an ancient connection. Their fathers had both been involved with the Saint-Simonians and had met at Ménilmontant. Sadi's father Hippolyte had been instrumental to the movement when it was still in embryonic form, recording and editing Saint-Amand Bazard's work for publication. Though Hippolyte Carnot's convictions had ultimately diverged from those of Barthélemy-Prosper Enfantin, his son Sadi, like Rosa, had been marked by the Saint-Simonian ethos and absorbed many of its tenets.[31]

Rosa had been anxious about her appearance in front of the esteemed guests, and she told Major Rousseau that she felt it best if she dressed in skirts. But when the Major shared Rosa's concerns, Mme Carnot exclaimed that Rosa simply must wear her usual attire. The fact was, this distinguishing feature had helped fix Rosa's renown.

Guests often felt short-changed if their visit did not afford at least a glimpse of this curious spectacle. Rosa was always mildly amused that her clothing should be such a point of fascination, but she obligingly dressed in her trousers and painting smock.

The slim-faced and dignified President, his wife, his son François and the naval officer Captain Edgard de Maigret (who had scaled the ranks of the navy to become the President's attaché), all arrived at By one afternoon in mid-September, where they were congenially welcomed and invited to tour the studio. As he worked through the sketches, drawings and paintings which were presented to him, President Carnot bestowed his compliments generously. The press reported how the visitors had lingered particularly in front of the canvas *Shepherd of the Pyrenees* (dated 1888), which Rosa was just completing.[32] At length, President Carnot's conversation drifted to the Saint-Simonians' ideas about the role of women, which he pronounced commendable. He shared his hope that France would soon grant its women as much liberty as England and America had done.

'I have met many sovereigns,' Rosa told Major Rousseau afterwards, 'but I have never met one as agreeable as M. Carnot.'[33]

The presidential visit proved an inspiriting interlude, but it was merely an ephemeral constellation in an otherwise gloomy sky. Once the eminent guests had left and the excitement dissipated, Rosa fell back into a more melancholy state of mind.

In the New Year, her mood had scarcely altered: 'I am not working much […] My solitude I am more attached to than ever […] I shall be delighted to leave no one behind me, thank God.'[34]

But her claim to autonomy was far from accurate. Rosa still had people to live for; there were her siblings – and that spring, she received an agonising reminder of just how very much they meant.

In April 1891, Juliette Peyrol passed away, aged 60. The news was reported in *Le Figaro* and *Le Matin* on 8 May, where the deceased's artistic achievements were summarily reviewed. If art lovers should visit the Salon that summer, they could still see the two pictures the youngest Bonheur sister had selected for submission. When they were hung, the creator could never have guessed that she would not live to see them taken down.[35]

Rosa had now seen three of her four younger siblings buried. Only Isidore remained.

'You see how much I have been afflicted during the last two years,' Rosa appealed to the sympathy of Paul Chardin.[36]

But she still had her work, and when she could rouse herself from her sense of despondency, that gave her purpose. Then there was her correspondence with Anna Klumpke.

Privately, Mr Arbuckle had suspected Rosa's amicable welcome to have been motivated more by the desire to make peace than the wish to establish any deeper kind of friendship. He urged Anna to be on her guard. But in practice, the exchange of pictures promised necessitated further communication. And as letters passed between the artist and the interpreter, a warm friendship began to blossom. In the summer of 1891, Rosa was crestfallen to learn that the young woman was planning to return to America. Her stay would be prolonged.

Miss Klumpke's letter concluded with a tentative but hopeful request: might she be able to pay Rosa one last visit before she left?

Rosa quickly assured her correspondent that she would be delighted if they could see each other again. If she wished, she could come chaperoned by her mother.

On 1 August 1891, Anna Klumpke left Paris for Fontainebleau, and not without trepidation; this would be the last opportunity she would have to speak to Rosa Bonheur for the foreseeable future.

24

Against the Odds

On Saturday morning, Anna and Mrs Klumpke stepped off the train in the little commune of Moret. The quaint, provincial station with its ticket office flanked by well-established trees made a striking contrast to the vast and crowded Gare de Lyon where they had boarded. Outside, Rosa's carriage was waiting.

The drive took the passengers along a quiet and picturesque route which cut through the forest and past green-shuttered farmhouses, their white walls laden with heavy vines. Besides the odd pedlar's cart, the route to By was usually deserted. It was easy to see why a reclusive artist had been drawn to the area.[1]

Within fifteen minutes, they had arrived at the Château de By, where a warm welcome and a delicious lunch were ready to greet them.[2]

The guests were immediately invited to take their seats at the solid wood dining table. As the meal commenced, both mother and daughter were struck by the easy coexistence of animals and humans; they were joined at table by Gamine, to whom Rosa offered some carefully prepared cuts of steak, then as they were eating, four Saint Bernard dogs bounded into the room seeking attention (and probably scraps). Only the clatter of the animals' food bowls being filled in the next room could lure them away. It was like dining on board Noah's Ark.

After lunch, Rosa proposed that her guests follow her to the studio to inspect some of her latest works. The presence of Mrs Klumpke, a fair-complexioned lady with a fuller, rounder face than her daughter and a button nose, had prompted Rosa to dress in skirts. But as they were entering the studio, Anna spotted her men's garments draped over the back of a chair. Catching her mother's eye, Anna tried to draw her attention to the outfit with a meaningful look. Noticing the silent exchange, Rosa explained her motivation for dressing as a man: it was a practical rather than a principled choice.

Pushing on the door in a ceremonial fashion, Rosa invited them into her 'sanctuary'. Anna was just as awestruck as on her first visit.

People who knew Rosa were frequently impressed by her remarkably unpossessive attitude towards completed works. As soon as she was satisfied she had done her best, she happily sent her 'children' out into the world. Now, Anna Klumpke was the lucky beneficiary. In little time, she had become the overjoyed recipient of an armful of signed pictures, including an engraving and a study of a lion.

Rosa took advantage of Anna's artistic opinion to discuss an idea she had had for an Indian composition. The only prop she lacked was the Native American grass needed to authenticate the foreground. How wonderful it would be, she exclaimed, if Miss Klumpke were able to source some on her trip back to the States. Unhesitating, the American promised that she would make it her priority.

As the day unfolded, Anna began to relax. A tour of the estate tempted her to pose questions about the lion she had seen on her first visit, when she came to By in Rosa's absence as Mr Arbuckle's interpreter and was greeted by Céline. Rosa recounted the sad tale of Fathma, before lightening the conversation with an ironic aside about the 'masculine intelligence' just exhibited by her gardener, whose over-zealous pruning of a yucca plant would likely prove fatal.

In too little time, the visit was drawing to a close. But as the mother and daughter made to board their carriage, Rosa sensed her younger acquaintance to be wrestling with a burning yet unspoken desire. Rosa believed she could second-guess her yearning: of course she would sign Miss Klumpke's autograph book.

Climbing into the carriage, the mother and daughter were thrilled to find a basket of the grapes Anna had enjoyed on her first visit – a present for her sisters, Rosa explained.

The hostess had one further request: at their last meeting, she had given Miss Klumpke her photograph. She now asked if she might have a copy of Anna's photograph in return. Anna promised that she would send one the moment she returned to Paris.

Then, her head still buzzing with her experience, Anna Klumpke took her seat on the train bound for Paris and watched the Forest of Fontainebleau disappear out of view.

That autumn, she boarded a steamer and set sail for America.

⚮

'I muse a good deal, only half living in this world,' Rosa told Paul Chardin at the end of December. 'Painting still pleases me, especially when I begin a picture,' but 'before I finish it, I find it tiresome.'[3]

Age was impressing itself. Memories of Nathalie haunted her and in every corner of the château, an object, a picture, a piece of furniture, brought recollections rushing to the surface in an overwhelming torrent. Losing her companion's favourite dog Gamine that year provided just one more reminder that the past, like her beloved friend, was slipping away.

But with renown came responsibility. And in the emotional wasteland in which Rosa now found herself, duty forced her to rally her spirits. When England's future king, Edward, Prince of Wales, travelled out to Fontainebleau for the day on 1 May 1892, Rosa hosted a warm reception. The portly eldest son of Queen Victoria with his greying beard had long been an admirer of Rosa's paintings. Then with their shared acquaintance of Alexandrine of Saxe-Coburg-Gotha and their love of the Riviera, where they had already crossed paths, the Prince and the painter had ample topics of conversation. His Highness arrived in the afternoon with his wife, his son Prince George, his daughters Princesses Victoria and Maud, and an entourage including Major

General Arthur Ellis and the diplomat Henry Austin Lee. Rosa proved herself a most obliging hostess. A member of the party recounted how she had even agreed to pose for a photograph in her men's clothing.[4]

Yet if social obligations helped restore Rosa's equilibrium, the greatest motivation came from her work. The stifling hot summer of 1892 induced a degree of lethargy which made it hard to concentrate, but her determination to paint gave her the stamina to persevere.

'My days being counted, I must use the precious moments in a way that brings in cash,' Rosa explained to Valérie Fould, whom she had developed the peculiar quirk of calling 'grandmother'.[5] Acutely aware of the contemporaries disappearing around her, Rosa was investing her extant relationships with even deeper meaning. In her letters, she often cast herself as a young man, allowing her gender to remain fluid. She did so partly in jest, but there was a more serious process of self-exploration at work beneath the affectation, too. Her own legend provided still another source of stability onto which she now clung. Visitors to By found a decorative 'RB' upholstered on cushions, cast in iron on a fireguard and painted on a plaque set above the fireplace. At times, remarks in her letters even carried an air of self-importance. But those close to her knew them to disguise an earnest quest for reassurance. As her important cornerstones gradually fell away, Rosa was left grappling for security. Rosa Bonheur the artist had become a convenient screen behind which Rosa Bonheur the woman could hide – and frequently did.

Nevertheless, Rosa's continued correspondence with Anna Klumpke breathed colour and interest into her life. Anna represented Buffalo Bill's America, and the contact with such a fascinating, far-off country served as an antidote to excessive introspection.

In her correspondence, Anna Klumpke tentatively explained the difficulty she was encountering attempting to source Rosa's buffalo grass. The plant only grew in wild, unpeopled terrains which were difficult to access and devoid of trains. Rosa did not retract her assignment; she merely waited. Meanwhile, Anna frantically wrote, enquired and scoured America, determined to find the plant.[6]

Finally, after some months, a package arrived at By.

Anna's sister Mathilda had managed to obtain a sample of the coveted buffalo grass from a horticultural society in Colorado. Relieved to finally be able to show the artist proof of her efforts, Anna had sent the sample straight to By, along with a photograph which she had obtained from a well-meaning schoolteacher.

Rosa wrote saying that she was delighted (if privately a little disappointed that the sample had not been fresher). Her affection for Miss Klumpke was growing. The attachment was not solely inspired by Anna's usefulness as a source of rare props or the exotic appeal of the country she represented. Rosa was finding young people increasingly necessary to her existence. They injected her life with vitality and they exercised her mind. She acted as willing mentor to a number of aspiring artists.

Rosa took a particular interest in the careers of Valérie Fould's daughters, Consuélo and Achille. Now in their mid-twenties, both girls had been showing works at the Salon for some years. Between them, Consuélo and her sister (who now signed her canvases Georges Achille-Fould) could boast the tutorship of both the academic painter Léon Comerre and the award-winning realist painter Antoine Vollon. With close associates like the Foulds, Rosa's wisdom was generously imparted and gratefully received.[7]

Valérie Fould had witnessed the powerful and beneficent effect of youth on her friend. She also knew the value of Rosa's artistic advice. It occurred to her that it might be in all the parties' interest if her daughters were to paint Rosa's portrait.

So congenial was the reception at By that an invited guest might scarcely have believed that, at heart, Rosa was still wedded to her sequestered existence. But she was; that solitude was intrinsic to her work. She had experienced years of success, but even more of victimisation. Reclusion had become her unthinking default, a form of self-protection. Nonetheless, Rosa consented to Valérie's request and Achille remembered how for three glorious weeks, she and her sister spent their afternoons at By. All the materials an artist could desire were provided and Rosa's precious reflections on art unstintingly shared.

It was decided that one portrait of Rosa would be sufficient for the Salon, so when the girls' works were nearing completion, Rosa suggested that they draw lots for this privilege. Achille emerged victorious.[8]

Her painting showed Rosa seated in her studio, dressed in her velvet trousers and the famous blue painting smock which had often prompted comparisons with the late male artist Camille Corot. The studio was depicted as a hive of artistic industry, with models and props scattered haphazardly here and there among dark, rich furnishings. To the left, a cropped view of *Wheat Threshing in the Camargue* (1899) could just be glimpsed, offering a tantalising foretaste of masterpieces yet to come, while on the right, the surface of a table could barely be seen for papers, a vase, a bust and a sculpture of an animal which littered it. And in the middle of this creative chaos, Rosa sat working on a picture her admirers already knew, pertinently, *Royalty at Home* (1885). Rosa herself twisted round awkwardly, as though surprised by the viewer. She looked mildly put out, but supremely confident and self-assured.

'The portrait of Mme *Rosa Bonheur* in her studio by Mlle Georges Achille-Fould is in itself a fascinating document of art historical interest,' remarked Charles Yriarte in *Figaro-Salon*.[9] Since Dubufe had captured Rosa at the height of her fame, she had all but vanished from view, remaining an enigma to the Paris art world; this work filled in the temporal gap. With the picture appearing just as Rosa's four contributions to the World's Columbian Exposition in Chicago were causing France to swell with pride, the portrait was well timed. It offered viewers a fascinating peek into the secret life of France's most elusive and eccentric painting heroine.

The praise which flooded in was heartening.[10] But Rosa was conscious of the disappointment Consuélo must be feeling not having received such recognition for the portrait of Mme Jean Rameau which she exhibited at that year's Salon. Rosa urged Valérie to counsel her eldest daughter not to fret.

'Rewards are much like blisters on wooden legs,' Rosa opined, 'they don't affect much [...] If you have done about the best you can, you cannot do more.'[11]

But Rosa knew how futile such reassurances were. And she was in a position to help.

Without telling Consuélo, Rosa wrote to Gambart's representative Lefèvre in London. The portrait of her exhibited at the Salon that year had met with great acclaim; surely he could find a patron to commission another such portrait, one also signed Fould? Lefèvre agreed that he very likely could.

Consuélo Fould was no more disposed to accept defeat than her mother and when she was offered the commission, she made no hesitation. Six weeks of sittings would begin at the end of the summer. The work would form a sequel to the portrait by Édouard Dubufe, now more than 40 years old. And as in that painting, Rosa would be pictured with an animal, this time one of her Saint Bernard dogs.

However much she claimed a fondness for travelling, whenever the day of a planned trip arrived, Rosa was increasingly reluctant to leave By. In the autumn of 1893, her nephew René's voyage to the Auvergne encouraged fond memories to resurface. In her mind, Rosa travelled with him. But these days, a spiritual journey sufficed. She was most comfortable at home, and Consuélo Fould encountered the same resistance to stray from her patch. Rosa stipulated that the sittings for the portrait should take place at By. Likewise, she declined the invitation to attend Consuélo's wedding breakfast at the end of the year when the portrait artist married Marquis François Foulques Marie de Grasse, on the basis that 'fine ladies and castles frighten me dreadfully'.[12] Rosa was at her best – and her happiest – when those she wished to see came to her. Her charm in such circumstances was clearly demonstrated that November, when Georges Cain brought the journalist and writer Jules Claretie to see her to gather material for an article. Rosa's cordial reception was rewarded by a flattering piece in *La Vie Parisienne*.

But if she shrank from participating in society outside By, there was one area in which Rosa insisted on her central involvement.

'Once the portrait is finished,' she instructed Consuélo, 'or even before, if you prefer, you can send me the canvas and I will paint the dog.'[13]

After Dubufe's portrait, Rosa could be in no doubt of the value her contribution would add. But her offer was not entirely self-sacrificing; the representation of an animal was an area in which she judged perfection to be critical.

✼

Despite her work and her tutoring, Rosa had not forgotten her American friend. By the time the name Klumpke appeared on the front page of *Le Figaro* at the end of 1893, Anna had been gone two years. During that time, the American had lost her sister Mathilda to diphtheria. Coming to terms with the loss of a beloved sister was a challenge Anna and Rosa had in common.

The article announced that a true 'feminine victory' had been won. Dorothea Klumpke had obtained her mathematical science doctorate with a highly acclaimed thesis on Saturn's rings. Her expertise in the field of astronomy had already earned her a position at the Observatoire de Paris, and according to the paper, a triumph such as this did 'more for the cause of women than a whole battalion of feminist lecturers'.[14]

A woman proving rather than proclaiming her worth was an approach Rosa could applaud. 'Women's rights! – Women's nonsense!', Rosa had been heard to scoff. 'Women should seek to establish their rights by good and great works, and not by conventions […] I have no patience with women who *ask permission to think!*'[15] Rosa had always venerated her literary counterpart, George Sand, whose independent spirit and creative zeal she considered to be the mark of 'a great genius'.[16] She had only one reproach to make of the trouser-wearing writer: she was 'too womanly'.

Aware of the friendship which had blossomed between her elder sister and the unintentional figurehead of women's equality, Dorothea sent Rosa a copy of the thesis. Rosa was touched by the gesture and impressed by the science, but she admitted that she understood virtually nothing of what was written. Receiving the thesis did bring one personal benefit though: it gave her good reason to recontact her friend.

Besides acknowledging Dorothea's achievement, Rosa shared her hope that she would see Anna again in Paris, and soon – 'before the advent of a better world,' she wrote weightily.[17]

Still working on portrait commissions in Boston, Anna Klumpke cherished the letter. But she made no plans to return to Europe immediately.

⁂

Rosa would turn 71 that March; no one was more conscious than she of her life's impending finale. That awareness injected her usual work ethic with a heightened sense of urgency. Every so often, her terror of running out of time translated into impatience, even faced with those people and projects she enjoyed. Whenever she felt she was being robbed of the little time she might have left, her responses could sound offhand. At such moments, she became like a protective mother. Her work was in jeopardy and her reflex was to defend.

A letter written to Georges Cain on 5 January 1894 recounted a 'surprise visit' she had received which she 'ought to have appreciated and didn't', since it upset her routine and she had caught a chill which had lost her two days' work. A certain lady had wished to paint her portrait and Rosa had been 'obliged' to offer hospitality 'both to her husband and herself'.[18] The note was written just two days after the date Rosa had agreed to sit for Consuélo Fould. When her painting hours were compromised, Rosa's mood could swing without warning and pre-existing arrangements were likely to be forgotten, however dear the friend.

Still, these outbursts were never the result of malice and they seldom reflected Rosa's true feelings; rather, her patience with obstacles which impeded her progress was waning. For if Rosa was unpossessive regarding individual paintings, work was her life. With family and friends and above all, Nathalie, disappearing around her, painting was the only reliable foothold she had left. Time was finite – and she was terrified; there was still so much she wanted to do.

The people of Thomery could vouch for Rosa's inherent kindness. In the locality, she was known as 'the good lady' of By.[19]

'We have lived here for fifteen years and in all that time, we have never seen Mlle Rosa refuse anything to anyone,' confided a female factory worker that year.[20]

'The years have often been hard on us,' seconded the wife of a farmer. 'Without Mlle Rosa, we would never have got through it.'

An innkeeper added: 'You know, Mlle Rosa is the salvation of our village.'

In any case, that spring, Rosa's attention was diverted from pressures on her timetable. Just a few weeks later, something incredible happened.

⌘

The World's Columbian Exposition in Chicago had proved a show of conflicting outcomes for France. Organisers had remained committed to the American system of awards, which dispensed with graduated medals and allowed objectors to declare their displays *hors concours*. Nations still wedded to the traditional system of juries and awards had been dismayed and many countries, including France, withdrew their exhibits from the competition, refusing to be judged. Commemorative plaques seemed a feeble recompense for outstanding talent in such circumstances. The French government decided that their best artists deserved further recognition.[21]

One day in February, Isidore arrived at By in a state of excitement. He had it on good authority that Rosa was to be promoted to Officier de la Légion d'Honneur, the rank above that of Chevalier which she already held.

Rosa was incredulous. It was impossible; no woman had ever received that coveted distinction. But Isidore seemed convinced.

Unsettled and uncertain, the very next day, Rosa wrote to Auguste Cain, whose prominence on the Paris art scene would surely make him privy to such an initiative.[22]

But before anything conclusive could be ascertained, a few days later, Rosa was preparing to retire for the night when she was startled by the clang of the bell at the gates of By. It was past 9.00pm; nobody called at that hour.

The nocturnal visitor was the Prince Stirbey – and he had come to deliver a very special gift: Rosa soon found herself holding an exquisite box bearing her initials and the insignia of an Officier de la Légion d'Honneur. Something was clearly in the offing.

In the next few days, Auguste Cain wrote confirming his certainty that the rumours were true. And the assertion was apparently well-founded; letters of congratulations now started arriving at By.

With such a radical possibility mooted but not yet formalised, it was hard to remain focused on work. Rosa needed an enthralling project in which she could lose herself. Consuélo Fould's portrait demanded just such a commitment.

Since the beginning of the year, Rosa had been writing persistent letters to Consuélo, now the Marquise de Grasse, asking when she would be able to paint the dog's head in her picture. At last, in the middle of March, the work arrived. The task came just as one of Rosa's dogs had died giving birth, leaving her to nurse an orphaned puppy with a bottle. The loss of an animal was always saddening, but the call to maternity was not altogether unpleasant to her. Like Consuélo's painting, it gave her another distraction, particularly valuable when she was afflicted with shingles at the end of the month and her blotched, itching skin provided another unwelcome reminder that she was, after all, only human.

At last, early in April, the announcement came: Rosa Bonheur would indeed be the first woman ever to be promoted to the rank of Officier de la Légion d'Honneur.

The news was revolutionary. This was not just a symbol of recognition for Rosa; it reflected a dramatic shift in perspective for the whole country. Historically, French women had been denied access to this most prestigious of ranks. But Rosa had proved that a woman could meet the criteria. Silently, through action alone, she had convinced an entire board of French officials that women deserved to be venerated.

Rosa now insisted on knowing how her unwitting triumph had come about.

It was no secret that she had shone at the World's Columbian Exposition in Chicago, a show which had placed particular emphasis on female achievement. Georges Stirbey and Auguste Cain had spied an opportunity to honour their old friend. Over the last few months, they had been lobbying and campaigning tirelessly. Stirbey had approached President Carnot and having successfully overcome the objections advanced that Rosa's greatest work, *The Horse Fair* (1853), had been sent to the States and she herself notably absent from the Paris Salon for many years, Stirbey gained Carnot's assent.[23]

The people of France were exultant.

'Parisian studios have been delighted by the news that Rosa Bonheur has been promoted to the rank of Officier de la Légion d'Honneur,' *Le Figaro* reported.[24]

'Genius has no sex,' seconded *Le Journal*, citing an oft-quoted phrase which had frequently been linked to Rosa.[25]

'A sign of the times,' observed *Le Matin*. 'Success, fortune, glory – by virtue of her own merits, Rosa Bonheur has achieved them all. Her sex might have delayed her success momentarily; it could not impede her forever.'[26]

'Not a single voice spoke out against this promotion to Officier de la Légion d'Honneur, the first ever issued to a woman,' wrote the reporter for *Le Voleur illustré*. 'And why would one object [...] what does the sex of an artist matter if it has not prevented them entering the first rank of the French school?'[27]

'Everyone has agreed that the act of making a woman Officier de la Légion d'Honneur should be applauded,' the *Journal du Dimanche* chimed in.[28] And it was not only a triumph for gender, but also for genre; for Rosa had single-handedly elevated animal painting to a respected status, thus shattering the traditional hierarchy which pitched history and religious painting as superior to landscape.

The *Petit Parisien* reminded its readers that when Rosa had presented *Haymaking in the Auvergne* at the Exposition Universelle of 1855, the state had protested that 'the author of the canvas was a woman and therefore could not be decorated'.[29] Just a few years later, officials had been obliged to retract the rebuff.

Friends and acquaintances were quick to respond with congratulatory messages. Still, Rosa could think of no better way of celebrating than in the company of family.

Rosa wrote to Isidore, asking him to join her for a meal. Céline would roast a leg of mutton, there would be a pie and they would mark the occasion with a bottle of champagne, courtesy of Mme Fould (sent in Prince Stirbey's name). The invitation marked an important shift. When Nathalie had died, Rosa's gastronomic streak had withered and perished with her. Her partiality to a good wine or liquor remained (or as Major Rousseau noticed, markedly increased), yet food ceased to be the source of pleasure it had always been. The evening meal had become a scant and passionless affair. But now, with good news to celebrate, Rosa's first thought was of food. For her close acquaintances, it was a heartening sign of her spiritual regeneration.[30]

For all her aversion to society, Rosa found it impossible to resist being swept up in the flurry of euphoria generated by her decoration. Her diary was suddenly studded with important receptions.

Shortly after the news was released, she was invited to be the guest of honour at the Duc d'Aumale's home. Henri d'Orléans, Duc d'Aumale, was the fifth son of King Louis-Philippe. His inheritance had included the Château de Chantilly, which now reflected his penchant for fine and costly paintings. The palatial residence was an exercise in artistic opulence and the guest list at the reception held to honour Rosa, constellated with high-ranking dignitaries.[31]

The Duc d'Aumale's secretary later reported that Rosa had given the host her medal from the Salon of 1845, since it bore the effigy of his father. Secretly, Rosa's ego was always plumed by such demonstrations of pomp and ceremony. But as the secretary noticed, not even the presence of royal blood could motivate Rosa to refrain from smoking.[32]

A few days later, Rosa made her way to the magnificent Élysée Palace, home of France's presidents since the mid-19th century, to formally thank and receive the official congratulations of Sadi Carnot. She was reassured to go accompanied by her sponsor Auguste Cain, himself an Officier de la Légion d'Honneur since 1882.[33]

With Auguste Cain also hosting a star-studded honorary banquet, the line-up of grand receptions was exhilarating. However, Rosa's predisposition towards reclusion meant that she desperately needed to withdraw between such events. Consuélo Fould's painting became a grounding form of retreat. By May, Rosa had completed the dog's head – and offered the artist an unembellished tutorial into the bargain:

'With what did you prepare those impastations? Not dry yet.'[34]

Notwithstanding, when Consuélo saw the finished canvas, she was overcome with emotion and refused to sign the painting. Rosa insisted, but the protégé held firm.

'Very well,' Rosa sighed, 'I will sign the dog and you sign my head!'

'I cannot sign my name next to yours,' the young woman exclaimed in dismay. 'It is already an enormous honour to be asked to produce your portrait.'

'Yes, you must, I want you to my *dear little sister*,' Rosa urged, laughing.[35]

As usual, Rosa got her way.

Consuélo's finished work was simpler than her sister's. She showed Rosa in a three-quarter-length portrait, her palette and brushes gripped firmly in her left hand. With the right, the artist absentmindedly fondled the head of one of her Saint Bernard dogs, while she held herself upright, her head raised, dignified and assured. The dark clothes and background accentuated the bright colours on her palette and the glossy sheen of the dog's chocolate-coloured coat. Meanwhile, the radiant flesh tones applied to the model's cheeks and forehead drew attention to her face.

The simplicity was just to Rosa's taste. Over the course of their sittings, Rosa had told Consuélo emphatically how she hated 'fashionable' painting which pleased the undemanding eye in the same way that a spicy dish gratified the uncultured palate. Similarly, she stressed the importance of referring to the old masters, her abhorrence of siccative or drying agent, her conviction that all equipment should be cleaned until it was spotless, that oil should be used sparingly – and that work should be allowed to dry properly. The money offered for a painting was unimportant; the quality was everything.

Her own position assured, Rosa's attention now turned to what she considered to be a brilliant plan. With her nephew Hippolyte, she began conspiring to get Isidore made Chevalier de la Légion d'Honneur.

As Rosa wrote letters, contacted friends and badgered fellow artists, the warm glow of the recent celebrations lingered. It had been an unforgettable start to 1894 – all the more so, because just a few weeks later, France was rocked by some devastating news.

At the end of June, President Sadi Carnot was making his way from the Chamber of Commerce in Lyon, where he had gone to deliver a speech, to a gala performance at the Grand-Théâtre. Suddenly, a man burst out of the crowd and rushed towards the statesman's carriage brandishing a knife. Gasps and cries of panic rippled through the mass of onlookers as Italian anarchist Sante Caserio jumped onto the vehicle's running board and plunged his weapon into the President. The attacker was punched to the ground by Préfet Rivaud, and the crowd set about him, while the President's driver rushed him to safety. But it was too late; shortly after midnight, France's leader was declared dead.

The country was horrified; Europe was stunned – and Rosa was profoundly shaken. Just a matter of days ago, she had been conversing with the President, standing close enough that she could have reached out and touched him. For some days, Rosa struggled to work and battled to overcome her shock.

Grief soon assumed a more personal character, too. In August, Rosa's friend and benefactor, Auguste Cain, passed away suffering from an affliction of the larynx. Henceforward, Rosa would look down to the cross with its rosette pinned to her left breast with poignancy. Auguste Cain had been the same age as her.

'Every day that I see slip away worries me,' Rosa shared her anxiety with Consuélo Fould.[36]

In such times, routines were reaffirming. That winter of 1894, Rosa returned as usual to the pied-à-terre she still kept in Paris. A brief bout of one of her seasonal maladies had soon passed and before long, she was back in By and hard at work. Industry remained her solace and she admired and encouraged the same quality in others.

'When I think what a worker you are and your sister, too, it makes me jubilate,' Rosa wrote to Consuélo Fould in March 1895, 'I see Woman marching on while the men fret and fume.'[37]

Though written in a playful mood, Rosa's cheeky feminist flourish was timely. She would soon need all the spirit she could muster – for in the summer of 1895, past, present and future rushed together in a spectacular collision. Within a matter of weeks, Rosa learned tragic news concerning one of her oldest friends, Isidore Bonheur received a wonderful surprise – and Anna Klumpke returned to Paris.

25

Four Loves

'At last, my dear old Brother, you've got IT!'[1]

Rosa had spotted the news in *Le Figaro*: finally, Isidore was to be made Chevalier de la Légion d'Honneur.[2]

In that moment of writing and receiving, the siblings were transported back to their teens and twenties, when shared excitement at the realisation of long-held dreams had animated the family gatherings at the Rue Rumford.

If Isidore's achievement came of his own merits, Rosa's campaign had certainly done him no harm. It was in a state of triumph that she spent two days striding around that year's Salon. Her nephew René had a landscape on show and his brother Hippolyte, a sculpture of a Gordon Setter. Flu having prevented Rosa attending Hippolyte's wedding the previous autumn, it was a chance to present a show of familial solidarity.

Rosa may have just turned 73, but that spring, she felt energised. Good news and young people were rejuvenating her. And the positive trajectory looked set to continue.

At the start of the summer, a letter arrived from Anna Klumpke. She was back in Paris.

Her important commissions fulfilled, Anna had been unable to resist the call of Europe's artistic capital any longer. Though she was disappointed to learn that the portrait artist François Thévenot, whose tutorship she had hoped to enlist, did not take students, she had instead re-enrolled at the Académie Julian. Setting herself up in her own studio, she began preparing work for next year's Salon. And now, above all, she wanted to see Rosa.

But before Rosa had a chance to reply, she received some harrowing news: on 10 July 1895, her intimate friend Caroline Carvalho passed away suffering from a complication of the kidneys. The singer died at her villa in Puy near Dieppe, where Rosa had often stayed.

'The death of Mme Carvalho has been a great blow to me,' Rosa opened her heart to Georges Cain and his wife. 'How hard life is sometimes! Now and again I grow very discouraged with art as with the rest.'[3]

Bereavement had become an all-too-familiar companion. Rosa was not yet conditioned to it. For the moment, she could not face people and she wrote to Anna Klumpke asking to postpone their reunion.

Yet from the world outside By, the voice of a younger generation was calling persistently. It would not be ignored. Through all the personal storms Rosa had weathered in recent years, engaging with less experienced artists had always compelled her to lift her vision to the future. And once she felt able to resume such communication, little by little, Rosa found herself able to reintegrate in society.

Mlle Delphine Gabrielle Keller was an inoffensive and mild lady whom Rosa liked immensely. She had started coaching Mlle Keller as an adolescent and though the student was now in her 50s, she had remained fixed in Rosa's mind as a delicate young fledgling. Having debuted at the Salon at the end of the 1850s, Mlle Keller had subsequently won multiple awards, becoming proficient in both painting and lithography, so much so that she now took students of her own. Rosa had developed an especially protective attitude towards her 'little wren'. That August, she urged Mlle Keller to experiment with outdoor painting. But the counsel came with a caution: she should not venture out alone to the more isolated corners of the Bois. Not everyone was to be trusted.

A few, select friends like Mlle Keller provided a vital line of communication with the outside world. But otherwise, for the remainder of the summer and the early autumn, Rosa sequestered herself at By, painting and allowing the familiar surroundings to work their curative magic.

Every morning, she rose at 5.00am and, dressing promptly, was ready to start her day by sunrise. In the summer months, by 7.00am, Rosa had clambered up into her horse-drawn tilbury and was trundling towards the narrow wooden door in the west wall, often with her dogs (and sometimes even her monkey) scampering or trotting beside her. In little time, she had reached the cool and shady heart of the forest and was greedily inhaling the damp, earthy scent of the leaf mould beneath the ancient oak trees. Though Moret station was not far away and beyond it, Paris, only occasionally did the faint rumble of a train in the distance remind a person of civilisation. For the most part, all that could be heard was the rustle of the breeze combing through the oak leaves, the shrill song of a bird, and sometimes, nothing – silence.[4]

Whenever a particular spot or effect of sunlight caught her eye, Rosa settled down to sketch. There, she could lose herself. She seldom returned to the château within two hours. In the winter, her expedition had to be delayed until late morning or early afternoon. But that it took place was indubitable. Rosa's daily drive was as necessary to her as air or water. The forest was like a drug, a form of deep meditation. It lifted her mood, it fuelled her creativity. She knew each shaded grove, every gnarled tree, thoroughly, intimately, as though it were part of her own body. In the forest, she became as a child and her troubles melted away, if only for a while.

When Rosa returned to the château, her skin flushed with morning and her eyes sparkling, it was as though she had lost ten years. Friends were struck by the rapidity of the forest's restorative effect. Now, Rosa was ready to start work.

An impassioned picture was consuming her that year. *The Duel* (1895) took as its subject the story of the legendary Godolphin Arabian. The fine bay steed was said to have been presented as a gift to Louis XV in the 18th century, but subsequently discarded on account of his diminutive size compared to European stallions, which were then in vogue. The animal was sold and subjected to gruelling labour. But salvation came when an Englishman transported the beast to Britain, where he was acquired by Francis, the Second Earl of Godolphin. Lord Godolphin owned a stud farm and he planned to use the new arrival (named El Scham in Eugène Sue's 1845 version of the story) as a teaser to test whether a mare would be receptive to another stallion's advances.

English painter George Stubbs had been inspired by the tale and Rosa had long admired an engraving of one his paintings. Her own picture showed the dramatic moment when a grey mare named Roxana sparks a ferocious battle between the Arabian and Hobgoblin, a superb and strapping grey. Rosa set the showdown in a contrast-ingly tranquil meadow, where she depicted El Scham rearing up on his hind legs and closing his jaws on Hobgoblin's neck. Locked in a vicious confrontation, the horses' eyes were wild, the sound of snorting and high-pitched protest vividly evoked. Rosa had lingered over Sue's description of Roxana, who 'tied to a post [...] seemed to be egging the Arabian on with urgent whinnies'.[5] Accordingly, in the far dis-tance, Rosa showed Roxana watching this fierce display of masculine prowess. The work was startlingly aggressive, quite unique in Rosa's oeuvre. It possessed the energy of *The Horse Fair* (1853), the simplicity of *Royalty at Home* (1885) – and the assurance that came with decades spent reconstructing animal life for enthralled spectators.

As the picture neared completion, that autumn, Rosa had the chance to gauge how it might be received when she was visited by a fellow artist for whom her respect was mounting.

ॐ

It was a bright and crisp morning in October when Anna Klumpke and her mother arrived at Moret station. Anna had scarcely stepped down onto the platform when a stout bundle of cloaks and coats she took to be a little old man marched up and embraced her. Horrified, Mrs Klumpke was on the point of intervening when the women recognised Rosa. Their mistake was the source of infectious laughter as the three boarded the carriage and sped back towards By.[6]

To Anna's delight, a hearty lunch was again a mere prelude to a tour of 'the sanctuary'. Rosa explained the story behind *The Duel*, which was mounted on an easel. The conversation then took an uncomfortable turn, when Rosa probed Anna about the buffalo grass: why had she not simply picked a fresh sample when it had been there just beneath her feet? Taken aback, Anna explained that the woman in the photograph she had sent was not her but the schoolteacher who had given her the picture. Rosa next wanted to know everything about her foreign visitor's trip. And as Anna spoke, Rosa listened intently. This was the closest she was ever likely to come to experiencing America.

Though Anna's idolisation showed no signs of waning, she was growing more confident around the artist and now felt able to ask a few favours of her own. Might Rosa be able to introduce her to the great portrait painter François Thévenot, she enquired? Rosa did not know him personally but assured Anna that she would write a letter of introduction. Then came another question: could Anna return to By with Sophie Walker, an American whose portrait she had painted and who wished to buy a picture for an art museum in Brunswick? Rosa agreed to that too.

When Anna returned a few weeks later with Miss Walker, Rosa astounded the American customer by promising to paint her a copy of a picture she liked for a mere fraction of what she had expected.

Still, Rosa was careful not to allow many such visits to compromise her work time that winter. Her prudence paid off; before Christmas, she had finished *The Duel* and her satisfaction with the result was ample recompense for her efforts. The 50,000 francs she received was merely a pleasant sweetener.[7]

Meanwhile, as Rosa formed new acquaintances, some older ones were being reconfigured. Valérie Fould's marriage to Prince Stirbey should not have come as a surprise, but Rosa was nonetheless struck by the appearance of a crown on her 'grandmother's' headed notepaper.

It would take some getting used to, Rosa joked, since that would nat-urally make her a prince.[8]

⊗

The flurry of sociability which concluded 1895 did not abate as the New Year began. In January, Anna Klumpke announced that one of her buyers from Pittsburgh, a Mrs Thaw, also wished to meet the great Rosa Bonheur. Mrs Thaw was a wealthy and well-regarded patron of the arts in the United States, a formidable woman of some 50 years whose determination, generosity and buying power had earned her a prodigious reputation. With Rosa's consent, Anna reappeared at By one day accompanied by a gaggle of American ladies, including Mrs Thaw, her sister and two daughters. Well versed in the art of providing visitors with the spectacle they craved, Rosa dressed in her men's garments and even produced a hasty sketch for the wide-eyed guests.[9]

Anna watched the performance admiringly, glowing with pride. Her reaction did not pass unnoticed. Before the visitors left, Rosa sud-denly made an impromptu suggestion: Anna should come and work at By. The American need not forfeit her independence, for Rosa would find her lodgings in the locality and would coach her as her career developed. It was an unparalleled opportunity. Anna left By that day visibly stupefied.

Finding her prospective student accommodation now became Rosa's new project. And she was pleased when a few enquiries in the village led her to find just what she was looking for and not far from By. She wrote to Miss Klumpke, suggesting that she begin work the following May.

But Anna's response was not the one Rosa had expected.

On returning to Paris, Mrs Thaw had declared herself eager to meet François Thévenot and their visit had an unexpected consequence; a few days later, Anna received a letter from Thévenot, informing her that he would take her on as a temporary student after all, for three months starting in May.

Now, the American found herself in an impossible position. She would have to reject either the acclaimed portrait artist or the revered painter of animals who – she fancied – was becoming her friend. It was a torturous decision, but Anna allowed her professional nous to guide her. She was a portrait painter; she must think of her career.

Rosa was understanding. In fact, she admired such objective self-appraisal and precedence being given to professional advancement. Rosa encouraged Anna to continue visiting whenever she wished, and the American promised that she would.

Still, Rosa knew the all-consuming nature of the Paris art world. A student had to dedicate him- or herself wholeheartedly to their work, while all around them, old masters and contemporary talents vied for their attention. Time inevitably vanished among the demands and attractions of the capital. It was hardly surprising when the visits Rosa had been promised did not take place. All too quickly, the summer was over and Anna Klumpke was due to return to America. She came to By once more before she left.

The meeting was as congenial as ever. The prospect of Anna's imminent departure soon led Rosa onto the subject of American Indians, her passion for the tales of the Wild West and of her vivid memories of her meeting with Buffalo Bill. Somehow, in the exhilaration of the moment, Anna again found herself promising to harvest some Native American grass for Rosa's picture (a fresh sample this time, Rosa specified emphatically).

Rosa had now grown deeply fond of the American. She told her guest how she hoped that they would meet again. But at her age, Rosa had to accept that this might be the last time she would ever see Anna Klumpke.

ॡ

With Anna gone, Rosa reabsorbed herself in the cocoon of her routine – rising at five, breakfasting lightly on tea and a boiled egg, returning from her sortie in the forest to begin work by nine, taking a simple lunch at half past eleven, and following it with a cigarette and a glance at the papers before resuming work and continuing until five. After a modest supper (often soup and cheese), her evening was spent with a book on travel or hunting or history. Every day, the same, reassuring pattern would recommence. But there were disruptions that summer too. A fall from one of her horses upset her work schedule and worried her friends. Fortunately, she soon recovered, which was just as well; Ernest Gambart wanted her to join him on a trip.[10]

Now in his 80s, Gambart's health was faltering. He had suffered at least one stroke (though he suspected it might be two), and both his mind and his eyes were less sharp. The dealer had decided that the fresh Alpine air of the Swiss mountains would likely prove remedial, so had taken a villa in the town of Schwyz, near the two Mythen mountains. But Gambart was an inherently social creature. He needed company as much as Rosa craved her solitude. Yet at present, a break was essential to him, just as artistic inspiration was vital to her. Spending time together in a picturesque location, each found the perfect compromise.

'As poor Gambart is moping to death all alone in the antique dwelling-place of William Tell, I am invited to hunt the chamois in his amiable society,' Rosa informed the Princess Stirbey. 'Along with the fresh air of icy mountains, I will get six weeks of tranquillity.'[11]

The period of repose was apposite; Rosa's timetable was about to become considerably fuller.

That October, Paris was taken up with the arrival of the Russian Czar Nicholas II. As part of France's show of hospitality, the Directeur des Beaux-Arts, M. Roujon, was choreographing a reception at the Louvre, where the visitors would be able to meet some of France's greatest artists. Rosa was invited to be one of the number.[12]

Now a seasoned expert when it came to royal and ministerial visits, Rosa pulled on her uniform black velvet dress, heavy coat and a feathered bonnet. But upon arriving, she instantly regretted her outfit.

The guest list had been restricted to individuals holding a Légion d'Honneur – and that necessarily meant one composed almost exclusively of men.

At the sight of an Officier wearing a dress, all heads turned. Rosa later confided that, at that moment, she would have given anything to be wearing her smock and trousers. Had it not been for the chivalrous greeting of the artist Carolus-Duran, her embarrassment would have been unbearable.

To Rosa's relief, the staring eyes were soon distracted when the sovereign's arrival was announced.

Once the Czar had enjoyed the Italian primitives, Rosa was formally presented. The Empress Alexandra complimented her talent so sincerely that tears were seen forming in Rosa's eyes.[13] Indeed, for all that her stolid appearance remained the butt of cruel jokes, humbling words and recognition never failed to stir Rosa.

Even so, the emotion of the day was overshadowed by her initial discomfort – and far outweighed by her love of By.

'I am now back home again and not sorry,' she told Isidore the day afterwards.[14]

Rosa had plenty to attend to. She had agreed to mount an exhibition of pastels at the Galerie Georges Petit the following summer and though she never actively courted media attention, an autobiographical article for *La Revue des Revues* now seemed pertinent. Age was partly responsible for this sudden need to account for herself, coupled with her growing awareness that the time to complete her creative mission was running out. However, such a feature merely increased the pressure to complete the showpieces to an exceptional standard. Then with other canvases to finish and staffing difficulties at the château, Rosa was already stretched to her limit when, at the end of May, Alexandrine of Saxe-Coburg-Gotha requested a favour. Her niece, Queen Victoria's youngest and best-loved daughter, Princess Beatrice, wanted to visit By.[15]

Doted on in infancy, depended on as an adult, the golden-haired, blue-eyed, porcelain-complexioned Beatrice was at once her mother's unofficial secretary and her jealously guarded confidante. In 1885, Beatrice had irked her Majesty by marrying Prince Henry of Battenberg, but the daughter's assurance that she would remain by her mother's side eventually reconciled Queen Victoria to the arrangement. Beatrice and Henry had gone on to have four children when, in 1896, Henry contracted malaria and died during the Anglo-Ashanti War, leaving Beatrice traumatised. That spring, the family had tried to buoy the Princess's spirits with a 40th birthday celebration on the French Riviera. Shortly due to return to London for the Queen's Diamond Jubilee, Beatrice was to conclude her French sojourn in Fontainebleau. And of all the area's diversions and distractions, she especially desired to make the acquaintance of Rosa, whose work she had admired in London.[16]

The Duchess of Saxe-Coburg-Gotha assured Rosa that she would warm to Beatrice, but with Céline falling ill and the rest of her staff proving infuriatingly ineffectual, the timing was far from ideal. As the royal visit loomed, the stout, 75-year-old Rosa was left with no choice but to lay down her brushes, roll up her sleeves and set to work dusting, scrubbing and polishing the château herself. To compound matters, Rosa was given no indication of precisely when she should expect Her Highness. Beatrice was travelling incognito, and her civilian guise even extended to her means of exploring the region, which she did both on foot and by tricycle, the fashionable mode of transport for women at the time. She arrived at By unannounced on Monday 14 June accompanied by her entourage and her lady-in-waiting, Miss Minnie Cochrane, giving Rosa scarcely enough time to wriggle into a skirt.[17]

Major Rousseau received an irascible letter that month, in which Rosa grumbled about the incompetency of her staff, her impossible workload and the lack of time to herself.[18] However, secretly, Rosa found such royal attention tremendously flattering. She was invariably compliant when a grand personality impressed her. The Princess was naturally creative, so as *L'Abeille de Fontainebleau* observed, the women could 'exchange more than just pleasantries'.[19] Beatrice's special penchant was photography, so Rosa agreed to pose for a photograph with her dapple grey mare, Panther.

The reception successfully hosted, Rosa could at last turn her attention to her exhibition at the Galerie Georges Petit. The show was remarkable for two reasons. For one thing, Rosa disliked working in pastel, a practice to which she gave the damning qualification of 'artistic masonry'.[20] The second surprise was that the exhibition was taking place at all. Rosa had not shown her work in the capital for years. As a result, the display of four pastels became a major artistic event, prompting a stream of articles which pored over the spectacle of the hermit who had ventured out of hiding.

The proud, hard-working Rosa sought solitude 'as single-mindedly as others pursue awards', *Les Annales politiques et littéraires* declared.[21] For the journalist Santilane writing in *Gil Blas*, Rosa was 'the doyenne of female artists', and after the close of the Salon, her show offered 'a consolation' and 'a bit of real art'.[22]

'It pleased me very much to succeed in a kind of painting that I had never cultivated,' Rosa admitted to Paul Chardin.[23] Nevertheless, with fellow female painter Virginie Demont-Breton, she confided her overwhelm at the public interest: 'For the last three months, I have done nothing but thank people in relation to my pastels, to such an extent that my mind is completely befuddled with all the polite courtesies I have had to pay.'[24]

Not all the associated correspondence was tedious to write, however. The exhibition gave Rosa a point of interest around which to base another letter to Anna Klumpke. And to her delight, Anna replied promptly, announcing that Rosa would shortly be receiving specimens of the wild plant she had requested.

A letter could scarcely convey the lengths to which the American had been obliged to go. To access the remote terrains where the plant grew, Anna had been forced to sign up to an expedition bound for a Christian Alliance convention in San Francisco, and had departed from Cincinnati on a train travelling across the prairies. Using Rosa's name, Anna had coaxed the conductor into stopping the vehicle full of passengers so that she could gather the elusive plant. She had even lost her paintbrushes in the process. But to her mind, it had all been worth it.

Oblivious to the extent of Anna Klumpke's pains, Rosa waited expectantly. The grass did not materialise. What did arrive was another letter from Miss Klumpke, this time with a request of her own: if she returned to France, would Rosa do her the honour of sitting for her portrait?

Having posed for artists of varying abilities over the years, Rosa had reached the irrevocable conclusion that she disliked working as a model. She knew the stamina it required, the time it would consume and the inherent risk that, after all that effort, the outcome might still only prove moderately satisfactory. Nonetheless, Rosa had also witnessed Anna Klumpke's skill. And the idea of their reunion was far from unpleasant to her. She agreed to cooperate.

Eventually in January 1898, a package arrived at By. Anna had sent a beautifully illustrated alphabet book by way of a New Year's gift, as well as a tentative enquiry about Miss Walker's picture. She said nothing about the portrait.

Rosa thanked her for the book and confessed that she had not yet finished the painting. Perplexingly, when Anna wrote again, she renewed her request about the portrait. Rosa was confused, but nonetheless restated her assent, adding that the American could stay at the château for the duration of the project. This time the response was prompt and enthusiastic: Anna would arrive at By in a few weeks' time.

∞

On 11 June 1898, Anna Klumpke found herself once more contemplating the imposing entranceway to the Château de By. With its tall metal railings, stone and red-brick facade, timbered studio and expansive front courtyard, the property had scarcely changed since her last visit. But Anna had; this time, she came not as an interpreter or a guest or even an intermediary – now, she presented herself as an artist, one to whom Rosa Bonheur was about to entrust her public image.[25]

Once Rosa's overenthusiastic dogs had been pushed down and the women had embraced, conversation quickly turned to the portrait. It was agreed that the first sitting should take place on the 16th of the month (they had best not tempt fate by starting on the 13th, Rosa reasoned).

When the day arrived, Rosa announced that she intended to appear in women's clothes. The American risked no objection. Reaching for her equipment and wrestling with her nerves, Anna began her first sketch.

Almost immediately, the critique she had both anticipated and feared was launched: her range of paints was insufficient. They should mount to Rosa's studio and collect a better assortment.

With the subject satisfied and the portrait artist still struggling to believe her good fortune, the sitting began. And as Anna worked and Rosa watched, the natural evolution of conversation began to deepen their acquaintance. Only once were they interrupted when one of Rosa's friends called in unexpectedly. Still, it gave Anna the perfect opportunity to study the great artist's face while she relaxed.

Anna concentrated intently on the woman she had long admired from afar. As her eye took in the figure before her, steadily, her hand began tracing its form. She explored each contour, discovering how the body supported the clothes, becoming familiar with every wrinkle and distinguishing feature, from the fine fingers now yellowed from years of smoking, to the eyes, still bright and engaging.

During the afternoon, Rosa studied her guest intensely too. Over dinner, she ventured a gentle tease: Miss Anna had a nose like Cyrano de Bergerac. Once they had returned to the studio, Rosa produced a copy of the recently published play by Edmond Rostand. Opening it, she began reading 'the nose tirade', in which a big nose was proclaimed to be a sign of countless desirable character traits. Enunciating eloquently in a voice which danced with animation, Rosa had her listener transfixed. Anna found her initial hurt dissolving as her admiration and sense of wonder crept back in. Rosa closed the volume and bade her visitor good night, urging her to read more Rostand before bed.

But Anna did not. The moment she had returned to her bedroom and closed the door, she sat down and, taking pen and paper, began recording her impressions of the day. As the household gradually fell silent, she sat up late into the night, noting everything that had taken place: the development of the sitting, the conversations, the subjects discussed, the curious turns of phrase Rosa employed in her clear, lively voice with its childlike inflections, to the smallest fluctuations in her facial expressions as she passed from one mood to another. Not a thing was missed.[26]

Anna realised that living in such close quarters was going to afford her a privileged degree of intimacy with the artist. From the outset, Rosa proved herself hospitable and generous, yet forthright and tenacious. She stipulated that she was not prepared to sit for long periods, nor would she pose every day. If Miss Anna wished to produce her portrait, these were the conditions she would have to accept.

The next day, Rosa took Anna to inspect her wardrobe. As they browsed through potential outfits for the sitting, Anna's inhibitions began to melt away and she confessed how torturous it had been not to receive an answer when she first asked Rosa about painting her portrait. Rosa retorted that she had replied. All at once, both women realised the misunderstanding which had occurred: Rosa's letter had never reached its recipient. Overcome with both relief and frustration at time spent worrying unnecessarily, Anna promptly burst into tears. Rosa's defensive air softened. She consoled the visitor; it no longer mattered. She was here now and the project underway.

As the first week progressed, Rosa encouraged Anna to experiment with a number of different poses. But as the days passed, Anna became increasingly apprehensive about the intrusion she felt certain her presence must be imposing. Living so closely with someone she still did not know well enforced a level of intimacy which might not be palatable to her hostess. Eventually, Anna hazarded the suggestion that it might be preferable if she took lodgings in Moret, as her former tutor from the Académie Julian, Tony Robert-Fleury, had advised. Rosa's objection was terse: the present arrangement suited quite well.

And so the summer unfolded. During the sittings, Rosa sat or reclined, often puffing on a cigarette and talking – about friends and family and art. She shared stories – tales of travels and people, of places and the past. Anna watched and absorbed everything. Every so often, Rosa got up and came to inspect how the work was progressing. Compliments and criticism were delivered with equal liberality.

Anna soon realised, too, that she was going to learn as much about the business side of art as she was the mechanics of painting. Over the weeks, dealers arrived, work needed signing, and letters replying to. One young visitor from London, Gambart's lively great-nephew and junior picture dealer, Ernest Lefèvre, even asked to purchase Anna's portrait of Rosa when it was complete. But Rosa abhorred being confined to the house all day. She made certain that work was punctuated by recreation.

Anna Klumpke painting.

Collection Atelier Rosa Bonheur

The American now discovered a whole new sylvan existence. There were trips out into Fontainebleau Forest in the tilbury with the horses Grisette and Panther and the eager little Yorkies Charley and Daisy snuggled in their basket beside them; there were leisurely strolls around the grounds, evenings sat under the linden tree watching the late summer sunset, and always, animals to be fed and petted, many of them former models.

Back at the château, Rosa showed Anna her medals, went through old photographs, and regretted her family. Gradually, the two women were coming to know each other intimately. From Rosa's perspective, opening up to Anna was unexpectedly therapeutic. Meanwhile, for Anna, the experience was providing the richest kind of artistic training

Rosa Bonheur wearing her laurel crown, 10 July 1898, photograph by Anna Elizabeth Klumpke.

Collection Atelier Rosa Bonheur

she could ever have hoped for. Artistic debate preceded anecdote, and solemn discussions were interspersed with humour. One day, Rosa produced a hasty caricature of Anna at work, exaggerating her outsize nose, and even the victim had to laugh. On another occasion, Rosa invited her guest to join her for a smoke and quickly realised her error when the novice coughed and spluttered her way through a cigarette. When Rosa's friend, the landscape painter, illustrator and engraver Auguste Allongé passed away, it was Anna whom Rosa asked to attend the funeral in her stead. Then one evening, Anna fashioned Rosa a crown made out of laurel sprigs – a homage on behalf of her country which was yet to duly honour her, she explained. Rosa was profoundly moved by the innocent gesture. She allowed Anna to photograph her

Rosa Bonheur in her laurel crown.

Collection Atelier Rosa Bonheur

in the regal headwear, and declared that she wished to be buried with the item.

The Exposition Universelle of 1900 provided a source of common excitement, and Anna offered to help Rosa complete her *Wheat Threshing in the Camargue* (1899), proposing to clamber up the scaffolding to paint the sky, despite her lameness. Shared experiences accumulated – and as the older woman came to know the younger and vice versa, an impenetrable bond began to form. Their mutual admiration mounted and their happiness soared.

But as the weeks went by, Anna found Rosa's contrary approach to posing beginning to vex her. She wanted to show her portrait in a forthcoming exhibition in Pittsburgh. Yet Rosa appeared to be doing everything in her power to prolong the sittings. She refused to pose if it were too hot, if she had work to do or if there was someone she simply must see. Anna was instructed to do more studies before tackling the final portrait. One day, Mr Tedesco arrived and Rosa told Anna to paint a portrait of his wife. Then there were days off and even, to Anna's disbelief, cleaning, with which she was expected to help. Once or twice, Anna informed her hostess that she needed to return to Paris briefly to seek the opinion of her former tutors, Tony Robert-Fleury and Jules Lefebvre. The mention of the alternative mentors put Rosa on edge. Each time a trip to Paris was mooted, Rosa instantly mellowed, imploring Anna to return soon and retracting her refusal to pose. Then when Anna came back, Rosa insisted on a complete account of what the rival tutors had said.

As the summer neared its end and the day of Anna's departure loomed like an unspoken curfew, the pleasures and frustrations in the burgeoning friendship seemed magnified. On occasion, Rosa's abrupt asides provoked tears in the devoted student. But then Anna too was gaining the confidence to answer back and be wilful. However, the tension always dissipated and a sensitive exchange eclipsed it. More than once, Rosa told Anna how much she looked like her mother, that she had become sincerely fond of her, that with her she felt young again. She even wrote to Anna's mother, insisting that her affection was wholly virtuous. Anna too had now seen that while Rosa could be awkward, her sensitivity was profound and her goodness unparalleled. Anna remained reverent and anxious to impress her admiration, though her adulation was rarely taken seriously. Nevertheless, one day, Anna distinctly remembered her flattery leading Rosa to enquire whether she truly cared for her.

'*Vous m'aimez bien sincèrement?*' [both 'do you really like me?' and 'do you really love me?'] Rosa asked.

Recording her mentor's question in the French allowed Anna to flirt with the potential for semantic slippage inherent in the verb *aimer*.

'*Oui, croyez-le,*' ['Yes, believe me'] the American confirmed.[27]

A lifetime of celebrity had taught Rosa to be wary. Anna's announcement was greeted with prolonged, reflective silence. In her diary, the American wrote that she could not be sure what Rosa was thinking.

It was the end of July when Rosa came to speak to Anna while she was working in the studio one day. She had reached a decision: Anna should come and live with her – forever.

26

Signing a Life

Gender politics had come a long way since Rosa first donned a pair of trousers. Fin-de-siècle French women were enjoying opportunities that their forbears could scarcely have imagined. In the 1880s, the provision of secondary education for girls, the reintroduction of divorce (prohibited since 1816) and a woman's right to open a bank account without her husband's permission had all charted decisive victories on the path to female emancipation. Across France, 'new women' were mounting bicycles and pedalling away from their post at the hearth towards untold horizons. Their perception of the world around them and their place within it was changing. An education, a career and an income were now realistic aspirations for many women. Meanwhile, short hair, knickerbockers and a cigarette were no longer the exception, but the unofficial uniform of a burgeoning tranche of females who had sampled the irresistible taste of freedom.

Yet despite these noticeable changes, as an organised movement, feminism in France had not mushroomed on a scale comparable with Britain. Efforts to promote women's rights had remained primarily literary in nature, most visible in the emergence of journals like *La Fronde* (founded in 1897). Radical feminists were in a minority and the country's feminist societies, largely confined to Paris. Those more determined activists were concentrated in the upper classes and the higher echelons of the bourgeoisie; it was not in these women's interest to launch a serious assault on the moral fabric of the class to which they belonged. At heart, France was still underpinned by a deep-set conviction – that men were naturally called to the public sphere while women should occupy themselves with the home. For many, the family remained a microcosm of the state, with a clearly defined, male leader and a hierarchy of subordinate subjects.[1]

A legacy of the ancien regime, the gendered landscape was now being reinforced by a vocal school of social theorists and conservative thinkers who relentlessly denounced anyone who rejected heterosexual marriage. This collective voice was strengthened by medics alarmed about the consequences of sexual promiscuity, as it was by demographers still haunted by the spectre of the Franco-Prussian War and anxious to safeguard the population. Added to the sociopolitical mix came a wave of texts like Léon Taxil's *Fin-de-Siècle Corruption* (1891) and Julien Chevalier's *Sexual Inversion* (1893), written in response to that fashionable scourge, lesbianism, which had proliferated in the closing years of the 19th century, particularly in bohemian circles and on the pages of novels.

By and large, the female population recognised that the best way to effect change in this climate was to work with, not against, the historical status quo. For the most part, the French still expected their daughters to marry a respectable man.

But the concerns Anna Klumpke now had to weigh up were infinitely more complex. Social opprobrium was not in itself a deterrent. Her parents had granted their handicapped daughter preferential entitlements in their will, so Anna had grown up accepting that meaningful work, not a man, would govern her life. In any case, the day she won a third-class medal at the Exposition Universelle of 1889, she had made herself a promise: 'That day I married art,' she remembered.[2] Then Anna was American; Rosa had often marvelled at the enlightened social attitudes in the States, and Anna's own friendship with the journalist Lillian Whiting, the intimate companion of the journalist and actress Kate Field, made her no stranger to the concept of the 'Boston marriage'. Popularised by Henry James's novel *The Bostonians* in 1886, the expression signified a long-term relationship between a pair of unmarried women. Typically, the couple were financially independent, often involved in the arts. The relationships sometimes encompassed sex, but not always; love could be poetic rather than carnal. James himself had classed his fictionalised study of such an arrangement as 'a very American tale'.[3]

In announcing that she intended to live with another female, Anna had less to fear from her family than would most women. The Klumpkes had always held progressive views. But Dorothea Klumpke had raised her girls to be independent – and that meant answerable to no one, male or female. Mrs Klumpke was committed to her eldest daughter's progress in her chosen field, but professionally speaking, Anna and Rosa were leagues apart. In attaching herself to Rosa, Anna risked sidelining her career and accepting a life in another artist's shadow. Such an arrangement could be just as inhibiting as an oppressive heterosexual marriage.

Rosa had no cause to be surprised when, having made her proposal and countered the immediate protest that the Bonheur family would disapprove, an emotional and tearful Anna begged to withdraw to her room. But as the minutes ticked by and the woman who had rekindled Rosa's enthusiasm for life did not reappear, the impulse to self-scrutinise was overwhelming.[4]

Rosa was now 76. She was reaching the end of a fine career, one marked by renown, recognition and rewards. She was cushioned by a respectable fortune, surrounded by loyal friends and comfortably ensconced in an idyllic country retreat. Yet the confidence she should have felt was suddenly being undermined – because she now realised that for her happiness to be complete, she depended largely on another person.

In a few short months, Anna Klumpke had become indispensable to her. It was as though all the women Rosa had ever loved and lost had been returned to her in one individual. Anna may not have been young, but she was younger and had filled the château with her infectious, still-innocent enthusiasm for art, while encouraging Rosa to think like a woman half her age. She looked and played the piano like Rosa's mother Sophie, she possessed Caroline Carvalho's ability to converse intelligently about music, while she offered the companionship, support and artistic camaraderie Rosa had cherished in Nathalie. And like Nathalie, Anna was physically disadvantaged; if only tacitly, she gave the impression that she needed something of Rosa, too. Above all, Anna kept Rosa constantly interested with her alluring air of foreignness. Then she was deferential, almost to a fault, but in such a way that Rosa's confidence and sense of self-worth were continually being polished and renewed. Faced with the possibility that all that might be snatched away, Rosa had every reason to feel apprehensive.

When at last the women reconvened that evening, dinner was taken in uncomfortable silence, the food barely touched.

Returning together to the studio, Rosa broke the tension. She repeated her earlier proclamation, insisting that she truly cared for Anna – like the daughter she had never had.

Choked with sobs, Anna now broke her silence too: of course she would stay and dedicate her life to Rosa – she adored her.

Rosa was euphoric. With Anna by her side, the best of the past would be remembered, the present became delicious and the future, indescribably exciting.

Back in her room, Anna's true feelings tumbled out onto the pages of her diary:

'It's nearly midnight. I am still trembling as I write this. How can I say everything in my heart? In truth, I cannot believe this unexpected bliss of becoming the lady companion, the adopted daughter, of Rosa Bonheur.'[5]

Anna remembered Rosa's impatience to make their agreement public, but Anna asked that they delay; first, she must speak to her family.

Notwithstanding, everything now moved quickly. The women's new, shared existence was heralded the next day when Rosa made another, weighty proposal: Anna had confessed that she was keeping a diary – would she use her notes to write Rosa's life story, accounting for it in a way that none of the men previously charged with the task had been able to do? Though initially hesitant, Anna agreed. That afternoon, both women wrote to Mrs Klumpke apprising her of their affection.

For all Anna's assurances, Rosa could not suppress a mounting sense of unease. She had seen how close Anna was to her family, and that was to say nothing of any other factors – or people – which might discourage her from staying. Rosa pressed her for reassurance, checking repeatedly that there was not some sweetheart waiting for her in America. Anna promised. There was not; she loved Rosa and she would stay forever.

Slowly, Rosa started believing that this unimaginable happiness might really be possible. Theirs would be the 'divine marriage of two souls', she effused.[6]

But soon, the anxiously awaited letter arrived. Its message was courteous but uncompromising: Anna must come back to Paris that very week. Mrs Klumpke was calling a family meeting.

As Anna's train pulled away from Moret station to return her to the bosom of her family, Rosa could only wait in trepidation. Everything depended on the Klumpke family's response – and on whether Anna would succumb to the pressure.

When at last Anna returned, her report began bleakly. Her brother-in-law Jules Déjerine had pointed to the career she would be sacrificing in Boston, all for the sake of an old lady's fancy. Mrs Klumpke's concerns centred more on the loss of pride at being a 'lady companion'. She also feared for the portrait commissions which Anna would very probably lose not being based in Paris. The mother admired Rosa Bonheur; after all, it was she who had encouraged Anna's appreciation of the artist in the first place. But she could not accept that, at 41 years old, and having strived for autonomy and a career of her own, Anna was contemplating a life of obscurity. Rosa Bonheur's glory would be the abortion of her own.

Anna had left Paris dismayed, disappointed – but not discouraged. She assured Rosa that nothing, not even her family, could change her mind.

Relieved and rapturous, Rosa wrote again to Mrs Klumpke, pledging to make every possible provision for Anna's material comfort both before and after her death.

Then, a joyous new chapter could begin. The walks, the drives, the conversations and the confidences which had become part of Rosa and Anna's routine over the summer resumed with renewed vigour. Rosa talked about Nathalie and art and the forest, Anna about the disability which had pushed her towards a career as a painter. And of course, Anna had her portrait of Rosa to complete.

The painting showed Rosa from the waist up, seated next to an easel on which a cropped picture of horses could just be glimpsed. In her left hand, she gripped a document, presumably a supporting study, while her right hand rested on her knee, gently holding a paintbrush. Rosa had settled on her navy jacket with intricate braided frog fastening and pretty buttons. To its breast, she had pinned her cross of the Légion d'Honneur, while on her lower half she wore a skirt. Rosa's whole body was angled away, but her head turned towards the viewer. As a result, light emanating from the top left-hand corner of the canvas bathed the right side of her face in a biblical glow, while transforming her hair into a bouncing froth of soft white and grey. The subdued background emphasised Rosa's face and hands, as Anna's gentle touch and muted palette betrayed the influence of contemporary naturalistic trends. Her feathery brushstrokes distinguished the face and eyes of a woman who was assured, but approachable. Compared with previous portraits of Rosa, the subject's face appeared finer, less square – infinitely more feminine. In a single image, Anna had accounted for Rosa's quiet confidence as an artist and conveyed her gentleness as a human being. The subject was admirable but not untouchable – and she was, above all things, a woman.[7]

Gratified with the result, Anna was looking forward to accompanying the painting to Pittsburgh where it was to be shown at the Carnegie International Exhibition along with Rosa's own *Cows and Bulls in the Auvergne* (1898). The trip would give Anna the opportunity to settle her affairs before leaving the States for good and to reunite with the friends whom she had left so precipitately. But Rosa was anxious; early in July, the French ocean liner, La Bourgogne, had sunk, drowning hundreds of passengers. The catastrophe had dominated the front page of *Le Figaro* on 7 July 1898 and Rosa exhorted Anna not to go. In the end, reluctantly, the American renounced her trip.[8]

Still, with word of a new Rosa Bonheur portrait in circulation, Anna did not have to travel far to gauge its reception. Ernest Gambart was quick to express his interest. Anna was disinclined to part with the picture, but Rosa urged her not to refuse; she had already begun working on another painting based on the photograph of Rosa wearing her laurel crown. Rosa added that she would be glad to pose for still another picture, perhaps holding her little Yorkie, Charley. If it were equally accomplished (as Rosa expected), Gambart might consider a swap. Anna finally consented, but she remained adamant that unlike Édouard Dubufe and Consuélo Fould, this portrait artist would paint Rosa's pet herself.

Rosa was now happier than she had been in years. Eager to share her new-found joy, on 26 August 1898, she wrote to her nephew René: 'America has made an alliance with old Europe and, in addition, is working to preserve for the family and for France the portrait of your aunt, Rosa Bonheur.'[9]

Other, exciting projects were beginning to take shape too. Rosa had long desired a bigger studio with a skylight to be able to finish *Wheat Threshing in the Camargue* (1899), and at the end of August, the first stone in an enormous outbuilding was ceremoniously laid. Taking her paintbrush, Rosa inscribed hers and Anna's initials on the surface and added the date. It was agreed that the workspace would become Anna's studio after the canvas was finished.

In the meantime, Anna continued recording her observations in writing, referring reverently to her subject as Rosa Bonheur, never Rosa. Her study remained scrupulous. It was as though Rosa's life were being thrust under a microscope and dissected. Time became magnified.

Curious to see how she was being presented, one day, Rosa asked to read some of the text. Anna claimed that her subject was profoundly moved. And as Anna probed for answers and Rosa submitted to the irrepressible flow of memories, both women found themselves reliving a glittering career.

The process was at once thought-provoking, revealing and deeply cathartic. It was gradually dawning on Rosa that through Anna, it would be possible to perpetuate her work, her memory and everything she had toiled so hard to achieve. And if that were to happen, Anna must know everything.

Accordingly, the day came when Rosa bid Anna follow her to a door in the château which the American had scarcely noticed; it had always remained closed. Turning the key in the lock, Rosa explained that this was Nathalie Micas's bedroom.

The door swung open to reveal the room of Anna's predecessor, with its yellow wallpaper, fine furniture and dainty sewing table. Rosa produced a little rosewood box and, opening it, presented a lock of Nathalie's hair. When the time came, Rosa told Anna, she wished to die in Nathalie's bed and to be laid next to her at Père Lachaise. One day, many years from now, she hoped that Anna would join them there. In the meantime, there was another task she wished her to fulfil: it concerned the estate at By. She was going to make Anna her soul legatee.

By the time the disbelieving Anna wrote to inform her mother what had been said, she could add that, besides her rolling estate and most of its contents, Rosa had also given her Nathalie's ring, Mme Micas's watch and a chain belonging to M. Micas, and that she had implored her to move into Nathalie's bedroom.

Now that she had joined the household at By, Anna was beginning to comprehend the eminence of the company Rosa kept. On Tuesday 20 September 1898, Rosa interrupted Anna painting with the news that Queen Isabella of Spain was downstairs. Passing rapidly from disbelief to panic, the American finally watched wide-eyed as, heaving and panting, the deposed Isabella manoeuvred her corpulent person and heavy skirts up the stairs to the studio. Once the Spaniard had recovered from her ordeal and the American from her shock, Anna remembered standing back and admiring how Rosa blossomed. Charismatic and wholly at ease darting about the studio like a twenty-year-old in her smock and trousers, Rosa was the very essence of hospitality. Though the Queen's roving gaze hinted that the studio held far more interest than pictures, Her Majesty complimented Anna on her portrait of Mrs Klumpke and the American signed a photograph of another of her paintings for the Queen to take away.

Once Isabella had been escorted out by lamplight, Rosa thanked her companion profusely. Living at By, such a polite and cordial disposition would be a considerable advantage. As *L'Abeille de Fontainebleau* observed, Rosa received 'almost exclusively crowned heads'.[10] Consequently, Anna's respect was all the greater when a letter from an admiring English schoolboy had as profound an impact as the words of a sovereign and Rosa was moved to tears.

☙

'A change has occurred in my life,' Rosa enthused in a letter to the Verdiers on 21 September 1898. 'I have found a charming friend, a kind lady of great talent and most distinguished family. I am happy and proud of her friendship. I will tell you all about it when we meet, for I intend to introduce her to you soon [...] We have decided to work together for the rest of our days [...] She is a good musician, which is a charm for me.'[11]

That musical flair held a particular attraction for Rosa. She was overjoyed to have a cultured ear to accompany her to a performance of Richard Wagner's *The Valkyrie* at the Opéra in Paris that autumn. Then one evening, Rosa spotted the sheet music to the Swiss composer Abraham Louis Niedermeyer's *The Lake* in Anna's collection. It was a piece she knew well, Caroline Carvalho having often performed it for her. In little time, Anna's dexterous hands were tackling the stirring minor chords of Niedermeyer's opening bars, while Rosa joined in with the lyrics, losing herself in the emotion of the music they were making together.

'I feel quite young again, in spite of my seventy-seven years,' Rosa told the Verdiers.[12]

Notwithstanding, the ticking clock could not be silenced. Rosa's deteriorating eyesight provided just one more reminder that the body was not immortal. Early in November, Rosa signed the will which recognised her new relationship. Then at the end of the month, she handed Anna a letter to be passed to her *notaire* after her death.

With their 35-year age gap, Anna and Rosa were naturally driven by different priorities. Even so, Anna was perpetually dismayed by Rosa's talk of her encroaching demise and her chillingly pragmatic approach to her property. Anna consciously tried to spur her to maintain an optimistic mindset, whether enticing her with the Exposition Universelle of 1900 or by presenting her with future-focused causes which ignited her creativity.

Hence Anna's canny questions about Christmas in French schools kindled the idea of their throwing a party for the children at the institution opened on the terrain Rosa and Nathalie had offered the town. Decorations, a tree and a piano were set out, and at Rosa's request, a picture of Nathalie was displayed, while the French and American flags were hoisted. On Christmas morning, tiny candles twinkled on the tree and the whole room resonated with the sound of children's voices carolling as Anna's fingers danced merrily across the keys of the piano. 'Father Christmas' even made a surprise appearance. After floating back to the château, drunk on good cheer, Anna led Rosa upstairs, where she unveiled a tree of their own which she had set up in secret and loaded with presents.

Rosa's traditional New Year's greetings effervesced with happiness. On New Year's Day, she wrote to Georges Cain and his wife, begging them to visit so that 'at last, I shall be able to introduce you to the nose of the Lady of By'.[13] Rosa told Princess Stirbey how she was convinced that Anna, her 'mascot', had brought her luck, while in a letter to Mme Rousseau, she eulogised at length about her 'young and worthy companion, who "very much wants to meet Mme the Major of whom we sometimes speak".'[14] Rosa added that the new studio would be completed in March while that quintessentially modern commodity, electricity, was soon to be installed at By.

Rosa's existence had become truly thrilling. She was in no doubt: Anna Klumpke had restored her passion for life and with it, her health.

'My wife has much talent and the children don't prevent us from painting pictures,' she quipped in a letter to the Princess Stirbey.[15]

Rosa knew that earthly pleasures must be savoured. And now, there was just one more experience she dearly wanted her new 'wife' to share.

'Mlle Rosa Bonheur reached Nice a few days ago and is visiting M. Gambart,' the *New York Herald* informed its readers early in February 1899.[16]

Ernest Gambart was delighted to finally be graced with his old friend's company at Les Palmiers. The women only planned to be in Nice for ten days or so, but in that short window, Gambart managed to cram their itinerary full of extravagant luncheons and grand receptions, each one studded with illustrious guests, all waiting to be met and spoken with.

However, one of the first people he accompanied Rosa to see was not a new acquaintance at all, but a long-standing ally.

'M. Gambart and his guest, Mlle Rosa Bonheur, went to the Villa Cyranos, at Cap Martin, on February 1, to take déjeuner with the Empress Eugénie,' the papers reported.[17]

Rosa had been looking forward to her reunion with the Empress. She readied herself expectantly, taking particular care to pin the cross Eugénie had given her to her breast. Leaving Anna behind (according to Gambart's wishes), Rosa and the dealer journeyed to the elegant Villa Cyranos. But when they were shown through to greet the former consort, Rosa was taken aback. Eugénie was barely recognisable.[18]

Thin and wan and cloaked in black, Eugénie had lost her husband, her son, her empire and with them, much of her sparkle. Once a figurehead of fashion, now her whole persona exuded melancholy, heartache and deep, immutable sadness.

Through the commonalities of past pleasure and personal pain, Rosa and the Empress rekindled their mutual admiration. As they spoke, tears and nostalgia brought comfort.

Other celebrated personalities attending the Empress included the Duchess of Osuna, the Spanish town to the east of Seville. Anna remembered that they subsequently hosted the Duchess at Les Palmiers, a reception which resulted in Rosa being issued an invitation to visit Spain.

Thanks to Gambart, brilliant social engagements succeeded each other during Rosa and Anna's stay. A photo taken when the women accompanied their host to a ball at the prefecture showed Rosa seated, her back straight, her mien majestic, while standing on either side of her were the two people most intrinsic to her career. On her left, Ernest Gambart appeared solemn and composed, while to the right, Anna stood with great propriety, her body angled magnetically towards Rosa. The photo portrait exuded formality, dignity and decorum – but it also intimated tension.

Ernest Gambart, Rosa Bonheur and
Anna Klumpke in Nice, 1899.

Collection Atelier Rosa Bonheur

The truth was, Anna Klumpke and Ernest Gambart had got off to a bad start. Oblivious to the extent of Anna's reputation, Gambart had initially pronounced her asking price for her portrait of Rosa too high. Realising his faux pas, he apologised and professed himself pleased at the effect she was having on his old friend. Still, he held his ground where her price was concerned. For works by Rosa, he would always reach a little deeper into his pocket. But Miss Klumpke had still to prove herself in his eyes. Anna reduced her price as a gesture of goodwill, but Gambart took issue with her conditions of sale, which had implications for reproductions and entitled her to complimentary copies for her friends. Gambart's competitive spirit was excited still further when he discovered Anna to be working on another portrait of Rosa for the Salon. Gambart was a strategist; if Miss Klumpke were not careful, she would sabotage herself. Moreover, Gambart was growing suspicious of Anna's intentions.[19]

The women had not long returned from Les Palmiers when an explosive row erupted between Gambart and Rosa, appropriately, over *The Duel*. Gambart was horrified to learn that Rosa had reimbursed the purchaser, his nephew Lefèvre, the entire fee, judging the work to have been ultimately unsuccessful and overpriced. She refused to let Gambart restore family honour by accepting the due fee for the painting; if he insisted on paying her, she would donate the money to the widows of the Société des Artistes Français. Rosa became even more prickly when she sensed Gambart to be casting doubt onto the value of Anna's work and reproaching Rosa herself for a fall in her prices. As hotly worded letters flew backwards and forwards, Rosa's temper raged. Gambart had no wish to fall out with her. But if Anna Klumpke could not be coaxed into using her influence on Rosa, she had become an irritating obstacle. In his letter to the art critic Frederick George Stephens written just after the women's visit to Nice, Gambart revealed how he really felt:

Rosa Bonheur & Miss Anna Klumpke spent eleven days
at my house, during which time I had numerous and

select company at luncheon every day – Rosa Bonheur
as nice as ever, but to my mind too much taken up with
her friend the young (about 36 [sic]) American lady who
has lately painted her portrait.[20]

But Gambart's opinion was of no consequence. Even if he had con-
fronted her with his concerns, Rosa had preordained that nobody
would rob her of her new-found happiness. Anna Klumpke was more
than a life partner; she was the agent who would enable Rosa to perpetuate her work. Rosa now felt it her duty to groom her legatee in
preparation for that weighty task.

Happily re-ensconced at By, the Salon became Rosa and Anna's
shared goal and the Exposition Universelle of 1900, the grand finale.

No sooner had the halls of the Galerie des Machines on the
Champ-de-Mars begun to fill with Salon-goers that May than Rosa's
re-emergence was being celebrated in the press.

Le Petit Journal was one of the first papers to delight in her reappearance: 'Breaking what had become a habit, Mlle Rosa Bonheur,
who has not exhibited at the Salon for many years, has sent *Cows and
Bulls in the Auvergne*'.[21] Describing Rosa's animals as 'perfection', the
reviewer set the tone for a rush of articles, all eulogising her continued
skill, few resisting the temptation to flag up her still 'virile' quality.

Before long, word spread that Rosa might even be in line for the
medal of honour. But on 13 May, an anonymous article appeared in
Le Journal which put an end to the matter:

> This year, Mme Rosa Bonheur has sent a small work;
> she has been absent from the Salon for the last 40 years.
> Therein lies a first area of contention.[22]

The author speculated that Rosa was being honoured purely on
account of her age, her name being promoted by dealers anxious to
improve their sales.

Rosa was outraged. She immediately penned a terse letter to the

President of the Société des Artistes Français, Jean-Paul Laurens, fore-stalling any such commendation for a painting she considered to be a mere 'calling card' with a flat refusal.[23]

At 77, Rosa's pride remained her most fiercely guarded attribute. Though she had made no secret of her pleasure at receiving a Légion d'Honneur, at heart, she believed artistic merit to be determined not by the glint of a medal, but by the quality of the work. That could be greatly enhanced or hindered by the context of its reception. As such, Rosa saw a visit to the Salon as the most truthful indicator of how she had fared.

Rosa and Anna arrived at the Galerie des Machines one morning in May to begin their tour. Rosa led the way in a smart, purposeful march, as though subconsciously, she felt her time here were limited.[24]

Every now and then, something caught her eye and she paused to evaluate the piece. Before long, Rosa and Anna had found their pictures.

Rosa declared herself satisfied with her own painting, and she complimented Anna on her picture of her with Charley. In the portrait, Rosa was shown seated against a brown drape in an antique, upholstered chair and an outfit almost identical to that worn for the Pittsburgh painting. Once again, the cross of the Légion d'Honneur was pinned to her left breast and her body angled away, while her face turned back towards the viewer. However, this time, her petite foot, one of her proudest features, could just be seen peeping out from underneath her long black skirt. And there was another difference, too: her face appeared graver, wiser – older. Anna had made her less an approachable woman and more a priest-like deity to be worshipped and admired.

Between their two pictures, Rosa and Anna had masterfully staged her triumphant return to the Paris art scene. The show was a resounding success.

During the course of the day, the couple's discussion had turned to the Musée du Luxembourg, and as they left the Salon, Rosa confessed that she had never visited that sanctuary of contemporary art. Anna could scarcely believe that the home of Rosa's *Ploughing in the Nivernais* (1849) should be unknown to the great painter. The itinerary for the following day was set.

ℂ

Within a few hours, Rosa found herself meandering through the uncharted halls of the Musée du Luxembourg, praising, pondering and perusing, while in her stilted walk, Anna moved along beside her, greedily drinking in what she knew to be valuable lessons. Presently, they found themselves standing before *Ploughing in the Nivernais* (1849). Rosa fell silent.

As her eyes travelled over the painting, reacquainting her with that once-familiar surface, forgotten memories and unanticipated emotions came flooding to the forefront of her mind. As a 27-year-old, she had strived to create a scene which was timeless. Conversely, that ageless quality now highlighted how very much had changed. A given brushstroke recalled now a person, now a place, now a conversation, while the memory of its creation brought a surge of multisensory recollections rushing to the surface – the pain of her father's death, the unmistakable smell of paint and straw of her studio in the Rue de l'Ouest, sounds of Nathalie bustling about the workspace, her siblings' supportive words, letters and visits. In that frozen instant, Rosa's whole life was replayed.

Leaving the gallery, Rosa informed Anna that before returning to By, she wanted to see her *notaire* to add a codicil to her will. Anna protested: it surely did not need attending to today. But Rosa insisted. She saw no reason to delay her relinquishment of By. Inheritance tax would be crippling. The particulars – how much to pay Céline, what to do with her paintings and the type of funeral she desired – could be briefed later. For now, it was time for Anna to take ownership of the estate.

ℂ

On 20 May, the weather in and around Paris had turned unseasonably dismal. The temperature had dropped, unremitting showers soaked the streets and around 11 o'clock, Parisians were astonished to see the rain turn to sleet. The sky set a forbidding mood for the public holiday of Pentecost.[25]

Notwithstanding, the household at By readied itself in anticipation of a pleasurable weekend. Mrs Klumpke had arrived a few weeks earlier, and Rosa was delighted. Though considerably younger, somehow Mrs Klumpke's motherly presence recalled that of Mme Micas. When Anna's sisters Julia and Dorothea joined them later that day, the 'family' seemed complete and the holiday could begin.

Presently, Céline's head appeared at the door of the studio with the news that the architect and the locksmith working on the new studio wished to have a word about fixtures and fittings. Rosa moved to the door and Anna got up to follow, but Rosa objected; there was no need for both of them to interrupt what they were doing. She would surely be back in a minute or two.

Outside in the courtyard, with the icy breeze grating Rosa's skin and a moist blanket of cold wrapping itself around her neck, one query spotlighted another and the few minutes quickly became 30. The foul-smelling breath of one of the men brought waves of nausea mounting from her stomach. When she finally returned to the warmth of the château, Rosa felt the sickening presentiment that she would have to pay for her self-neglect.

It was not until the next morning, the day of Pentecost, that Rosa suspected something to be seriously amiss. Having taken her guests to admire the new studio with its great skylight, she admitted to Anna that she had not felt quite right since breakfast. She would not join them for lunch, but would take a lie down. No doubt that would restore her. But by early evening, Rosa was clearly quite unwell.[26]

Noticing that Rosa's speech sounded a little odd, Anna asked to inspect the inside of her mouth. An icy chill ran through her veins when she saw Rosa's tongue to be white. She knew such an oral membrane to be symptomatic of diphtheria, the condition which had claimed the life of her sister, Mathilda. Terrified, Anna summoned the doctor.

Her primary fear was quickly allayed; it was not diphtheria but flu. However, the relief was short-lived.

Over the next two days, the Château de By transformed into an emotional pressure cooker, its epicentre being Rosa's enormous bedroom, with its extraordinary decor of hanging birdcages housing all manner of chirruping avian friends. One moment, Rosa seemed a little better and hope was restored. Then she took a turn for the worse and the state of panic resumed. Anna raised the alarm, the doctor came and went, Céline and the Klumpke mother and sisters rushed to and from the bedroom, fetching what was needed, anticipating what very soon would be. The cloying atmosphere of sickness and angst became virtually palpable.

On the fourth day of her illness, Rosa asked to be taken into Nathalie's bedroom. There, she collapsed into the armchair and began looking about her. Anna asked whether she would like to take a lie down in the bed. Rosa hesitated. At length, she said that she would prefer to return to her own bed.

When the doctor made his call that afternoon, he became solemn. Rosa's malady had developed into pulmonary influenza. It was time to fetch Dr Apostoli.

A telegram was dispatched to Paris alerting Isidore, the Peyrols and M. Tedesco.

Throughout the following day, 25 May, Anna and her mother attended Rosa in a state of heightened anxiety. Every so often, another inquisitive face appeared at the bedroom door. The team of carers now included Rosa's nephew, Hippolyte Peyrol, Anna's brother-in-law Jules Déjerine, and her sister Augusta. During one, fleeting moment of lucidity that day, Rosa asked Anna to sing her Niedermeyer's *The Lake*. Going to the studio, opening all the doors so that the patient would be able to hear, Anna sat down at the piano. Battling to control her emotions, she began to play.

Suddenly, the sound of footsteps racing to the room she had just left caused her to stop. Rushing back, Anna found that Rosa's condition had plummeted and the bedroom was a flurry of frantic activity. Anna passed out. When she came to, she went straight to her companion. A few hours later, Rosa's pulse was barely detectable.

As she had promised, Anna wrapped her arms around Rosa and held her. Moving her head next to the patient's, Anna struggled to hear as Rosa whispered a drawn-out, breathy promise: she would always be the American's guardian angel. Then Anna felt the body in her arms turning cold. Rosa Bonheur was gone.

So ended the most perfect love story. Because Rosa's life was just that – a love story. As early as 1859, she had pledged her heart: 'I wed art. It is my husband – my world – my life-dream – the air I breathe. I know nothing else – feel nothing else – think nothing else. My soul finds in it the most complete satisfaction.'[27]

'I still have energy to paint,' Rosa had assured her friend Virginie Demont-Breton just a few months previously. 'That kind of energy only dies with your last breath.'[28] That moment had come – and Rosa Bonheur had fulfilled her ultimate promise to the world.

Epilogue

Stepping back outside onto the Rue de Sèze and closing the door of the Galerie Georges Petit behind her, Anna Klumpke could submit to her emotions. If she had foreseen trauma following Rosa Bonheur's death, she could scarcely have envisaged the ordeal which lay before her.[1]

When the Drs Gilles and Apostoli had pronounced Rosa's body dead, the ensuing grief and sense of denial were chastened by the formalities. At the request of Rosa's family, the very next day the rooms were *mises sous scellés*, or officially sealed, a legal measure employed in France to protect the assets pending the reading of the will; nothing was left to chance.

Anna was distraught. It took her sister Julia to remind her about Rosa's wish to be buried wearing her laurel crown. Special permission had to be granted by the *Juge du paix* in Moret to re-enter the room and place it with Rosa.

As soon as the news of Rosa's death was released, journalists across the world set to work penning obituaries. Meanwhile, visitors to the Salon could still admire *Cows and Bulls in the Auvergne* (1898), the painting which had heralded Rosa's long-awaited return. There it hung in room fourteen, only now, it was draped in black fabric.

Rosa's funeral took place on 29 May. On the morning of the ceremony, the temperature had risen, the rain had eased and the sky over Thomery promised a fine spring day, one quite different from the unseasonable eve of Pentecost just a week earlier.[2]

Though she had spurned the presence of a priest when she died, Rosa's determination to be buried next to Nathalie had meant consenting to a religious ceremony. Her coffin was accordingly draped in white and loaded onto the hearse to begin its journey to the church. And as the vehicle's wheels started crunching over the ground outside the gates of By, a heartrending noise turned the heads of passers-by; Rosa's dogs, who had been enclosed in the courtyard, were howling pitifully.[3]

A crowd of mourners gathered at Thomery church at 11.00am to watch the procession arrive. Most were local – farmers, labourers and housewives, all of whom had some fond memory of Rosa or a personal encounter to share. But among the townsfolk, a correspondent from Chicago provided a salient reminder that Rosa's reputation stretched far beyond the boundaries of provincial Thomery.[4]

The hearse arrived preceded by a carriage loaded with flowers, many species native to Thomery and Bordeaux. The doors of the church were draped in white and thrown open to allow the priest to lead in a procession of choirboys, locals and children from the nearby school. Inside, from nave to chancel, long black hangings echoed the mood as a stirring ceremony unfolded, with the choir from the church of Saint-Louis-en-l'Île performing selected hymns.[5]

Afterwards, the coffin was loaded onto a train and transported to Paris to be laid in the Micas family vault at Père Lachaise. The hearse arrived shortly before five o'clock, the vehicle in front of it decked with wreaths and flowers.

Just as Rosa had stipulated (and irrespective of her entitlements as an Officier de la Légion d'Honneur), there were no military honours, no official escort and categorically no speeches. Isidore Bonheur's friend, the painter William-Adolphe Bouguereau, had arrived with a few lines prepared. The folded document had to be returned to his pocket, his tribute left unread.[6]

Still, if eulogies were forbidden, admirers would hear of no embargo on flowers. Once the coffin had been set down, the spot was quickly hidden beneath a sea of floral tributes.

'If only we had known that she would die so suddenly, my colleagues and I would have certainly voted for Rosa Bonheur,' Tony Robert-Fleury told Anna Klumpke shortly after the funeral, referring to the Salon's medal of honour for which Rosa had refused nomination. 'We had hoped to mark her career with an even higher distinction, by awarding her the medal of honour at the Exposition Universelle of 1900.'[7] The recognition came too late; the committee made its decision on the day Rosa died.

Ernest Gambart had been travelling to his villa in Schwyz, Switzerland, when a stomach upset forced him to break his journey in Lugano. It was there that the news reached him. The dealer was devastated. The day after Rosa's funeral, he wrote to the Minister of Fine Arts from his sick bed, offering to donate a selection of his pictures by Rosa Bonheur to the Louvre.[8]

Once Rosa had been laid to rest, the next step was the publication of her last wishes.

The will stated that the entire estate at By was to be given to Anna Klumpke. Rosa's goddaughter, Rosa Mathieu, and her sister Jenny would receive an annual allowance of 1,200 francs (to be shared but not to be reduced when one or other of the sisters died), while Céline would be paid an annuity of 800 francs (a sum Rosa had asked Anna to supplement). In the document, Rosa defended her allocation of funds, proclaiming that she was not as rich as people supposed and that she had provided her family with ample financial support during her lifetime; today, she judged none of them to be in need of contingency. Therefore, and in view of the fact that Anna Klumpke had sacrificed so much to become her companion, she should now be compensated. In the event of Anna's death, the remaining Klumpke sisters would inherit By.[9]

The resulting furore was something Rosa had anticipated. She used the letter she had instructed Anna to pass to her *notaire* to give further reasons for her actions.

It explained that when Nathalie Micas had passed away, Rosa had been left alone. None of her family was in a position to come and look after her. Auguste had catered handsomely for his daughters and as for her nephews, Rosa considered all to be fit, strong and able to work. She hoped them to have sufficient pride not to expect money from a dead woman who had had to fight for her career. Rosa added that if Isidore should ever find himself in financial difficulty, she trusted Anna Klumpke would assist him.

The will sparked outrage among Rosa's relatives. Most notably riled was her nephew, Juliette's son Hippolyte Peyrol, the bespectacled sculptor now in his 40s who had been at Rosa's bedside in her final hours. Quite apart from his own interests, there were those of his sexagenarian father, Rosa's stepbrother and brother-in-law Hippolyte senior, and of his 72-year-old uncle and sculpting mentor Isidore to defend. And that was to say nothing of family honour. The document was furiously contested – and Anna Klumpke immediately felt the effects.

When a trip to Paris induced Anna to call on Bouguereau, a frosty reception greeted her. Rosa's wider circle of friends and associates were equally troubled by her last decisions and suspicious of her young American legatee.

'Through circumstances which I cannot understand, Mlle Rosa has disinherited all her numerous family, that she loved sincerely,' Ernest Gambart exclaimed in a letter to the Mayor of Fontainebleau.[10]

Gambart's correspondence had another purpose besides voicing incredulity. He wished to fund a monument to be erected in Fontainebleau in memory of Rosa. And since Rosa had not seen fit to recognise her family in her will, Gambart felt it only right that Isidore Bonheur and Hippolyte Peyrol father and son should be entrusted with the statue's creation.

While the resentment towards her mounted, Anna Klumpke was far from comfortable with the arrangement herself. She felt it her duty to offer Isidore Bonheur some form of inheritance. Yet she was at a loss as to how she could accomplish that. Rosa's words still echoed in her ears: 'I am entrusting you with the conservation of this property in which I have experienced such success and glory.'[11] To Anna at least, that signified that Rosa wished neither the house nor any of the contents belonging to the Micases to be sold. She concluded that the only reasonable option was to give Isidore half of Rosa's remaining fortune of 300,000 francs.

But when Anna spoke of her intention to the Tedescos, she received a shock: did she not realise, M. Tedesco enquired, that Rosa had left around 2 million francs' worth of assets in the form of studies and miscellaneous artwork? His father, Tedesco senior, had tried to purchase the collection more than 40 years ago, only to be met with the impatient rebuff: 'Get lost, Tedesco!'[12] Today, he would pay Anna 1.5 million francs for it.

It was a fortune. Afterwards, Anna willingly admitted that she had been sorely tempted by the offer. But she could not dismiss the gnawing sense that Rosa would have been horrified. 'I would rather spend my whole life eating nothing but stale bread than sell my studies,' Rosa had often proclaimed.[13] Each one represented a landmark in the story of her life. Anna was in no doubt: her companion had wished the house and its contents to remain intact and under Anna's jurisdiction. If she accepted Tedesco's offer, she would relinquish control and could donate nothing to museums, nor give any pieces to Rosa's friends or even photograph them for posterity.

It occurred to Anna that handing over three-quarters of the studies to Isidore yet retaining reproduction rights might be the shrewdest compromise. But when she informed the *notaire* Maître Tollu of her plan, he was indignant; Anna could not just apportion the legacy like pieces of a birthday cake. She must do one of two things: accept Tedesco's offer or hold an auction. Anna insisted that it was Tollu who advised her that, in view of the expenses she would incur, she should hand over just half, not three-quarters, of any profits to the Peyrol-Bonheurs.

The proposal did nothing to mitigate the family's wrath. Charged emotions animated the rival households of the Château de By and 14, Rue de Crussol, the shared Paris address of the Peyrols and Isidore Bonheur. The apartment was now a simmering cauldron of discontent, the views of its individual members lost beneath a united front of contention. Not until the middle of June did Rosa's family resentfully agree to accept the 50 per cent being offered. But they quickly retracted their consent two weeks later. And it was then, Anna reported, that she started receiving a deluge of offensive letters: Miss Klumpke had hypnotised the great artist, abused her trust, encouraged Rosa's penchant for alcohol as a way of manipulating her into making these outrageous decisions.[14]

'The disinherited family members are going to attack this testament,' *L'Abeille de Fontainebleau* informed its readers, 'resorting to evidence which we will not disclose here but which is currently the subject of intense discussion and the source of sensational gossip. Either way, word is that a big court case is in the offing.'[15]

But on that matter at least, Paris's gossips were to be disappointed; eventually, Rosa's family had to concede that the will was incontestable and the men agreed to accept half the profits from the sale. One disgruntled branch of the family dealt with, Anna's attention was soon solicited by Rosa's cousin, Louise Lagrolet, intent on staking her claim on the painting (and maybe more) that she knew she had been bequeathed.

By the summer of 1899, Anna Klumpke was emotionally exhausted. In the midst of the tumult, an idea came to her: if a sale must take place, she would purchase *Wheat Threshing in the Camargue* (1899) and keep it permanently on display at By.

Throughout the upheaval, Anna derived some comfort from that plan. But hers was not the only spirit fractured by Rosa's demise. While Anna painstakingly worked through her thoughts and feelings on paper, mindful of her promise to publish Rosa's life story, Isidore Bonheur was of a different character. A man of few words, it was not in his nature to air his emotions. Friends remembered him as industrious, goodhearted and charming, but taciturn and fearfully timid. He never married. Of all the Bonheur siblings, he and Rosa had shared a unique and especially close bond. His true thoughts and feelings regarding his sister's death and decisions could be inferred but they could never be known.

Rosa Bonheur, *Wheat Threshing in the Camargue*, 1872–1899, oil on
canvas, 313 x 651 cm, Musée des Beaux-Arts-Mairie de Bordeaux.
Photo: L. Gauthier. No. d'inventaire: RF2388

That October, the Paris press announced Anna Klumpke's decision to
hold a sale and split the profits with the Peyrol-Bonheur family. The
story implied an amicable resolution; it was far from accurate.

As she stood outside the Galerie Georges Petit that same month,
Anna realised that reaching an agreement about the auction did not
equate to a truce. Her meeting with the Peyrols had been acrimoni-
ous. Hippolyte Peyrol's animosity particularly startled the American,
who remembered Rosa's nephew demanding that all the engravings
dedicated to Nathalie Micas be destroyed.

Struggling to remain coolheaded, Anna was still set on doing what
she felt to be right. Early in December, a letter appeared in Paris's leading papers. It was addressed to the President of the Société des Artistes
Français, Jean-Paul Laurens:

> Sir, I am pleased to inform you that in honour of my
> friend Mlle Rosa Bonheur, I wish to offer a gift of
> 50,000 francs to the Société des Artistes Français. The

interest earned on this sum will fund an award to be called the Rosa Bonheur Prize.[16]

The letter was signed Anna E. Klumpke.

᠁

The sale of Rosa Bonheur's atelier was the talk of *Paris artistique*. For weeks before, the papers had been whipping up a frenzy and 350 pictures had even been sent to London's Hanover Gallery on New Bond Street to generate interest among English and American buyers. The sale finally opened on 25 May 1900, a year to the day of Rosa's death.

L'Abeille de Fontainebleau quickly confirmed it to be 'a spectacle of which an examination cannot be too highly recommended'.[17] Amateurs and serious collectors pushed their way through the crowded salesroom to inspect the work on show. The sheer quantity was breathtaking; there were over 1,800 pieces. Few people had grasped the enormity of Rosa's oeuvre.

The press were in raptures over the pictures, most of them by Rosa, but some by other artists, works she had collected over the years. Critics tended to agree that backgrounds were not Rosa's particular forte. But the verisimilitude of her animals beggared belief.

On the first day alone, over 500,000 francs was taken. A few days into the sale, *Le Figaro* reported how 'despite the miserable weather and the waiting around, throughout the morning and the afternoon, the public fought over studies by the famous artist, paying astronomical prices.'[18] A watercolour of a tiger reached a staggering 7,700 francs.[19] By the sale's close, takings had tipped 1,180,880 francs.[20]

The expenses paid, Anna Klumpke could finally turn over half the profits to Rosa's family, and the residents of the Rue de Crussol and the new chatelaine of By could each begin a fresh chapter. Anna felt certain that she had done the right thing by Rosa's family. Whether she had satisfied Rosa's wishes, she was less sure.

But then, on 15 June 1900, an article appeared in *L'Abeille de Fontainebleau*. A quantity of Rosa's letters had been found. Among them was one Rosa had written in 1898, startling in its perspicacity.

'If I were to die, they could have quite a lucrative sale of my works,' spoke a voice from beyond the grave. Then came the twist: 'people would have been taken in; I have already destroyed a vast quantity of them which I was unsatisfied with.'[21]

Anna need not have worried; Rosa had always been strong-willed and fastidious where her work was concerned. The pictures that now went out into the world had each been toiled over and evaluated, reworked and vetted. There could be no better ambassadors of Rosa's oeuvre. Every item represented a little piece of her creative project – and of herself. As they scattered to all four corners of the globe like ashes on the wind, something of Rosa's character and life journey travelled with them.

Afterword

In 1855, Rosa Bonheur was described as 'the greatest painter of rustic subjects in France – perhaps in the world'; by 1899, the artist William-Adolphe Bouguereau placed her 'in the front rank, with the masters.'[1]

Rosa's drawings, paintings and sculptures defy enumeration, while even her own family lost track of the titles, medals and commendations she accumulated. From the Cross of San Carlos of Mexico, to the Belgian Order of Léopold, the Cross of the Order of Isabella the Catholic of Spain, the Order of Merit for the Fine Arts of Saxe-Coburg-Gotha, the Order of Saint-Jacques of Portugal, honorary presidency of the Union des Femmes Peintres et Sculpteurs and of course, Chevalier then Officier de la Légion d'Honneur: at the time of her death, few could dispute that Rosa Bonheur had earned her rightful place in the tomes of art history.

Yet her imprint has faded over time. The crumpled, unread eulogy found in Bouguereau's possessions after he died elucidates this perplexing conundrum: 'Among the women of her century, the position of Rosa Bonheur has been unique.'[2] In life, that quality was Rosa's personal salvation and her professional calling card; in death, it has become an obstacle.

Though she revered the old masters, Rosa espoused no painting school, aligned herself with no artistic movement which might have cemented her place in the layman's compendium of art history. Committing early to her specialism, she worked persistently, single-mindedly, aware of but undistracted by passing trends in contemporary art. Though her lifestyle was radical, her painting style remained conservative. By depicting timeless vignettes of unspoiled, rural France, Rosa gave a post-Revolutionary public just the visual reassurance it craved. Artistically speaking, she was of her time – both literally and inadvertently a victim of fashion. With the rise of photography, new generations have made different demands of the art they consume; the enthusiasm Rosa's work once generated has been transferred onto other styles and movements.

Rosa never made it her mission to subvert established pictorial conventions. On the contrary, she wanted to paint as she had seen others do. Her perpetual challenge was that those 'others' were men.

Still in the 1880s, a critic could write that 'women have never produced any great masterpieces in any genre' and expect to find supporters.[3] When Rosa began her career, the division between the sexes was even more conspicuous, the barriers keeping women from opportunity, less penetrable. For a well-bred woman, to have a career in the mid-19th century was remarkable; to triumph was exceptional; to surpass many men was virtually unheard of. Rosa's conquest was a silent one. For generations of artists and women, she effected measurable change – and she did so through action, not words. Rosa firmly established the *animalier*'s place in the 19th-century art world, while helping normalise the figure of the female artist. Rosa never called for equality; she ensured that her work earned her that right.

If the painter instigated a quiet revolution in the art world, the woman left a gaping hole in the lives of those who knew her.

The friction between the Peyrol-Bonheur and the Klumpke dynasties did not immediately dissipate with the conclusion of the sale. In January 1901, reporters from *La Liberté* telephoned the Observatoire de Paris hoping to engage Dorothea Klumpke in a discussion about Anna's recent donation of some 50 works to the Musée du Luxembourg. Dorothea was mistakenly recorded as saying that her sister had known Rosa 'since the very early days', a claim Isidore Bonheur demanded that the astronomer publicly refute. Dorothea obliged – but was sure to add that Anna's gift would certainly have been more substantial had the Peyrol branch of the family not been so obstinate.[4]

Just a few months later, the monument Ernest Gambart had commissioned, an enormous bronze bull, was unveiled in Fontainebleau under the watchful eye of the Parisian press. Isidore Bonheur only survived a few more months. His body succumbed little more than two years after his beloved sister was taken from him. The monument created in her honour remained in Fontainebleau until the 1940s, when the Germans' hunger for munitions overruled the French desire to mark collective memory.

Monument to Rosa Bonheur at Fontainebleau,
English photographer (20th century).

Private Collection/Look and Learn/Illustrated Papers
Collection/Bridgeman Images
Illustration for *The Illustrated London News*,
23 November 1901

After Rosa's death, Anna Klumpke continued to live at By, making occasional visits back to America. In 1908, the biography she had promised Rosa was published in French, while Rosa's atelier was opened to the public with the entrance fee going to fund a bed in the Hôpital de Fontainebleau in Rosa's name. During the First World War, Anna, her mother and her sisters Dorothea and Augusta ran a military hospital from the château. Afterwards, Anna's commemorative projects included curating an exhibition of Rosa's work at the Château de Fontainebleau in 1924 and attempting to found a women's art school in Rosa's name. For her services to art, Anna Klumpke was made Chevalier de la Légion d'Honneur in 1924 then Officier de la Légion d'Honneur in 1936.

In the mid-1930s, Anna returned to San Francisco, where she was to die in 1942, her ashes sent to Père Lachaise to be scattered with Rosa and Nathalie. The Château de By passed to her sister Augusta's children. It remained in the Sorrel-Déjerine family and operated as a museum until 2014, when the surprise announcement of its sale provoked dismay among locals and Rosa Bonheur aficionados. A movement to have the building classed as a historic monument was hastily launched, but the fate of the paintings remained uncertain. Bonheur enthusiasts could soon feel reassured; into Anna Klumpke's shoes stepped another extraordinary woman. Former student of the École du Louvre Katherine Brault purchased the property in 2017 and made it her mission to revive the museum, while striving to retain the original ambience and integrity of Rosa's home. At the time of writing, the museum is open every day by appointment and the team at the château are currently working to establish an International Research and Study Centre dedicated to Rosa Bonheur's work. A tearoom and space which can be hired for functions complete Mme Brault's vision, with a *chambre d'hôtes* facility due to open soon.

Inside, Rosa's atelier stands frozen in time. A painting smock lies discarded on the back of a chair, a half-finished canvas rests on an easel awaiting completion, while brushes and a palette have been set

Rosa Bonheur's studio at By.
Collection Atelier Rosa Bonheur

down, as though momentarily, as if Rosa has just rushed downstairs to greet Gambart or sauntered out to the gardens to feed one of her deer.

Beyond Thomery, Rosa has given her name to landmarks as diverse as her menagerie. Claude François Denecourt dedicated one of Fontainebleau's wooded valleys to the sylvan painter. Maps of Paris, Bordeaux and Fontainebleau all boast a Rue Rosa Bonheur (with the former location also displaying a profile of the painter in marble), while schools in France and Belgium have adopted Rosa's name. Sculptor Gaston Leroux presented a statue of Rosa at the Salon of 1902 which was subsequently transferred to Bordeaux. Further afield, in Elkridge, Maryland, the Rosa Bonheur Memorial Park, founded in 1935, operated as a pet cemetery until 2002, during which time it welcomed some notable four-legged celebrities, including Gypsy Queen, the horse who travelled more than 11,000 miles in the mid-1920s in an aim to visit all 48 states, and the Doberman Corporal Rex Ahlbin, a

combat dog who saved lives serving with the US Marine Corps during the Second World War. Meanwhile, Paris's pleasure-seekers can be
found sipping cocktails aboard the floating bar, the Rosa Bonheur sur
Seine, or against the backdrop of the Pont d'Asnières at the waterside
Rosa Bonheur à l'Ouest, just as the original Rosa Bonheur bar still
brings landlubbers and lesbians flocking to the Buttes Chaumont for
pizza and tapas.

Statue of Rosa Bonheur at the Jardin
Public, Bordeaux by Gaston Leroux.
Ageev Rostislav/Alamy Stock Photo

But we perhaps come closest to Rosa through the paintings she has left us. *Wheat Threshing in the Camargue* (1899) remains unfinished. It was held in Anna Klumpke's collection until 1922, when it was passed to the Musée des Beaux-Arts in Bordeaux. In New York, *The Horse Fair* (1853) constitutes one of the jewels of the Metropolitan Museum of Art's collection, while in Paris's Musée d'Orsay, *Ploughing in the Nivernais* (1849) still stops visitors in their tracks as they move closer to check whether the work before them is not a photograph. Not to be outdone, the National Gallery in London displays a second version of *The Horse Fair* (1855), completed with Nathalie Micas's assistance. Every now and then, the art world receives a reminder of the kind of excitement a Rosa Bonheur painting could generate; in February 2019, Rosa's *Ploughing* (1845) came up for auction at Sotheby's in New York. Experts believed it might reach between $80,000 and $120,000. The painting fetched $423,000.

Today, whether on display, hidden from view or yet undiscovered, each of these pictures and sculptures stands as proof of one woman's single-minded resolve to do what she loved, to shape her oeuvre, to cast aside the manuals of convention and to write her own story. Every one illustrates what can be achieved with industry and self-belief. And together, they testify to Rosa Bonheur's determination to make her mark – against the odds and whatever the cost.

In each of Rosa's paintings, hours, months, sometimes years of industry still allow us to experience a moment of magic. All over the world, in cities intoxicated with fumes and traffic, retreating to the stillness of a gallery and finding a work by Rosa, the viewer is transported to a rural idyll. We can almost smell the warm grass, hear the chirruping of the birds circling overhead, as we come face-to-face with a deer, a horse or a sheep. Or else we find ourselves carried to a sun-parched plain, marvelling at the breathtaking majesty of a lion. And in that moment, something wondrous happens: we look into the animal's eyes and we feel certain we can see its soul. Through the canvas in front of us, Rosa reaches through time and holds us entranced.

And if the reader happens to walk down the Rue Saint-Antoine in Paris, take a moment to stop outside the butcher's shop at number 49. There in the entranceway, the life-sized boar Rosa ran her fingers over as a child waits to greet us. Ghosts of the past are all around us if we will only choose to look.

The boar outside Au Sanglier, 49, Rue Saint-Antoine, Paris.
Author's photograph

Acknowledgements

Stepping off a train into the heart of the snow-covered Forest of Fontainebleau to discover Rosa Bonheur's kingdom, I could tell that I was embarking on a magical adventure. What I could not have predicted was where that journey would lead me, nor how many generous people would assist me on my path to telling Rosa's story.

The Royal Literary Fund committee were most generous in awarding me a grant early on in this project. I am also grateful to The Society of Authors and the Authors' Foundation for the grant which assisted me in the final stages of writing this book.

Once again, it has been both a pleasure and a privilege to work with the publishing team at Icon Books. Duncan Heath, Robert Sharman, Andrew Furlow, Victoria Reed and Lydia Wilson have made every step of the publication process gratifying and enjoyable. I have been overwhelmed (but not surprised) by the energy demonstrated by my tireless agent, Andrew Lownie, and by his commitment to this project from the outset.

When I first started unravelling Rosa's story, it quickly became clear that to fully understand the woman and the painter, a researcher must first acquaint him- or herself with By. I am indebted to Katherine Brault at the Musée Rosa Bonheur in By for having welcomed me so warmly into her and Rosa's home that cold February morning and guided me around the château and its archives, then patiently responded to my ongoing queries once I returned to England. I am especially humbled by the generosity and dedication of By's historian, Michel Pons, who has been an invaluable source of knowledge and wisdom throughout the process of research and writing. This book simply would not have been the same without him.

Beyond By, a great many scholars, associations, museums and galleries have assisted me in my project. Some have been confirmed experts; others have proved to be unsung heroes.

Marie Borin was kind enough to respond to my questions via Michel Pons. I am also grateful to Agnès Vatican at the Archives Départementales de la Gironde for helping me locate M. Dublan's address in Bordeaux. I am indebted to Hélèna Salmon at the Musée des Beaux-Arts de Bordeaux for sharing the museum's archives with me, particularly those relating to Pierre Lacour and Raimond Bonheur, and most especially for the copy of Major Rousseau's memoirs and letters. Frédéric Laux at the Archives Bordeaux Métropole was instrumental in helping me locate Rosa's original birth certificate. Thanks must also be extended to Véronique Bancel at the Mairie in Magny-les-Hammeaux for helping me source Françoise Bonheur's death certificate. Valérie Renaud at the Service des Archives Municipales de Fontainebleau proved a fount of knowledge on the monument commissioned by Ernest Gambart, and I am enormously thankful for the time she spent discussing this with me. I am equally grateful to Edouard Gouteyron at the Service de l'Etat-Civil at the Mairie of the 11e arrondissement in Paris for directing me to René Peyrol's death certificate.

Further afield, in the States, I was thrilled to make contact with Sue Whitaker at the Worthington Historical Society's Doll Museum and was most grateful for her insights into their Rosa Bonheur doll. My sincere thanks are also due to Howard L. Rehs at Rehs Galleries, Inc., New York for his generous supply of images.

I am of course exceedingly grateful to all the museums, galleries and collections who have kindly allowed works to be reproduced in this book, in particular the Musée des Beaux-Arts de Bordeaux, the Musée des Beaux-Arts de Nice, the Archives Départementales de Seine-et-Marne, Brown University Library in Providence and the Eskenazi Museum of Art at Indiana University. Staff at the Courtauld Institute of Art and the British Library have also been of great assistance.

ACKNOWLEDGEMENTS

Throughout this project, information has come coupled with inspiration. I will always be indebted to the late Professor John House for introducing me to Rosa Bonheur and encouraging me to look beyond as well as at Impressionism. I am also grateful to Professor Colin Davis at Royal Holloway, University of London, for his support when I first set out on my path in biography.

On a personal note, my very sincere thanks must go to Mary-Beth Hawrish for her assistance in navigating life's inevitable rites of passage while writing was underway.

As ever, my family have provided a tremendous source of support, as well as an occasional proofreading service. John and Elaine Hewitt – words will never be able to express the gratitude I feel. Sam Hewitt and Emelie Larsson have also been consistent in their encouragement throughout. In addition, Rosa Bonheur would not have rested easy without some mention being made of Alfie and his valiant attempts to help with footnotes.

Last but not least, my deepest gratitude must go to my very own King of the Forrest, Alex – for loving, supporting, living with Rosa Bonheur for the last two years and, most of all, for not being inspired to make rat pâté after reading chapter 17.

Select Bibliography

Ashton, Dore and Denise Browne Hare, *Rosa Bonheur: A Life and a Legend* (New York: The Viking Press, 1981)

Badsey, Stephen, *The Franco-Prussian War, 1870–1871* (Oxford: Osprey Publishing, 2003)

Bonheur, Rosa, 'Souvenirs inédits de Rosa Bonheur', *La Revue des revues*, 1 January 1897, 131–142.

Bonnefon, Paul, 'Une Famille d'artistes: Raimond et Rosa Bonheur', *L'Art*, 1903, 419–428 (pp. 424–425).

Borin, Marie, *Rosa Bonheur: Une Artiste à l'aube du féminisme* (Paris: Pygmalion, 2011)

Browne, Julia Margaret, 'Rosa Bonheur's Plowing in the Nivernais (1849): The Circumstances of Success' (unpublished master's thesis, University of British Columbia, 1989)

Buettner, Stewart, 'Images of Modern Motherhood in the Art of Morisot, Cassatt, Modersohn–Becker, Kollwitz', *Women's Art Journal*, 7 (1986–1987), 14–21.

Bury, J.P.T., *France 1814–1940* (London: Methuen & Co. Ltd, 1969)

Carlisle, Robert, B., *The Proffered Crown: Saint-Simonianism and the Doctrine of Hope* (Baltimore and London: The Johns Hopkins University Press, 1987)

Claretie, Jules, 'Une Visite à Rosa Bonheur', *La Vie à Paris* (Paris, 1896), pp. 400–411.

Cope, Susan, and others, eds, *Larousse Gastronomique* (London: Mandarin, 1990)

Crastre, François, *Rosa Bonheur* (New York: Frederick A. Stokes Co., 1913)

Demont-Breton, Virginie, 'Rosa Bonheur', *La Revue des revues*, 15 June 1899, 605–619

Dwyer, Britta C., *Anna Klumpke: A Turn-of-the-Century Painter and Her World* (Pennsylvania: Northeastern University Press, 1999) de F., Mme, *Les Jeunes voyageurs dans Paris, ou les tablettes de Jules* (Paris, 1829)

Fould, Consuélo, 'Rosa Bonheur', *La Revue illustrée*, 1 November 1899, NP

Frith, W.P., *A Victorian Canvas: The Memoirs of W.P. Frith*, ed. by Nevile Wallis (London: Geoffrey Bes, 1957)

Galignani's New Paris Guide (Paris, 1830)

Galignani's New Paris Guide (Paris, 1852)

Gélis, Jacques, *History of Childbirth: Fertility, Pregnancy and Birth in Early Modern Europe*, trans. by Rosemary Morris (Cambridge: Polity, 1991)

Gervais, Suzanne, 'Honoré de Balzac 1799–1850: Splendeurs et misères parisiennes' in *Paris dans les pas des grands hommes*, ed. by Christophe Barbier (Paris: L'Express, 2015), p. 86.

de Goncourt, Edmond et Jules, *Journal – Mémoires de la vie littéraire, I, 1851–1861*, ed. by Robert Ricatte (Paris: Robert Lafont, 1989)

Goubert, Pierre, *The Course of French History*, trans. by Maarten Ultee (London and New York: Routledge, 1991)

Henderson, Anne and Zoë Urbanek, *Rosa Bonheur: Selected Works from American Collections* (Dallas, Texas: The Meadows Museum, 1989)

Hervier, Paul-Louis, 'Lettres inédites de Rosa Bonheur', *La Nouvelle Revue*, January–February 1908, 187–203.

Hippler, Thomas, 'The French army, 1789–1914: Volunteers, pressed soldiers and conscripts', in *Fighting for a Living: A Comparative History of Military Labour, 1500–2000*, ed. by Jan-Erik Zürcher (Amsterdam: University of Amsterdam Press, 2014), pp. 419–446.

Horne, Alistair, *Seven Ages of Paris* (London: Pan Macmillan, 2003)

Iruzun, Françoise, 'Pierre Lacour' (unpublished master's thesis, Université Michel de Montaigne, Bordeaux III, 1997)

Jones, Colin, *Cambridge Illustrated History of France* (Cambridge: Cambridge University Press, 1994), p. 201.

Kearns, James, *Théophile Gautier, Orator to the Artists* (London: Legenda, 2007)

Klumpke, Anna, *Rosa Bonheur, Sa Vie, son oeuvre* (Paris: Flammarion, 1908)

— *Rosa Bonheur: The Artist's [Auto] Biography*, trans. by Gretchen van Slyke (Michigan: The University of Michigan Press, 2001)

Kybalová, Ludmila, Olga Herbenová and Milena Lamarová, *The Pictorial Encyclopedia of Fashion*, trans. by Claudia Rosoux (London: Paul Hamlyn, 1968)

de La Forge, Anatole, *La Peinture contemporaine en France* (Paris, 1856)

Lambert, Monique, 'Enfants trouvés et abandonnés de la Gironde – 19ème siècle', *Cahiers d'Archives: Des archives … des histoires*, http://www.cahiersdarchives.fr/index.php?option=com_content&view=article&id=193:enfants-trouves-et-abandonnes-de-la-gironde-19eme-siecle&catid=18&Itemid=101 [accessed 7 December 2017]

Lepelle de Bois-Gallais, F., *Biographie de Mademoiselle Rosa Bonheur* (Paris, 1856)

— *Biography of Mademoiselle Rosa Bonheur*, trans. by James Parry (London, 1857)

Luez, Philippe, and others, *Rosa Bonheur et sa famille*, exhib. cat. (Magny-les-Hameaux: Musée du Port-Royal-des-Champs, 2016)

M., *Le Petit Diable Boiteux, ou Le Guide anecdotique des étrangers à Paris* (Paris, 1823)

Maas, Jeremy, *Gambart – Prince of the Victorian Art World* (London: Barrie and Jenkins, 1975)

Mansel, Philip, *Paris Between Empires 1814–1852* (London: John Murray, 2001)

McTavish, Lianne, *Childbirth and the Display of Authority in Early Modern France* (Aldershot: Ashgate, 2005)

Millais, John Guille, *The Life and Letters of Sir John Everett Millais*, vol. 2 (London: Fred鹿ick A. Stokes Company, 1899)

de Mirecourt, Eugène, *Rosa Bonheur* (Paris, 1856)

Montigny, Louis Gabriel, *Le provincial à Paris: esquisses des mœurs parisiennes*, 2 vols (Paris, 1825)

'A Morning with Rosa Bonheur', interview conducted on 10 August 1859, originally published in the *Home Journal,* reprinted in *Littel's Living Age* (October, November, December, 1859), pp. 124–126.

Peyrol, René, *The Life & Work of Rosa Bonheur*, trans. by J. Findon Brown (London, 1889)

Rebsamen, Léa, 'Rosa Bonheur, Artiste Animalière au XIXème Siècle' (unpublished doctoral thesis, École Nationale Vétérinaire d'Alfort, 2013)

Reid, Joyce M.H., ed, *The Concise Oxford Dictionary of French Literature* (Oxford: Oxford University Press, 1985)

Ribemont, Francis, and others, *Rosa Bonheur, 1822–1899*, exhib. cat. (Bordeaux: William Blake & Co., 1997)

Richardson, Joanna, *La Vie Parisienne 1852–1870* (London: Hamish Hamilton Ltd, 1971)

Robb, Graham, *The Discovery of France* (London: Picador, 2008)

Roger-Milès, L., *Rosa Bonheur: sa vie – son oeuvre* (Paris, 1900)

Mémoires du Commandant Rousseau, manuscript kindly supplied by the Musée des Beaux-Arts de Bordeaux.

Seward, Desmond, *Eugénie* (London: Sutton Publishing, 2010)

Stanton, Theodore, *Rosa Bonheur: Reminiscences* (London: Andrew Melrose, 1910)

Strumingher, Laura S., 'L'Ange de la maison: Mothers and Daughters in Nineteenth-Century France', *International Journal of Women's Studies*, 2 (1979), 51–61

Thoré, Théophile, 'Salon de 1845', *Salons de Théophile Thoré – 1844, 1845, 1846, 1847, 1848* (Paris, 1870)

Vigée-Lebrun, Élisabeth-Louise, *Souvenirs de Madame Élisabeth-Louise Vigée Lebrun* (Paris, 1835)

Weisberg, Gabriel, and others, *Rosa Bonheur: All Nature's Children*, exhib. cat. (New York: Dahesh Museum, 1998)

Notes

Chapter 1: Two Houses

1. On Sophie Marquis, see Anna Klumpke, *Rosa Bonheur: The Artist's [Auto] Biography*, trans. by Gretchen van Slyke, (Michigan: The University of Michigan Press, 2001), pp. 83–84. See also Dore Ashton and Denise Browne Hare, *Rosa Bonheur: A Life and a Legend* (New York: The Viking Press, 1981), pp. 6–13.

2. I am grateful to Agnès Vatican at the Archives Départementales de la Gironde for helping locate M. Dublan's address in Bordeaux.

3. On Jean-Baptiste Dublan de Lahet, see Marie Borin, *Rosa Bonheur: Une Artiste à l'aube du féminisme* (Paris: Pygmalion, 2011), p. 434. M. Dublan's wife's name is written as Jeanne Clothilde Julie Ketty Guilhem, Jeanne Clothilde Julie Kethy Guilhem, Jeanne-Kéty Guilhem or Jeanne Clothilde Julie Kelly Guilhem. Her year of death is also given as 1811 (Borin) and 1816 (geni.com).

4. Françoise Iruzun, 'Pierre Lacour' (unpublished Master's thesis, Université Michel de Montaigne, Bordeaux III, 1997). I am indebted to Héléna Salmon at the Musée des Beaux-Arts de Bordeaux for sharing the museum's archives with me.

5. On this conflict, see Theodore Stanton, *Rosa Bonheur: Reminiscences* (London: Andrew Melrose, 1910), p. 76. Ashton and Browne Hare, pp. 2–4.

6. On Raimond Bonheur's style, see F. Lepelle de Bois-Gallais, *Biographie de Mademoiselle Rosa Bonheur* (Paris, 1856), pp. 8–10.

7. Klumpke, p. 84.

8. Stanton, p. 1; Ashton, p. 2.

9. On Cambacérès, see: Mme Junot, *Memoirs of the Duchess d'Abrantès*, 2 vols (London, 1831), II, pp. 328–329.

10. Stanton, p. 2.

11. See Susan Cope and others, eds, *Larousse Gastronomique* (London: Mandarin, 1990), pp. 271–272.

12. Raimond and Sophie lived at number 29. Saint-Seurin became a basilica in 1823.

13. Madeleine Lassère, *Histoire de Bordeaux* (Bordeaux: Éditions du Sud Ouest, 2017), pp. 137–146.

14. Philippe Ariès, *Centuries of Childhood* (Harmondsworth: Penguin Books, 1986), pp. 370–401; Michelle Perrot, 'The Family Triumphant' in *A History of Private Life*, ed. by Philippe Ariès and George Duby, trans. by Arthur Goldhammer, 5 vols (Cambridge, MA and London: Belknap Press of Harvard University Press, 1987–1991), vol. 4: *From the Fires of Revolution to the Great War*, ed. by Michelle Perrot (1990), pp. 99–129 (p. 101).

15. Stewart Buettner, 'Images of Modern Motherhood in the Art of Morisot, Cassatt, Modersohn-Becker, Kollwitz', *Women's Art Journal*, 7 (1986-1987), 14–21 (p. 15); Laura S. Strumingher, 'L'Ange de la maison: Mothers and Daughters in Nineteenth-Century France', *International Journal of Women's Studies*, 2 (1979), 51–61 (p. 51.)

16. Jacques Gélis, *History of Childbirth: Fertility, Pregnancy and Birth in Early Modern Europe*, trans. by Rosemary Morris (Cambridge: Polity, 1991), p. 99.

17. Lianne McTavish, *Childbirth and the Display of Authority in Early Modern France* (Aldershot: Ashgate, 2005), pp. 1–3.

18. On Victoria, see: 'Le web de l'Espagne', http://espagne01.perso.infonie.fr/femigracion.htm [accessed 21 November 2017]

19. On Manuel Silvela, see: https://www.museodelprado.es/en/the-collection/art-work/manuel-silvela-y-garcia-aragon/2b2dcd7c-d733-4673-ad63-625b99f51c3c [accessed 21 November 2017]

20. I am grateful to Frédéric Laux at the Archives Bordeaux Métropole for helping me to locate the original birth certificate.

21. George Sussman, 'The Wet-Nursing Business in Nineteenth-Century France', *French Historical Studies*, 9 (1975), 304–328.

22. Abbé Besnard, *Périls auxquels sont exposés les enfants que leurs mères refusent d'allaiter, malheurs que par ce refus ces mères attirent sur elles-mêmes* (Paris, 1825)

23. On the family in art at this time, see Louis Hautecoeur, *Les Peintres de la vie familiale* (Paris: Galerie Charpentier, 1945)

24. Sussman, pp. 307–308.

25. *Bonnes et nourrices: la domesticité féminine à Paris au XIXe siècle*, Musée Carnavalet – Dossier pédagogique, June 2011, p. 2.

26. *Calendrier de la Gironde*, 1813, p. 132.

27. Sussman, p. 308.

28. Klumpke, p. 86.

29. On Elisabeth, see Stanton, p. 1.

30. M. Dublan's rights over the property were contested in court after his purchase. See Ledru-Rollin, *Journal du Palais, Receuil général des lois et arrêts fondé par J.B. Sirey, 1822–June 1823* (Paris, 1840), vol. 17, pp. 1203–1204.

31. Roger Price, *A Social History of Nineteenth-Century France* (London: Hutchinson, 1987), p. 87.

32. On the growth of these cities, see Magali Talandier, Valérie Jousseaume and Bernard-Henri Nicot, 'Two centuries of economic territorial dynamics: the case of France', *Regional Studies, Regional Science*, 3, (2016), 67–87.

33. Monique Lambert, 'Enfants trouvés et abandonnés de la Gironde - 19ème siècle', *Cahiers d'Archives: Des archives … des histoires*, http://www.cahiers darchives.fr/index.php?option=com_content&view=article&id=193:enfants-trouves-et-abandonnes-de-la-gironde-19eme-siecle&catid=18&Itemid=101 [accessed 7 December 2017]

34. As indicated by Auguste's birth certificate.

35. Correspondence transcribed in Klumpke, p. 86.

36. The birth certificate records the baby's name as François-Auguste.

37. On Rosalie's memories, see Klumpke, pp. 86–88.

38. On this and the following memories of Rosalie's childhood, see Klumpke, pp. 87–88.

39. Letter dated 8 February 1824, reproduced in Stanton, p. 13.

40. Klumpke, p. 88.

41. The name Sophie gave to her daughter. See Klumpke, p. 88.

42. Stanton, p. 35.

43. *Encyclopaedia Britannica Online*, https://www.britannica.com/biography/Leandro-Fernandez-de-Moratin [accessed 21 December 2017]

44. L. Roger-Milès, *Rosa Bonheur: sa vie – son oeuvre* (Paris, 1900), pp. 10–11.

Chapter 2: Where Angels Fear

1. M, *Le Petit Diable Boiteux, ou Le Guide anecdotique des étrangers à Paris* (Paris, 1823), xii.

2. Alistair Horne, *Seven Ages of Paris* (London: Pan Macmillan, 2003), p. 241.

3. J.P.T. Bury, *France 1814–1940* (London: Methuen & Co Ltd, 1969), pp. 33–34.

4. Colin Jones, *Cambridge Illustrated History of France* (Cambridge: Cambridge University Press, 1994), p. 201.

5. On this institution, see: http://www.academiedesbeauxarts.fr/presentation/grandes-dates.php [accessed 16 January 2018]

6. Suzanne Gervais, 'Honoré de Balzac 1799–1850: Splendeurs et misères parisiennes' in *Paris dans les pas des grands hommes*, ed. by Christophe Barbier (Paris: L'Express, 2015), p. 86.

7. Gervais, p. 86.

8. Gervais, p. 86.

9. Jones, p. 202.

10. Horne, p. 248.

11. Horne, p. 247.

12. On *diligences*, see A. Carlier, *Histoire du Véhicule – Diligences et Malles-poste* (Cannes: L'Imprimerie à l'École, 1932). See also Patrick Marchand, 'Voyager en France au

temps de la poste aux chevaux', *Comité pour l'histoire de la poste*, https://www. laposte.fr/chp/mediasPdf/PMarchand.pdf [accessed 10 January 2018]

13. Mme de F., *Les Jeunes voyageurs dans Paris, ou les tablettes de Jules* (Paris, 1829), p. 7.

14. Carlier, p. 8. On Rosa's experience of this journey, see Anna Klumpke, *Rosa Bonheur: The Artist's [Auto] Biography*, trans. by Gretchen van Slyke, (Michigan: The University of Michigan Press, 2001), p. 89.

15. Carlier, p. 19. Raimond Bonheur spent 78 francs 16 sous on board and lodging when he arrived in Paris. See Theodore Stanton, *Rosa Bonheur: Reminiscences* (London: Andrew Melrose, 1910), p. 5.

16. Stanton, p. 4.

17. Stanton, pp. 4–5.

18. Letter dated 30 April 1828, L. Roger-Milès, *Rosa Bonheur: sa vie – son oeuvre* (Paris, 1900), p. 14.

19. Stanton, p. 13.

20. Letter dated 20 July 1828, Roger-Milès, p. 14.

21. Stanton, p. 13.

22. Letter dated 20 July 1828, Roger-Milès, p. 14.

23. Stanton, p. 5.

24. Stanton, p. 47.

25. On Saint-Simonianism, see Robert B. Carlisle, *The Proffered Crown: Saint-Simonianism and the Doctrine of Hope* (Baltimore and London: The Johns Hopkins University Press, 1987)

26. Stanton, p. 16.

27. Stanton, p. 13.

28. See Klumpke, p. 89.

29. Stanton, p. 5.

30. On the area, see Stanton, pp. 6–7.

31. This sculpture still stands outside the Charcutier Traiteur, Au Sanglier, at number 49, Rue Saint-Antoine.

32. Stanton, p. 7.

33. Stanton, p. 7.

34. On M. Antin and the apartment, see Stanton, pp. 6–7.

35. Now the Place des Vosges.

36. Stanton, pp. 7–8; Klumpke, pp. 89–90.

37. On this period, see Bury, pp. 33–44. See also Jones, pp. 201–203.

38. Bury, p. 40.

39. Bury, p. 40.

40. On the events of July 1830, see Philip Mansel, *Paris Between Empires 1814–1852* (London: John Murray, 2001), pp. 226–279.

41. Cited in Mansel, p. 246.

Chapter 3: Hear the People

1. Cited in Philip Mansel, *Paris Between Empires 1814–1852* (London: John Murray, 2001), p. 244.
2. On the July Revolution of 1830, see: Mansel, pp. 226–279; Colin Jones, *Cambridge Illustrated History of France* (Cambridge: Cambridge University Press, 1994), pp. 200–203; Alistair Horne, *Seven Ages of Paris* (London: Pan Macmillan, 2003), pp. 252–256; J.P.T. Bury, *France 1814–1940* (London: Methuen & Co. Ltd, 1969), pp. 38–49.
3. Juste Olivier, cited in Mansel, p. 241.
4. William Hone, *Full Annals of the Revolution in France, 1830* (London, 1830), p. 53.
5. Rosa told Stanton it was Raimond who fell from the porte cochère. Speaking to Klumpke, she remembered the victim as Auguste. Given Raimond's size, Klumpke's version seems more plausible. See Anna Klumpke, *Rosa Bonheur: The Artist's [Auto] Biography*, trans. by Gretchen van Slyke, (Michigan: The University of Michigan Press, 2001), pp. 90–91. All references to Klumpke refer to this edition unless otherwise stated. See also Theodore Stanton, *Rosa Bonheur: Reminiscences* (London: Andrew Melrose, 1910), p. 8.
6. Hone, p. 53.
7. Hone, p. 54.
8. On Rosalie's memories, see: Klumpke, pp. 90–91; Stanton, p. 8.
9. Hone, p. 53.
10. Hone, p. 54.
11. Hone, p. 54.
12. Hone, p. 56.
13. Charles Ledré, *La Presse à l'assaut de la monarchie* (1960), p. 112. Cited in Mansel, p. 249.
14. Hone, p. 54.
15. 'Journée du 29 juillet 1830', *Le Figaro*, 30 July 1830, p. 1.
16. Honoré de Balzac, cited in Mansel, p. 267.
17. On Louis-Philippe, see: Mansel, pp. 266–267; Bury, pp. 45–71.
18. On the Saint-Simonian response, see Robert B. Carlisle, *The Proffered Crown: Saint-Simonianism and the Doctrine of Hope* (Baltimore and London: The Johns Hopkins University Press, 1987), pp. 133–150.
19. Carlisle, p. 127.
20. See Stanton, p. 8.
21. Stanton, p. 8.
22. On the Micases, see: Stanton, pp. 8, 83–87; Klumpke, pp. 113–114.
23. Anna Klumpke, *Rosa Bonheur, Sa Vie, son oeuvre* (Paris: Flammarion, 1908), p. 140.
24. Klumpke, *Rosa Bonheur, Sa Vie, son oeuvre*, p. 140.

25. Stanton, p. 76. Raimond was probably referring to Louis Boulanger, one of Victor Hugo's followers and a figure admired by the Romantics. He was active in the Romantic circles whose ideas Lacour had discouraged.

26. Stanton, p. 76.

27. Stanton, p. 77.

28. On the Saint-Simonian project, see Stanton, pp. 72–73. See also Klumpke, pp. 94–95.

29. Stanton, p. 75.

30. Carlisle, p. 185.

31. On the epidemic, see Mansel, pp. 283–285.

32. Stanton, p. 8.

33. On the routine at Ménilmontant, see Carlisle, p. 191.

34. Stanton, p. 73.

35. Klumpke, p. 97; Stanton, pp. 8–9.

36. Klumpke, p. 114.

37. Klumpke, *Rosa Bonheur, Sa Vie, son oeuvre*, p. 148.

38. Klumpke, *Rosa Bonheur, Sa Vie, son oeuvre*, p. 148.

39. Mansel, p. 284.

40. Klumpke, p. 97.

41. Carlisle, p. 185.

42. Stanton, p. 71.

43. Klumpke, p. 98.

44. Klumpke, p. 98.

45. On the indictment, see Carlisle, p. 186.

46. On the trial, see Carlisle, pp. 214–232.

47. Klumpke claims Raimond Bonheur's work with the Saint-Simonians ended at this point. See Klumpke, p. 100. However, Stanton insists he continued to promote the doctrines. See Stanton, pp. 72–75.

48. Klumpke, p. 102.

49. See Klumpke, pp. 102–103.

Chapter 4: Trying for Size

1. See Louis Hautecoeur, *Les Peintres de la vie familiale* (Paris: Galerie Charpentier, 1945), pp. 64–98.

2. W. de Monnières, *Guide Perpétuel dans la capitale* (Paris, 1838), p. 26.

3. On Rosalie's schooling, see: Anna Klumpke, *Rosa Bonheur: The Artist's [Auto] Biography*, trans. by Gretchen van Slyke, (Michigan: The University of Michigan Press, 2001), p. 104; Theodore Stanton, *Rosa Bonheur: Reminiscences* (London: Andrew Melrose, 1910), p. 9. Eugène de Mirecourt and Anna Klumpke state that Rosa was educated by nuns in the parish of Chaillot. (See Eugène de Mirecourt, *Rosa Bonheur* [Paris, 1856], p. 8.) The Soeurs de la Sagesse did open

a school in Chaillot in 1823. It was inaugurated by the Archbishop of Paris. (See *L'Ami de la Religion et du Roi*, vol. 36, 1823, p. 149.) However, neither Rosa nor any of her other biographers, including René Peyrol, her nephew, make any mention of this school. Rosa declared de Mirecourt's biography to be riddled with errors, and given that Anna Klumpke's mention of the school occurs just before she quotes a passage from de Mirecourt's biography, it seems likely that she drew this fact from de Mirecourt's study, not Rosa.

4. See Klumpke, p. 105.

5. Élisabeth Louise Vigée-Le Brun, *The Memoirs of Mme Élisabeth Vigée-Le Brun, 1755–1789*, trans. by Gerard Shelley (London: Forgotten Books, 2017), p. 83.

6. Vigée-Le Brun, pp. 83, 80.

7. Louis Lazare, 'Revue d'arrondissements', *Gazette Municipale – Revue Municipale*, 1 June 1852, pp. 806–809.

8. On Bernard-Raymond Fabré-Palaprat see: *World Heritage Encyclopedia*, http://www.gutenberg.us/articles/eng/Bernard-Raymond_Fabre-Palaprat [accessed 26 February 2018]; A.V. Arnault, A. Jay, E. Jouy and J. Norvins, *Biographie nouvelle des contemporains, ou Dictionnaire historique et raisonné de tous les hommes qui, depuis la Révolution française, ont acquis de la célébrité par leurs actions, leurs écrits, leur erreurs ou leurs crimes, soit en France, soit dans les pays étrangers*, vol. 7, 1822, p. 9.

9. On the Knights Templar, see: *The Knights Templar – A History*, http://www.theknightstemplar.org/history/ [accessed 2 March 2018]

10. Stanton, p. 11.

11. 'Mosaique', *Messager des Dames*, 14 February 1833, pp. 103–104.

12. Colin Heywood, *Childhood in 19th-Century France: Work, Health and Education Among the 'Classes Populaires'* (Cambridge: Cambridge University Press, 2002), p. 217.

13. Stanton gives this employer's name as Gendorf. However, Rosa, Klumpke and Roger-Milès affirm that the seamstress's name was Ganiford. The most reliable sources here are Rosa herself and Klumpke, whose study was based on conversations with Rosa. See Rosa Bonheur, 'Souvenirs inédits de Rosa Bonheur', *La Revue des revues*, 1 January 1897, pp. 131–142.

14. Baron Vaerst, cited in Ludmila Kybalová, Olga Herbenová and Milena Lamarová, *The Pictorial Encyclopedia of Fashion*, trans. by Claudia Rosoux, (London: Paul Hamlyn 1968), p. 262.

15. 'Modes', *Messager des Dames*, 14 February 1833, p. 97.

16. On fashion in the 1830s, see Kybalová, Herbenová and Lamarová, pp. 261–270.

17. Stanton, p. 10.

18. On the Bissons, see Stanton, p. 11.

19. Stanton, p. 11.

20. On Étienne Geoffroy Saint-Hilaire, see: *Encyclopaedia Britannica – Étienne Geoffroy Saint-Hilaire*, https://www.britannica.com/biography/

Etienne-Geoffroy-Saint-Hilaire [accessed 2 March 2018]; Isidore Geoffroy Saint-Hilaire, *Vie, Travaux et Doctrine Scientifique d'Étienne Geoffroy Saint-Hilaire* (Paris, 1847)

21. *Encyclopaedia Britannica* – Joseph-Louis Gay-Lussac, https://www.britannica.com/biography/Joseph-Louis-Gay-Lussac [accessed 2 March 2018]

22. *The Concise Oxford Dictionary of French Literature*, ed. by Joyce M.H. Reid (Oxford and New York: Oxford University Press, 1985), p. 330.

23. *The Concise Oxford Dictionary of French Literature,* pp. 14, 20.

24. Robert B. Carlisle, *The Proffered Crown: Saint-Simonianism and the Doctrine of Hope* (Baltimore and London: The Johns Hopkins University Press, 1987), pp. 93–94.

25. Stanton, p. 11.

26. Stanton, p. 36; Klumpke, pp. 106–107.

27. Stanton, p. 11.

28. Stanton, p. 10. On another occasion, Rosalie remembered this episode as having taken place at night. Stanton, p. 36.

29. Stanton, p. 9.

30. On this episode see: Stanton, p. 12; Klumpke, p. 109.

31. Stanton, p. 12.

32. Stanton, p. 12.

Chapter 5: Beasts and Benefactors

1. Élisabeth-Louise Vigée-Lebrun, *Souvenirs de Madame Élisabeth-Louise Vigée-Lebrun*, 3 vols (Paris, 1835), I, p. 3.

2. Vigée-Lebrun, p. 2.

3. Germaine Greer, *The Obstacle Race: The Fortunes of Women Painters and Their Work* (New York: Farrar, Straus and Giroux, 1979), pp. 95–96.

4. Louis Gabriel Montigny, *Le provincial à Paris: esquisses des mœurs parisiennes*, 2 vols (Paris, 1825), I, p. 144.

5. Montigny, p. 145.

6. Montigny, p. 60.

7. *Galignani's New Paris Guide* (Paris, 1830), p. 748.

8. On Mont Valérien, see: http://www.mont-valerien.fr/en/ [accessed 8 March 2018]

9. Anna Klumpke, p. 111.

10. S, 'Le Salon de 1836', *Musée des Familles* 1835–1836, p. 208.

11. S, 'Le Salon de 1836', p. 208.

12. On this first visit, see Klumpke, *Rosa Bonheur: The Artist's [Auto] Biography*, trans. by Gretchen van Slyke, (Michigan: The University of Michigan Press, 2001), p. 110.

13. Klumpke, p. 110; L. Roger-Milès, *Rosa Bonheur: sa vie – son oeuvre* (Paris, 1900), p. 27.

14. Klumpke, p. 110; Roger-Milès, p. 27.

15. https://www.louvre.fr/en/oeuvre-notices/parade-fatted-ox-also-known-parade-easter-ox [accessed 15 March 2018]

16. S, 'Le Salon de 1836', *Musée des Familles* 1835–1836, p. 211.

17. On Rosalie's copies see: Klumpke, p. 113; Stanton, p. 37.

18. S, 'Le Salon de 1836', p. 211.

19. Stanton, p. 37.

20. Stanton, p. 17; Klumpke, p. 113.

21. Stanton, p. 46.

22. *The Concise Oxford Dictionary of French Literature*, ed. by Joyce M.H. Reid (Oxford: Oxford University Press, 1985), pp. 236–239.

23. Stanton, p. 20.

24. Stanton, pp. 130, 371.

25. On Lamennais, see: *The Concise Oxford Dictionary of French Literature*, pp. 331–332; *Encyclopaedia Britannica* – Félicité Lamennais, https://www.britannica.com/biography/Felicite-Lamennais [accessed 9 April 2018]

26. Léon Roger-Milès, *Atelier Rosa Bonheur*, 2 vols (Paris: Georges Petit, 1900), p. XI.

27. *Encyclopaedia Britannica* – Pierre Leroux, https://www.britannica.com/biography/Pierre-Leroux [accessed 9 April 2018]

28. Stanton, p. 36.

29. Stanton, p. 14.

30. Klumpke, p. 114.

31. Stanton, p. 26.

32. Klumpke, p. 114.

33. Klumpke, p. 115.

34. Klumpke, p. 115.

35. Stanton, p. 47.

36. Stanton, pp. 47–49.

37. Stanton, pp. 47–49.

38. Now the Rue du Faubourg-Saint-Honoré

39. Stanton, p. 34.

40. Stanton, p. 34.

41. Stanton, p. 15.

42. Klumpke, p. 115; Stanton, p. 15.

43. On Félix-Sébastien Feuillet de Conches, see: Institut National d'histoire de l'art – Feuillet de Conches, Félix-Sébastien, https://www.inha.fr/fr/ressources/publications/publications-numeriques/dictionnaire-critique-des-historiens-de-l-art/feuillet-de-conches-felix.html [accessed 13 April 2018]

44. In 1837, the Princess lived at number 25, Rue Faubourg-du-Roule. *La Presse*, 24 December 1837, p. 3.

45. *La Presse*, 24 December 1837, p. 3.

46. *La Presse*, 2 February 1839, p. 3.

47. On this acquaintance, see: Roger-Milès, p. 24; Stanton, pp. 15–17.

48. Stanton, p. 16. On Admiral George Cockburn and Napoleon, see: *Fondation Napoléon*, https://www.napoleon.org/en/history-of-the-two-empires/articles/napoleon-and-saint-helena-1815-1816/ [accessed 15 April 2018]; *Shannon Selin – Imagining the Bounds of History*, https://shannonselin.com/tag/admiral-cockburn/ [accessed 15 April 2018]

49. Roger Morriss, *Cockburn and the British Navy in Transition: Admiral Sir George Cockburn, 1772–1853* (Exeter: University of Exeter Press, 1997), p. 7.

50. Stanton, p. 16; Roger-Milès, p. 24.

51. Rosalie Bonheur was listed as nos. 185 & 186.

52. Klumpke, p. 116.

Chapter 6: True Nature

1. In 1869, Gustave Flaubert would have the protagonist of his *Education Sentimentale* take an apartment in the Rue Rumford.

2. Félix Lazare, *Dictionnaire administratif et historique des rues de Paris et de ses monuments* (Paris, 1844), p. 605.

3. Alistair Horne, *Seven Ages of Paris* (London: Pan Macmillan, 2003), p. 255; Pierre Goubert, *The Course of French History*, trans. by Maarten Ultee (London & New York: Routledge, 1991), p. 242.

4. *Encyclopaedia Britannica* – Giuseppe Maria Fieschi, https://www.britannica.com/biography/Giuseppe-Maria-Fieschi [accessed 15 April 2018]

5. J.P.T. Bury, *France 1814–1940* (London: Methuen & Co Ltd, 1969), pp. 62–63; Goubert, p. 245.

6. Horne, pp. 250–251.

7. On the apartment, see Hippolyte Peyrol's reminiscences, in Theodore Stanton, *Rosa Bonheur: Reminiscences* (London: Andrew Melrose, 1910), pp. 19–20.

8. On Auguste, see Hippolyte Peyrol's reminiscences in Stanton, pp. 49–50, 54.

9. Stanton, p. 26.

10. On Isidore, see Hippolyte Peyrol's reminiscences in Stanton, pp. 54–55.

11. See Hippolyte Peyrol's reminiscences in Stanton, p. 20.

12. *Galignani's New Paris Guide* (Paris, 1830), p. 584.

13. *Galignani's New Paris Guide*, p. 584

14. Stanton, p. 21.

15. L. Roger-Milès, *Rosa Bonheur: sa vie – son oeuvre* (Paris, 1900), p. 28. The village of Villiers was eventually absorbed into the commune now known as Levallois-Perret.

16. Stanton, p. 17.
17. Roger-Milès, p. 28.
18. Roger-Milès, p. 28.
19. Stanton remembers Rosa saying that Isidore carried the sheep. See Stanton, p. 37. Roger-Milès claims Rosa told him Auguste did this. See Roger-Milès, p. 28.
20. Roger-Milès, p. 28; Stanton, p. 37.
21. Stanton, p. 339.
22. Klumpke, pp. 121–122.
23. Stanton, p. 18.
24. Stanton, p. 18.
25. On this episode, see Stanton, pp. 18, 339. See also Roger-Milès, pp. 29–30.
26. Stanton, p. 20.
27. 'Salon de 1842', *Revue étrangère de la littérature, des sciences et des arts*, vol. 42, April 1842, pp. 1–13.
28. Roger-Milès, p. 40.
29. On the date of Hippolyte Peyrol's arrival, see his memories in Stanton, p. 19.
30. Rosa insisted that the princess she taught was Ida. However, Princess Czartoryska's daughter was named Izabela Elzbieta. It seems likely that this was the princess Rosa taught. She would have been around eleven at the time and was often referred to as Iza, which could explain the confusion. (https://books.google.co.uk/books?id=oZYmAQAAIAAJ&q=princess+izabela+Elzbieta+czartoryska+Paris&dq=princess+izabela+Elzbieta+czartoryska+Paris&hl=en&sa=X&ved=oahUKEwid7YjJ_uvaAhXmA8A KHS8UB4oQ6AEIRzAE.) However, Rosa's nephew René Peyrol claimed that it was Princess Czartoryska's niece that Rosa taught. See René Peyrol, *The Life and Work of Rosa Bonheur* (London, 1889), p. 4. See Stanton, pp. 15–17; Klumpke, pp. 115–116.
31. On the Hôtel Lambert, see: https://family.rothschildarchive.org/estates/82-hotel-lambert [accessed 15 April 2018]
32. Stanton, p. 16.
33. Lepelle de Bois-Gallais notes that her submissions were awarded a third-class medal when they were shown in Rouen. See F. Lepelle de Bois-Gallais, *Biographie de Mademoiselle Rosa Bonheur* (Paris, 1856), p. 24.
34. Stanton, pp. 20–21.
35. On Rosa's working method, see Roger-Milès, p. 32.
36. Fabien Pillet, 'Le Salon de 1844', *Le Moniteur Universel*, 1 April 1844.
37. Stanton, p. 26.
38. An image of the abattoir appeared in the *Illustrated London News*, 21 July 1849.
39. *Galignani's New Paris Guide* (Paris, 1845), p. 118.
40. Félix Lazare, *Dictionnaire administratif et historique des rues de Paris et de ses monuments* (Paris, 1844), p. 399.

41. *Galignani's New Paris Guide* (Paris, 1845), p. 118.
42. F. Lepelle de Bois-Gallais, *Biographie de Mademoiselle Rosa Bonheur* (Paris, 1856), p. 21.
43. Stanton writes that Émile Gravel prepared and sold calves' heads and calves' and sheep's feet wholesale and that he later made money investing in property at Levallois-Perret. Stanton adds that Gravel invited Rosa and Raymond to paint portraits of his family. See Stanton, pp. 22–23.
44. Stanton, p. 22.
45. Roger-Milès, pp. 48–49.
46. Stanton, p. 37.
47. On this trip, see: Klumpke, p. 117; Stanton, pp. 26–28.
48. Rosa told Anna Klumpke that this individual was assassinated at the same time as a mayor of Bordeaux. See Klumpke, p. 117.
49. Stanton, p. 27.
50. Stanton, p. 27.

Chapter 7: Life and Death

1. Theodore Stanton, *Rosa Bonheur: Reminiscences* (London: Andrew Melrose, 1910), p. 27.
2. Théophile Thoré, 'Salon de 1845', *Salons de Théophile Thoré – 1844, 1845, 1846, 1847, 1848* (Paris, 1870), p. 189.
3. Thoré, p. 189.
4. L. Roger-Milès, *Rosa Bonheur: sa vie – son oeuvre* (Paris, 1900), p. 44.
5. Roger-Milès, p. 44.
6. Stanton, pp. 28–29.
7. Stanton, pp. 28–29.
8. Roger-Milès, p. 159.
9. On Juliette, see Hippolyte Peyrol's reminiscences in Stanton, pp. 52, 55.
10. *Galignani's New Paris Guide* (Paris, 1830), pp. 652–653.
11. Stanton, p. 23.
12. Stanton, p. 23.
13. Thoré, 'Salon de 1846', p. 321.
14. On Rosa's working method, see Anna Klumpke, *Rosa Bonheur: The Artist's [Auto] Biography*, trans. by Gretchen van Slyke (Michigan: The University of Michigan Press, 2001), pp. 218–221.
15. On the use of tubes versus ground colour in the 19th century, see Anthea Callen, *Techniques of the Impressionists* (London: Tiger Books International, 1990), pp. 22–25.
16. Anna Klumpke remembered Rosa using tubes of paint. Klumpke, p. 32. Annie-Paule Quinsac, 'Rosa Bonheur ou la probité du metier' in Francis Ribemont and others, *Rosa Bonheur, 1822–1899*, exhib. cat. (Bordeaux: William

Blake & Co., 1997), pp. 103-111. I am grateful to Katherine Brault for confirming Rosa's use of paint based on the material found at By.

17. Klumpke, p. 218.

18. Stanton, pp. 32–33.

19. Stanton, p. 40.

20. Graham Robb, *The Discovery of France* (London: Picador, 2008), p. 221.

21. Anna Klumpke, *Rosa Bonheur, Sa Vie, son oeuvre* (Paris: Flammarion, 1908), pp. 185–186.

22. On the Saler breed, see: '15 Things You Should Know About Salers Cattle!', http://www.thatsfarming.com/news/salers [accessed 1 June 2018]

23. Klumpke, *Rosa Bonheur, Sa Vie, son oeuvre*, p. 184.

24. Klumpke, *Rosa Bonheur, Sa Vie, son oeuvre*, p. 186.

25. Stanton, p. 340.

26. Signed letter, unreferenced copy held by the Witt Library, Somerset House. On Adolphe Moreau fils, see: http://www.musee-delacroix.fr/fr/actualites/expositions/delacroix-en-heritage-autour-de-la-collectiond-etienne-moreau-nelaton [accessed 1 June 2018]

27. Théophile Gautier, 'Salon de 1847', *La Presse*, 8 April 1847, cited in Dominique Dussol, 'La place de Rosa Bonheur dans l'art animalier à travers la presse de 1841 à 1899' in Francis Ribemont and others, *Rosa Bonheur, 1822–1899*, exhib. cat. (Bordeaux: William Blake & Co., 1997), pp. 39–50 (p. 41).

28. Paul Mantz, *Salon de 1847* (Paris, 1847), p. 32.

29. Théophile Thoré, 'Salon de 1847', *Salons de Théophile Thoré*, p. 475.

30. Klumpke, *Rosa Bonheur, Sa Vie, son oeuvre*, p. 186.

31. Klumpke, *Rosa Bonheur, Sa Vie, son oeuvre*, p. 186.

32. Klumpke, *Rosa Bonheur, Sa Vie, son oeuvre*, pp. 186–187.

33. Klumpke, *Rosa Bonheur, Sa Vie, son oeuvre*, pp. 188–189.

34. Klumpke, *Rosa Bonheur, Sa Vie, son oeuvre*, p. 189.

35. On the 1848 Revolution and its build up, see: Philip Mansel, *Paris Between Empires 1814–1852* (London: John Murray, 2001), pp. 383–422; J.P.T. Bury, *France 1814–1940* (London: Methuen & Co Ltd, 1969), pp. 64–87; Pierre Goubert, *The Course of French History*, trans. by Maarten Ultee (London & New York: Routledge, 1991), pp. 244–251.

36. On this Salon, see Roger-Milès, pp. 45–47. See too *Journal des Beaux-Arts*, 20 August 1848, pp. 1–2.

37. On Paul Delaroche, see: https://www.britannica.com/biography/Paul-Delaroche [accessed 1 June 2018]. On the École des Beaux-Arts, see: https://www.britannica.com/topic/Ecole-des-Beaux-Arts [accessed 1 June 2018]

38. Klumpke, p. 127.

39. 'Salon de 1848', *La Revue critique*, 1848, p. 193.

40. James Kearns, *Théophile Gautier, Orator to the Artists* (London: Legenda, 2007), p. 38; Théophile Thoré, *Salons de T. Thoré*, pp. 560–561.

41. Théophile Gautier, 'Salon de 1848', *La Presse*, 7 May 1848, cited in Dominique Dussol, 'La place de Rosa Bonheur dans l'art animalier à travers la presse de 1841 à 1899' in Francis Ribemont and others, *Rosa Bonheur, 1822–1899*, exhib. cat. (Bordeaux: William Blake & Co., 1997), pp. 39–50 (pp. 41–42).

42. A J D, 'Beaux-Arts; Salon de 1848', *L'Illustration*, 3 June 1848, p. 227.

43. A J D, p. 227.

44. Mansel, p. 409.

45. On Germain Bonheur's size, see Marie Borin, *Rosa Bonheur: Une Artiste à l'aube du féminisme* (Paris: Pygmalion, 2011), p. 105.

46. Colin Jones, *Cambridge Illustrated History of France* (Cambridge: Cambridge University Press, 1994), pp. 210–211.

47. Bury, pp. 79–80.

48. The order of events that summer becomes clear from a letter of Raymond Bonheur's to Pierre Lacour dated 9 August 1848. See Bonnefon, pp. 424–425.

49. Bonnefon, pp. 424–425.

50. On Republican art policy, see Kearns, pp. 7, 38–66.

51. The changing art policy and Rosa's commission is the subject of an excellent thesis by Julia Margaret Browne. See Julia Margaret Browne, 'Rosa Bonheur's Plowing in the Nivernais (1849): The Circumstances of Success' (unpublished Master's thesis, University of British Columbia, 1989)

52. Browne, pp. 19–22. See also: Sheila D. Muller, *Dutch Art: An Encyclopedia* (London: Routledge, 2013), p. 145, https://books.google.co.uk/books?id=ZPhLoy0FICMC&pg=PA146&dq=frances+suzman+jowell+revival&hl=en&sa=X&ved=0ahUKEwim5e7o7KrbAhVrDcAKHa9dA_AQ6AEIPDAE#v=snippet&q=Republic%20France&f=false [accessed 5 June 2018].

53. Kearns, p. 56.

54. Browne, p. 18.

55. Kearns, p. 55.

56. Browne, p. 18.

57. Stanton, p. 28.

58. Now the Rue Dupuytren. See Raymond's letter to Pierre Lacour dated 9 August 1848. See Bonnefon, pp. 424–425.

59. *Galignani's New Paris Guide* (Paris, 1830), p. 452.

60. Thomas Hippler, 'The French army, 1789-1914: Volunteers, pressed soldiers and conscripts', in *Fighting for a Living: A Comparative History of Military Labour, 1500–2000*, ed. by Jan-Erik Zürcher (Amsterdam: University of Amsterdam Press, 2014), pp. 419–446.

61. Browne, p. 18.

Chapter 8: Cometh the Hour

1. Theodore Stanton, *Rosa Bonheur: Reminiscences* (London: Andrew Melrose, 1910), p. 152.
2. Stanton, p. 286.
3. On Raymond Bonheur and money, see Stanton, p. 286.
4. Paul Bonnefon, 'Une Famille d'artistes: Raimond et Rosa Bonheur', *L'Art*, 1903, p. 426.
5. Bonnefon, p. 426.
6. Julia Margaret Browne, 'Rosa Bonheur's Plowing in the Nivernais (1849): The Circumstances of Success' (unpublished Master's thesis, University of British Columbia, 1989), pp. 23–29.
7. See: http://chateau.de.la.cave.free.fr/ [accessed 1 June 2018]; https://www.chateauduchene-dtripod.com/single-post/2016/05/10/Rosa-Bonheur-au-Ch%C3%A2teau-de-la-Cave-actuellement-Ch%C3%A2teau-du-Ch%C3%AAne [accessed 1 June 2018]; https://www.lejdc.fr/beaumont-sardolles/loisirs/2013/08/18/le-domaine-du-chene-une-renovation-dans-les-regles-de-lart_1660110.html mastic [accessed 1 June 2018]
8. Stanton, p. 151.
9. Stanton, p. 152.
10. Stanton, p. 152.
11. Hippolyte Peyrol remembered Rosa taking the studio towards the end of 1848. See Stanton, p. 382. Roger-Milès claims the move took place in the middle of 1849. L. Roger-Milès, *Rosa Bonheur: sa vie – son oeuvre* (Paris, 1900), p. 46. Since Hippolyte Peyrol lived at the Rue Rumford, his account seems most reliable. Rosa gave the Rue de l'Ouest as her address in the Salon catalogue in June 1849.
12. Roger-Milès notes that the building also housed the studios of the painters Adolphe Yvon, Jules-Antoine Droz, Émile Signol and François Joseph Heim. The Salon catalogues for 1849–1852 confirm only that Signol worked from the Rue de l'Ouest during this period. Yvon was based in the next street, Rue Notre-Dame-des-Champs. Roger-Milès, p. 48.
13. See Edmond Texier, *Tableau de Paris*, 2 vols. (Paris, 1852–1853), II, pp. 46–47.
14. Anna Klumpke, *Rosa Bonheur: The Artist's [Auto] Biography*, trans. by Gretchen van Slyke, (Michigan: The University of Michigan Press, 2001), p. 121.
15. Raymond Bonheur died on 23 March 1849.
16. *Journal des Beaux-Arts*, 8 April 1849, p. 3.
17. Letter dated 14 October 1848. See Bonnefon, p. 426.
18. Stanton, p. 47.
19. Cited in Stanton, p. 71.

20. Stanton, p. 29.
21. On this Salon, see James Kearns, *Théophile Gautier, Orator to the Artists* (London: Legenda, 2007), pp. 97–101.
22. On Louis-Napoleon, see J.P.T. Bury, *France 1814–1940* (London: Methuen & Co. Ltd, 1969), pp. 81–82.
23. Bury, pp. 72–87; Pierre Goubert, *The Course of French History*, trans. by Maarten Ultee (London & New York: Routledge, 1991), pp. 246–251.
24. F. de Lagenevais, 'Le Salon', *Revue des Deux Mondes*, 1 July 1849, p. 585.
25. 'Salon de 1849', *Journal des Beaux-Arts*, 8 July 1849, p. 42.
26. Théophile Gautier, 'Salon de 1849', *La Presse*, 10 August 1849, p. 1.
27. Lagenevais, p. 585.
28. Louis Desnoyers, 'Salon de 1849', *Le Siècle*, p. 2.
29. Desnoyers, p. 2.
30. Francis Ribemont and others, *Rosa Bonheur, 1822–1899*, exhib. cat. (Bordeaux: William Blake & Co., 1997), p. 157. On the Nivernais, see: https://www.britannica.com/place/Nivernais [accessed 1 June]
31. Desnoyers, p. 2.
32. A J D, 'Le Salon de 1849', *L'Illustration*, 1849, p. 342.
33. Jeremy Maas, *Gambart – Prince of the Victorian Art World* (London: Barrie and Jenkins, 1975), p. 24.
34. Stanton, p. 372. Léonide also became a painter.
35. On the Tedesco empire, see: https://www.labreuche-fournisseurs-artistes-paris.fr/fournisseur/tedesco-freres [accessed 1 June 2018]
36. Stanton, p. 391.
37. Stanton, pp. 391–392.
38. The recollections of Mlle Keller, Stanton, p. 399.
39. Stanton, p. 42.
40. Roger-Milès, pp. 112–115.
41. Stanton, pp. 153–154.
42. Stanton, p. 154.
43. On the delay to the Salon, see T.J. Clark, *Image of the People – Gustave Courbet and the 1848 Revolution*, p. 85.

Chapter 9: Changing Views

1. The text is cited in Christine Bard, 'Le <<DB58>> aux Archives de la Préfecture de Police', *Clio. Femmes, Genre, Histoire*, 10/1999, pp. 1–2.
2. Bard, p. 5.
3. On women and trousers, see also: Gretchen van Slyke, 'Women at War: Skirting the Issue in the French Revolution', *L'Esprit Créateur*, Spring 1997, Vol XXXVII, No. 1, pp. 33–43; Laure-Paul Flobert, 'La femme et le costume masculin', *Le Vieux Papier*, 1 July 1911, pp. 349–366.

4. Bard, p. 5.

5. Occasionally, permanent permissions were granted. See Flobert, p. 359.

6. Flobert, p. 360.

7. *A Handbook for Travellers in France*, 5th edn (London: John Murray, 1854), p. 225.

8. Anne Martin-Fugier, 'Bourgeois Rituals' in *A History of Private Life*, ed. by Philippe Ariès and George Duby, trans. by Arthur Goldhammer, 5 vols (Cambridge, MA and London: Belknap Press of Harvard University Press, 1987–1991), vol. 4: *From the Fires of Revolution to the Great War*, ed. by Michelle Perrot (1990), pp. 261–337 (p. 301); Graham Robb, *The Discovery of France* (London: Picador, 2008), p. 277.

9. *A Handbook for Travellers in France*, p. 223.

10. *A Handbook for Travellers in France*, p. 230.

11. Stanton, p. 105.

12. Stanton, p. 106.

13. Stanton, p. 155.

14. Stanton, p. 155.

15. Stanton, p. 106.

16. Stanton, p. 105.

17. *A Handbook for Travellers in France*, p. 232.

18. *A Handbook for Travellers in France*, p. 232.

19. *A Handbook for Travellers in France*, p. 234.

20. Stanton, p. 106.

21. *A Handbook for Travellers in France*, p. 230.

22. *A Handbook for Travellers in France*, p. 234.

23. Stanton, p. 155.

24. Stanton, p. 155.

25. Stanton, pp. 109–110.

26. Stanton, p. 109.

27. Catherine Van Casselaer, *Lot's Wife: Lesbian Paris 1890–1914* (Liverpool: The Janus Press, 1986), p. 10; Lillian Faderman, *Surpassing the Love of Men: Romantic Friendship and Love between Women from the Renaissance to the Present* (London: The Women's Press Ltd, 1997), pp. 254–269.

28. Van Casselaer, p. 13.

29. Van Casselaer, p. 10.

30. Stanton, p. 249.

31. Stanton, p. 99.

32. Stanton, p. 99.

33. Stanton, pp. 97–98.

34. Stanton, p. 85.

35. Stanton, p. 102.

36. Stanton, p. 40.
37. Stanton, p. 41.
38. 'A Morning with Rosa Bonheur', interview conducted on 10 August 1859, originally published in the *Home Journal*, reprinted in *Littel's Living Age* (October, November, December, 1859), p. 124.
39. Stanton, pp. 102–103.
40. Stanton, p. 110.
41. Stanton, p. 112.
42. Stanton, p. 113.
43. *A Handbook for Travellers in France*, p. 230.
44. M. le docteur Pressat, *Notice médicale sur les eaux minérales d'Ems* (Paris, 1857), pp. 5–6.
45. Stanton, p. 120.
46. Stanton, p. 120.
47. Stanton, p. 121.
48. Stanton, p. 122.
49. Stanton, p. 122.
50. Stanton, p. 122.
51. Stanton, p. 124.
52. See: https://www.louvre.fr/en/oeuvre-notices/tenth-metope-south-facade-parthenon [accessed 22 July 2018]
53. Dore Ashton and Denise Browne Hare, *Rosa Bonheur: A Life and a Legend* (New York: The Viking Press, 1981), pp. 82–87.
54. Probably *De la conformation du Cheval* (Paris, 1847)
55. *Galignani's New Paris Guide* (Paris, 1830), p. 312; *Galignani's New Paris Guide* (Paris, 1852), p. 463.
56. *Galignani's New Paris Guide* (Paris, 1830), p. 312.
57. Stanton, p. 383.
58. Stanton, p. 288.
59. *Bury and Norwich Post and Suffolk Herald*, 18 June 1851, NP.
60. 'Exhibition of Paintings, Lichfield House, St. James's Square', *Daily News*, 12 June 1851, p. 5; Dante Gabriel Rossetti, writing in the *Spectator*. Cited in Jeremy Maas, *Gambart – Prince of the Victorian Art World* (London: Barrie and Jenkins, 1975), p. 56.
61. *Le Palais de Cristal*, 5 July 1851, p. 139.
62. 'Nouvelles dramatiques, *Le Nouvelliste*, 9 August 1851, NP.
63. They married on 2 August 1851. See Paul Bonnefon, 'Une Famille d'artistes: Raimond et Rosa Bonheur', *L'Art*, 1903, p. 541.
64. On the events, see: J.P.T. Bury, *France 1814–1940* (London: Methuen & Co. Ltd, 1969), pp. 85–91; Pierre Goubert, *The Course of French History*, trans. by Maarten Ultee (London & New York: Routledge, 1991), pp. 250–251;

Philip Mansel, *Paris Between Empires 1814–1852* (London: John Murray, 2001), pp. 416–422.

65. On Louis-Napoleon and Saint-Simonianism, see: https://www.napoleon.org/ en/history-of-the-two-empires/articles/napoleon-iii-and-abd-el-kader/ [accessed 22 July 2018]; https://books.google.co.uk/books?id=UYOvBwAAQ BAJ&pg=PA108&lpg=PA108&dq=napoleon+iii+Saint+Simonianism&source =bl&ots=nO6sstEArC&sig=r3cHqZuQqLxCCEaTqifWc6wWdLU&hl=en& sa=X&ved=0ahUKEwjjlsffyJncAhXGVhQKHT_HAw84ChDoAQgmMAA #v=onepage&q=napoleon%20iii%20Saint%20Simonianism&f=false [accessed 22 July 2018]

66. Stanton, p. 66.

67. On Charles de Morny, see: Joanna Richardson, *La Vie Parisienne 1852–1870* (London: Hamish Hamilton Ltd, 1971), p. 67; Desmond Seward, *Eugénie: The Empress and her Empire* (Stroud: Sutton Publishing, 2004), p. 45; SR, 'Morny, Charles Auguste Louis Joseph, Duc de (1811–1865)', https://www.napoleon. org/en/history-of-the-two-empires/biographies/morny-charles-auguste-louis-joseph-duc-de-1811-1865/ [accessed 22 July 2018]

68. Alain Decaux, *L'Empire, l'amour et l'argent*. (Paris: Libraire Académique Perrin, 1982), pp. 89–94.

69. See Anna Klumpke, *Rosa Bonheur: The Artist's [Auto] Biography*, trans. by Gretchen van Slyke, (Michigan: The University of Michigan Press, 2001), pp. 148–150.

70. James Kearns, *Théophile Gautier, Orator to the Artists* (London: Legenda, 2007), p. 142.

71. Claire Dupin de Beyssat, 'Un Louvre pour les artistes vivants? Modalités d'appropriation du musée par et pour les artistes du XIXe siècle', https:// journals.openedition.org/cel/684?lang=en#text [accessed 22 July 2018]

72. *'Ce Salon à quoi tout se ramène': Le Salon de peinture et de sculpture, 1791–1890*, ed. by James Kearns and Pierre Vaisse (Bern: Peter Lang, 2010), https://books. google.co.uk/books?id=yNB7_zYd_skC&pg=PA70&lpg=PA70&dq=Salon+ 1853+James+H%C3%B4tel+des+Menus-Plaisirs&source=bl&ots=-olMgkeo6 R&sig=Y34Rotdso_5BSATuAleTkxg1WGc&hl=en&sa=X&ved=0ahUKEwj Ll43e2pncAhXHuxQKHXMNBwQQ6AEIUzAI#v=onepage&q=Salon%20 1853%20James%20H%C3%B4tel%20des%20Menus-Plaisirs&f=false [accessed 22 July 2018]

73. On Gambart, see Maas.

74. Borin, pp. 275–277.

75. See the *Athenaeum*, 21 April 1849, p. 416; Maas, pp. 54, 61. Gambart attended the sale of the Duc d'Orléans' collection in the Rue des Jeûneurs. See *Gazette des Beaux-Arts*, 23 January 1853, p. 2; *Collection du Journal La Lumière – Revue de la Photographie* (Paris, 1853)

Chapter 10: A Woman's Work

1. Simon Horsin-Déon, *Rapport sur le Salon de 1853, lu le 19 juin à l'assemblée générale annuelle de la Société Libre des Beaux-Arts* (Paris, 1853), p. 12.
2. Horsin-Déon, p. 12.
3. See Gabriel Weisberg, 'Rosa Bonheur's Reception in England and America: The Popularization of a Legend and the Celebration of a Myth' in Gabriel Weisberg and others, *Rosa Bonheur: All Nature's Children* (New York: Dahesh Museum, 1998), pp. 1–22. On Émilien de Nieuwerkerke, see: Joanna Richardson, *Princess Mathilde* (London: Weidenfeld & Nicolson, 1969), p. 50; Desmond Seward, *Eugénie: The Empress and her Empire* (Stroud: Sutton Publishing, 2005), pp. 75, 139.
4. Horsin-Déon, p. 12.
5. 'Exposition de 1853', *La Mode*, 25 June 1853, p. 602.
6. N. Berthon, *L'Eventail*, 21 June 1853, p. 4.
7. 'Art in Continental States', *Art Journal*, 1 July 1853, p. 174.
8. Richard Sincère, 'Un Souvenir du Salon', *Le Nouvelliste*, 6 August 1853, pp. 1–2.
9. *Journal de Eugène Delacroix (Complete)* (Alexandria: Library of Alexandria, 2017), 10 July 1853.
10. Courtois, 'Les moutons de Mlle Rosa Bonheur', *Le Nouvelliste*, 18 July 1853, NP.
11. Théophile Gautier, 'Salon de 1853', *La Presse*, 22 July 1853, p. 3.
12. Henri Delaborde, 'Salon 1853', *La Revue des Deux Mondes*, volume 2, June 1853, pp. 1142–1144.
13. On the emergence of feminism, see: Lillian Faderman, *Surpassing the Love of Men: Romantic Friendship and Love between Women from the Renaissance to the Present* (London: The Women's Press Ltd, 1997), pp. 178–189; Theodore Zeldin, *France 1848–1945: Ambition and Love* (Oxford, New York, Toronto and Melbourne: Oxford University Press, 1988), pp. 343–357.
14. *La Mode*, p. 602; E. Pierre de Boesse, 'Revue de l'Exposition', *Gazette des Beaux-Arts*, September 1853, p. 112. It was later suggested that Rosa depicted herself in the central figure mounted on horseback, dressed in a blue smock and black flat cap. Inspection of the hands throws doubt onto this hypothesis: this figure's hands are large and manly. Rosa's delicate and feminine hands were often remarked on. It has also been said that Antoine Richard (du Cantal), who gave her his book on horses, posed for one of the figures. See Francis Ribemont and others, *Rosa Bonheur, 1822–1899*, exhib. cat. (Bordeaux: William Blake & Co., 1997), p. 158.
15. *A Handbook for Travellers in France*, 5th edn (London: John Murray, 1854), p. 230.
16. Stanton, p. 114.
17. Stanton, p. 114.
18. See the review in the *Art Journal*, 1 October 1853, p. 262.

19. Stanton, p. 114.
20. Stanton, p. 115.
21. Joan DelPlato, *Multiple Wives, Multiple Pleasures: Representing the Harem, 1800–1875* (Vancouver: Fairleigh Dickinson University Press, 2002), p. 185.
22. Stanton, p. 16.
23. Stanton, p. 116.
24. Stanton, p. 117.
25. 'Art in Continental States', *Art Journal*, 1 September 1853, p. 227.
26. 'Exposition de la Société des Amis des Arts de Bordeaux', *Echo des coulisses*, 1 January 1853, NP.
27. *L'Illustration*, 31 December 1853, p. 438.
28. 'Exposition des oeuvres des artistes vivants en province', *Gazette des Beaux-Arts*, 15 December 1853, p. 304.
29. Stanton, p. 218.
30. Stanton, p. 383.
31. Roger-Milès claims the move took place in 1854. L. Roger-Milès, *Rosa Bonheur: sa vie – son oeuvre* (Paris, 1900), pp. 61–62. Anna Klumpke situates the move shortly after the exhibition of *The Horse Fair* at the Salon. Anna Klumpke, *Rosa Bonheur: The Artist's [Auto] Biography*, trans. by Gretchen van Slyke, (Michigan: The University of Michigan Press, 2001), p. 150. However, Hippolyte Peyrol remembered Rosa moving in 1851. The Princess Stirbey also recollected seeing Rosa working on *The Horse Fair* in this new studio. If this was the original version of the painting, Rosa would have had to be working there before 1853. See Stanton, p. 30 and p. 383. In 1853, the Salon catalogue gave Rosa's base as the Rue de l'Ouest, while in 1855 it had become 32, Rue d' Assas.
32. Roger-Milès, p. 61.
33. Stanton, p. 41.
34. P. Ludow Vigé, 'Société des Amis des Arts, 4e Exposition Publique des Artistes vivants', *Echo des coulisses*, 19 November 1854, NP.
35. On Gambart, see Jeremy Maas, *Gambart – Prince of the Victorian Art World* (London: Barrie and Jenkins, 1975).
36. Stanton quotes Gambart, who said that Bordeaux had been asked for 12,000 francs. Anna Klumpke reported that Bordeaux refused the canvas at 15,000 francs. See: Stanton, pp. 379–380; Klumpke, pp. 150–151.
37. Klumpke, pp. 150–151; Stanton, pp. 384–385.
38. Rosa's words reported by her friend, the Prince Georges Stirbey. See Stanton, p. 385.
39. Stanton, pp. 379–380.
40. *Revue des Beaux-Arts* (Paris, 1855), p. 169.
41. Stanton, p. 23. I am grateful to Michel Pons at the Château Rosa Bonheur for the biographical information on Céline Rey.

42. Stanton, p. 30.
43. Stanton, p. 33.

Chapter 11: Beyond the Sea

1. Louis Énault, *Angleterre, Écosse, Irlande – Voyage Pittoresque* (Paris, 1859), p. 4.
2. Theodore Stanton, *Rosa Bonheur: Reminiscences* (London: Andrew Melrose, 1910), p. 218.
3. On cross-Channel travel, see: Thomas Muller, *The History of the Channel Ferry* http://www.sailingandboating.co.uk/history-channel-ferry.html [accessed 5 August 2018]; Thomas James Holidays – *Travelling to France with the Ferry or Channel Tunnel*, http://www.thomasjamesholidays.co.uk/ferry-or-eurotunnel-to-france/ [accessed 5 August 2018]; *Channel Ferries – History*, https://www.theotherside.co.uk/tm-heritage/background/ferries.htm [accessed 5 August 2018]; Ambrose Greenway, *Cross Channel and Short Sea Ferries: An Illustrated History* (Barnsley: Seaforth Publishing, 2014)
4. Lady Eastlake travelling on 23 August 1855. See Charles Eastlake Smith, *Journals and Correspondence of Lady Eastlake*, volume 2, (London, 1895), p. 45.
5. *Galignani's New Paris Guide* (Paris, 1852), p. x.
6. *The Times*, 19 July 1855, p. 12.
7. C.H. Rolph, *London Particulars* (Oxford, New York, Toronto and Melbourne: Oxford University Press, 1980), pp. 10–11.
8. Énault, p. 5.
9. Énault, p. 5.
10. Énault, p. 6.
11. On Charles Eastlake, see: *The National Gallery* – Sir Charles Lock Eastlake, https://www.nationalgallery.org.uk/paintings/history/directors/sir-charles-lock-eastlake [accessed 8 August 2018]
12. On Edwin Landseer, see *Encyclopaedia Britannica* – Sir Edwin Landseer, https://www.britannica.com/biography/Edwin-Landseer [accessed 8 August 2018]
13. On the weather, see *The Times*, 19 July 1855, p. 12.
14. Eastlake, pp. 42–43; Jeremy Maas, *Gambart – Prince of the Victorian Art World* (London: Barrie and Jenkins, 1975), pp. 74–75.
15. Maas, p. 75.
16. Eastlake Smith, *Journals and Correspondence of Lady Eastlake*, volume 2, pp. 42–44.
17. Stanton, p. 136.
18. Maas, p. 75.
19. *Guide dans l'Exposition Universelle* (Paris, 1855), p. 174.
20. Stanton, pp. 117–118.
21. Stanton, p. 118.
22. Stanton, p. 118.

23. Stanton, p. 119.
24. 'L'Exposition de la Société des Amis des Arts de Bordeaux,' *Echo des coulisses*, 1 January 1853, NP.
25. Stanton, p. 119.
26. Virginie Demont-Breton, 'Rosa Bonheur', *La Revue des revues*, 15 June 1899, 605–619 (p. 612).
27. *Athenaeum*, 8 September 1855, p. 1034.
28. 'Rosa Bonheur', *New York Times*, 9 August 1855, p. 4.
29. *Athenaeum*, p. 1034.
30. Stanton, pp. 218–219.

Chapter 12: The Lady of the Lakes

1. Walter Scott, *The Lay of the Last Minstrel* (London, 1805), p. 170.
2. On the British, the French and the Crimean War, see J.P.T. Bury, *France 1814–1940* (London: Methuen & Co. Ltd, 1969), pp. 94–96.
3. Bury, pp. 94–95.
4. Jeremy Maas, *Gambart – Prince of the Victorian Art World* (London: Barrie and Jenkins, 1975), p. 78.
5. Theodore Stanton, *Rosa Bonheur: Reminiscences* (London: Andrew Melrose, 1910), p. 125.
6. *Athenaeum*, 8 March 1856, p. 303.
7. 'French School of the Fine Arts – Exhibition at the Royal Institution', *Manchester Times*, 5 April 1856, NP
8. *Athenaeum*, 10 May 1856, p. 591.
9. *Athenaeum*, 28 June 1856, p. 810.
10. Stanton, pp. 132–133.
11. Stanton, p. 125.
12. Stanton, p. 125.
13. Stanton, p. 125.
14. *The Horse Fair* was shown in Liverpool in April 1856.
15. On Rosa's time in Scotland, see Frances Fowle, 'Picturing the Highlands: Rosa Bonheur's Grand Tour of Scotland', *Journal of the Scottish Society for Art History*, 18, (2012), pp. 40–48.
16. Stanton, p. 133.
17. Stanton, p. 125. Edwin Bullock lived at Hawthorne House. He was an iron founder, hinge maker, art collector. See: Sue Young Histories – Edwin Bullock, http://sueyounghistories.com/archives/2009/11/14/edwin-bullock-1802-1870/ [accessed 20 August 2018]
18. Quoting Nathalie's letter to her mother dated 16 August 1856. See Marie Borin, *Rosa Bonheur: Une Artiste à l'aube du féminisme* (Paris: Pygmalion, 2011), pp. 150–151.

19. Frederick Goodall, *The Reminiscences of Frederick Goodall R.A.* (London and Newcastle-on-Tyne: The Walter Scott Publishing Co. Ltd, 1902), p. 129.
20. See Stanton, pp. 129–131.
21. BBC History – Scottish History – Victorian Glasgow, https://www.bbc.co.uk/history/scottishhistory/victorian/trails_victorian_glasgow.shtml [accessed 30 August 2018]; Stana Nenadic, 'Second City of the Empire: 1830s to 1914 – Everyday Life', *The Glasgow Story*, https://www.theglasgowstory.com/story/?id=TGSDA [accessed 30 August 2018]
22. *Encyclopaedia Britannica* – Daniel Maclise, https://www.britannica.com/biography/Daniel-Maclise [accessed 30 August 2018]; Maas, p. 65.
23. Letter dated 5 September 1856, see Borin, p. 151.
24. Stana Nenadic, 'The Rise of Edinburgh', BBC History – British History in Depth, http://www.bbc.co.uk/history/british/civil_war_revolution/scotland_edinburgh_01.shtml [accessed 30 August 2018]
25. Stanton, p. 127.
26. On Bass Rock, see Neil Wilson and Andy Symington, *Lonely Planet – Scotland* (London: Lonely Planet Publications, 2013), p. 100.
27. Stanton, p. 128.
28. 'Fine Arts', *Morning Post*, 23 September 1856, p. 5.
29. *Glasgow Herald*, 10 September 1856, NP.
30. This article appeared in: *Caledonian Mercury*, 26 August 1856, NP; *Glasgow Herald*, 27 August 1856, NP; *Freeman's Journal and Daily Commercial Advertiser*, 27 August 1856, NP; *Aberdeen Journal*, 3 September 1856, NP.
31. 'Falkirk Tryst', *Morning Post*, 11 September 1856, p. 8; *The Glasgow Herald*, 10 September 1856, NP.
32. Stanton, p. 369.
33. Tim Hilton, *John Ruskin* (New Haven and London: Yale University Press, 2002), pp. 181–184. On the episode, see Maas, pp. 85–86.
34. Stanton, p. 134.
35. A.M.W. Stirling, *Victorian Sidelights* (London: Ernest Benn Ltd, 1954), p. 30.
36. Stirling, p. 30.
37. Maas, p. 87.
38. Goodall, p. 129.
39. On John Ruskin see: *Encyclopaedia Britannica* – Sir John Ruskin, https://www.britannica.com/biography/John-Ruskin [accessed 30 August 2018]; John Ruskin Museum – 'Who was John Ruskin (1819–1900)?', http://www.ruskinmuseum.com/content/john-ruskin/who-was-john-ruskin.php [accessed 30 August 2018]
40. Stanton, p. 132.
41. On this exchange, see Goodall, pp. 130–131.
42. Stanton, p. 132.

43. Stanton, p. 132.
44. Goodall, p. 131.
45. Maas, p. 87.
46. Maas, p. 88.
47. 'Sporting Intelligence', *The Times*, 17 October 1856, p. 7.
48. See: 'Exhibition of French Art', *Standard*, 5 May 1856, p. 1; 'French Exhibition', *Athenaeum*, 10 May 1856, p. 591; 'The Fine Arts', *Examiner*, 17 May 1856, NP.

Chapter 13: Such Stuff as Dreams
1. On this episode, see Theodore Stanton, *Rosa Bonheur: Reminiscences* (London: Andrew Melrose, 1910), p. 342.
2. See Stanton, pp. 380–382.
3. Stanton, p. 394.
4. Stanton, p. 373.
5. Stanton, pp. 30, 372.
6. Stanton, pp. 39–40, 369. Rosa's goddaughter, Rosa Mathieu, claimed that the performance Rosa attended was *The Magic Flute*. This cannot be the case; *The Magic Flute* was not performed at the Opéra Comique until 3 April 1879. See: Nicole Wild, *Éditions de la Bibliothèque nationale de France –Décors et costumes du XIXe siècle –* 'Théâtre de l'Opéra-Comique', pp. 158–211, https://books.openedition.org/editionsbnf/835?lang=en [accessed 5 September 2018]
7. Maxime du Camp, *Le Salon de 1857* (Paris, 1857), p. 135.
8. 'Salon de 1857', *Revue des Beaux-Arts*, 1857, p. 251.
9. 'Salon de 1857', *Revue des Beaux-Arts*, p. 251.
10. Louis Auvray, *Exposition des Beaux-Arts – Salon de 1857* (Paris, 1857), p. 57.
11. See Hélène Lafont-Couturier, 'The Dissemination of Rosa Bonheur's Works by the House of Goupil', trans. by Henry Krawitz in Gabriel Weisberg and others, *Rosa Bonheur: All Nature's Children* (New York: Dahesh Museum, 1998), pp. 59–60.
12. Lafont-Couturier, pp. 59–60.
13. *New York Times*, 17 September 1857, p. 4.
14. *New York Times*, 1 October 1857, p. 4.
15. On the Goncourts, see: *Encyclopaedia Britannica* – Edmond and Jules Goncourt, https://www.britannica.com/biography/Edmond-and-Jules-Goncourt [accessed 5 September 2018]
16. Edmond et Jules de Goncourt, *Journal – Mémoires de la vie littéraire, I, 1851–1861*, ed. by Robert Ricatte, (Paris: Robert Lafont, 1989) p. 241.
17. de Goncourt, *Journal*, I, p. 399.
18. Stanton, p. 393.
19. Stanton, p. 393.
20. *Gardeners' Chronicle*, 26 February 1859, p. 162.

21. Auguste Villemont, 'Chronique Parisienne', *Le Figaro*, 6 August 1854, p. 1.
22. On Rosa's purchase of By, see Florent Tesnier, 'Rosa Bonheur, Jules Saulnier et l'achat du domaine de By à Thomery' (2017), http://amisderosabonheur.asso.fr/wp-content/uploads/2017/09/Article-2017-Achat-By-H04-1.pdf [accessed 5 September 2018]
23. *La Presse*, 4 April 1859, NP.
24. *Le Constitutionel*, 8 April 1859, NP.
25. *Indicateur Officiel des environs de Paris*, 15–31 March 1859, p. 15.
26. Tesnier, pp. 1–7.
27. Tesnier, pp. 8–26.
28. Stanton, p. 265; Marie Borin, *Rosa Bonheur: Une Artiste à l'aube du féminisme* (Paris: Pygmalion, 2011), p. 165. Rosa had already given up her studio in Chevilly by this point. She relinquished her tenancy in the late 1850s.

Chapter 14: Pure Invention

1. Florent Tesnier, 'Rosa Bonheur, Jules Saulnier et l'achat du domaine de By à Thomery' (2017), http://amisderosabonheur.asso.fr/wp-content/uploads/2017/09/Article-2017-Achat-By-H04-1.pdf [accessed 5 September 2018], pp. 9–11; Anna Klumpke, *Rosa Bonheur: The Artist's [Auto] Biography*, trans. by Gretchen van Slyke, (Michigan: The University of Michigan Press, 2001), pp. 162–164.
2. Theodore Stanton, *Rosa Bonheur: Reminiscences* (London: Andrew Melrose, 1910), p. 302.
3. Stanton, p. 303. Mme Lagrolet was Isidore Dublan's daughter.
4. Stanton, p. 220.
5. Stanton, pp. 359–361.
6. Stanton, p. 341.
7. Stanton, p. 357.
8. Chantal Georgel, 'La forêt de Fontainebleau: une nature monumentale, un monument naturel?', *Perspective – actualité en histoire de l'art*, vol. 1, 2017, pp. 137–138.
9. *Annuaire des Artistes et des Amateurs* (Paris, 1861), p. 7.
10. Stanton, p. 157.
11. Stanton, p. 157.
12. Stanton, p. 221.
13. On this episode, see: Gerald M. Ackerman, *The Life and Work of Jean-Léon Gérôme* (London: Sotheby's, 1986), p. 59; Wendelin Guentner, *Women Art Critics in Nineteenth-Century France: Vanishing Acts* (Delaware: University of Delaware Press, 2013), pp. 307–309; 'Cours et Tribunaux', *Le Temps*, 21 February 1862, p. 3; 'Cours et Tribunaux', *La Presse*, 21 February 1862, p. 3; Stanton, p. 221.
14. Georgel, pp. 137–138.

15. Stanton, p. 302.
16. Stanton, p. 303.
17. Stanton, p. 158.
18. Rosa Bonheur to Paul Chardin, Letters of Rosa Bonheur, 19, reproduced in Anne Henderson and Zoë Urbanek, *Rosa Bonheur: Selected Works from American Collections* (Dallas, Texas: The Meadows Museum, 1989), NP.
19. Rosa Bonheur to Paul Chardin, Letters of Rosa Bonheur, 2. See Henderson and Urbanek, NP.
20. Stanton, p. 86.
21. Stanton, p. 87.
22. Stanton, p. 87.
23. Stanton, pp. 90–91.
24. Stanton, p. 90.
25. Stanton, p. 92.
26. Stanton, p. 93.
27. Such as the International Exhibition in London in 1862.
28. Stanton, p. 163.
29. Stanton, p. 223.
30. Stanton, p. 96.

Chapter 15: All That Glitters

1. See Hippolyte Peyrol's account in Theodore Stanton, *Rosa Bonheur: Reminiscences* (London: Andrew Melrose, 1910), pp. 95–97; Desmond Seward, *Eugénie* (London: Sutton Publishing, 2010), p. 50.
2. On the crinoline, see Ludmilla Kybalová, Olga Herbenová and Milena Lamarová, *The Pictorial Encyclopedia of Fashion*, trans. by Claudia Rosoux (London: Paul Hamlyn, 1968), pp. 271–272.
3. Joanna Richardson, *Princess Mathilde* (London: Weidenfeld & Nicolson, 1969), p. 68.
4. Seward, p. 39.
5. Seward, p. 40.
6. Stanton, p. 96.
7. Stanton, p. 161.
8. Stanton, p. 161.
9. Stanton, p. 362.
10. Stanton, p. 161.
11. On the Château de Fontainebleau, see: https://www.chateaudefontainebleau.fr/spip.php?lang=en [accessed 8 October 2018]
12. Seward, p. 51.
13. Anna Klumpke, *Rosa Bonheur: The Artist's [Auto] Biography*, trans. by Gretchen van Slyke, (Michigan: The University of Michigan Press, 2001), pp. 168–174;

Rosa Bonheur, 'Souvenirs inédits de Rosa Bonheur', *La Revue des revues*, 1 January 1897, p. 140.

14. Seward, p. 46.
15. Seward, pp. 46–47.
16. See Klumpke, pp. 170–174.
17. Joanna Richardson, *La Vie Parisienne 1852–1870* (London: Hamish Hamilton, 1971), pp. 237–239.
18. On Pauline de Metternich, see Seward, pp. 121–123.
19. Klumpke, p. 170.
20. Stanton, p. 276.
21. See Stanton, pp. 386–391.
22. See: 'Un tableau de Mlle Rosa Bonheur', *La Chronique des Arts et de la Curiosité*, 1865, p. 261; Hippolyte Philibert, 'Chronique départementale', *Le Petit Journal*, 17 February 1865, p. 3.
23. Stanton, pp. 164–165.
24. See: 'Maison des Bonheur', https://www.magny-les-hameaux.fr/content/maison-des-bonheur [accessed 20 October 2018]
25. Klumpke, p. 172.
26. Stanton, p. 165.
27. For Hippolyte's account, see Stanton, pp. 95–97. For an alternative account, see Klumpke, pp. 172–174.
28. Stanton, p. 97.
29. Klumpke, p. 173.
30. Eugène de Mirecourt, *Les Contemporains: Rosa Bonheur* (Paris, 1856), pp. 93–94.
31. *Le Moniteur Universel*, 11 June 1865, p. 1.
32. *Le Journal des Arts*, 1 July 1865, p. 1.
33. *Le Monde illustré*, 17 June 1865, p. 372. On Sister Marthe, see: *Biographies des hommes vivants, ou histoire par ordre alphabétique de la vie publique de tous les hommes qui se sont fait remarquer par leurs actions ou leurs écrits* (Paris, 1818), vol. 4, pp. 362–363. On women and the Légion d'Honneur, see: Haryett Fontanges, *La Légion d'Honneur et les Femmes Décorées: Étude d'Histoire et de Sociologie Féminine* (Paris: Alliance Co-opérative du Livre, 1905). Breton Double, alias Duconde Laborde, was made a regimental quartermaster by Napoleon Bonaparte in 1806. She served until 1840 as a soldier and a spy. She received the Légion d'Honneur in the 1830s. *Colburn's United Service Magazine and Naval and Military Journal* (London, 1843), Part 3, pp. 75–77.
34. *La Salle à Manger*, 20 June 1865, p. 140.
35. Stanton, p. 224.
36. Stanton, p. 225.
37. Stanton, p. 225.
38. Stanton, p. 166.

Chapter 16: Gathering Storms

1. E.A. Spoll, *Mme Carvalho: notes et souvenirs* (Paris, 1885), p. 9.
2. *Men of the Time: A Dictionary of Contemporaries*, ed. by Thompson Cooper (London, 1872), p. 195. Ultimately, the union proved 'a most unhappy one'. When Léon Carvalho was made bankrupt in the late 1860s, 'a judicial separation was obtained by his wife, who, it appeared, had not received for four years a single shilling of her salary'.
3. *Athenaeum*, 14 April 1860, p. 515.
4. Auguste Cain married Pierre-Jules Mêne's daughter before fathering two sons, Henri and Georges. Nearly every member of the family was involved with sculpture, painting, writing or music.
5. Theodore Stanton, *Rosa Bonheur: Reminiscences* (London: Andrew Melrose, 1910), p. 102.
6. Stanton, pp. 225–226.
7. Stanton, p. 226.
8. Stanton, p. 228.
9. G.A.A. Storey, *Sketches from Memory* (London: Chatto and Windus, 1889), p. 325. See also Jeremy Maas, *Gambart – Prince of the Victorian Art World* (London: Barrie and Jenkins, 1975), p. 24; Joanna Richardson, *La Vie Parisienne 1852–1870* (London: Hamish Hamilton Ltd, 1971), pp. 189–199.
10. Stanton, pp. 166–167.
11. Stanton, p .168.
12. Stanton, p. 169.
13. C. Spéranza, 'Exposition Universelle', *L'Indépendance Dramatique*, 11 May 1867, p. 1.
14. C. Spéranza, p. 1.
15. 'Revue', *Journal des Arts*, 15 April 1867, p. 1.
16. Alphonse de Calonne, *Revue Contemporaine*, pp. 726–727.
17. M. de Saint-Saintin, 'J.R. Brascassat', *Gazette des Beaux-Arts*, 1 June 1868, pp. 575–576.
18. *Les Curiosités de l'Exposition Universelle de 1867* (Paris, 1867), pp. 140–141.
19. *La Chronique des Arts*, 12 May 1867, pp. 150–151; 'Nouvelles et Faits Divers', *L'Indépendance Dramatique*, 11 May 1867, p. 4.
20. Stanton, p. 169.
21. Stanton, p. 243.
22. Stanton, p. 169.
23. See Maas, p. 208.
24. Stanton, p. 170.
25. Rosa remembered this being awarded in 1867. See L. Roger-Milès, *Rosa Bonheur: sa vie – son oeuvre* (Paris, 1900), p. 131.
26. Stanton, p. 274.

27. Stanton, p. 170.

28. I am indebted to Sue Whitaker at the Worthington Historical Society's Doll Museum for her insights into their Rosa Bonheur doll. Britta C. Dwyer, *Anna Klumpke: A Turn-of-the-Century Painter and Her World* (Pennyslvania: Northeastern University Press, 1999), p. 5. On antique dolls, see Lydia and Joachim F. Richter, *Collecting Antique Dolls* (Cumberland, Maryland: Hobby House Press, 1991); Karen Chernick, '160 Years Before the Frida Kahlo Barbie, a Rosa Bonheur Doll Celebrated a Queer Woman Painter', *Hyperallergic*, 22 March 2018, https://hyperallergic.com/433726/frida-kahlo-barbie-rosa-bonheur-doll/ [accessed 7 November 2018]

29. Stanton, p. 175.

30. Stanton, p. 169.

31. On Bismarck and the Franco-Prussian War, see: Pierre Goubert, *The Course of French History*, trans. by Maarten Ultee (London and New York: Routledge, 1991), pp. 262–263; 'Otto von Bismarck (1815–1898)' – *BBC History*, http://www.bbc.co.uk/history/historic_figures/bismarck_otto_von.shtml [accessed 7 November 2018]

32. Stanton, p. 319. On the drought, see *Le Journal Officiel de l'Empire Français*, 30 June 1870, p. 13: 'The drought and the heat which have continued for several months have led to an excessive consumption of water in Paris.' See also: 'Rapport indiquant les moyens d'atténuer les effets de la sécheresse sur les productions fourragères en 1870', *Le Journal Officiel de l'Empire Français*, 22 June 1870, p. 1.

Chapter 17: Knowing the Enemy

1. Theodore Stanton, *Rosa Bonheur: Reminiscences* (London: Andrew Melrose, 1910), pp. 172–173.

2. Stanton, p. 173.

3. The Prince hailed from the Catholic branch of the Hohenzollern family headed by King Wilhelm of Prussia. On the Franco-Prussian War, see Stephen Badsey, *The Franco-Prussian War, 1870–1871* (Oxford: Osprey Publishing, 2003). See also: J.P.T. Bury, *France 1814–1940* (London: Methuen & Co. Ltd, 1969), pp. 120–137; Alistair Horne, *Seven Ages of Paris* (London: Pan Macmillan, 2003), pp. 282–313; Desmond Seward, *Eugénie* (London: Sutton Publishing, 2010), pp. 177–254.

4. Alexandre Duvernois, *Le Figaro*, 18 July 1870, p. 1.

5. Stanton, p. 173.

6. Stanton, p. 173.

7. On pineapples, see Susan Cope and others, eds, *Larousse Gastronomique* (London: Mandarin, 1990), pp. 959–960.

8. Stanton, p. 320.

9. Stanton, pp. 174–175.

10. Stanton, p. 320.

11. Stanton, p. 320.

12. Stanton, p. 321.

13. Stanton, pp. 321–322.

14. Stanton, p. 322.

15. Stanton, p. 323.

16. Stanton, p. 326.

17. Stanton, p. 325.

18. Stanton, p. 324.

19. Stanton, p. 326.

20. Anna Klumpke, *Rosa Bonheur: The Artist's [Auto] Biography*, trans. by Gretchen van Slyke, (Michigan: The University of Michigan Press, 2001), p. 177; Stanton, p. 326.

21. See *Rosa Bonheur: Une Artiste à l'aube du féminisme* (Paris: Pygmalion, 2011), pp. 203–204.

22. Stanton, p. 327.

23. Stanton, pp. 327–328.

24. Stanton, pp. 329–330.

25. Stanton, pp. 328–330.

26. The pass, which is still held at the Château de By, is dated 26 September 1870.

27. A. Lacroix, 'The State of Nice', *The Times*, 20 September 1870, p. 8.

28. Hollis Clayson, *Paris in Despair: Art and Everyday Life under Siege (1870–71)* (Chicago and London: University of Chicago Press, 2002), p. 174.

29. Sée, *Aujourd'hui Paris*, pp. 267–269, cited in Clayson, p. 86.

30. On the siege and the Commune, see Alistair Horne, *Seven Ages of Paris* (London: Pan Macmillan, 2003), pp. 282–313.

31. Stanton, p. 332.

32. Stanton, p. 332.

33. Stanton, p. 332.

34. Stanton, p. 333.

35. Francis Ribemont and others, *Rosa Bonheur, 1822–1899*, exhib. cat. (Bordeaux: William Blake & Co., 1997), no. 104, p. 178.

36. Letters of Rosa Bonheur, 19, cited in Anne Henderson and Zoë Urbanek, *Rosa Bonheur: Selected Works from American Collections* (Dallas, Texas: The Meadows Museum, 1989)

37. Stanton, p. 333.

38. *The Indianapolis News*, 6 March 1871, p. 1.

39. Klumpke, p. 180.

40. Stanton, p. 318.

41. See Stanton, pp. 316–317.

42. Stanton, pp. 318–319.

43. Stanton, p. 318.

44. Stanton, p. 316.

45. On the Commune, see: Bury, pp. 133–134; Horne, pp. 301–302; Badsey, pp. 81–86.

46. Paul-Louis Hervier gives only the recipient's initial. Stanton confirms the identity. Hervier dates this letter as 23 May 1876, which, knowing the dates of the Commune, must be an error. Stanton, pp. 228–229; Paul-Louis Hervier, 'Les Lettres inédites de Rosa Bonheur', *La Nouvelle Revue*, January–February 1908, pp. 187–203, (p. 198).

47. A.M.W. Stirling, *Victorian Sidelights* (London: Ernest Benn Ltd, 1954), p. 104.

48. Stanton, p. 397.

49. Stanton, p. 176.

50. Stanton, p. 177.

51. Stanton, p. 244.

52. Stanton, p. 178.

53. Stanton, p. 400.

54. I am grateful to Michel Pons for the information on the darkroom at By. On Rosa's use of photography, see Francis Ribemont, 'Rosa Bonheur telle qu'en elle-même: L'artiste et ses animaux' in Francis Ribemont and others, *Rosa Bonheur*, pp. 85–99 (p. 95).

55. Stanton, p. 245.

56. On Louis Dejean, see: 'Cirque d'hiver' – *Circopedia*, http://www.circopedia. org/Cirque_Fratellini [accessed 1 November 2018]. On Louis Dejean and the Château de Saint-Leu, see: 'Guide de Visite – Château de Saint-Leu' – *Journées Européennes du Patrimoine 2016*, https://www.vert-saint-denis.fr/wp-content/uploads/book/Support-de-Visite-Cha%CC%82teau-de-Saint-Leu. pdf [accessed 1 November 2018]

57. On Pierrette, see Anna Klumpke, pp. 182–184.

58. On this episode, see Borin, pp. 182–183.

59. Stanton, p. 180.

Chapter 18: Standing Out From the Pack

1. On life expectancy in 19th-century France, see Roger Price, *A Social History of Nineteenth-Century France* (London: Hutchinson, 1987), pp. 62–71. I am grateful to Véronique Bancel at the Mairie in Magny-les-Hammeaux for helping me source Françoise Bonheur's death certificate. No cause of death is noted. She died at her parents' home.

2. Anna Klumpke, *Rosa Bonheur: The Artist's [Auto] Biography*, trans. by Gretchen van Slyke, (Michigan: The University of Michigan Press, 2001), pp. 185–186.

3. Theodore Stanton, *Rosa Bonheur: Reminiscences* (London: Andrew Melrose, 1910), pp. 180–181.
4. Rosa Bonheur, 'Coming from the Fair', *The Times*, 3 April 1875, p. 10.
5. Louis Brall, 'Coming from the Fair', *The Times*, 8 April 1875, p. 8.
6. Stanton, p. 181.
7. 'Les Femmes Artistes au Salon de 1875', *Les Gauloises*, June 1875, p. 18.
8. Stanton, pp. 181–182.
9. See the letter to Juliette dated February/March 1865. Stanton, p. 164.
10. I am grateful to Katherine Brault at the Musée Rosa Bonheur for confirmation of this point.
11. Méry, 'Le Dernier tigre', *Le Figaro*, 20 August 1876, pp. 1–2.
12. Letter dated 22 November 1876. Stanton, p. 182.
13. On tigers as pets, see: 'Tigers as Pets', *The Spruce Pets*, https://www.thespruce pets.com/pet-tigers-1238150 [accessed 1 December 2018]; 'Guidance on Keeping Lions and Tigers – Dangerous Wild Animals (Northern Ireland) Order 2004' – Northern Ireland Environment Agency, https://www.daera-ni.gov.uk/sites/default/files/publications/doe/natural-guidance-keeping-lions-tigers.PDF [accessed 1 December 2018]
14. Stanton, p. 183.
15. Stanton, p. 183.
16. 'Télégrammes et Correspondances', *Le Figaro*, 22 March 1877, p. 2.
17. Stanton, p. 185.
18. Stanton, p. 186.
19. 'Rosa Bonheur à Anvers', *L'Echo du Parlement*, 30 August 1877, p. 2.
20. On the Exposition Universelle of 1878, see Alistair Horne, *Seven Ages of Paris* (London: Pan Macmillan, 2003), p. 329; Marc Gaillard, 'Les Expositions Universelles de Paris' – Académie des Beaux-Arts, séance du 27 avril 2005, pp. 70–71, http://www.academiedesbeauxarts.fr/upload/Communication_seances/2005/05-Gaillard.pdf [accessed 11 December 2018]. See also Le Bureau International des Expositions: https://www.bie-paris.org [accessed 11 December 2018]
21. 'Opening of the Paris Exhibition', *The Times*, 2 May 1878, p. 5.
22. Jeremy Maas, *Gambart – Prince of the Victorian Art World* (London: Barrie and Jenkins, 1975), pp. 257–258.
23. Frith situated this episode when he and Millais came to see the 'Great Exhibition' in 1868. However, there was no Exposition Universelle in 1868 and the Exposition of 1867 finished in November. He mentions that Rosa's health had been unsatisfactory lately and that he saw a picture of threshing corn in Spain on her easel, a work Rosa had been struggling to complete. This was undoubtedly *Wheat Threshing in the Camargue*. This painting took Rosa many years and was never completed. In 1882, she wrote to Jean-Léon

Gérôme, saying that she had been working on this piece 'for 12 years'. Frith could only have seen this painting in 1878, not 1868. Jeremy Maas concurs. See Maas, pp. 257–258. W.P. Frith, *A Victorian Canvas: The Memoirs of W.P. Frith*, ed. by Nevile Wallis (London: Geoffrey Bes, 1957), pp. 181–182; John Guille Millais, *The Life and Letters of Sir John Everett Millais*, vol. 2 (London: Fredrick A. Stokes Company, 1899), pp. 13–14.

24. Frith, pp. 181–182.

25. Stanton, p. 187; *La Nature – Revue des sciences et de leurs applications aux arts et à l'industrie*, 28 September 1878, p. 303.

26. Stanton, p. 187.

Chapter 19: The Call of the Wild

1. *Les Gauloises*, 10 September 1879, p. 1.

2. Theodore Stanton, *Rosa Bonheur: Reminiscences* (London: Andrew Melrose, 1910), p. 187.

3. *Mémoires du Commandant Rousseau*, manuscript kindly supplied by the Musée des Beaux-Arts de Bordeaux.

4. Stanton, p. 188.

5. Stanton, p. 188.

6. Stanton, p. 189.

7. Maxime Gérard, 'Paris à Nice', *Le Gaulois*, 16 November 1879, p. 2.

8. Rachaumont, 'Chronique Parisienne', *Le Constitutionnel*, 26 January 1878, p. 3.

9. 'La Colline de Fabron', *Collection 'Les Sites', Ville de Nice*, https://www.nice. fr/uploads/media/default/0001/15/FDP%20La%20CollineDeFabron_FRAN_ WEB.pdf [accessed 4 December 2018]; Jeremy Maas, *Gambart – Prince of the Victorian Art World* (London: Barrie and Jenkins, 1975), pp. 246–257.

10. Rachaumont, 'Chronique Parisienne', p. 3.

11. *L'Indépendance Belge*, 18 December 1877, p. 2.

12. La Condamine, 'Gil Blas à Nice', *Gil Blas*, 1 January 1880, p. 2.

13. Pierre Borel, 'Les Hôtes de Nice – Rosa Bonheur', *L'Éclaireur du dimanche*, 2 January 1921, p. 8.

14. Stanton, p. 189.

15. Rachaumont, 'Chronique Parisienne', p. 3. See for example Francis Pattison, 'The Collection of M. Gambart at Les Palmiers, Nice', *Athenaeum*, 26 August 1876, pp. 276–278.

16. On the lions, see Anna Klumpke, *Rosa Bonheur: The Artist's [Auto] Biography*, trans. by Gretchen van Slyke (Michigan: The University of Michigan Press, 2001), pp. 183–184.

17. On M. Grivot, see Stanton, p. 281; Parisis, 'La Vie Parisienne', *Le Figaro*, 27 August 1884, p. 1.

18. Stanton, pp. 189–190.
19. See 'Nécrologie', *L'Indépendance Belge*, 3 July 1880, p. 2.
20. Stanton, p. 190.
21. On Gambart's domain, see 'La Colline de Fabron', *Collection 'Les Sites', Ville de Nice*, https://www.nice.fr/uploads/media/default/0001/15/FDP%20La%20CollineDeFabron_FRAN_WEB.pdf [accessed 4 December 2018]
22. *Mémoires du Commandant Rousseau*.
23. *Mémoires du Commandant Rousseau*.
24. See Rosa's letter to Auguste on 25 March 1851, in Stanton, pp. 190–191.

Chapter 20: Mastering the Moon

1. On the event, see D., 'Incendie du Théâtre de Nice', *Le Figaro*, 25 March 1881, pp. 1–2.
2. An illustration of the disaster appeared on the cover of *L'Univers Illustré*, 2 April 1881.
3. D., 'Incendie du Théâtre de Nice', p. 2.
4. Theodore Stanton, *Rosa Bonheur: Reminiscences* (London: Andrew Melrose, 1910), p. 190.
5. Letter dated 8 May 1881, in Stanton, p. 191.
6. See Stanton, p. 191.
7. On Alexandrine, Duchess of Saxe-Coburg-Gotha, see: Susan Flantzer, 'Unofficial Royalty – Alexandrine of Baden, Duchess of Saxe-Coburg-Gotha', http://www.unofficialroyalty.com/alexandrine-of-baden-duchess-of-saxe-coburg-and-gotha/ [accessed 15 December 2018]
8. 'Alexandrine of Baden, Duchess of Saxe-Coburg-Gotha (1820–1904), by Sir William Ross', *Royal Collection Trust*, https://www.rct.uk/collection/420420/alexandrine-of-baden-duchess-of-saxe-coburg-gotha-1820-1904 [accessed 15 December 2018]
9. Anna Klumpke, *Rosa Bonheur: The Artist's [Auto] Biography*, trans. by Gretchen van Slyke (Michigan: The University of Michigan Press, 2001), p. 190.
10. Stanton, pp. 191–192.
11. Stanton, pp. 346, 350.
12. Theodore Stanton transcribes Rosa's letter of 27 March 1881 using the spelling 'Manger'. However, Rosa's handwriting was notoriously illegible. The journal *La Basse-Cour* was headed by L. Mauger at this time.
13. Stanton, pp. 340–341.
14. Stanton, p. 341.
15. L. Niesten, 'La Grande Comète de 1807 et de 1881', *La Science Populaire*, 28 July 1881, p. 1212.
16. Stanton, p. 192.
17. Stanton, p. 193.

18. Stanton, p. 195.
19. Stanton, p. 348.
20. 'Les Travaux du Jardin des Plantes', *La Presse*, 7 August 1882, p. 2.
21. See Jules Claretie, 'Une Visite à Rosa Bonheur', *La Vie à Paris* (Paris, 1896), p. 410. See also Klumpke, pp. 183–184.
22. Frédéric Gilbert, 'Mlle Rosa Bonheur', *Le Gaulois*, 12 December 1883, p. 1.
23. See George J. Engelmann, 'The Early History of the Vaginal Hysterectomy', *American Gynaecological and Obstetrical Journal*, May 1895, 1–15.
24. P. Bazy, 'Hystérectomie – Rapport', *La France Médicale*, 1883, 739–741 (p. 740).
25. P. Bazy, 'Hystérectomie – Rapport', p. 740.
26. Stanton, p. 195.
27. Stanton, p. 63.
28. *Journal des Connaissances Médicales Pratiques et de Pharmacologie*, Paris, 1881, p. 144.
29. Dr Georges Apostoli, 'Sur une nouvelle application de l'éléctricité aux accouchements', *Annales de Gynécologie*, Tome XV, 1881, 327–337. This article also provides an overview of Dr Apostoli's methods and approach.
30. Letter dated 9 April 1883 to M. & Mme Rousseau, reproduced in *Mémoires du Commandant Rousseau*, manuscript kindly supplied by the Musée des Beaux-Arts de Bordeaux.
31. On Alfred Borriglione, see: 'Alfred Borriglione' – *Sénat* – *Un site au service des citoyens*, https://www.senat.fr/senateur-3eme-republique/borriglione_alfredo114r3.html [accessed 19 December 2018]
32. Stanton, p. 349.
33. Stanton, p. 197.
34. On Rosa's attack, see: Frédéric Gilbert, 'Mlle Rosa Bonheur', p. 1; Le Masque de fer, 'A Travers Paris,' *Le Figaro*, 10 December 1883, p. 1; 'Nos Echos', *Le Gaulois*, 11 December 1883, p. 2.
35. *Mémoires du Commandant Rousseau*. Rousseau dates this episode as 'around 1886' but Rosa's letters suggest that this is an error. Rosa was apparently cured by 1884. Borin concurs. See Marie Borin, *Rosa Bonheur: Une Artiste à l'aube du féminisme* (Paris: Pygmalion, 2011), p. 216.
36. *Athenaeum*, 24 November 1883, p. 676.
37. *Athenaeum*, 8 December 1883, p. 746.
38. 'A Travers Paris', *Le Figaro*, 10 December 1883, p. 1.
39. *Le Radical*, 12 December 1883, p. 2.
40. Frédéric Gilbert, 'Mlle Rosa Bonheur', p. 1.
41. 'Boite aux lettres', *Le Gaulois*, 15 December 1883, p. 3.
42. Borin, p. 217.
43. *Athenaeum*, 22 December 1883, p. 822.

44. Dr Georges Apostoli, 'Sur une nouvelle application de l'éléctricité aux accouchements', p. 335.
45. *Mémoires du Commandant Rousseau.*

Chapter 21: A Question of Pride
 1. Le Masque de fer, 'A Travers Paris', *Le Figaro*, 23 February 1884, p. 1.
 2. Theodore Stanton, *Rosa Bonheur: Reminiscences* (London: Andrew Melrose, 1910), p. 197.
 3. Letter dated 26 February 1884, in Stanton, p. 245.
 4. Le Masque de fer, 'Echos de Paris', *Le Figaro*, 21 March 1884, p. 1.
 5. Le Masque de fer, 'A Travers Paris', *Le Figaro*, 24 March 1884, p. 1.
 6. 'Vingt-cinq chefs d'oeuvre', *Le Figaro*, 3 May 1884, p. 3.
 7. Stanton, p. 198.
 8. For samples of her drawing, see: http://percheron-international.blogspot.com/2016/02/la-mort-horrible-de-voltaire.html
 9. Stanton, pp. 283–284. On the court case, see 'Un Accouchement laborieux', *Le Rappel*, 12 June 1880, p. 3.
10. Un Domino, 'Le Monde et la ville', *Le Gaulois*, 14 December 1884, p. 1.
11. Stanton, p. 199.
12. Stanton, p. 246.
13. Stanton, p. 199.
14. On Rosa's correspondence, see Joseph Mischka, *The Percheron Horse in America* (Wisconsin: Heart Prairie Press, 1991), p. 130.
15. Mischka, p. 130.
16. See letter of 4 January 1885 to Major Rousseau, *Mémoires du Commandant Rousseau*, manuscript kindly supplied by the Musée des Beaux-Arts de Bordeaux.
17. See the letter of 27 May 1885, *Mémoires du Commandant Rousseau*; 'Sport', *Le Gaulois*, 24 April 1885, p. 3.
18. Anna Klumpke, *Rosa Bonheur: The Artist's [Auto] Biography*, trans. by Gretchen van Slyke (Michigan: The University of Michigan Press, 2001), pp. 183–184.
19. Rosa mentioned also painting 'big horses' at this time. She was almost certainly referring to *Wheat Threshing in the Camargue*, the great canvas which remained unfinished when she died. See Stanton, p. 291.
20. Stanton, p. 350.
21. Letter dated 7 January 1886, *Mémoires du Commandant Rousseau*.
22. Letter to Mme Rousseau dated 8 April 1886, *Mémoires du Commandant Rousseau*.
23. Stanton, p. 298.
24. Stanton, p. 350.
25. Letter dated 28 October 1886, in Mischka, p. 133.

26. Virginie Demont-Breton, 'Rosa Bonheur', *La Revue des revues*, 15 June 1899, 605–619 (p. 605).

27. See Stanton, p. 397. One figure given for an average wage of a postman in 1890 is 600 francs. See: http://nlghistoire.fr/documents/NLGH%20-%20prix%20 &%20salaires%2019-20%C3%A8me%20si%C3%A8cles%20a.pdf [accessed 23 January 2019]

28. See Stanton, p. 396.

29. 'Echos du Jour', *Le XIX Siècle*, 18 November 1886, p. 2.

30. 'Echos de province', *Le Gaulois* 20 November 1886, p. 1. The journalist compares the man's fortune to that of a recently deceased multimillionaire described in the paper a few days earlier. See Tout Paris, 'Un Roman de 80 millions', *Le Gaulois*, 17 November 1886, pp. 1–2.

31. On the earthquakes, see 'Les Tremblements de Terre', *Le Petit Parisien*, 25 February 1887, pp. 1–2; 'Les Tremblements de Terre', *Le Petit Parisien*, 28 February 1887, p. 2.

32. Stanton, p. 285.

33. Consuélo Fould, 'Rosa Bonheur', *La Revue illustrée*, 1 November 1899, NP.

34. Dom Pedro II of Brazil fell ill in February 1887. A trip to Europe was prescribed. Mary Williams, *Dom Pedro the Magnanimous: Second Emperor of Brazil* (London: Routledge, 2013), p. 279.

Chapter 22: The Price of Fame

1. On the sale, see: 'Two Great Masterpieces', *New York Times*, 26 March 1887, p. 1; 'For the People to Enjoy', *New York Times*, 27 March 1887, p. 9.

2. Theodore Stanton, *Rosa Bonheur: Reminiscences* (London: Andrew Melrose, 1910), pp. 201–202.

3. Anna Klumpke, *Rosa Bonheur: The Artist's [Auto] Biography*, trans. by Gretchen van Slyke (Michigan: The University of Michigan Press, 2001), p. 192.

4. See the letter to Juliette dated 11 May 1887, reprinted in Stanton, p. 202.

5. Maxime Serpeille, 'Dom Pedro II à Paris', *Le Gaulois*, 21 July 1887, p. 2.

6. On Dom Pedro, see: *Encyclopaedia Britannica* – Pedro II, https://www. britannica.com/biography/Pedro-II [accessed 15 January 2019]

7. Le Masque de fer, 'Hors Paris', *Le Figaro*, 22 November 1887, p. 1.

8. See the letter dated 22 November 1887, *Mémoires du Commandant Rousseau*, manuscript kindly supplied by the Musée des Beaux-Arts de Bordeaux. On the visit, see M., 'Au Pays du soleil', *Le Gaulois*, 27 November 1887, p. 2.

9. Stanton, p. 281.

10. Stanton, pp. 280–281.

11. Un Domino, 'Echos de province', *Le Gaulois*, 11 December 1887, p. 2.

12. The couple were in Nice during the spring of 1887. They left Paris in May. *Le Figaro*, 18 February 1887, p. 1; *Le Figaro*, 22 May 1887, p. 1.

13. 'La Vie en plein air', *Le Figaro*, 2 November 1887, p. 4.
14. Klumpke, p. 9.
15. Klumpke, p. 9.
16. Letter dated 9 March 1888, *Mémoires du Commandant Rousseau*.
17. Stanton, p. 229.
18. Stanton, p. 204.
19. *Le Figaro*, 11 September 1888, p. 4.
20. Klumpke, p. 184; Stanton, pp. 342–344; Virginie Demont-Breton, 'Rosa Bonheur', *La Revue des revues*, 15 June 1899, 605–619 (pp. 609–610).
21. Stanton, p. 230.
22. Stanton claims that Auguste Cain was on the jury. However, his name does not appear in *Exposition Universelle Internationale de 1889 – Liste des membres du jury* (Paris, 1889).
23. Stanton, p. 280.
24. See Stanton, pp. 99–100.

Chapter 23: The Final Awakening

1. Theodore Stanton, *Rosa Bonheur: Reminiscences* (London: Andrew Melrose, 1910), p. 80.
2. Stanton, p. 82.
3. *Le Figaro*, 23 June 1889, p. 3.
4. Letter dated 27 June 1889, *Mémoires du Commandant Rousseau*, manuscript kindly supplied by the Musée des Beaux-Arts de Bordeaux.
5. Stanton, p. 80.
6. On Gustave Fould and Valérie Simonin, see: *Gazette Anecdotique, littéraire, artistique et biographique*, Tome 1 (Paris, 1876), pp. 260–261; Faber, 'Nouvelles du jour', *La Presse*, 20 August 1884, p. 2; Jean Raimond, 'Un Ennemi de lui-même', *Le Gaulois*, 4 September 1884, p. 2; *Le Gaulois*, 4 September 1884, p. 2; *Le Cri de Paris*, 19 October 1919, p. 3.
7. Stanton, p. 251.
8. Stanton, pp. 102–103.
9. On Colonel William Frederick Cody, see: 'A Brief History of William F. "Buffalo Bill" Cody' – *The Buffalo Bill Museum and Grave*, http://www.buffalo bill.org/History%20Research%20on%20the%20Buffalo%20Bill%20Museum/ index.html [accessed 1 February 2019]; *Encyclopaedia Britannica* – Buffalo Bill, https://www.britannica.com/biography/William-F-Cody [accessed 1 February 2019]; Steve Friesen, 'Paris Catches Wild West Fever', *True West Magazine*, 19 February 2016, https://truewestmagazine.com/buffalo-bill-comes-to-paris/ [accessed 1 February 2019]
10. 'La Première de Buffalo Bill', *Le Petit Journal*, 20 May 1889, p. 2.
11. 'Théâtres et divertissements', *La Lanterne*, 26 May 1889, p. 15.

12. Paul Verner, 'Le Musée Catlin et les Indiens O-jib-be-wa's', *La France Théâtrale*, 18 September 1845, NP.

13. Dick, 'Les Indiens Ioways', *La France Théâtrale*, 29 May 1845, NP.

14. Juliette Lormeau, 'Causeries', *Journal des Femmes*, June 1845, pp. 277–281.

15. Stanton, p. 251.

16. 'Choses et gens', *Le Matin*, 13 September 1880, p. 3.

17. 'Buffalo Bill and Rosa Bonheur', *Galignani's Messenger*, 26 September 1889, p. 3; 'Chronique Locale', *L'Abeille de Fontainebleau*, 27 September 1889, pp. 1–2.

18. *Mémoires du Commandant Rousseau.*

19. See 'Au Jour le jour', *La Presse*, 29 September 1889, p. 2. Jules Claretie mentions two mustangs, but in a letter to Paul Chardin dated 19 January 1890, Rosa refers to only one. See Jules Claretie, 'Une Visite à Rosa Bonheur', *La Vie à Paris* (Paris, 1896), pp. 400–411. See also Stanton, p. 246.

20. See Anna Klumpke, *Rosa Bonheur: The Artist's [Auto] Biography*, trans. by Gretchen van Slyke (Michigan: The University of Michigan Press, 2001), pp. 5–11.

21. On the Klumpkes, see Britta C. Dwyer, *Anna Klumpke: A Turn-of-the-Century Painter and Her World* (Pennsylvania: Northeastern University Press, 1999), pp. 3–31.

22. On the Académie Julian, see Germaine Greer, '"À tout prix devenir quelqu'un": the women of the Académie Julian', in *Artistic Relations: Literature and the Visual Arts in Nineteenth-Century France*, ed. by Peter Collier and Robert Lethbridge (New Haven and London: Yale University Press, 1994), pp. 40–58.

23. Gaston Calmetto, 'La Première interne des hôpitaux', *Le Figaro*, 3 February 1887, p. 2.

24. Gaston Calmetto, p. 2.

25. See *Le Bulletin Mensuel du Club Alpin Français*, May 1889, p. 157.

26. Stanton, p. 252.

27. Stanton, p. 246.

28. Stanton, p. 254.

29. *Mémoires du Commandant Rousseau.*

30. *Mémoires du Commandant Rousseau.*

31. Robert B. Carlisle, *The Proffered Crown: Saint-Simonianism and the Doctrine of Hope* (Baltimore and London: The Johns Hopkins University Press, 1987), p. 88; Klumpke, pp. 193–194.

32. 'Echos et Nouvelles', *Le Petit Parisien*, 17 September, 1890, p. 2.

33. *Mémoires du Commandant Rousseau.*

34. Letter to Paul Chardin dated 6 January 1891. See Stanton, pp. 246-247.

35. 'A Travers Paris', *Le Figaro*, 8 May 1891, p. 1; 'Echos du Matin', *Le Matin*, 8 May 1891, p. 3.

36. Stanton, p. 247.

Chapter 24: Against the Odds

1. On the approach to By, see Jules Claretie, 'Une Visite à Rosa Bonheur', *La Vie à Paris* (Paris, 1896), pp. 400–411.

2. See Anna Klumpke, *Rosa Bonheur: The Artist's [Auto] Biography*, trans. by Gretchen van Slyke (Michigan: The University of Michigan Press, 2001), pp. 12–15.

3. Theodore Stanton, *Rosa Bonheur: Reminiscences* (London: Andrew Melrose, 1910), p. 247.

4. Stanton mistakes this for Princess Beatrice's visit five years later. The description remains pertinent. Stanton, p. 212. See 'Chronique locale', *L'Abeille de Fontainebleau*, 6 May 1892, p. 1.

5. Letter dated 24 September 1892, Stanton, pp. 254–255.

6. See Klumpke, pp. 16–17.

7. On the Foulds, see: *Dictionnaire Universel et Contemporain* (Paris, 1893), pp. 1544–1545; Charles Virmaître, *Paris-Palette* (Paris, 1888), pp. 252–253; 'Les Artistes' – *Musée Roybet Fould de Courbevoie*, https://www.museeroybetfould.fr/les-artistes/ [accessed 20 February 2019]

8. See Stanton, p. 257.

9. Charles Yriarte, *Figaro-Salon* (Paris, 1893), pp. 37–39.

10. See 'Le Salon des Champs Elysées', *Le Panthéon de l'Industrie*, May 1893, pp. 94–95.

11. Stanton, p. 258.

12. Letter quoted in Stanton, pp. 257–258.

13. Stanton, p. 259.

14. Guy Tamel, 'Une Doctoresse Ès-Sciences', *Le Figaro*, 16 December 1893, p. 1.

15. 'A Morning with Rosa Bonheur', interview in the *Home Journal*, 10 August 1859, reproduced in *Littell's Living Age*, October, November, December 1859, pp. 124–126.

16. 'A Morning with Rosa Bonheur', p. 124.

17. Klumpke, p. 18.

18. Stanton, pp. 232–233.

19. 'Rosa Bonheur', *Le Matin*, 4 April 1894, pp. 1–2. See also Jacques Lefranc, 'Courrier de la semaine', *Le Petit Parisien*, 15 April 1894, p. 114.

20. 'Rosa Bonheur', *Le Matin*, pp. 1–2.

21. On the World's Columbian Exposition, see Bruno Giberti, *Designing the Centennial: A History of the 1876 International Exhibition in Philadelphia* (Kentucky: The University Press of Kentucky, 2002), pp. 171–172; Auguste Lemoine, 'La France à l'Exposition de Chicago', *Le Figaro*, 29 May 1893, p. 2.

22. See letter dated 26 February 1894 in Paul-Louis Hervier, 'Lettres inédites de Rosa Bonheur', *La Nouvelle Revue*, January–February 1908, 187–203 (pp. 202–203).

23. For Georges Stirbey's account, see Stanton, pp. 383–384.
24. Boyer d'Agen, 'Les Décorés de Chicago', *Le Figaro*, 6 April 1894, p. 2.
25. Georges Docquois, 'La Croix de Rosa Bonheur', *Le Journal*, 4 April 1894, p. 2.
26. 'Rosa Bonheur – La Première Officier de la Légion d'Honneur', *Le Matin*, 4 April 1894, pp. 1–2.
27. 'Mlle Rosa Bonheur', *Le Voleur illustré*, 19 April 1894, p. 248.
28. Petit-Jean, 'Causerie', *Journal du Dimanche*, 13 May 1894, p. 1.
29. Jacques Lefranc, 'Courrier de la semaine', *Le Petit Parisien*, 15 April 1894, p. 114.
30. Stanton, p. 209; *Mémoires du Commandant Rousseau*, manuscript kindly supplied by the Musée des Beaux-Arts de Bordeaux.
31. 'The home of a prince and collector' – *Domaine de Chantilly*, http://www.domainedechantilly.com/en/accueil/history/duke-aumale/ [accessed 8 March 2019]
32. See Klumpke, p. 196.
33. See 'A Travers Paris', *Le Figaro*, 24 April 1894, p. 1.
34. Letter dated 10 May 1894, Stanton, pp. 263–264.
35. Consuélo Fould, 'Rosa Bonheur', *La Revue illustrée*, 1 November 1899, NP.
36. Stanton, p. 264.
37. Stanton, p. 266.

Chapter 25: Four Loves

1. Letter dated 10 May 1895, in Theodore Stanton, *Rosa Bonheur: Reminiscences* (London: Andrew Melrose, 1910), p. 211.
2. 'Les Décorations des Expositions de Lyon, d'Anvers, etc', *Le Figaro*, 8 May 1895, p. 3.
3. Letter dated 16 July 1895, Stanton, p. 237.
4. On Rosa's routine, see: Letter to René Peyrol dated 26 August 1898, Stanton, p. 214; Stanton, pp. 297–299; Virginie Demont-Breton, 'Rosa Bonheur', *La Revue des revues*, 15 June 1899, 605–619 (pp. 612–613).
5. Eugène Sue, *The Godolphin Arabian*, trans. by Alex de Jonge (Lanham and New York: The Derrydale Press, 2004), p. 130.
6. On the weather, see *Le Figaro*, 27 October 1895, p. 1. See Anna Klumpke, *Rosa Bonheur: The Artist's [Auto] Biography*, trans. by Gretchen van Slyke (Michigan: The University of Michigan Press, 2001), pp. 19–25.
7. See letter dated 11 December 1895, Stanton, pp. 210–211.
8. See letter dated 30 December 1895, Stanton, pp. 266–267.
9. On Mrs Thaw, see Britta C. Dwyer, *Anna Klumpke: A Turn-of-the-Century Painter and Her World* (Pennsylvania: Northeastern University Press, 1999), pp. 80–82.
10. Letter dated 19 June 1896, Stanton, p. 267. On Rosa's routine, see Jacques Evrard, 'Rosa Bonheur – Notes et souvenirs', *La Liberté*, 30 May 1899, p. 2.

11. Letter dated 19 June 1896, Stanton, p. 267.

12. On the event, see: 'Quatrième Journée – Paris-Versailles', *Le Gaulois*, 9 October 1896, p. 1; 'Les Souverains russes à Paris', *Le Figaro*, 9 October 1896, p. 1.

13. 'Quatrième Journée – Paris-Versailles', *Le Gaulois*, p. 1.

14. Letter dated 9 October 1896, Stanton, p. 212.

15. Rosa Bonheur, 'Souvenirs inédits de Rosa Bonheur', *La Revue des revues*, 1 January 1897, pp. 131–142.

16. On Beatrice in France, see 'Royalty on the Riviera', *New York Herald*, 6 April 1897, p. 5.

17. See Klumpke, p. 191; 'Chronique Locale', *L'Abeille de Fontainebleau*, 18 June 1897, p. 1.

18. See letter dated 20 June 1897, *Mémoires du Commandant Rousseau*, manuscript kindly supplied by the Musée des Beaux-Arts de Bordeaux.

19. 'Chronique Locale', *L'Abeille de Fontainebleau*, 18 June 1897, p. 1.

20. See letter dated 28 March 1897, *Mémoires du Commandant Rousseau*.

21. Sergine, 'Les Echos de Paris', *Les Annales politiques et littéraires*, 20 June 1897, pp. 392–393.

22. Santilane, 'Le Roi de la forêt', *Gil Blas*, 13 June 1897, pp. 1–2.

23. Letter dated 9 July 1897, Stanton, p. 247.

24. Virginie Demont-Breton, 'Rosa Bonheur', p. 611.

25. See Klumpke, pp. 31–38.

26. On Rosa's voice and appearance, see Virginie Demont-Breton, 'Rosa Bonheur', pp. 606–607.

27. Anna Klumpke, *Rosa Bonheur, Sa Vie, son oeuvre* (Paris: Flammarion, 1908), p. 100.

Chapter 26: Signing a Life

1. On feminism in 19th-century France, see: James F. McMillan, *Twentieth-Century France: Politics and Society 1898–1991* (London, New York, Sydney and Auckland: Arnold, 1992), pp. 58–61; Theodore Zeldin, *France 1848–1945: Ambition and Love* (Oxford, New York, Toronto and Melbourne: Oxford University Press, 1988), pp. 345–350; Claire Goldberg Moses, *French Feminism in the 19th Century* (Albany: State University of New York, 1984)

2. Anna Klumpke, *Rosa Bonheur: The Artist's [Auto] Biography*, trans. by Gretchen van Slyke (Michigan: The University of Michigan Press, 2001), p. 70.

3. On the 'Boston marriage', see Lillian Faderman, *Surpassing the Love of Men: Romantic Friendship and Love between Women from the Renaissance to the Present* (London: The Women's Press Ltd, 1997), pp. 190–230.

4. See Klumpke, pp. 63–75.

5. Anna Klumpke, *Rosa Bonheur, Sa Vie, son oeuvre* (Paris: Flammarion, 1908), p. 104.

6. Klumpke, *Rosa Bonheur, Sa Vie, son oeuvre*, p. 112.

7. On this portrait, see Britta C. Dwyer, *Anna Klumpke: A Turn-of-the-Century Painter and Her World* (Pennsylvania: Northeastern University Press, 1999), pp. 89–115.

8. 'Le Naufrage de la Bourgogne – 628 victimes', *Le Figaro*, 7 July 1898, p. 1.

9. Letter dated 26 August 1898, Stanton, p. 214.

10. 'Chronique Locale', *L'Abeille de Fontainebleau*, 23 September 1898, p. 1.

11. Stanton, p. 276.

12. Stanton, p. 276.

13. Letter dated 1 January 1899, Stanton, pp. 240–241.

14. Letter to Mme Rousseau dated 4 January 1899, *Mémoires du Commandant Rousseau*, manuscript kindly supplied by the Musée des Beaux-Arts de Bordeaux.

15. Letter dated 26 January 1899, Stanton, p. 269.

16. 'Riviera', *New York Herald*, 3 February 1899, pp. 2–3.

17. 'Riviera', *New York Herald*, 10 February, 1899, p. 2.

18. The French press during April 1899 reveals that Eugénie looked unwell.

19. Marie Borin has recently discovered correspondence which sheds light onto these tensions. See Marie Borin, *Rosa Bonheur: Une Artiste à l'aube du féminisme* (Paris: Pygmalion, 2011)

20. Letter dated 8 May 1899, in Jeremy Maas, *Gambart – Prince of the Victorian Art World* (London: Barrie and Jenkins, 1975), p. 278.

21. 'Les Salons de 1899', *Le Petit Journal*, 30 April 1899, p. 1.

22. 'La Ville', *Le Journal*, 13 May 1898, p. 1.

23. See for example 'Lettres, sciences et arts', *L'Univers et le Monde*, 21 May 1899, p. 3.

24. See Klumpke, pp. 236–244.

25. On the weather, see *Le Figaro*, 21 May 1899, p. 1.

26. On Rosa's last days, see Klumpke, pp. 245–254. See also Hippolyte Peyrol's recollections in Stanton, pp. 402–403.

27. 'A Morning with Rosa Bonheur', interview conducted on 10 August 1859, originally published in the *Home Journal*, reprinted in *Littel's Living Age* (October, November, December, 1859), pp. 126.

28. Virginie Demont-Breton, 'Rosa Bonheur', *La Revue des revues*, 15 June 1899, 605–619 (p. 605).

Epilogue

1. On the aftermath, see Anna Klumpke, *Rosa Bonheur: The Artist's [Auto] Biography*, trans. by Gretchen van Slyke (Michigan: The University of Michigan Press, 2001), pp. 245–261; Marie Borin, *Rosa Bonheur: Une Artiste à l'aube du féminisme* (Paris: Pygmalion, 2011), pp. 383–415.

2. On the weather, see *Le Figaro*, 30 May 1899, p. 1.

3. See Hippolyte Peyrol's reminiscences in Theodore Stanton, *Rosa Bonheur: Reminiscences* (London: Andrew Melrose, 1910), pp. 402–403.

4. On the funeral, see 'Rosa Bonheur', *L'Abeille de Fontainebleau*, 2 June 1899, p. 5.

5. 'Rosa Bonheur', *L'Abeille de Fontainebleau*, 2 June 1899, p. 5.

6. Stanton, pp. 403–405.

7. Anna Klumpke, *Rosa Bonheur, Sa Vie, son oeuvre* (Paris: Flammarion, 1908), p. 404.

8. Jeremy Maas, *Gambart – Prince of the Victorian Art World* (London: Barrie and Jenkins, 1975), pp. 279–280.

9. Klumpke, *Rosa Bonheur: The Artist's [Auto] Biography*, pp. 263–268.

10. Letter dated 5 June 1899, cited in Maas, p. 280.

11. Klumpke, *Rosa Bonheur, Sa Vie, son oeuvre*, p. 362.

12. Klumpke, *Rosa Bonheur, Sa Vie, son oeuvre*, p. 406.

13. Klumpke, *Rosa Bonheur, Sa Vie, son oeuvre*, p. 408.

14. On the tensions, see Borin, pp. 387–401.

15. *L'Abeille de Fontainebleau*, 16 June 1899, p. 2.

16. *Le Temps*, 9 December 1899, p. 2.

17. 'L'Oeuvre de Rosa Bonheur', *L'Abeille de Fontainebleau*, 1 June 1900, p. 1.

18. Valmont, 'Les Grandes Ventes – Atelier Rosa Bonheur', *Le Figaro*, 2 June 1900, p. 3.

19. 'La Vente Rosa Bonheur', *L'Abeille de Fontainebleau*, 8 June 1900, p. 2.

20. 'La Vente Rosa Bonheur', *Le Matin*, June 1900, p. 3.

21. 'Un Millier de lettres de Rosa Bonheur', *L'Abeille de Fontainebleau*, 15 June 1900, pp. 5–6.

Afterword

1. *Daily News*, 19 July 1855, cited in F. Lepelle de Bois-Gallais, *Biography of Mademoiselle Rosa Bonheur*, trans. by James Parry (London, 1857), pp. 45–47; Theodore Stanton, *Rosa Bonheur: Reminiscences* (London: Andrew Melrose, 1910), p. 403.

2. Stanton, p. 403.

3. Tamar Garb, 'Gender and Representation' in Francis Frascina and others, *Modernity and Modernism: French Painting in the Nineteenth Century* (New Haven and London: Yale University Press, 1993), pp. 219–289 (p. 231).

4. 'La Succession de Rosa Bonheur', *La Liberté*, 21 January 1901, p. 2.

Index

ALSO AVAILABLE

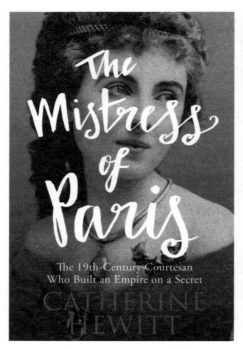

THE MISTRESS OF PARIS

Comtesse Valtesse de la Bigne was a celebrated 19th-century Parisian courtesan. She was painted by Édouard Manet and inspired Émile Zola, who immortalised her in his scandalous novel *Nana*. Her rumoured affairs with Napoleon III and the future Edward VII kept gossip columns full. But all was not as it seemed. Who was this Valtesse? Where had she come from? And was she really a comtesse? Catherine Hewitt tells the story of a remarkable woman's journey from obscurity to the stratosphere of Parisian society, and the creation of a cultural icon.

ISBN 9781785780448 (paperback) / 9781848319271 (ebook)

RENOIR'S DANCER

Once considered the Impressionists' most beautiful model, Suzanne Valadon sensationally emerged as a talented artist in her own right. Some found her vibrant still lifes and frank portraits as shocking as her bohemian lifestyle. But she refused to be confined by tradition or gender and in 1894 her work was accepted to the Salon de la Société Nationale des Beaux-Arts, an extraordinary achievement for a working-class woman with no formal art training. Catherine Hewitt tells the remarkable tale of an ambitious, headstrong woman fighting to find a professional voice in a male-dominated world.

ISBN 9781785784040 (paperback) / 9781785782749 (ebook)

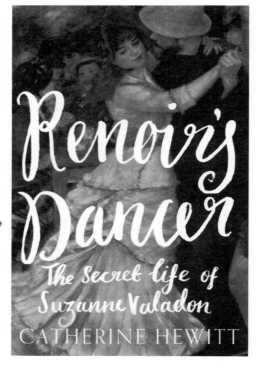